TURKEY & AMERICA

EAST & WEST – WHERE
THE TWAIN MEET

HENRY P. (PHIL) WILLIAMS III

NEW DEGREE PRESS

COPYRIGHT © 2019 HENRY P. (PHIL) WILLIAMS III

TURKEY & AMERICA

East & West – Where the Twain Meet

LCCN   2019937619

ISBN   978-1-64137-206-0   *Paperback*
          978-1-64137-207-7   *Ebook*

This book is dedicated to the peoples of Turkey and America, the peoples of the East and West, the Orient and the Occident, in hope that they, like grapes ripening in the sun together, side by side, or as the Turks might say, üzüm üzüme baka baka kararır, may grow closer in understanding of, and better appreciation for, each other.

CONTENTS

IN APPRECIATION

This book, based on a lecture series, is the culmination of an odyssey on the Mediterranean that began nearly a half a century ago with my wife Marilyn. Even when I was quite sure I didn't know what I was doing upon arrival in Ankara (1977) to undertake doctoral research, she stayed true to the belief that my course was in Divine Hands. She was always encouraging, during challenging, even dangerous, times and circumstances. I am indebted to her steadfast love and commitment.

Additionally, and critically, credit for the opportunity to be hired to combine my life's adult passions into a lecture series and teach at Koç University in Istanbul thirty-eight years later goes to the dearest of friends, Can and Aslı Kıraç. Without their foresight, I would never have met the Rector, Umran İnan, and this book might never have happened. In that teaching endeavor, I am further indebted to Ali Çarkoğlu, then Dean of the International Relations Department, and to the wonderfully supportive staff at the University.

PREFACE

My lecture series, which later became this book, was written in fifteen strenuous months. However, it was conceived in an adult lifetime, first as a master's candidate, then a doctoral researcher in Ankara. Later, I worked as an investment banker in Istanbul, and then as a U.S.-based Turkey-related business consultant. Subsequently, I began lecturing on Turkey and the Middle East and on the American Revolution. In 2013, I was invited to lecture at Koç University in Istanbul.

My purpose in creating the lectures, and ultimately this book, was to guide the audience to bridges where others see chasms, transporting the reader, back and forth, from East to West, across the centuries, juxtaposing geography and discovery, politics and war, religion and the arts, terrorism, key figures, and human triumph. The goal of the journey is a better appreciation for both the controversy and the extraordinary contributions that lie at the heart of the East-West dynamic. This book is but my own small attempt at decoding some of the facile presumptions behind misconceptions that become the prisms through which perception is filtered.

The ambitious breadth of this work risks the suggestion that the audience should include scholars for whom my analyses may seem to be wanting, or are found to be at odds with their own findings and interpretations, or even old hat. Even there, they might find my comparative work in areas with which they are less familiar to have some redeeming value. Additionally, the book should be of interest to students of the many disciplines and topics, which I use to weave together a brilliant and tragic story that inescapably belongs to us all. Finally, there are readers who may sharpen their understanding of these subjects in light of the experiences and perceptions of other cultures and peoples. If I am not fooling myself, there is much to be learned or considered, by a rather wide and diverse range of readers. It is hoped that my presentations of these many subjects will be edifying, stimulating thought, debate, and some "ah ha" moments along the way.

My knowledge of the subjects in this book is based both on considerable scholarship and, importantly, deep and abiding personal experiences engaging the heart and mind in pursuit of a deeper understanding of the American Experience, the Mediterranean World in general, and Turkey. I am steeped in the history of the Near and Middle East, of Europe and America. And, I remain a commentator on current events in each of these areas.

As the book covers two millennia, I am indebted to so many scholars whose earlier work undergirds my knowledge and commentary. These authorities are duly noted both in the text and the bibliography. Their works have served as the better part of my peer review process. I encourage the reader to use my Selected Bibliography to explore in greater depth the myriad topics and eras considered here. I have studied at their feet and am in awe of their scholarship and commentary.

This book synthesizes the specializations of others, together with my own areas of expertise and experience, resulting perhaps in a few possibly novel insights. My analysis and discussion of these many subjects has benefited from what I would like to think of as a near bi-cultural vision. Where to start thanking the men, women and children, friends, associates, teachers and table companions, on both sides of the Atlantic who have nurtured my vision and experience defies contraints of space and memory. Let me just say I have been more than lucky with thanks to all.

I would, however, like to give credit for the multi-disciplinary approach taken in this book to the extraordinary training I received in Graduate School at the Fletcher School of Law and Diplomacy, Tufts University, where I took two Masters and a Doctorate in International Law and Diplomacy. Here I would like to give special mention to my Dissertation adviser, the late Professor Robert Meagher. His approach to teaching and insistence on conjuring up "the right questions" to ask before embarking on any inquiry, proved to be an enduring inspiration in my life. Moreover, I would be remiss if failed to note that he owned a fabulous wine collection whose fruits he generously shared during his senior "in home" seminars.

Since I do not fit the usual molds in fields where I tread, the list of thanks for those who directly contributed to this work does not include the customary recognition of a large cast of supporting actors, peer reviewers, and well-wishers, with a few notable exceptions. I am indebted to my IWP academic colleague Professor Doug Streusand, whose expertise on early Islamic history served to refine my knowledge and understanding of that period. The encouragement and hawkeyed editing of dear friend Patricia Taylor were invaluable. Similarly, dear friend Professor C. Brian Kelly generously shared his editing skills. The members of the New Degree Press team of editors, especially Gina Champagne, graphic artist Gjorgji Pejkovski, and layout and marketing specialists have combined to raise the quality and expand the outreach of this book. As this work has otherwise been in the main a "solo effort," all shortcomings readers will surely find, and interpretations with which they might take issue, remain the responsibility of the author.

SPELLING CONVENTIONS AND ABBREVIATIONS

Regarding the spelling of words of Arabic and/or Turkish origin, I have opted for the Turkish spelling, as in *Ümmet* for Umma, referring to the Muslim Faithful, or for the Islamic School of Jurisprudence, *Hanefi*, rather than Arabic transliteration of *Hanafa*. When Turkish spelling is used, it will appear in italics, as with Latin terms, *jus sanguinis* for example. For words that are easily recognizable in English, such as Sharia and Caliph, their common English spelling is used. Where I think it useful, I will use the conventional English spelling, but include the Turkish equivalent in parentheses immediately after, such as Şeyhulislam after the word Grand Mufti or *Sheik ul-Islam*.

Regarding dating conventions, I have opted for BCE and CE, Before the Common Era and the Common Era, rather than BC and AD. I use these abbreviations for dates related to historical events that took place during the period conventionally described as the Middle and Late Antiquity, more traditionally known as the Dark Ages, Medieval, and Late Medieval periods.

Where appropriate and useful, I have added to CE dates the Islamic Calendar date of AH, meaning Anno Hegirae, the year of the Hegira, or flight of Muhammad from Mecca to Medina which is set at 622 AD, or 622 CE. This date begins the first year of the Islamic Calendar, which is a Lunar, rather than a Solar Calendar. As such, over time, the Muslim Calendar date cannot be calculated simply by just subtracting 622 from the CE/AD date. For example, the end of the Umayyad Caliphate and Dynasty of 750 CE, is 132 AH, not 128 AH.

From the 17th century going forward, I do not specify CE or AH on the assumption that the reader will understand by the context that we are in the Modern Era.

Chapter 1

IN THE BEGINNING – THE ABRAHAMIC TRADITION

"Oh, East is East and West is West, and never the twain
shall meet, Till Earth and Sky stand presently at God's
great Judgment Seat; But there is neither East nor West,
Border, nor Breed, nor Birth, When two strong men stand
face to face, though they come from the ends of the earth!"

—RUDYARD KIPLING, 1889

"In the beginning God created the heaven and the earth...
And God said let there be light...[and on the sixth day] And
God said, let us make man in our own image, after our
likeness: and let them have dominion...over every creeping
thing that creepeth upon the earth...in the image of God
created he him: male and female created he them. And
God blessed them, and God said be fruitful, and multiply...
And on the Seventh day God ended his work which he had
made: and he rested."

—GENESIS 1. THE HOLY BIBLE, KING JAMES
VERSION, 1714 ED., PRINTED BY JAMES WATSON,

Pentateuch/Bible, New Testament, Koran

The first five books of the Old Testament Bible are known as the The Pentateuch. These are the Books of Genesis, Exodus, Leviticus, Numbers and Deuteronomy. From these Books stem three monotheistic religions with a common Abrahamic origin, Judaism, Christianity and Islam. It is thought that the first five Books of the Old Testament were written between 600 and 400 BCE (Before the Common Era) in Hebrew by Jews during their Babylonian capitivity. To the Jews, it is known as the Torah – the instruction or guide for the faithful. After this period, the Torah and the rest of the Old Testament Books were translated into Aramaic, the language spoken by Jews and non-Jews in and around the Mesopotamian area. With the success of Alexander the Great's Empire, there arose a demand for the Old Testament in *"koine"* or common Greek – said to be of Attic and Ionian Greek dialectic origins. A group of Jewish scholars, about 200 BCE, translated the Hebrew Bible, all the Books and Commentaries (Septuagint) into *koine*, or what was sometimes termed Alexandrian Greek, the language of Egyptians trading and intellectual capital where non-Hebrew-speaking, but rather, Greek-speaking, Jews lived.

In keeping with the theme of this book, it is important to note that the first five Books are common to all three religions and are based on God's Revelation to Moses (*Hazreti Musa Peygamber* in Turkish). At this point, there was no "East is East and West is West." The "twain" might be "believers in one God, the God of Abraham" and everyone else – polythiests, such as the Romans, and shamanists like the early Turks and Native Americans.

Family Feuds, Isaac, Ishmael, and Tribal Divisions
However, seeds of difference, seeds of bitterness, may have already been planted in Abraham's time. These differences may in today's parlance be the result of Abraham's dysfunctional family. Scripture tells us that Abraham and his wife Sarah had followed the commands of God, journeying from Haran to Egypt, and from there to Canaan. Abraham had been promised that from his seed would grow a nation. Sarah came to believe, as she found herself well beyond childbearing years, that she could not be the genesis of a nation. The Old Testament then tells us, *"Now Sarai, Abram's wife, bore him no children. She had an Egyptian slave-girl whose name was Hagar, and Sarai said to Abram, You see that the Lord has prevented me from bearing children; go into my slave-girl; it may be that I shall obtain children by her."* Genesis 16.8, *The New Revised Standard Version of the Bible*, Oxford University Press.

Hagar bore a child. God said to her that her son should be called Ishmael, foretelling that he shall be a, "wild ass of a man, with his hand against everyone, and everyone's hand against him; and he shall live at odds with all his kin." But God also promised Hagar that her son's seed would multiply greatly.

The story gets more complicated in Chapter 17 of Genesis because Sarah learns that in her older age she would bear a son who will be named Isaac. She, of course, becomes even more jealous of Hagar and Ishmael than she was before, fearing God's promise to Abraham that from him a nation would be born might, instead, pass through Ishmael. In her anxiety, Sarah prevailed upon her husband to banish Hagar and her son Ishmael. God then promised Abraham that Isaac would carry the seed of the Covenant of His people. As for Ishmael, he would father twelve princes. It is these princes who are said to have founded the twelve tribes of Arabia. His first born, Qaidar, founded the north Arabian Quraysh Tribe – the tribe into which the Prophet Muhammad is said to have been born. From this point on, Abraham's seed was divided into two lines of descent. A case may be made that these two Nations came to be separated geographically, one remaining in the area of Israel, and the other, in Jordan (Nabatea) and the Arabian Peninsula.

From the initial writing of the Old Testament, it would be another five or six centuries before Christianity would challenge Judaism and Mosaic Law. The Disciples of Jesus would proclaim the revealed word of Jesus as the Son of God. The Gospels would begin to be written within a generation of Christ's Crucifixion, and assembled in a few more generations to be become the New Testament. By Divine Revelation and Christian tradition, without getting into the details, the concept of God being Triune, Father, Son and Holy Ghost (The Holy Trinity), was born. This Gospel message, after the death of Christ, was carried by the Evangelists from the Holy Lands South to Egypt and Ethiopia, East to Persia and India and West to the Gentiles (Greek speakers) of Asia Minor and later into Europe. Rulers of many of these lands, who worshipped many dieties, but the Romans in particular persecuted the Christians for some 250 years.

By 325 CE, Roman Emperor Constantine moved his capital from Rome to the shores of the Bosphorus and named it Constantinople. Additionally, under pressure from his mother, Helen, who had accepted Christianity, he proclaimed Christianity to be the official religion of the Empire. Before doing so, he insisted that the Christians, already beset by various opposing interpetations of the Gospels, sort out their differences. He ordered Bishop Marcellus of Ankara to assemble the bishops of the Church in Nicea (İznik in Turkey, near Istanbul). The Bishops agreed on the basic Articles of Faith known as the Nicene Creed. Interpretations deviating from this orthodoxy were deemed heretical. It will come as no surprise that adherents of these differing interpretations and their successors went "underground" but did not die out. Some differences would resurface in subsequent Lateran

Councils over succeeding centuries, giving rise to some doctrinal compromises. Other differences persisted, resulting in the great Schism of the 11th century CE (Christian Era) – a divide between what became the Orthodox and Catholic Churches.

It would be several more hundreds of years, when the Prophet Muhammad at the age of 40 (610 CE) while living in Mecca, and surrounded by Christians, Jews, Mithrates, and other polytheists, would have a series of Revelations from the Angel Gabriel giving rise to a new faith, Islam. This new religion accepted the shared monotheistic Abrahamic tradition (Koran: Chapter 37/ Verse 112), thereby giving respect to "Peoples of the Book," Jews, Christians, and Zoroastrians. Jesus was accorded the status of Prophet, although not accepted as the Son of God (Koran: 3/45; 57/27; 5/110,111). And Mary, the Mother of Jesus, is revered in the Koran, but is not recognized as the bearer of the Son of God.

Mohammad's Revelation (Koran), was systematically written down over some time, with the San'a palimsest vellum document discovered in 1972 during the restoration of the dome of the Great Mosque of San'a Yemen being the oldest known manuscript. The underlayer of the washed vellum is estimated by several scholars, such as Asma Hilali, to date back to approximately 669 CE. The overlayer is thought to date to 705 CE, pointing to a process known as "canonization" whereby the Koran is edited, corrected, and organized. While much of the Koran was standardized by that later date, during the reign of the Fifth Umayyad Caliph, 'Abd al-Malik al Marwan, within a generation of the Prophet's death, the evolution continued until 1924, the date of the current standard text (The Cairo Edition). And still, the process continues. Chase F. Robinson, in his book on 'Abd al-Malik, writes that the process of the recordation and organization of the Koran, along with the stories about the Prophet's life and teachings (Sunna) and the Holy Traditions (Hadith), was a "fluid process," that grew to become the basis for the new law, the Sharia. For Muslims, Sharia Law, unlike Judeo-Mosaic Law and Christian Canon, will come to define all aspects of life.

For the new followers of the Prophet Muhammad, the Koran is accepted as the last and true Revelation of God, now called in Arabic, Allah. Similar to Christianity, not long after the death of The Prophet, Islam would also experience divisions in the Successsion of Caliphs entitled to rule the Faithful, as well as in interpretations of the Koran that follow from the original divide, or controversy, of succession. These are the Sunni (Orthodox) Schools of Hanefi, Hanbali, Maliki and Shafi'i and Shia interpretation, Jafari.

Having seen examples of what religious tradition is shared, and what is not, between and among Judaism, Christianity, and Islam, one should not forget that the original adherents of these Faiths were all ethnically Semitic peoples of the Levant. Time, competition, and conflict among men have compounded the differences between the adherents of these three religions. Similarly divisive forces, of course, predate the advent of these monotheistic religions. Here Thucydides, on the subject of human nature, comes to mind where he opines that man is motivated by fear (*phobos*), self-interest (*kerdos*), and honor (*doxa*). The thoughtful, if debatable, words of Edward Atiyah in his book, *The Arabs*, also sheds some insight, "*The God of the Muslims is the same as the God of the Jews and the Christians, but without the racial exclusiveness attributed to him by the former, or the intricate metaphysical theory woven about him by the latter. The Prophet Mohammed not only learned his monotheism from Jewish and Christian sources, but he also accepted and venerated Moses and Jesus as his forerunners, merely claiming to complete their message and be the last of the prophets.*"

Asian Turkic Migration, the Bering Strait, and native Americans

As this discussion has centered on what one might call "Biblical" times, it is *a propos* to imagine that Eastern and Western, Turkic and American, relations, might have been literally "bridged" much earlier in time than more conventional dates and events such as the Crusades (in the case of Europeans) or Barbary Coast Piracy (in the case of Americans). Curiously, on the matter of "bridging," it is interesting to speculate about the theory regarding the possibility that North-East Asian Turkic peoples from the Altai-Ural region may have crossed the Bering Strait onto, and into, the North American land mass at the end of the last Ice Age, some 10,000 years ago. If there is any truth to this theory, this would help to explain the Shaman practices of Native American peoples. It would also give some rationale to the uncanny similarities in culture and art, from totems to rug design, sug-

gestive of the possibility of common ancestry. Note the seemingly Turkic word for these water falls in the Grand Canyon, Havasu Falls (*havasu*, translated as "water from the sky" in Turkish).

The next chapter will look at a later migration of Turkic peoples who began to move West and South West, off the Central Asian plain, with several of the tribes moving into the Middle East beginning in the 7th and 8th centuries CE. They will bring with them their Shamanistic practices, but will give them up over time and convert to Islam.

Chapter 2

ISLAM, CHRISTIANITY, AND THE HOLY LANDS

Turkic Migrations into the Middle East

Much of what we know about the equestrian pastoral and nomadic peoples of the Asian Steppe comes from Chinese accounts. Turkic peoples are said to have come from the Altai-Ural area of Upper Mongolia. The Orkhon Inscriptions found in Mongolia, carved on stone monuments dating from the 8th century, illustrate the existence of an Old Turkic Script. It appears that food scarcity precipitated their migrations. For our purposes, we will focus on the Western Göktürk tribes which began to move to the Aral-Caspian area. From there, branches of this tribe, the Kipchaks, Oğuz, and later, Seljuk dynasty which sprang from the Qiniq branch that ruled over a confederation of Oğuz tribes, came into contact with Umayyad Arabs as far back as the 6th and 7th centuries. Efforts to convert the Turks, by sword or religious beliefs, were variously resisted for nearly 300 years. They seemed to have been perfectly happy with their Shaman pagan practices. The earliest recorded conversions began with the Kara-Khanids of Transoxiana in the mid-tenth century, when Sultan Satuk Bughra Khan converted.

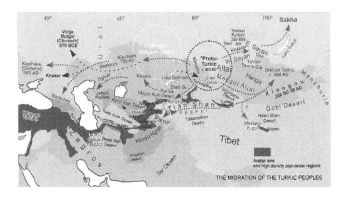

THE MIGRATION OF THE TURKIC PEOPLES

From Shaman Worship to Conversion to Islam

It would not be until the late 10th century that Seljuk himself, now a conqueror, found it useful to convert to Islam. From there, the Seljuk Islamic Empire would begin in the East, with its capital located in Nishapur in 1037 CE, under the leadership of Tuğrul Bey. Later in that century, they continued to expand primarily in a Westerly direction, into the Levant and across Anatolia, where they fought against the Christian Byzantines. These Seljuks of Rum would establish their capital in Konya.

Being geographically removed from the brunt of the Mongol invasions, another descendant of the Oğuz tribe, Osman I, whose clan was located in Western Anatolia, would continue where the Seljuks left off. His descendants, the Ottomans, would carry the banner of Islam to its geographic zenith.

For all the military prowess of the Turks, by the time mass conversion of Turks was taking place, the Turkish ruling elites had become inheritors of a Persian-Arab culture that had attained very high levels of civilization.

Abbasid Caliphate – A Golden Age of Expansion and Tolerance

Upon verifying the death of the Prophet Muhammad, Abu Bakr, his father-in-law and the first Caliph (successor), famously proclaimed to the followers, *"Whoso worshippeth Mohammed, let him know that Mohammed is dead; but whoso worshippeth God, let him know that God liveth and dieth not".* Under the direction of the second Caliph, Omar, Arab conquests, often in search of the riches of Persia and Byzantium, were swift. The cities of Jerusalem, Damascus, and Alexandria fell quickly. By 750 CE (132 AH), the Umayyad rule came to a bloody end, when its army was defeated in the Battle of Zab and all but one of the ruling family was murdered. To the burgeoning Arab Civilization, the Umayyads brought their language and their religion as a lasting legacy. Arabia and Islam were now poised to give to and receive from the many peoples that came under their influence.

The Abbasids were descended from an uncle of the Prophet, al Abbas. They moved the capital from Damascus to Baghdad, the legendary city of the "Arabian Nights" and the court of Caliph Harun al Rashid. Into the Arab elite flowed non-Arab blood, Persian culture, Greek philosophy, science, mathematics, and medicine translated (mostly by Greeks and Persian scholars) from Greek or Syriac under the patronage of the Abbasids. Abbasid textiles, taffeta, organdy, wood, and metalwork were prized in the church and courts of Western Europe. The House of Wisdom in Baghdad (*Bayt Al-Hikma*) and some of the prime thinkers and scientific minds of the time will be discussed further in the Chapter concerning the learning that was transferred both directly to Europe and via *Al Andalus* (Moorish Spain). Both Harun and his son Ma'mun were scholars themselves. One can hardly imagine the notable differences between Baghdad and Paris in Charlemagne's time. City lighting, plumbing, hospitals, fountains, and gardens describe Baghdad at that time. Paris was truly primitive by comparison.

From Praetorian Guard to the Sword of Islam

The culture of the Abbasids needed to be protected. Having a great respect for the equestrian warriors from the Steppe with whom the Arabs were skirmishing in the northern reaches of their empire (today's Iran), over time, either by capture or slave market purchase, the Turks, mostly Perso-Sunni Kipchaks, were brought in to form a non-Arab "Praetorian" guard committed to the protection of Abbasid Caliphs. Their systematic recruitment began in the early ninth century under the Seventh Abbasid Caliph, al-Ma'mun, son of the famed Harun al-Rashid. They were called Mamluks, coming from the Arabic word for property, or slave. In time, they became the military rulers of the Caliphate and were proclaimed Sultans.

The Caliphs were the spiritual leaders of the Islamic Faithful, while the administration and expansion of the Arab Empire fell to the Sultan and his army and tax collectors. This diminution of Caliphal power that began with the Abbasid defeat by the Shi' i Buyids, when they captured Baghdad (945 CE), resulted in disunity in the Empire, with Egypt then falling under control of Ali's line (the Prophet's son-in-law and nephew cousin), the Fatimid Shias. Moorish Spain, *Al Andalus*, came under the rule of the one Umayyad to escape the slaughter of his family at the hands of the Abbasids. About him, we will hear more in the Chapter on *Al Andalus*. The Maghreb (North African Muslim States West of Egypt, meaning where the sun sets in Arabic, as opposed to Mashriq, including Egypt, and Muslim States to the East, where the sun rises) came to be governed by the Ifriqiya, Aghlabid, and Idrisid dynasties. And finally, as noted above, the Seljuks in the 11th century CE, established an empire centered in Konya (Biblical Iconium), known as the Sultanate of Rum, which extended east to include the Levant.

In spite of all these centrifugal tendencies dividing the Abbasid Empire, Baghdad, as a center of learning, continued to personify the meaning of the Golden Age of Islam. Tolerance for new ideas, different races, and ethnicities made it a cultural and political melting pot. Christians, Jews, Greeks, Persians, Turks, Berbers all joined in the Arab language and the religion of Islam, either voluntarily or at the point of a sword. Truly, the contribution of the Abbasids might best be characterized in the Koranic injunction and Hadith, "the ink of a scholar is more holy than the blood of a martyr."

All of this grandeur, already in decline, came to a frightening halt with the Mongol invasions and the burning of Baghdad in 1258 CE (625 AH). However, the Mongols would prove to be no different from other conquerors. They would in many ways be conquered by the civilization and religion of the people conquered. They accepted Islam in the same manner that the conquering Goths and Visigoths in the West accepted Christianity, more often than not through intermarriage with European Christians.

Some would like to minimize the achievements of the Abbasids and the Golden Age as being limited to a resurrection, via Arabic translation, of the Wisdom of earlier civilizations. If this were true, it was so only in the beginning. The re-discovered wisdom and learning was then subjected to critical questioning and testing. Earlier science was amended and improved. New science was generated. The many words of Arabic origin that have come down to us today such as algebra, algorithm, alchemy, zero, tariff, checkmate (shah mat, the king is dead), lemon, rice, sugar, atlas, damask, syrup, ginger, sofa, divan, Guadalquivir, wadi, and admiral and, most importantly, Arabic numerals are a testament to just some of the most widely recognized words and concepts handed on to the world by Islamic civilization. The cultural and scientific borrowing, or adoption, is even greater in Spanish and Portuguese because of long Muslim rule in the Iberian Peninsula.

Islam, Christianity, and the Holy Lands would be intertwined forever and usually not in peace, as we will learn in the next chapter about conflict around the Mediterranean.

Chapter 3

COMPETITION AND CONFLICT AROUND THE MEDITERRANEAN BASIN

The Battle of Manzikert – Alp Arslan

The spread of Islam is nothing if not a continuation of competition and conflict around the Mediterranean Basin. By the 11th century, the driving military force behind the spread of Islam came from a dynastic branch of the Oğuz tribe, the Seljuk Turks. The original Seljuk Empire extended from its home south of the Aral Sea east to Afghanistan. The founder of the Empire was Tuğrul Bey. After converting to Islam, the Seljuks moved south in Persia, where Persian was spoken at Court and Oğuz Turkish in the army. From there, they began to move into Eastern Anatolia. At this time, Islam was flourishing across North Africa and into Spain. Baghdad remained the cultural center of Islam. The geographic front lines of Islam continued to be defined by the Franks and the Pyrenees in Northern Spain and the Byzantines and their eastern border, Anatolia and the Holy Lands.

During the reigns of two successive Byzantine Emperors, Constantine IX and Constantine X, the strength and command of the Byzantine army was falling into disarray due to elites infighting and a failing economy. Skirmishes with the Turks had begun in the 1030s and 1040s CE. In 1067 CE, the Turks captured Ani, the Armenian capital and shortly thereafter, Caesarea (*Kayseri*), a key trading center along the Great Silk Route. However, preoccupied with a more pressing enemy, the Fatimids of Egypt, the Seljuks signed a treaty with the Byzantines. It may be interesting to note that the year before, in the West, William the Conqueror, a Norman-French king of Viking ancestry, conquered the English King Harold of Wessex at the Battle of Hastings. While England was his target, his successors would eventually do battle with the Muslims of *Al Andalus* (Moorish Spain), capturing Sicily from them in the same year, 1071 CE (463 AH), as the Battle of *Manzikert*.

The significance of the Battle of Manzikert (Malazgirt in Eastern Turkey) continues to be debated in the West. Clearly, the defeat and capture of the Byzantine Emperor Romanos IV Diogenes and the disarray of the Byzantine Army, itself a collection of Byzantine, European, Armenian, and Turkish mercenary forces, opened the way for the victorious Seljuk ruler, Alp Arslan (notice the Persian spelling, which in Turkish is Aslan, meaning lion) to begin to overrun Anatolia. One important geo-political fact is that crossing the Anatolian plain began to close for Christian Pilgrims, and later, more tightly, for the Crusaders after the Battle of Myriokephalon in 1176 CE in Phrygia (west central Anatolia). They were then forced to use sea routes – thereby bolstering the wealth and power of the Genoan and Venetian republics and their commercial and military fleets. Writing only a few decades after this battle, an historian and the Princess daughter of Byzantine Emperor Alexios I Komnenos wrote, *"...the fortunes of the Roman Empire had sunk to their lowest ebb. For the armies of the East were dispersed in all directions, because the Turks had over-spread, and gained command of, countries between the Euxine Sea [Black Sea] and the Hellespont [Dardanelles], and the Aegean Sea and Syrian Seas [Eastern Mediterranean Sea], and the various bays, especially those which wash Pamphylia, Cilicia, and empty themselves into the Egyptian Sea [Alexandria]"*.

The Seljuks, from their capital of Konya (Iconium), in the century between these two battles, secured much of Anatolia as well as key Mediterranean and Black Sea ports. If Manzikert was the beginning of the end of the Byzantine Empire, the Battle of Myriokephalon left the remnants of this once great empire isolated in Constantinople and its immediate surroundings.

The significance of the Manzikert defeat is perhaps best seen in the Western response. Under the leadership of Pope Urban II, the first Crusade was launched to wrest control of Jerusalem from Seljuk rule. The Christian heritage of Jerusalem and the Holy Lands had everything to do with the legitimacy of Christian rule, from the Papacy to the kingdoms of Western Europe and Latinate Kingdoms of the Holy Lands. The fact that these lands were also holy for the Muslims was beside the point to the West, the Christian claims of which antedated Muslim claims by six centuries, not to mention even older Old Testament claims. Protecting pilgrims and their access to Jerusalem came to be the rationale for the First Crusade, which did succeed in regaining control of Jerusalem in 1099 CE. A Latinate Kingdom was "re-established." The second King of which, Baldwin II, with a Papal blessing, gave permission to two groups of Knights, the Templars and the Hospitalers, to provide safety and health care, respectively, to Christian travelers and pilgrims (1119 CE) on their way to the Holy Lands. The Christian West took some solace in this achievement. The pride of Western Christendom was temporarily restored – but only temporarily. The Muslims would capture the Christian stronghold of Edessa and a Second Crusade to recapture it was launched (1147-1149) and failed.

Significance of the Battle of Hattin –
Saladin and the Ayyubs

On July 4, 1187 CE (583 AH), Muslim forces led Saladin the Sultan of Egypt and Syria, defeated the Crusader army led by the King of Jerusalem, Guy de Lusignan, and Raymond III of Tripoli. The battle involved 50,000 soldiers and took place some six miles west of the Sea of Galilee along the main road from the coast at Acre. Legend has it that remnants of the "True Cross" carried by the Bishop of Tyre were captured when the bishop was killed in battle. It is said that Saladin then dishonored these, but that story may be apocryphal.

Without getting into the details of the battle, King Guy's decision to leave their stronghold in Sephora where they had water and to move east to engage Saladin's forces in the open, with no access to water for the soldiers, was reckless and ill-advised. The net result was that Jerusalem was lost to Christendom.

Almost immediately, a third Crusade was organized and led by Richard I (the Lionheart), Phillip II of France, Holy Roman Emperor Barbarossa, and Byzantine Emperor Isaac II Angelus. In 1189 CE, they returned to the Holy Lands and recaptured much of what had been lost. Due to dissention within Richard's war cabinet, with Jerusalem in sight, a decision to retreat was made. They established their new capital in Acre (Akko, Israel today) on the coast two years later.

Richard and Saladin did negotiate a treaty whereby Christian pilgrims and traders would be allowed safe passage to and from Jerusalem. Richard succeeded in reestablishing control of the profitable trading ports from Jaffa to Antioch. However, neither side was really satisfied. Saladin's critics were fearful that Crusader forces would return in large numbers and retake Jerusalem and the Levant. In the Catholic West, Richard was criticized for his failure to retake Jerusalem. In response, a fourth Crusade would be organized five years later. This Crusade never reached the Near East for reasons to be discussed in the chapter concerning schisms in Islam and Christianity. Jerusalem would remain in Muslim hands. Even Acre would fall to the Mamluks (Kipchak Turks), successors to the Ayyubs of Egypt, a century later, in 1291 CE (690 AH). Christian forces would not have a presence in the Levant until Napoleon's army captured Cairo five centuries later.

It is interesting to note that Saladin (born in Tikrit, where the Iraqi ruler Saddam Hussein was born and was captured during the First Gulf War) and the Ayyub elite were Sunni Kurdish. Saladin's rise to notoriety began in the service of Sunni Turkic ruler of Mosul, Nur al-Din Zangi, by first fighting the Crusaders and later conquering Egypt. Under the watchful eye of Nur al-Din, he began his political rise as Vizier under the Shia Fatimid dynasty of Egypt. He quickly rose through the ranks, overthrowing the Fatimids and realigning his kingdom with the Sunni Abbasid Caliphate of Baghdad. It is also worth remembering that the Mamluk successor dynasty to Saladin and the Ayyubs negotiated with the Christians a rite of passage through Crusader-controlled territory in order to engage the Mongols in what became the Battle of Ain Jalut in 1260 CE in Galilee. This battle proved to be significant as the first sustained defeat of a Mongol Army. The Crusaders granted permission to the Mamluks to cross their territory because the Mongols represented a more imminent threat than did the Mamluks.

The Crusades and Failure to Hold
Jerusalem, a Western View

In summary, Crusader failure to recapture Jerusalem from
the "Muslim infidels" remained an obsession and a scar in
the heart of Western Christendom until the end of World
War I, when Britain and France, under the terms of the
Versailles Treaty, gave England and France "mandated"
influence over the Levant more than six centuries after
the fall of the Latinate Kingdom of Jerusalem.

Arguably, the defeat of the Crusaders remained in the
memory of Muslim culture as a source of pride in the
"rightness" and superiority of Islam and fulfillment of the
Will of Allah. In their eyes, they retained their spiritual
homeland. Such victories reinsured the message that Islam
must be the "True Faith," but who should carry the banner
of Islam was the more abiding concern for the Muslims.
Internecine warfare was incessant, in spite of the warning
given by Muhammad that his tribes should rise above their
ignorant tendency to continually war with one another
(*Cahiliyya*). Some Muslim kingdoms allied themselves with
the Crusaders if they thought it would help them defeat
rival Muslim kingdoms or principalities. Arguably, this
tendency in many ways persists down to present times.

The Fall of Constantinople – Another Victory
for Islam, Another Scar for Christendom

Symbolically, the capture of the capital of the Holy Roman
Empire in 1453 CE (857 AH), home to the Byzantine

successor to the great empire of Constantine, dealt yet another blow to the psyche of Christian Europe. The idea that Emperor Justinian's great Saint Sophia Basilica, by then the seat of the Greek Orthodox Patriarchate, had been turned into a Mosque, was a public shame to the head, and heart, of Christendom.

In fact, the fall of Constantinople happened slowly. With the Seljuk tribes in disarray in the face of continued Mongol incursions, Osman I and his tribe in Western Anatolia were able to flourish and, by 1299 CE, claim independence from the Seljuks. Over the next 250 years, his descendants would grow his achievements into an empire that would last almost six centuries. At the invitation of the Byzantine Emperor John V Palaeologus, the Ottoman Turks crossed the Dardanelles into Europe and began to seize areas in the Balkans. By the time Fatih Sultan Mehmet II conquered Constantinople, with the exception of Karamanid territory around Konya, the Ottomans controlled most of Anatolia and some of Thrace. When Constantinople fell, it was but a ghost of its former glory – and by then virtually surrounded by Turks.

As the Eastern seat of the Caesars, it had been an objective and a thorn in the flesh of Islam, mentioned by the Prophet Muhammad himself as recorded in a Hadith. Mehmet II even added *"Rum Kayseri (*Roman Caesar*)"* to his many titles. For more than 1100 years, Christian Emperors had ruled from Constantine's capital. The psychological impact of this conquest is duly noted in the first lines from Alan Parker's book, *The Decline and Fall of the Ottoman Empire*,

> "'There Never Has Been And Never Will Be A More Dreadful Happening,' wrote a monastic scribe in Crete when in June 1453 reports reached the island that Constantinople had fallen to the Turk. His tone of horror was echoed in Papal Rome and Republican Venice...in the trading cities Aragon and Castile as the shock wave spread across the continent."

It should be remembered that when push came to shove, that is when the Emperor Palaeologus called for help from his Christian brothers in the West, it was not forthcoming. Western Catholic concern for more local issues, compounded by what had become a substantial linguistic, theological, and cultural divide, growing for several centuries, left the Byzantines with less sympathy from their Western brethren, especially after the Ottoman defeat of the Kingdoms of Poland, Hungary, and the Holy Roman Empire and the Papal States at the Battle of Varna in eastern Bulgaria in 1444 nearly a decade earlier with no help then offered from Constantinople. That the Byzantines had come to take a less bellicose posture toward the Muslims regarding its own shrinking borders, being by then more given to diplomactic maneuver, even with the Muslims, had not sat well in Western Europe where Islam was being rolled back militarily in Spain, for example.

The next chapter examines the enormous cultural and scientific exchange of Mediterranean and Asian cultures occasioned by trade and conflict. Turks, Chinese, Indians, Afghans, Persians, Arabs, Berbers, Byzantines, Iberians, Franks, Latins, Normans, and Slavs borrowed significantly from one another's civilizations. Globalization was a process well underway via the Silk Road connecting the Asian world to the Mediterranean world.

Chapter 4

COMMERCE, CARAVANS AND CULTURAL – SCIENTIFIC EXCHANGE

"This civilizational closure of the earth's relatively empty spaces, mainly in the temperate zone, began in a fundamental way with the voyages of discovery: those of da Gama, Columbus, Magellan, and others."
—ROBERT D. KAPLAN, *THE REVENGE OF GEOGRAPHY*

Anatolia and the Silk Route of Commerce and Ideas

As developments in technology progressed from the Iron and Bronze ages forward, societies and then entire civilizations began to increasingly form and rub shoulders. Conflict and competition acclerated the spread of commerce, languages, cultures, and ideas. Mesopotamia and Anatolia came to be a geographic crossroads, first by land and then by sea, in the predominately east-west, west-east movement of peoples and goods. Along the route, food and materials production benefitted from the abundant water supplies and plains of a temperate zone that stretched from the Far East to Western Europe and England. Long stretches of flat lands, rivers and seas further facilitated the migration of peoples along what became major arteries of tribes and then civilizations spreading along what came to be called the Silk Route.

The bandwidth of this zone allowed for some North-South migrations as well, with geography playing a critical role in the cultural interplay. This area was bounded on the South by the Sahalian desert and in the North by mountain ranges and colder climates. In time, even these impediments were gradually overcome by advances in seamanship, less by moving across the zone than by sailing around it. As peoples moved beyond survival, they organized themselves into societies with members divided into functional specialities, and finally into civilizations. As Kaplan notes above, the earth's empty spaces began to be filled. This process accelerated between what has been called the Golden Age of Islam and the Rennaissance – between the 8th and 16th centuries CE. We will discuss this in more detail below but, as Kaplan has observed, while rulers and the boundaries of their domains change, *"The only thing enduring is people's position on a map. Thus in times of upheaval, maps rise in importance. With the political ground shifting rapidly under one's feet, the map, though not determinative, is the beginning of discerning a historic logic about what might come next."*

In the world of Ancient Greece and Rome, the *Oeukoumene*, or the "known inhabited quarter of the world," began with the Mediterranean, about which the Greek historian and geographer, Strabo writes in the first century CE, *"Most of all it is the sea that delineates precisely the layout of the land, creating gulfs, sea-basins, traversable narrows and, in the same way, isthmuses, peninsulas and capes; in this the rivers and mountains also play their part."*

At right is a printed map from the 15th century depicting Ptolemy's ancient description of the *Oecumene* (1482, Johannes Schnitzer, engraver).

The Romans would then call this map the *"orbis terrarum,"* later becoming the basis for the title of what is said to be the world's first true atlas, *"Theatrum Orbis Terrarum"* written by Abraham Ortelius and printed in Antwerp in 1570 (seen at bottom).

The Silk Route was primarily a Eurasian land bridge for the movement of commodities as noted in the map below. For our purposes, the Silk Route is equally a conduit for languages, cultures, and ideas. At its Western edge, it begins in the Mediterranean basin wherein the lingua franga was initially Greek. The Phonecians make the first significant and abiding connections

by establishing outposts on a sea frontier, from Tyre to the second Tripoli, to Carthage, Sicily, and Gibraltar. To this world are subsequently added Hellenistic, Roman, and Byzantine cultures linked through conquest and trade from England, across Southern Europe, along North Africa, all linked by the Mediterranean and land routes running as far East as the Indus Valley and China.

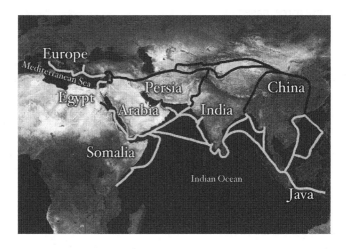

At the center of this matrix of exchange is the Mediterranean Sea. As noted by the first great modern scholar of the history of the Mediterranean region, Fernand Braudel, with the publication of the second French edition of *The Mediterranean and the Mediterranean World in the Age of Phillip II*, [in translation] he observed the following, *"Today in 1972, I think I can say that two major truths have remained unchallenged. The first is the unity and coherence*

of the Mediterranean region. I retain the firm conviction that the Turkish Mediterranean lived and breathed with the same rhythms as the Christian, that the whole sea shared a common destiny... And the second is the greatness of the Mediterranean, which lasted well after the age of Columbus and Vasco da Gama."

With the fissure between the Eastern and Western Holy Roman Empire, between Rome and Constantinople, a new force, based in Damascus, came into the gap, sweeping out of the Arabian Peninsula – Islam under the banner of the Umayyad Caliphs in the 7th and early 8th centuries CE. The expansion followed shortly thereafter by the Abbasids, who settled in Kufa (in modern Iraq) and then later moved their capital to Baghdad initiating what has come to be known as the Golden Age of Islam – both its cultural flowering and its conquests, from Persia, across North Africa to Spain and into the Balkans.

Coming from Moorish Spain, Islam waged war northward against the Merovingian Franks, led by Charles Martel, at the Battle of Tours (Loire Valley) in France in 732 CE and were there stopped, retreating back south of the Pyrenees. The geographical frontier of Islam in Western Europe was then largely fixed for centuries. Yet, the cultural and intellectual exchange was only just beginning.

Moving our attention back to the Levant, what was happening in the court of Arab Caliph Harun al Rashid in his capital of Baghdad? What were its effects on *Al*

Andalus, the Arab-Berber controlled Iberian Peninsula, Spain, and Portugal?

Harun al Rashid is remembered for many reasons. The focus will be on the House of Wisdom (*Bayt al-Hikma*) established in Baghdad during his reign (786-809 CE). This became the center of learning and translation of works in Greek, Persian, and Indian texts. By the middle of the 9th century, it is said to be the largest repository of books in the world – only to be destroyed during the Mongol invasions of the 13th century. As a center, it was unrivaled in the study of the humanities, science, mathematics, astronomy, alchemy, cartography, and philosophy. Islamic scholars gathered here to study and to translate the Ancient Works into Arabic. From there, Western scholars began to translate the works of Aristotle, Plato, and others from Arabic into Latin. Later, translations from Latin into the early vernacular languages of Christian Europe would help fuel the renaissance. This burst of learning would spread to Europe not just from the Abbasids in Baghdad, but notably from Moorish Spain.

Al Andalus, the Epicenter of Cultural and Scientific Exchange in the West

In the words of Anwar Chejne in his book, *Muslim Spain – Its History and Culture*, he notes, *"Muslim Spain was always an integral part of the literary and intellectual mainstream of the East and, as such, was as Islamic as Syria or Egypt."* The Arabs were present in Spain for almost eight centuries, from 711 to 1492. Those remaining thereafter, during the Inquisition, converted to Christianity (Mudéjares, Moriscos), willingly or not, though as many of their Christian counterparts (Mozarabs) during Moorish rule, in private, retained their ancestral faiths. Muslim Spain was the most advanced country of Western Europe and it served as a cultural bridge between Europe, Africa, and Asia. Its cities such as Cordova, Seville, Granada, and Toledo were renowned for their architectural beauty and the immense body of literature held in the areas of science, medicine, *belles lettres*, geography, history, religion, and speculative sciences. Arabic was the language for most of this work and was spoken by all educated people, Romans, Visigoths, Arabs, Jews, Berbers, and others. Its scholars and future rulers traveled east, especially to centers of learning – most particularly, Baghdad. One of these was Abd al-Rahman II who traveled to Medina, studied under the great jurisprudent Maliki, then returned to *Al Andalus* where he established the Maliki School of interpretation of Islamic law. Let us briefly look at two of the more influential and better known of these scholars, Averröes and Ibn Khaldun, who traveled to the Arab East and returned to the Arab-Spanish Courts with Arabic translations of the works of earlier civilizations. In turn, they and other scholars imparted their knowledge via these translated works of science, philosophy, and art well beyond the borders of Muslim Spain.

Already by the 12th century CE, scholars from England, France, Italy, and Germany were coming to study works of the Ancients from which they had largely been cut off for centuries. These scholars learned Arabic in order to translate the works of towering figures of the Ancient world such as Aristotle, Plato, Socrates, Euclid, Galen, and Herodotus, into Latin, and then later into European vernacular languages. Indian works on astronomy, such as the Sindhind, re-introduced Greek usage of the astrolabe in navigation. A Chinese invention probably, the Arabs also brought with them parchment paper, a critical improvement in cost over vellum (animal hide), then still being used in Western Europe. Moorish architecture came to influence all of Europe and continues to this day especially in Spain, Latin America, Florida, and California.

For the Moorish influence to be significant and lasting, an environment had to be created conducive to an explosion of learning. The procuring cause came through the guidance of an escaped Umayyad-family refugee, Abd al-Rahman I, the rest of whose family had been treacherously murdered by the new ruling Abbasid Caliphs. He re-founded an Umayyad Dynasty and Emirate that lasted in Spain from 756 CE to 929 CE. His grandson, Abd al Rahman III, proclaimed a Caliphate lasting from 929 CE to 1031 CE (see map below). Thereafter, Muslim Spain began to break into feudal city-states ruled tribally by Arabs and Berbers who maintained order in their cities with mercenaries and alliances with Christian kings in the northern reaches of the Iberian Peninsula. In the contest for control, Arabized Christian Mozarabs had divided loyalties between the Muslim Andalusians and their co-religionists in the North. This was also true of the Mudéjares, Muslims who lived in Christian territories. Perhaps the handwriting was on the wall when Spanish King Alfonso VI retook the City of Toledo in 1075 and El Cid took Valencia in 1085.

In an effort to stanch a crumbling Muslim Spain, the support of the Berber Kings of the Maghreb, the Almoravids, were welcomed into *Al Andalus*. They did not leave until the final Catholic *Reconquista* of Iberia in 1492, when King Ferdinand and Queen Isabella, with support from Christian Europe and the Holy Roman League, took back control of the Iberian Peninsula.

The impact of this on Muslims and Jews was profound. All were forced to convert to Catholicism, were killed or fled to other countries. The story of the Sephardic Jews is well known – many going to the Ottoman Empire where they were given safe haven. What is not so well known is the trauma that impacted the much larger population of Muslims who suffered the same fate. Some converted, some escaped to the Maghreb, and many perished. Many of those who converted and remained, Jew and Arab alike, continued to worship their ancestral faith in the privacy of their homes.

In spite of strife during the slow Christian re-conquest, counter-intuitively, the intellectual and cultural life of Muslim Spain continued in the various Kingdoms onto which they managed to hold. Great architectural works come down to us that are a blend of Moorish and Christian artistic influences such as the Alhambra in Grenada and the Grand Mosque of Seville (See below).

Averroes (Ibn Rushd), Polymath, and Conduit for Western Rediscovery of Aristotle and Plato

While other great philosophers came out of *Al Andalus*, such as Ibn Tufayl, and Maimonides, Ibn Rushd, (pictured here) better known as Averröes (1126-1198 CE), was remarkably influential on Western thought. He was a polymath, a master of Aristotelian and Islamic philosophy, as well as theology, math, science, medicine, Maliki law and jurisprudence, astronomy, and music. He is recognized in the West as being the "Father of secular thought." His influence was felt well beyond the borders of *Al Andalus*. He popularized Aristotle and, in the process, fostered Scholasticism in Medieval Europe. His influence is seen in the teachings of Anselm, Abelard, Duns Scotus, and Thomas Aquinas. Alas, his works came to be considered heretical by Islamic authorities, and he was banished from his home in Cordova to Morocco.

Ibn Khaldun, Islamic World Traveler and the Father of Sociology

The other towering figure of influence on Western and Eastern thought was Ibn Khaldun (1332-1406 CE). Of Yemeni and then Andalusian ancestry, Ibn Khaldun was born in the cosmopolitan city of Tunis, where he would return later in life to write *The History of the World (The Muqaddima)* about which British historian Arnold Toynbee observed reveals a, *"philosophy of history which is undoubtedly the greatest of its kind that has ever yet been created by any mind in any time or place."*

This is a man who witnessed and lived in a time of great upheaval, including the Black Plague, which took his parents in Tunis, the continuing Christian re-conquest of Spain, The Hundred Years' War, the Mongol destruction of Damascus and Baghdad, and the rise of the Ottomans. He traveled from Tunis to Grenada, Seville, then to Morocco, Western Algeria, and back to Tunis. He then went on a Pilgrimage (*Haj*) to Mecca. He later moved to Egypt where he was a judge (*Kadı*). From there, he was sent by Egyptian Muslim officials to Damascus to negotiate a peace with Tamerlane, the Turco-Mongol Conqueror. The mission failed and he returned to Egypt where he died.

Ibn Khaldun was born into an educated family whose members had served in various official capacities. Ibn Khaldun followed in their steps with a substantial political career in many courts in addition to his academic and intellectual pursuits. He is considered in the West as a "Founding Father of Modern Sociology (*umran al-basharı*), Historiography and Economics." His development of the concept of "*asabiyya*" or "social solidarity" on the cycles of formation of tribes, societies, nations, and of civilizations, found in his seminal work, *The Muqaddima*, was greatly influential on Western social and political thought. His work on this subject must surely have influenced the analysis of Edward Gibbon's *The Rise and Fall of the Roman Empire*. An example of his insights into economics is seen in the following passage of the *Muqaddima*, *"When civilization [population] increases, the available labor again increases. In turn, luxury again increases in correspondence with the increasing profit, and the customs and needs of luxury increase. Crafts are created to obtain luxury products. The value realized from them increases, and, as a result, profits are again multiplied in the town. Production there is thriving even more than before. And so it goes with the second and third increase. All the additional labor serves luxury and wealth, in contrast to the original labor that served the necessity of life."*

Influenced by Aristotle, Ibn Khaldun synthesized a practical marriage between theory and practice. He did not begin with a pre-conceived notion and then seek to prove it by arranging facts to support his theory. He began with real observations from which he developed theory. As noted by Chejne, *"… the historian should have a clear knowledge of customs, facts of politics, the nature of civilization, and the conditions governing social organization. Furthermore, he should use critical judgment in dealing with the past, duly regarding changes that occur in the course of time; and he should be fully aware of accounts not properly verified, partisan, or ignorant of the true nature of various conditions arising in a civilization."*

On the subject of taxes, Ibn Khaldun's observations are prescient. He observed that, *"In the early stages of the state, taxes are light in their incidence, but fetch in a large revenue; in the later stages the incidence of taxation increases while the aggregate revenue falls off. ...Now where taxes and imposts are light, private individuals are encouraged to actively engage in business; enterprise develops, because businessmen feel it worth their while, in view of the small share of their profits which they have to give up in the form of taxation. And as business prospers the number of taxes increases and the total yield of taxation grows. However, governments become progressively more extravagant and start to raise taxes. These increases [in taxes and sales taxes] grow with the spread of luxurious habits in the state, and the consequent growth in needs and public expenditure, until taxation burdens the subjects and deprives them of their gains. People get accustomed to this high level of taxation, because the increases have come about gradually, without anyone's being aware of exactly who it was who raised the rates of the old taxes or imposed the new ones. But the effects on business of this rise in taxation make themselves felt. For businessmen are soon discouraged by the comparison of their profits with the burden of their taxes, and between their output and their net profits. Consequently, production falls off, and with it the yield of taxation. The rulers may, mistakenly, try to remedy this decrease in the yield of taxation by raising the rate of taxes; hence, taxes and imposts reach a level, which leaves no profit to businessmen, owing to high costs of production, heavy burden of taxation and inadequate net profits. This process of higher tax rates and lower yields (caused by the government's belief that higher rates result in higher returns) may go on until production begins to decline owing to the despair of businessmen, and to affect the population. The main injury of this process is felt by the state, just as the main benefit of better business conditions is enjoyed by it. From this you must understand that the most important factor making for business prosperity is to lighten as much as possible the burden of taxation on businessmen, in order to encourage enterprise by giving assurance of greater profits."*

After the Reconquista, the Spanish Kings sought to remove from memory *Al Andalus* and the many great achievements of Moorish culture. However, the Muslim legacy was ingrained in the culture too deeply to be erased. It took until the late 18th and early 19th centuries for a Western School of Orientalism to begin to recover the great significance of Arab culture on the West. *Al Andalus* was the focal point of that influence for centuries.

There are those Western scholars who have sought to trivialize the Arab contributions to civilization as having lacked originality of thought. The implication is that Arab wisdom was merely a copy of the Greek, Roman, and Persian sources that they translated. A much deeper understanding of Arab cultural extraction and subsequent augmentation of the wisdom of the Ancients have largely replaced that school of thought. The role of *Al Andalus* as a conduit for that learning, science, and medicine is now firmly established.

As Byzantine power subsided and was succeeded by Norman (Viking) energy and conquest from Scandinavia to France, then to England and south to Sicily, it is patently clear that Arab culture's imprint, itself the beneficiary of preceding cultures and civilizations, on the West goes well beyond Arabic numerals. The influence on Dante, the interplay of faith and reason, Humanism and the Renaissance, after centuries of primitive Western culture, is undeniable. One might argue that the Renaissance would not have happened when it did without Arab learning transferred directly from the Middle East and Muslim Spain. Chejne sums up this observation with the following.

> "In a sense, the process becomes confrontation between two societies in which one side gains ascendency over the other in some respects and, at the same time, is itself influenced. This can be illustrated by the Greek and Roman confrontations with other peoples in antiquity, and the Arab confrontation with the West in Medieval and modern times. In all three instances, great empires comprising enormous territories which came into contact with peoples of different cultures and languages. The outcome was invariably that the conquering minority succumbed in many ways to the majority, but preserved certain features of its own, which became the distinctive mark of its civilization. By these processes, composite cultures were born under what may be called Pax Hellenica, Pax Romana, and Pax Arabica."

**Piri Reis, The Ottoman Lake and the European
Response – Magellan and Drake**

Competition, commerce and confrontation were the hallmarks of the relations of Muslim and Christian, East and
West, around the Mediterranean. As long as the Ottoman
Navy commanded the Eastern portion, with its strategic
control of shipping and caravans traveling to the Orient
and back, pressure to circumvent
Ottoman control and taxes would
spur technological innovation. Piri
Reis, Admiral of the Ottoman fleet
and cartographer at the time of
Sultan Selim I, is well known by
cartographers and students of Maritime history in the Renaissance. His
famous map of 1513 seen here not
only shows his skill as a cartographer, but importantly illustrates the
exchange of technology between the East and the West.
It is said to be composed of Ptolemaic maps of the 2nd
century CE, an Indian map in Arabic, and new Portuguese Maps obtained in Pakistan (Sind) and a Columbus
map. What remains is about a third of the original. Note
the mapping of North, Central, and South America, the
New World.

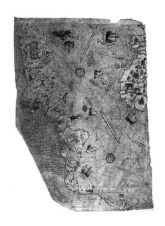

The Battle of Lepanto off the Western coast of Greece in
1571 wherein the Holy League of maritime Catholic States
defeated the Ottoman Navy was strategically important.

Some have argued that had the Ottomans won that battle, Western Europe might have fallen to the Ottomans. In any case, the Mediterranean having been seen as "the Ottoman Lake" for more than two centuries gave rise to Western exploration and circumnavigation of a world in which the "sphericity" of the earth, and the impetus to trade and bring back gold, silver, spices, and foodstuffs, triggered robust efforts to develop new trade routes.

In 1498, the Portuguese explorer Vasco Da Gama was the first to reach the Indian Ocean and the Spice Islands successfully, without traveling through the Mediterranean and the Arabian Peninsula, by sailing around the Cape of Good Hope, the southern tip of Africa. As important as this was, Ferdinand Magellan, Portuguese by birth, but sailing under the auspices of Spanish King Charles V, had the then original idea of sailing West to the Indies, not East around the tip of Africa. His fleet sailed to South America and around its Southern tip through what came to be known as the Magellan Straits. He then sailed into what he called, "the Peaceful Sea" from which we get the term Pacific Ocean. His voyage began in 1519 and reached the West Indies, returning to Spain in 1521. While he himself was killed in an encounter with a native in the Philippines, his crew completed the first-ever circumnavigation of the earth.

The pursuit of riches also put the Europeans in competition with each other. In 1580, after a 3-year voyage, Francis Drake, a privateer, successfully completed the second circumnavigation of the earth. His ship was laden with treasure, including spices and Spanish gold which he grabbed by attacking Spanish ships. Drake returned to a hero's welcome, providing Queen Elizabeth treasure worth a year's tax revenues. He went on to lead the English fleet in the defeat of the Spanish Armada in 1588, becoming Sir Francis Drake.

However, the risks of exploration were high. Mariners and ships lost at sea or dashed on rocks were the norm. Determining latitude had long been relatively easy using a sun reading at noon and cross-referencing it with sun chart tables. It would be another two hundred years before seafarers could successfully calculate longitude. This would wait for an English clockmaker, John Harrison, who would invent a marine chronometer that was stable at sea, by which calculations could be made of distance traveled from the time of the homeport clock. This allowed an alternative to dead reckoning, easy enough on land, but hugely difficult at sea. It allowed for shortening the distance traveled by sailing on arcs using the curvature of the earth.

The European powers made very good use of the Arab rediscovery of the astrolabe and how it works. The European gain in navigation and shipbuilding was just the beginning of technology transferred from the East, and daringly capitalized on by countries seeking to avoid Ottoman middleman trading taxes. This Western response to the Ottoman challenge also greatly reduced trade revenues to the Sublime Porte. Finally, great seafaring and trading

City States like Venice and Genoa developed powerful navies to challenge for control of "the Ottoman lake." This truly was a case of Kaplan's "revenge of geography." As we will see, geography will play a role in religious controversy, not just between the Christian West and the Muslim East, but within the two religions.

Chapter 5

RELIGIOUS CONTROVERSY AND WARS – THE MUSLIM EAST AND THE CHRISTIAN WEST

> *"For the resolutions of the just depend rather on the grace of God than on their own wisdom; and in Him they always put their trust, whatever they take in hand. For man proposes, but God disposes; neither is the way of man in his own hands."*
>
> —THOMAS À KEMPIS, THE IMITATION OF CHRIST.

The 15th century CE quote above is probably based on the Bible, Proverbs 16:9. In his book, *Conflicts and Tensions in Islamic Jurisprudence*, author Noel Coulson seems to stand that message on its head by suggesting that, "God proposes: Man disposes." Man's interpretation of Divine Revelation opens an ineluctable diversity. Diversity of interpretation of sacred and profane, religious and secular, laws has always yielded both unity and division – often in response to external threats or the absence thereof. Christianity and Islam are no exception. Conflicts and tensions in both will be examined. As Christianity precedes Islam chronologically, we begin with the Christian experience. Needless to say, the intention here is to be aware that the fact that there are differences in the experiences of both religions does not change the important observation that both have had controversy. This has resulted in different traditions, pain, war, and suffering within the body of the two Faiths.

Schism in Christianity, Orthodoxy, and Catholicism

Controversy began, if not before, already by the year 50 CE over the issue of the applicability of strict Mosaic Law when it came to evangelizing the Gentiles, the non-Jews of Asia Minor (modern day Turkey). Many, like Saul, who had persecuted Christians on behalf of Roman rule, who himself later converted to Christianity on the road to Damascus, was a Roman citizen of Hellenic background from the Tarsus Mountains. As a Greek speaker (and Latin and Aramaic), formerly Saul, now Paul, was "called" to proselytize the pagan Greek speakers in Asia Minor where the first seven churches of Western Christendom were eventually founded.

The first issue with which he had to deal in particular was the subject of circumcision – an obligation under Mosaic Law. In his Gospel letter to the Galatians, Paul argued for a liberal interpretation of the law whereby non-Jews need not be circumcised to be in covenant with the God of Abraham. He argued that with the Word of Jesus, the covenant was in fact a spiritual commitment for which the physical act of circumcision was not a prerequisite for becoming Christian.

It has been argued that in the lifetimes of the Apostles, a certain amount of deviation in the telling and interpreting of the events in Jesus' life, and the understanding of who He was, was thought to be understandable. After all, the Evangelists had been party to these events and had heard Him speak. In the succeeding centuries, the issue of doctrinal purity and orthodoxy of "the correct" understanding of Jesus, and the events surrounding his life, became subject to some hardening of beliefs. Presciently, the Apostle Peter speaks to this concern when writing, *"But false prophets also arose among the people, just as there will be false teachers among you, who will secretly bring in destructive opinions. They will even bring denial of the Master who bought them – bringing swift destruction on themselves. Even so, many will follow their licentious ways, and because of these teachers the way of truth will be maligned."* (2nd Peter, 2:1-3, New RSV)

The instinct to conform to "an orthodoxy" was only enhanced in succeeding centuries in the face of the sometimes-horrific persecution of Christians. While tortured and executed martyrs, such as Saints Stephen and Polycarp, served either to increase the zeal of those who continued to believe in the face danger, while scaring others away from the early Church. Among those whose faith increased, also did the tendency to devise differing interpretations of exactly who Jesus was and was not. What came to be deemed heresies typically centered on the meaning of the Divinity of Christ. Was He just a prophet? Was He both man and God? Was He a Triune being, the earthly manifestation of the Trinity, Father, Son, and Holy Ghost? Was He resurrected from the dead? Was man inherently evil or good and did human will play a role in the equation. From each of these questions arose differing interpretations offered by their advocates.

Our purpose here is not to explore these heresies or the "heretics" who espoused them. Some of the more enduring heresies include: Manicheanism, Arianism, Apollinarism, Monophysitism, Nestorianism, and Iconoclasm. Each of these would be dealt with in succeeding Councils over the centuries, but not until the Roman strictures against the profession of Christian faith were removed. This happened with the Edict of Milan in 312 CE. From that time forward, practicing Christianity was no longer illegal in the Roman Empire.

Constantine, who co-authored the Edict, would later, under his mother Helen's influence, who had famously converted to Christianity, offer to make Christianity the official religion of the Empire. This would replace the pantheon of pagan deities observed by Romans since Rome's founding by the legendary demi-gods Romulus and Remus over a millennium earlier. He had only one condition and that was that an official creed, setting the cornerstones of Christian faith, be uniformly agreed to by the Church

Fathers. Differing practices and belief systems tended to be geographically centered where the proponents of the different interpretations resided – such as Rome, Alexandria, Antioch, and Carthage. To this end, Constantine called upon the Bishop of Ancyra (Ankara), Marcellus, to assemble the Bishops and hash out the definitions of orthodoxy. Beliefs and practices not in that doctrine were to be deemed heretical and declared anathema to the True Faith.

Emperor Constantine invited all 1800 Bishops from the East and the West of the Empire. Some 318 are said to have attended the meeting in Nicaea (*Iznık Turkey today*) in 325 CE. From the debate came a common summary of "official" Christian beliefs known as the Nicene Creed. The primary achievements of this first Ecumenical Council included: resolution of the Christological attributes wherein Jesus is deemed to be the Son of God and of one substance with the Father; an agreement on the date of Easter; the actual writing of the Creed and, the uniform promulgation Canon Law within the churches. In keeping with the purposes of the Council, Arius, for example, and his followers were branded heretics and he was banished from the Empire. It would actually not be until 380 CE, with the Edict of Thessalonica, that Paganism was outlawed and Christianity actually became the sole official religion of the Empire.

Some "heresies" survived, even when officially outlawed, such as Nestorianism, promoted by the Bishop Nestorius of Constantinople, at the Third Council in Ephesus in 431 CE held under the oversight of Emperor

Theodosius II. While he was permitted to retire to a monastery, the belief system did not die out and was popular in Persia and supported by the Zoroastrians. With new outbreaks of Nestorian belief, a Fourth Council was held just twenty years later to stamp out the notion that Christ had two separate natures, human and divine, as advocated by Nestorius. With this Council of Chalcedon (*Kadıköy in Turkey*), the beginnings of a permanent split in the Church led by the Oriental Patriarchies, with significant following in the areas of Armenia, Syria, Persia, Egypt, the Sudan, and Ethiopia, began to manifest itself.

In total there were seven Councils, the last of which was the Second Council of Nicaea in 787 CE. Here it was hoped that agreement could be reached between the Eastern Orthodox Church in Byzantium and the Western Latin Church centered in Rome/Europe. The veneration of icons was restored after the wholesale destruction of them occurred during the reign of Emperor Leo III (born in Commagene, Syria, now *Kahramanmaraş, Turkey*). During this period, with weakness in the Byzantine rule, an Umayyad Muslim army besieged Constantinople. Leo was aware that his Muslim enemies had outlawed the veneration of icons as a form of idolatry from Islam's very beginning, and on the subject of icon veneration, he was roundly opposed by the Pope and the Church of Rome. Within thirteen years, the Pope would be crowning an Emperor in the West of the Holy Roman Empire, Charlemagne. While this Council restored the practice of veneration of Icons, giving appearance to a uniformity of belief and practice in Christendom, the truce was fragile at best. It would be almost three more centuries before the Great Schism would break the Church into parts. The Oriental Patriarchates had already separated from the Eastern Orthodox Church after Chalcedon. The later Councils had already shown signs of disagreements exacerbated by linguistic differences between Greek- and Latin- speakers as well as from those speaking Syriac and Persian.

The Great Schism of 1054 was the culmination of centuries of gradual estrangement of the Eastern and Western Churches based on doctrinal, ecclesiastical, linguistic, and political reasons, including geographic jurisdictional disputes. At this time, the Pope in Rome and Western Christendom saw himself as *primus inter pares* (first among equals). Issues in dispute included the Western practice of using unleavened bread and the Western claim that Rome and its Pontiff should be recognized as the head of the Universalist Church by virtue of Papal interpretation of the New Testament Gospel of Mark, where Jesus is quoted as saying, *"Blessed are you, Simon [Peter] son of Jonah! ... And I tell you, you are Peter, and on this rock I will build my* church (Matthew 16: 17,18, New RSV)." According to the Roman interpretation, Jesus was setting up the precedent for one Disciple to be above the others. The Eastern Church disagreed, but it was beset by Arab conquest of some of its most important Patriarchates, in cities such as Alexandria and Antioch. In fact, Byzantium was about to experience its first defeat by a Muslim army at Manzikert seventeen years later as discussed in an earlier Chapter.

The net result of these irreconcilable disagreements is that the Catholic Pope and the Patriarch of the Orthodox Church excommunicated each other and their respective followers. The rift was now official. It would not be until 1965 that Pope John Paul VI and the Ecumenical Patriarch of Constantinople Athenagoras I nullified the anathemas of 1054 CE. Both sides remained friendly enough, but the Fourth Crusade would show just how fragile the peace between them was.

The growing separation between the Latin and the Greek churches was further exacerbated in 1182 CE when the Greek Byzantines, probably out of envy for their wealth related to sea trade, attacked the Catholic community of Latins (Venetians, Pisans, Genovese) killing or forcing them to flee Constantinople, upwards of 10,000 Latins. Their churches and homes were looted and several thousand of them were sold as slaves to the Muslim Sultan of Rum. In retaliation, three years later, Norman Catholics from Sicily attacked and pillaged Thessalonica (Greece today), the second largest city in the Byzantine Empire.

Upon succeeding to the Papacy, Pope Innocent III issued a Papal Bull (*Post Miserabile*) in 1198 CE calling for a Fourth Crusade to regain control of Jerusalem. Rather than crossing over Anatolia, largely in the control of the Seljuks, his plan was to launch a sea-borne army, which would land in Egypt and move North to recover the Holy

Lands. Raising the money, ships, and army to mount this effort was complicated by the fact that France and England were at the time fighting each other. Nevertheless, by 1202, arrangements for a fleet and army to sail from Venice had been completed.

As the debt to the Venetians for the fleet had not been fully paid, the Doge (Duke) suggested that the balance might be made up by raiding some of the Byzantine Christian ports along the Adriatic. While the Pope had specifically advised that the expedition was not to harm fellow Christians in Byzantine Orthodox realms, this communiqué was, it is thought, intentionally or not, not conveyed to some of the forces. Miscommunication or not, the net result was that a portion of the fleet crossed the Adriatic and pillaged the Dalmatian port city of Zara. The Pope was appalled, accepted the tragic fact, and ordered the expedition to sail on for Egypt. Through a truly "Byzantine" intrigue, in the context of a succession struggle going on in Constantinople, large sums of money were secretly promised to the Crusaders by Parties to the dispute as an incentive to attack Constantinople. This/these offer(s), together with the lure of establishing a Latinate Catholic Kingdom in place of the Greek Byzantine Constantinople, was too tempting. The orders for the Expedition were disregarded. The Pope's objective of Jerusalem could wait while the Latins redressed their long-held and festering grievances with the Byzantines.

The Crusaders laid siege to the city in the summer of 1203 CE and breached the walls in the following year. Thousands of fellow Christians, albeit Orthodox, were not spared. Rape, incest, burning and killing knew no bounds. Orthodox churches were looted. A short-lived Latinate Kingdom was established. The Pope was said to be ashamed and thoroughly embarrassed by these events. The promised objective of Jerusalem had been abandoned. Efforts were taken to repair the damage, first at The Council of Lyons in 1272 CE and again at the Council of Ferrara-Florence in 1439 CE. Both efforts failed, leaving Constantinople ultimately vulnerable to Muslim encirclement. Muslim conquest would follow a little more than a century later.

It is important to note that these wounds within the body of Christendom, 800 years later, prompted Pope John Paul to apologize profusely to the Ecumenical Patriarch of Constantinople, Bartholomew in a speech in 2004. A year later, the Patriarch accepted the apology in the spirit of Easter saying, *"The spirit of reconciliation of resurrection... incites us to reconciliation of our churches."*

Schism in Islam, Sunni – Shia

As reported in the New Testament in the Gospel of John (Chapters 14-17), Jesus commands his Disciples the night before His crucifixion at the Last Supper, to love one another as He has loved them. Maintaining unity, bound together as he prophesies by the Holy Spirit, is clearly His most vital message.

That succession of leadership will always be contentious, the Prophet Muhammad, in his Farewell Sermon while on Haj in March of 632 CE (11 AH) in the Uranah Valley of Jabal Arafat, cautioned his followers not to revert to old tribal ways, tribal animosities. He refers to this as the Era of Ignorance (*Cahiliyya*).

Upon the Prophet's death, the issue of his succession resulted in factions within the leadership. These factions were partially occasioned by distinctions between the Prophet's original Meccan supporters (*muhajirun*) and the families of Medina/Yathrib *(ansar)* who had given safe haven and subsequently joined forces with the Prophet after his flight *(icra, 622 CE, 1 AH))* from pagan Meccans who opposed him. Their issue came down to who could best represent the Faithful (*Ümmet*) without distinction as to whether one was from Mecca or Medina, or the tribe of the candidate. The initial contenders were Abu Bakr (*muhajirun*), the father of Muhammad's wife Aisha (*Ayşe*) and Saad ibn Ubada *(ansar)*, who met in a small group in Saqifa. In the end, supporters of Abu Bakr prevailed and he became first Sunni Caliph.

While the Prophet's cousin and son-in-law, Ali ibn Talib (Ali), married to Fatimah (*Fatma*), the daughter of another of the Prophet's wives, Khadijah (*Hatice*), had been designated by the Prophet as his successor in a sermon at Ghadir Khumm shortly before his death, he is said to have been busy with the Prophet's funeral arrangements. Though he made no claim to be the next legitimate successor, there were those who believed that he should have been. Fatimah was the mother of two of the Prophet's grandsons, one of whom, Hussein, would die a violent death over this continuing issue.

Within 25 years of the Prophet's death, a civil war (*fitna*) broke outfollowing the assassination of the third Caliph, Uthman. Ali was elected the fourth Sunni Caliph, but became involved in a disagreement about the timing of the revenge killing of those responsible for Caliph's Uthman's death. By 657 CE, Ali and his forces found themselves lined up for battle with the forces of the Governor of Syria, Muawiyah. The ensuing Battle of Şiffın on the banks of the Euphrates near Raqqah Syria (latter day ISIS capital) was bloody and lasted three days. Cooler heads then prevailed. Invoking the Koran, it was agreed to arbitrate their dispute. By 661 CE, he would be assassinated by the Kharijites (the "Outsiders") and Muawiyah would become the fifth Caliph. As Tom Holland writes in his book, *The Shadow and the Sword*, of the Kharijites, they argued that Ali as a true believer *"would have trusted his fate, not to diplomacy, but to ongoing warfare and the will of God."* It should be noted that records indicate that as many as 70,000 had perished in the battle of Şiffın prior to an agreement for arbitration.

Ali's son, Hussein, would take up the banner. His followers would not recognize Muawiyah. As noted by Vali Nasr in his book *The Shia Revival*, *"Hussein rejected the rule of the caliph at the time... He stood up to the caliph's very large army on the battlefield. He and 72 members of his family and companions fought against a very large Arab army of the caliph. They were all massacred."* After being decapitated, his body left on the battlefield at Karbala (680 CE, 60 AH), his head was taken to Damascus to be paraded in front of the Caliph. This act may have been the critical event in sealing the divide between the Sunni (*Rashidun*) followers and those following Ali. The Sunnis recognize all four of the first Caliphs. At this point, the Shia now divide from the Sunnis, recognizing Ali as the true First Caliph, the First Imam, and spiritual leader of the Faithful. As Nasr observes, with this event, *"An innocent spiritual figure is in many ways martyred by a far more powerful, unjust force. He becomes the crystallizing force around which a faith takes form and takes inspiration."* Hussein's death is commemorated by public mourning and self-flagellation annually, known as Ashura.

Parallel practices, though not so widely spread in Christianity, are found in 13th and 14th century Flagellants, in Catholic monasticism and in the 20th century lay order, *Opus Dei*, made famous by author Dan Brown's, *The Da Vinci Code.*

As with Christianity, the basic tenets of Islam are observed by both Sunni and Shia Islam, including the Koran and the "Five Pillars" of obligation for Believers. The Sunni view that the Shia engage in an almost cult-like reverence for their Imams, due to this bloodline claim, holds that this is an inclination which The Prophet himself seemed at pains to discourage as verging on idolatry.

This claim might be particularly leveled against the "Twelvers," those who believe that the Shia Imam, the final "ordained" Imam, Muhammad ibn al-Hassan (b. 869 CE) disappeared, and that the last of the Twelvers, the Mahdi, will reappear to render the final interpretation of the Prophet. In this sense, this belief offers a messianic "Second Coming" similar to that professed in Judaism and Christianity.

Later in the Chapter, we will revisit this schism in Islam and see how it has played out in the intervening centuries by looking at the contest between the Ottomans and the Safavids, both Turkic, but one Sunni and one Shia. We will see how that contest, one set in Levantine culture and the other in Persian, played out in the late 1500s-early 1600s CE continuing to this day. Also, just as we have seen divisions within Islam, and will later discuss jurisprudential differences of interpretation of the Law within Sunni Islam, the focus now returns to consider differences within Christian belief and practice.

We have already seen schisms in the Christian Faith, breaking into major fault lines between Eastern Orthodoxy and Western Catholicism. We have seen a further divide between Eastern and Oriental Orthodoxy where the two are in "communion" with one another but operate separately with separate Patriarchs and Synods. At this point, we now turn our attention to Catholicism and its contest with its newest offshoot, Protestantism, beginning in the 16th century CE, the Protestant Reformation, and the Catholic Counter-Reformation.

The Protestant Reformation, The Holy Roman Empire, *Reconquista*

While each of the subjects in this Chapter deserves its own book, I will keep the discussion brief. It is intended here to illustrate some of the comparative factors of division within Christianity as we have seen in Islam. And, just as Christianity influenced the Prophet Muhammad and Islam, perhaps more especially in Sufi mysticism to be discussed later, so the spread of Islam influenced Christianity in general, and contributed, both directly and indirectly, in significant ways to division within Catholicism in the West.

We have discussed one influence already – the rediscovery of Ancient Wisdom and its transmission through centers of learning and culture in Baghdad, Tunis, and *Al Andalus* Spain. Augmenting this effect was the Muslim introduction of parchment into Western Europe, replacing the more expensive and cumbersome vellum. Not wishing to oversimplify, but arguably the "Wisdom of the Ancients" opened debate between temporal and spiritual power, between Monarchs and the Pope. This is a debate that had begun centuries before in Islam between the powers of a Sultan and those of a Caliph at least by the time of Seljuk rule. And, it was seen from Christianity's genesis when Jesus draws a distinction between rendering unto Caesar what is Caesar's and unto God what is God's. This "Wisdom" also helped to usher in science and reason as critical components of standards to be reckoned with in the ordering of society. Such considerations contributed substantially to the Renaissance in Western Europe. Cheaper parchment opened the debate beyond the confines of royalty and clergy. The next quantum technological invention, Guttenberg's printing press, appeared in Europe just as Mehmet II was conquering Constantinople. While the Han Chinese had invented movable type in the 11th century CE, in its Renaissance application, the press appeared in time to begin a process of "democratizing" learning, paving the way for Humanist Thought and the Protestant Reformation. Less than a hundred years after its appearance, copies of the books and writings of the two leading proponents of both movements alone, Erasmus and Luther, sold in the hundreds of thousands – in their lifetimes.

The second direct influence of Islam on the divide within European Catholicism was military – following the control of Bulgaria, defeat of the Hungarians at the Battle of Mohacs and the siege of Vienna laid by Sultan Suleiman in 1529 CE. This threat had a galvanizing influence on the Holy Roman Empire and the Catholic Church. Catholic preoccupation with this existential threat provided critical breathing room for Protestantism to incubate in "safe harbors" in parts of Northern Europe.

The Protestant Reformation may have its origins in the work of Oxford University Don John Wycliffe, a philosopher, theologian, preacher, and reformer of the late 1300s CE. He had preached against the preoccupation of the Popes with material wealth at the expense of the spiritual growth of the Faithful. He dared to question the authority of the Clergy. He translated into vernacular English (Chaucerian) the New Testament portion of the Holy Latin Vulgate of St. Jerome, the official Bible since the 5th century CE. He believed that not just the bread, but the wine should be offered to lay members of the Church during Communion, not just the clergy. His followers, the Lollards translated the rest of the Bible and soon found themselves excommunicated, but not before a Czech (Bohemia then) theologian and priest, John Hus had taken up the mantle. As noted by Dairmaid MacCulloch in his seminal tome, *The Reformation*, *"The Lollard defeat in England came at the same time that an allied dissenting movement triumphed against Rome. An accident of royal matchmaking ...linked England to the far off Kingdom of Bohemia in Central Europe... resulting [in] contacts between English and Czech nobility and Universities in Prague."* In the end, Hus was burned at the stake but launched a precursory reform movement in Prague, the Hussites, some of whose followers continue down to this day. In addition, the Moravian Church of Bohemia, an offshoot, continues to this day in the Czech Republic and in America. While these movements may be said to have sown the seeds of the Protestant Reformation, great credit must be given to priest and theologian Martin Luther (Lutheranism). His disaffection was with the selling of indulgences and a litany of abuses of the Catholic Church, which he enumerated and posted on the door of the church in Wurttemberg in Southern Germany known as the 95 Theses in 1517 CE. He did this just as Sultan Selim the Grim was conquering the Mamluks and bringing Egypt and Syria into the Ottoman fold. As argued by Prof. Andrew Hess, in a 1973 article (Jan., Vol. 4. Issue 1) titled, "The Ottoman Conquest of Egypt (1517) and the Beginning of the 16th Century World War," this event established Ottoman control of its Eastern Front fortuitously allowing for his successor, Suleiman, to push westward through the Balkans into Europe. The Holy Roman League would be distracted and preoccupied with this threat. This fact proved to be welcome news for the Protestant Reformers, who would enjoy some breathing room as a result.

Protestant Reformers in England such as Tyndale, Coverdale, and Cranmer, and in France, John Calvin (Calvinism underlying the Scottish Reform of John Knox and Presbyterianism) and Zwingli in Switzerland broadened the appeal and produced martyrs along the way. Henry VIII also played a role in the Anglican Protestant Reformation, though his incentives had more to do with annulling marriages and producing a male heir. Lastly, after a long period of Protestant reaffirmation during the Reign of Queen Elizabeth I, Anglican Protestant luminaries, at the behest of King James I, brought forth, in Elizabethan

English, the English of William Shakespeare, the iconic King James Version of the Bible. That Bible was carried around the earth as England began its part in global conquest and trading. The King James Version of the Bible and the works of Shakespeare, Marlowe and others would all carry Protestant Christianity and English culture around the world. This Bible also served as the primary written source for Christian practice for many of the future subdivisions of Protestant belief, for Presbyterians, Episcopalians, Methodists, Congregationalists, Baptists, Quakers, and others.

The Counter-Reformation was quick to respond to this threat to Catholicism and the Papal hierarchy. As the Ottoman army would be turned back from the gates of Vienna, the Holy Roman Empire and its Kingdoms would join forces in now trying to quash the anti-clerical inclinations of Northern Europe.

The French, English, and Spanish had been fighting each other for dominion in Europe and around the newly discovered world at least since the beginning of what came to be known as the Hundred Years' War beginning in 1337 CE and ending with the Battle of Agincourt in 1415 CE. This last battle was made famous almost 200 years later by Shakespeare's play *Henry V.* As the Protestant Reformation began to take hold, the conflicts, while still motivated by trade, territory, and resources, the European wars began to take on religious overtones.

In response to Protestant criticism of the excesses of the Catholic Church, Pope Paul III called The Council of Trent in 1545 CE at which a commission of Cardinals was formed to undertake institutional reform of the Church and address the abuses of corrupt Bishops, veneration of the Virgin Mary bordering on idol worship, and excessive manipulation of the Faithful through the aggressive sale of indulgences, which had been used to rebuild and decorate St. Peter's Basilica and the Vatican. Objections included the nudity seen in the artwork of the Sistine Chapel funded with these indulgences all the while proclaimed to be dedicated to the saving of souls. While attempting reform within, especially after neutralizing the Ottoman naval threat at the Battle of Lepanto in 1571 CE, the attempts to crush the Protestant Movement began in earnest with the St. Bartholomew's Day Massacre a year later in Paris. In this case, the targets were French Calvinists who were known as Huguenots. The French King Francis I ordered that their leaders be assassinated. It got out of control, with Catholic mobs killing thousands of Protestants. This event sparked what came to be known as the French Wars of Religion, which continued through the balance of that century. The conflict spread well beyond French borders, including the defeat of the Catholic Spanish Armada in 1588, which had aimed at invading Elizabeth I's Protestant England. Some relief for the Protestants came with the signing of the Edict of Nantes in 1598 by French King Henry IV granting amnesty to the Huguenots and restoring to them certain rights and freedom of conscience. Neither side was very happy, but it did restore peace on the religious front for 20 years until the 30 Years' War began. The cause was initially a religious conflict between Catholics and Protestants. In the end, it became political and territorial. Physical destruction, "witch-hunts," burnings at the stake, combat deaths, and disease exacted an enormous toll in parts of Italy, Bohemia, the Low Countries, and Germany. In some of these areas, as much as 25% – 40% of the area populations died. In order to strengthen the hand of a Hungarian Prince of Transylvania and King Frederick of Bohemia, both of them Protestants, signed a treaty with Sultan Osman II and the Ottomans, further destabilizing the Catholic Holy Roman League.

In the end, at horrific cost, peace was reestablished on the continent with the signing of the Treaty of Westphalia (Treaties actually) about which we will speak in a later Chapter concerning the history of the concept of sovereignty. This put an end to the religious wars of continental Europe, just in time for a Protestant-led coup that resulted in the beheading of English Catholic King Charles I, and the beginning of the Puritan government of England under its leader Oliver Cromwell. This would not last a decade before the restoration of another Catholic King, Charles II. His successor, James II would be overthrown in a bloodless coup in what came to be known as The Glorious Revolution, which we will discuss later. The English Parliament reached across the water to usher in

Dutch Protestants William and Mary to rule over Protestant England.

In that same year, French King Henry's grandson, Louis XIV, who revoked the Edict of Nantes in 1685, again undermined religious tolerance. This resulted in an exodus of French Protestants with some going North to Germany, East to Switzerland, and West to America. Of those coming to America, many settled in New York (New Rochelle and New Pfalz) and in Virginia (Manakin-Sabot) and Charleston, South Carolina. One of their Huguenot descendants figured prominently in the American Revolution. I will speak later of Jack Jouett, whose famous nighttime ride during the American Revolution is legendary.

Having focused attention on Protestant clashes with the Catholic States and Principalities of the Holy Roman League, we will now briefly come to one of the principal actors in the Catholic Counter Reformation. For this we must return to Spain which, after finally driving the Arab and Berber rulers out of the Iberian Peninsula during what is known as the Reconquista, we shall focus on the purging of all those not willing to convert to Catholicism during the reign of King Ferdinand and Queen Isabella.

Spanish Inquisition, Impact on Jews and Muslims – Ottoman Safe Haven for Sephardic Jews

In 1492, the year Columbus set sail on behalf of the Spanish monarchs for the East Indies and discovered the West Indies, an Inquisition was established to rid the country of

Muslims and Jews. Many converted; some were burned at the stake, and most fled back to North Africa in the case of Muslims, or to Germany and the Ottoman Empire in the case of the Jews. Of course, the hardships were unspeakable. Those coming to Turkish lands settled largely in Istanbul, Smyrna (later Izmir) and Thessalonica. Interestingly, it would be a Jewish doctor who would deliver the baby Mustafa Kemal, later Atatürk, in Thessalonica. The author was living in Istanbul the year Jews came from all over the world, especially those of Sephardic background, to join those still living in Turkey (many of whom having lived in Anatolia/Asia Minor long before the Turks arrived) to commemorate this act of kindness and tolerance 500 years later in 1992.

Ottoman – Safavid Contest, Then and Now

Pictured below is Shah Ismail I, founder of the Safavid dynasty in 1500, based in Tabriz and lasted until 1736. The Safavids were Twelver Shia Sufis. Their army were

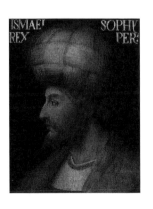

primarily Turkic tribes known as the *Kızılbaş* ("red head," the color of their military head ware), who might best be described as Azeri Turks. The Safavid Empire at its greatest extent included parts of eastern Turkey, the north Caucasus, Armenia, eastern Georgia, Iraq, Kuwait, Syria, Kuwait, Turkmenistan, Uzbekistan, and Pakistan. Like the Ottomans, both are descended from the Oğuz Turks who settled in the Caspian-Aral Sea area coming out of the Asian Steppe. As they were located in the middle of the Silk Road, they acquired wealth. With Persian influence, their capitals in Ardabil, Tabriz, Isfahan, and Baghdad became showcases of art and culture.

Continued expansion of the Empire placed the Safavids between two other Turkic powers, the Mughals of India to the East and the Ottomans to the West. Douglas Streusand, in his book, *The Islamic Gunpowder Empires*, provides important insights into the similarities and differences of the military structures and war-fighting strategies of each, while confirming the significance that all three of these empires introduced firearms and artillery into their armies over the course of the 16th century.

A series of wars between the Ottomans and the Safavids began in 1532 over Iraq (Mesopotamia) and the Holy Shia shrines. This war pitted Sultan Suleiman and Shah Tahmasp I against one another. After a series of three 2-year campaigns, by 1555, by treaty, the Ottomans returned Tabriz to the Shah but kept Baghdad, Erzurum, and Western Armenia.

War again broke out between the two Empires in 1623, ending in 1639 with the Treaty of Zuhab. The border wars largely ended and Mesopotamia (Iraq) and the South Caucasus remained in Ottoman hands until the aftermath of the First World War.

Divided by Sunni-Shia religious differences, compounded by what one might say are underlying Byzantine versus Persian cultural influences, their modern counterparts, Turkey and Iran, remain locked in contest for regional hegemony. Sometimes the contest is unspoken; sometimes it is violent. Current events and conflicts from Lebanon to Syria and Iraq are breaking out along historic religious and ethnic fault lines. Shias have formed a kind of geographic crescent surrounded by a sea of Sunni countries into which the Shia have spilled, from Alevi Turks, to Alawites of the Hatay/Jordan and Shia in Saudi Arabia and the Gulf States. That larger sea of Muslims worldwide is about 80% Sunni, 12% Shia, and the rest, smaller offshoot sects such as the Druze. The Silk Route, currently being re-activated by Chinese investment and foreign policy, has been covered with oil and gas – together with precious water. Over these resources, conflict will continue, both regionally and globally.

In conclusion, it may be helpful to think of Sunni vs. Shia as similar to Catholicism versus Eastern and Oriental Orthodoxy and Catholicism versus Protestantism. Two of the great Faiths of the world, Islam and Christianity, are themselves divided. Their sub-branches agree on the most fundamental tenets of their respective faiths. However, the divide in Christianity has, since the end of the Religious Wars of Europe and their empires, remained largely ideological and spiritual. This cannot be said of the differences and disputes in Islam. There area host of reasons for this important distinction, some of which will be discussed in future chapters.

Chapter 6

MYSTICISM IN THE
EAST AND WEST

Mysticism in Islam, Shams Tabriz, Mevlana

Attempting to define mysticism, Sufism and other manifestations of inner searches for truth, spiritual truth, and
divine truth are, by definition, only instructive at best.
Certainly, the objective here is limited to an effort to illustrate that the human urge to have a direct relationship
with the divine and may be found in all cultures. What
they have in common is some form of seeking to surrender
one's self, one's ego, as part of a process to achieve a closer
experience and connection to the Divine. This process may
be what the ancient Greeks were driving at with the aph-
orism inscribed at the entrance to the Temple of Apollo
at Delphi, *"Know thyself."* One is also prompted to think
of William Shakespeare's Polonius, in Hamlet, whose last
words to his son were, *" this above all; to thine own self be
true...".* Yunus Emre, the great 14th century Anatolian poet,
defines the essence of science when he posits that, *"True
science is self-knowledge".*

The origins of Islamic Sufism are said by some to stem from a number of sources including: the Greek Pythagoreans; Zoroastrianism; the vow of poverty and discipline of pre-Christian Essenes; the early Christian ascetics of Egypt and Syria, and Buddhist thought. Arguably, like Islam itself, Sufism may be thought to embody parts of all these traditions. It is based on a philosophy of Islam that seeks to know Allah's essence from the Koran and the Sunna – beyond the judgment of the law (Sharia), jurisprudence (*fiqh*) and the realities of mundane existence. The medium of communication and writing in the early centuries of Sufism was Persian. The well-developed traditions of Persian poetry and music readily lent themselves to mystical expression for the early Sufis.

Long before Shams and Rumi, Sufi ascetics and mystics are well-recognized by the 8th century CE. By the 10th century, their philosphy was articulated by the Muslim theologian, philosopher, jurist and musician, Al Farabi. While there were forces which sought to arrest Sufi influence on the Muslim faithful, by the 11th century, Imam Ghazali (c. 1057-111 CE) had written two treatises, "Revival of Religious Sciences" and "The Alchemy of Happiness" wherein he mainstreams Sufi practice and belief as having its origins in the Koran. The word Sufi is said by some to come from the Arabic *(tasawuff)*, "one who wears wool", a reference to the rough wool garb of ascetic mystics, and by others, to have been derived from the Greek word *"sofia"* meaning wisdom.

If Sufism's early origins are clouded in some historical vagueness, we can say that a man, originally from what is today Azerbaijan, came to study in the Persian city of Tabriz to learn the wisdom of his age. He came to be known as Shams (light of the sun). He was a true peripatetic in the Greek sense. He is said to have traveled widely in search of those who might help him better see and experience the truth and purpose of man's existence – a search for divine wisdom. Later in his life (1185-1250 CE), in the mid-1200s, he traveled west to the Seljuk capital of Konya during the time of the Mongol invasions. While he was traveling west, away from the center of Mongol depredations in the Levant, at that very time, Ibn Khaldun was traveling east to Damascus in an effort to negotiate peace with their leader, Tamerlane. As noted earlier, Ibn Khaldun failed in that effort, whereas, Shams succeeded in meeting his greatest student, Jalāl ad-Din Rumi, who would arguably become the single best known Sufi (*Sofu*), especially outside the Islamic world, in history. Within the Islamic world, the Mevlevi orders have been most prominent in the Ottoman heartland of Anatolia. In addition to the Bektashi and Nahkshibendi orders already mentioned, there are a significant number of other orders including the Christiyya and Qadiriyyah. What they all have in common is that they helped in the spread of Islam, beyond the Middle East to South Asia and across North Africa.

There are many wonderful stories, probably apocryphal, about Shams' first encounter with Rumi. What is important is that he proved to be the great teacher Rumi both discovered and needed. And when Shams left Konya, Rumi is said to have become desperate for their interaction and friendship. His words speak to that friendship and separation which anyone might feel.

"Listen to the reed and the tale it tells. How it sings of separation. 'Ever since they cut me from the reed bed, my wail has caused men and women to weep. Whoever has been separated from his source longs to return to that state of union.'" Rumi Mevlana, *Mathnawi*

Shams left for posterity his extraordinary "40 Rules of Love" and his protégé, Rumi. For Rumi, Shams was the true mentor described in Shams' Rule 12 below.

"There are more fake gurus and false teachers in this world than the number of stars in the visible universe. Don't confuse power-driven, self-centered people with true mentors. A genuine spiritual master will not direct your attention to himself or herself and will not expect absolute obedience or utter admiration from you, but instead will help you to appreciate and admire your inner self. True mentors are as transparent as glass. They let the light of God pass through them."

Who was Rumi, or Mevlana (Our Master) as he came to be known? He was born into a Persian-speaking family in the area of Balkh, a center of Persian culture and Khorasan Sufism that today borders Tajikistan and Afghanistan. His father was a highly regarded Sufi teacher. With the coming of the Mongols, his father began to move west where the young Rumi is said to have met the Persian poets Attar and Sanai in the city of Nisahpur in the province of Khorasan. Of them he said, *"Attar was the spirit, Sanai his eyes twain, And in time thereafter, Came we in their train.'* From there, it is said that the family traveled to Baghdad and Damascus, and from there to Mecca to make the Pilgrimage *(haj)*. They continued into Anatolia (Asia Minor), finally settling in Konya where the young Rumi continued to study under his father. After his father died, Rumi began to teach and preach, becoming a Jurist of Sharia Law and the *Tariqa* (head of the Dervish order). He also became the head of a Medresse (Muslim school).

During this time, Rumi became passionate about the value of combining poetry, music, and dance as a means of reaching Allah. From this came the practice of "whirling dervishes." Upon his death in 1273, his son, together with other followers, founded the Sufi order known as the *Mevlevi*. As earlier noted, it eventually spread throughout the Ottoman heartland. His legacy comes down to us today through his poetry, writings, and wisdom, and of course, the *Mevlevi* Sufi order. His appeal goes well beyond Islam. Under the auspices of UNESCO, on the 800th anniversary of his birth, 2007 was celebrated as the year of Rumi. His message of love and inclusiveness is famously evidenced in the following quote.

"Come, come, whoever you are, Wanderer, idolater, worshiper of fire, Come even though you have broken your vows a thousand times, Come, and come yet again. Ours is not a

caravan of despair." [In Turkish, *"Gel, gel, ne olursan ol yine gel, ister kâfir, ister mecusi, ister puta tapan ol yine gel. Bizim dergahımız, ümitsizlik dergahı değildir, Yüz kere tövbeni bozmuş olsan da yine gel..."*]

There are other well-known and influential Sufi groups such as the *Bektashi* and the *Nakshibendi*, but not with the same appeal outside of Islam as Rumi. Former Prime Minister and now President Recep Tayyip Erdoğan is reported to be a member of the politically significant *Nakshibendi* in Turkey. The Order traces its lineage to the First Caliph, Abu Bakr. Its followers are committed to the traditional tenets of orthodox Sunni Islam and the sufficiency of the (*kafi*) Koran and the Sunna as true and holy sources. President Erdoğan is said to be a member of the *Khaledi* branch. It is less esoteric than most other Sufi orders and more politically engaged. This is not a new tendency for this Order. As will be discussed later, during the 19th century, they were among the staunchest resisters of the 19th century Westernizing reforms (*Tanzimat*).

Before moving to Christian mysticism, I conclude with the *"breath"* of Rumi.

"Not Christian or Jew or Muslim, not Hindu Buddhist, Sufi, or Zen. Not any religion or cultural system. I am not from the East or the West, not out of the ocean or up from the ground, not natural or ethereal, not composed of elements at all. I do not exist, am not an entity in this world or the next, did not descend from Adam and Eve or any origin story. My place is placeless, a trace of the traceless. Neither body

or soul. I belong to the beloved, have seen the two worlds as
one and that one call to and know, first, last, outer, inner,
only that breath breathing human being." Jalāl ad-Dīn Rumi,
"Only Breath."

Mysticism in Christianity, Mt. Athos, and Monasticism

The urge to shed one's self-centeredness and be at one
with God, without clerical intermediaries, is as common
to the history of Christianity as it is to Islam. Many of the
same pre-Christian antecedents that influenced the rise of
Sufism also influenced mystical sects of Christianity. In
his book, *The Foundations of Mysticism: Origins to the Fifth
Century,* Bernard McGinn defines Christian Mysticism as,
"[T]hat part, or element, of Christian belief and practice that
concerns the preparation for, the consciousness of, and the
effect of... a direct and transformative presence of God."

As early as the 3rd century CE, Christian mystics were
living in small gatherings in the deserts of Egypt (*Wadi
Natroun*). The most famous was Saint Anthony the Great,
who is said to be the Father of Christian mysticism and
monasticism, influencing both the Orthodox and Catholic
branches of Christianity. The practices of these "Desert
Fathers" may be seen in both traditions, in the Orthodox
monasteries of Mt. Athos in Greece and those of the Catholic Benedictine Order in Italy and the West, for example.

While the organization of mystical and monastic traditions range from the individual hermit, to *sketes* or very
small groups of monks, to larger monastaries, what one

sees is the motivating factor – a kind of removal from the mundane exigencies of larger society. This tendency is aptly described by Richard King in *Orientalism and Religion: Post-Colonial Theory, India and "The Mystic East,"* who points out this disjunction between "mystical experience" and social justice:

> *"The privatisation of mysticism – that is, the increasing tendency to locate the mystical in the psychological realm of personal experiences – serves to exclude it from political issues as social justice. Mysticism thus becomes seen as a personal matter of cultivating inner states of tranquility and equanimity, which, rather than seeking to transform the world, serve to accommodate the individual to the status quo through the alleviation of anxiety and stress."*

St. Athanasius, named for the 4th century Bishop of Alexandria, and the namesake for Mount Athos (*Agion Oros*), is a good example of monastic asceticism. He was born in Trabzon in the 10th century CE. He studied Christianity in Constantinople, but found the monks there to be distracted by the pleasures of city life. He moved to Mt. Athos, the 3rd Peninsula of the Chalkidiki, east of Thessaloniki in the north Aegean. He found hermits there who initially objected to his building and development of what became a large monastery, the Grand Lavra. In the ensuing centuries, Mt. Athos became the center of Eastern Orthodox monasticism. Great monastaries were built under the patronage of Byzantine emperors, Russian Tsars, and

Patriarchs from Orthodox states in the Balkans. The Athonite Monasteries were tolerated throughout the centuries of Ottoman rule until 1912, when the area reverted to being a part of Greece after the Second Balkan War.*

The author had the opportunity to visit Mt. Athos twice in 1972 and observe the habits and practices of several monastic communities. These experiences began with my passport being stamped upon entrance to the capital, Karyes, with a date two weeks earlier than the rest of the world, as Mt. Athos has remained on the Julian (as in Julius Caesar, since 42 BCE) calendar.**

Pictured here is one of the monasteries I visited on foot. The mountain was dedicated to the Virgin Mary with the restriction that women not set foot on it. This restriction holds to this day. Even the goat's milk used to make their feta must be imported onto the peninsula. Mt. Athos remains a repository of extraordinary early biblical scrolls and writings, icons, frescoes, and monks living in primitive conditions  harkening back to earlier centuries. After seven hours of walking steep mountain trails bound for the first monastery (*Iviron*), with feet so sore I could hardly walk, my monastic dinner fare consisted of stale bread, boiled potatoes, poor feta, and retzina wine. Famished and exhausted, I found the meal fit for a king. After being jarred awake the next morning at 3:30 with the thudding sound of a wooden cudgel banging on an enormous block of wood known as a semandron, I arose from my simple bed, lighted the kerosene lamp, and prepared to join the monks in their daily ritual. I attended prayers that took the better part of three hours. The sun would not rise for the first two. I could see my breath as I gazed, mystified by the "oriental" setting. Candles were burning in front of icons, their soft light illuminating the reliquary, frescoed walls, and the domes in three separate churches/chapels. Moving from

one church, one service, to the next, I marveled at the bearded and stove-pipe hatted monks in black robes, singing their Kiriye's. The experience was literally, "enchanting." I was then given a simple breakfast, with fasoulia beans, more stale bread, cheese, ersatz coffee, and a fiery anise liquor called *tsipourou*. Still spellbound with what I had just witnessed, I was ever so thankful for the sustenance, Spartan as it was.

While working at the American Farm School near Thessaloniki, we sometimes visited Joice Nankivell Loch, MBE, and Australian by birth [her autobiography pictured here] in a tower (*Pyrgos*), in Ouranoupolis (City of Heaven) originally built in the early 14th century by the Byzantine Patriarch, Andronicus II Palaeologus, as a storehouse for his Monastery of Vatopedi. We stayed in the tower a number of times together with, it was said, the ghost of the monk killed by pirates from the nearby islands of the Ammouliani centuries earlier. His skull is perched on the exterior wall of the balcony one sees at the top of the pictured *Pyrgos*.***

Simply stated, Joice was a force, an old world character. Her story is well worth reading. We have several of the naturally-dyed rugs, with Byzantine motifs developed from her husband's (Sydney) photographic record of monastic art and artistry based on his extensive travels on the mountain. What makes the carpets so fascinating in their provenance is that they were hand-tied by Asia Minor Greek women, in a cottage industry developed by Joice to help these recently "repatriated" women of the Aegean Region of Anatolian Turkey. They had been part of a treaty exchange of populations after Turkish independence between the Muslim and Christian populations between Greece and Bulgaria and Turkey (1921-1923). These women were refugees, who contined to suffer through the world-wide Depression. Joice capitalized on the fact that these women knew how to weave carpets, with the Turkish knot (asymmetrical, unlike the Persian knot), having passed down the art for generations in Ottoman Turkey. ****

Before turning to later and more modern forms of mysticism in both the Christian and Islamic Faiths, it is important to credit early forms of Christian mystical and monastic practice to one, the Apologetics of St. Augustine of Hippo, through which NeoPlatonist concepts were used to help explain and legitimize monastic practices, and two, the work of St. Jerome, late 4th and early 5th centuries CE, compiler of the Holy Vulgate (the first combined Old and New Testaments), both contemporaries.

Puritanism in Christianity and Islam, Plymouth Bay and Wahhabism

Stemming from the Protestant Reformation, Puritanism began as a Reform Movement with the Anglican and other Protestant denominations, among them Calvinists, followers of Swingli and later Scots Presbyterians. Some followers believed the Protestant church had not gone far enough in removing the trappings of the Catholic Church and "Popery." Those who were dissatisfieid with attempts to change the situation from within came to be known, derogatorily, as "Separatists" and "Puritans." They originally fled James I and England to Holland. Led by William Bradford, a group of Separatists sailed in the Mayflower, a 100-foot ship with 102 passengers and crew. They set out for the Virginia Colony which had been established thirteen years earlier at Jamestown. They were blown off course and landed on the North Cape of what later became the Colony of Massachusetts. They named this place after a coastal town in England, Plymouth Bay.

They were initially focused on survival. By the 1640s, more and more Puritan Separatists were arriving. A high priority was placed on the work ethic, piety, and stark simplicity in their church rituals. Eventually, piety became so political and restrictive a way of life, because of the judgmental behavior of the Elders who oversaw it, that life became intolerable for many. Not surprisingly, it was not long before breakaway Separatist groups moved out, initially, to what became Rhode Island. Other Puritans subsequently came from England and purchased land from the Native Americans in what became Connecticut and Long Island.

Dutch people came in large numbers and settled New York. The Dutch and the English would eventually fight each other in the late 1600s, ultimately establishing a border between the predominantly Dutch Colony of New York, and the predominately English Colonies, in what became New England.

The rigors of Puritanism and its overbearingly pious lifestyle were brought to light in Nathaniel Hawthorne's, *The Scarlet Letter: A Romance*, a work of historical fiction, written in 1850. The book, set in the Massachusetts Bay Colony of the 1640s, describes the "shunning" of an adulteress. Hawthorne's novel dealt with the public shaming of sin and immorality in the context of strict Puritan moral codes. In the course of his research, having learned that his great-great-grandfather, John Hathorne, was a judge in the actual Salem Witch Trials of the early 1690s, Hawthorne added a "w" in the spelling of his name in an apparent effort to hide his family association with this shameful episode in the history of his Puritan forebears. It is interesting to note that his neighbors in Concord, Massachusetts included Ralph Waldo Emerson and David

Thoreau with whom he joined in the Transcendentalist movement to be discussed briefly later in the chapter.

Puritan reform and behavior in Christianity had its counterpart movements in Islam as well. Coming down to modern times, both religions have been "highjacked" at various times by extremist groups. In the case of America, beginning after the Civil War, the Ku Klux Klan terrorized Blacks, Jews, and Catholics in the name of their perverted "White Supremicist" interpretation of Holy Scripture.

Wahhabism is an ultraconservative, fundamentalist, and puritanical form of Orthodox Islam. Twenty-three percent of Saudis are Wahhabi and are concentrated in Najd where this reform movement was founded in the late 18th century by Mohammad Ibn Abd al Wahhab. It is also estimated that 47% of Qataris and 45% of Emiratis are Wahhabi. From this early movement have sprung today's Al Qaeda, Taliban, Salafis, and ISIS terrorists. Their "purist," and arguably "distorted and perverted" approach to Islam, justifies the targeting of Christians and Jews ("Peoples of the Book," otherwise protected in the Koran), Westerners and non-Wahhabi, non-purist Muslims, typically described as apostates by them. They believe that Islam was weakened from within, seduced by excessive dependence on modern comforts. The West, ultimately, is held to be responsible for a preoccupation with material culture and resultant immorality to have befallen their co-religionists.

In 1801 and 1802, the Saudi Wahhabis, under Abdul Aziz ibn Muhammad ibn Saud, attacked and captured the holy Shia cities of Karbala and Najaf in Iraq, and destroyed the tomb of Hussein ibn Ali, son-in-law and cousin of the Prophet Muhammad. Atrocities against fellow Muslims and Westerners continue, often bank-rolled by Persian Gulf oil profits and fanatical extremists. Of course, adherents and supporters believe the violence is in a "just and holy cause." Jihadis are but instruments and may be "martyred" in the cause – to be rewarded in heaven. Sadly, violent extremism has plagued mankind since history began. One need not think long to conjure up example after example in modern times. Our attention shifts back to non-violent Reform Movements in America.

The Second Great Awakening, Transcendentalism, Charismatics in America

The Second Great Awakening began in America not long after the American Revolution, less than a century after the First Great Awakening. The First Awakening gave rise to many new Protestant denominations and the establishment of America's oldest church-sponsored colleges, Harvard, Yale, Princeton, and Dartmouth. In some ways, this Second Great Awakening was a reaction to organized religion and its ornaments and trappings. It was also a reaction to Deism and its overweaning reliance on the "rationalism" of the Enlightenment. It was fueled by Baptists, Methodists, Quakers, and Congregationalists, who often met in the open for Revival Meetings and Camps, seeking to "purify" believers from the inroads of the devil. Church attendance soared. Great Evangelist preachers were the "rock-stars" of the day. Like Cotton Mather, Jonathan Edwards, and George Whitefield, famous orators and preachers of the First Great Awakening, Francis Asbury, Henry Ward Beecher, Alexander Campbell, and Timothy Dwight IV preached not just to the churched, but to the "unchurched" as well. This was the America through which Alexis de Toqueville, the famous French biographer of America at that time, travelled, duly noting the aspects of American life which contrasted with life in Europe.

Before this movement had run its course, it had helped to spawn other movements beginning in the first half of the 1800s, including Women's Rights groups (Elizabeth Cady Stanton) and Abolitionist anti-slavery groups. If the Second Great Awakening might be said to have focused on a visceral and more direct attachment to God through His word, not unlike the attraction of Sufism, Unitarianism, and Transcendentalism move away from the group dynamic of a Revival Meeting to a more intellectual approach to Christianity. In the process, they deviated from some of the orthodox tenets of mainstream Christian belief.

Both movements originated in New England, but have earlier antecedents in Poland, Transylvania, and England. Both were influenced by academics. The Unitarians, harkening back to Arius and the Arian heresy of the early

Christian church, see Jesus as a Prophet with Divine inspiration, but is not thought to be Divine or a part of a Triune God as defined by the Council of Niceae in 325 CE. This places their religious practice and Christology in a camp not far removed from position of the Prophet Muhammad regarding the Trinity. Joseph Stevens Buckminister and William Ellery Channing were the leading lights of the Unitarian movement.

Also coming out of New England Congregationalism is the Transcendental movement. Its followers rejected the concepts of Calvinist Predestination and, like the Unitarians, the concept of a Triune God. While the Unitarians had churches, the Transcendentalists did not, but many worshipped in Unitarian churches. Transcendentalism is an intellectual movement calling for self-reliance and a new world vision, with inspiration coming from many sources, a mixture of Eastern and Western religions. Scholars of the movement seem to agree that Ralph Waldo Emerson's essay "Nature" written and published in 1836 followed a year later by a speech titled, "The American Scholar," represented the beginning of what can best be described as both a cultural and a philosphical movement. In addition to Emerson, other mouthpieces of the movement included Unitarian preacher George Putnam and Henry David Thoreau, author of *Walden; or, Life in the Woods* (1854), a story based on the two years, two months and two days in which he lived a simple ascetic life communing with nature in a cabin owned by Emerson on Walden pond, located in Concord outside Boston, Massachusetts.

Critics included Nathaniel Hawthorne, about whom we spoke earlier, and poet Edgar Allen Poe, who referred to their followers as "frogpondians" in reference to these Bostonian intellectuals being like croaking frogs in the great pond of Boston Commons.

In some ways, modern Charismatics and Pentecostals exhibit worhip practices that emphasize the "gifts" that are received by the Holy Spirit. These gifts include healing, prophecy, and a kind of revelation stemming from the gift of "speaking in tongues." The liturgical rituals of mainstream Protestant and Catholic practice are not observed. Like Sufis, Charismatics seek a closer and more personal connection to God and His truth revealed through the medium of the Holy Spirit within us. Charismatic preachers, like Sufi teachers, serve as guides to finding the Holy Spirit within and to leading a life of godliness. It has been estimated that they number some 500,000 million, representing a quarter of all the Christians in the world today.

Following on the thematic purpose of this comparative study, the next chapter examines the concepts of Sovereignty, Secularism, and the Rule of Law. These concepts do not spring up from nowhere. Nor do they happen overnight. They have origins that go back to ancient Greece and Rome. But, rather than coming from the Eastern world, they find more fertile soil in the West. They developed in the West during the Enlightenment of the Rennaissance.

Their evolution and cultural inculcation benefited in some ways from a more conducive geography, plentiful water supplies, fertile pastures, and better naturally defined borders. Acceptance of these concepts came over the course of many centuries. And it is these same centuries that this awakening begins in no small measure, as we have already learned, with a debt to Islam by its preservation and sharing of the Wisdom of the Ancients with the West.

---

* As one drives across a narrow spit of land and onto the Athonite peninsula, one can see the remains of a story in ancient history. In 480 BCE, Xerxes' army gouged out this land bridge connection so that he could roll his ships on a land canal, rather than attempt to sail around the treacherous seas of Karoulia at the rocky southern tip of the peninsula. Eleven years earlier, in his first attempt to invade Greece, his fleet had been wrecked attempting to sail around the rock-laden seas of Karoulia at the southern tip of the peninsula.

** It is interesting to note that the Gregorian Calendar was introduced by Papal Bull in 1582 by Pope Gregory XIII and the Catholic Church and adopted in Catholic Countries at that time. Protestant churches and Orthodox countries resisted this new calendar. England, and her Colonies, did not accept the "New Style" calendar until 1752. Turkey accepted it in 1926.

*** Staying with Joice, then 84 (her husband by our time there in 1972 was deceased), and being regaled, waving her cane as she spoke, was a fascinating and colorful window on history. As an example, we learned that she and her husband, for their honeymoon, covered the Irish Sinn Fein "Easter Uprising" in 1916 as journalists. She told stories of Igor Sikorski visiting at the tower in 1937, who, after a tour of Third Reich industrial and military plants, foretold of an impending war. The Russian-born designer of early helicopters during WWII, came to America in 1919. He later founded an aircraft company, Sikorsky Chance Vought, which produced the first functional military helicopters used in WWII. So many stories were told while eating the most succulent figs we dropped from a collosal and ancient fig tree, often paired with smoked metzovo cheese. She told of their time working in rail cars with Quakers and with the Red Cross administering to Polish refugees fleeing south, as Germany and Russia went to war against each other in September of 1939. Joice and her husband would move with the refugees all the way to Palestine during the war. As it happens, one of those refugees was an acquaintance of ours, recently deceased, Wladyslaw Anders. He formed the basis of the Polish II Army Corps from those refugee camps. He and his army would join the Allies. He went on to become a general of great fame. His Corps distinguished itself as the spearhead force at the Battle of Monte Cassino in 1944. His daughter, a friend of ours, is now a Senator in Poland and a Minister-at-Large to Polonia (the Polish Diaspora, mostly in America).

**** Here is pictured a Tree of Life carpet made for us over a six-month period, from wool dying to completion. Note Argus, the 100-eyed dog, guarding the Gates of Hades. The light brown of the dogs comes from wool dyed with spring heather. The darker tree color comes from fall heather. The crimson red comes from tree beetles picked by shepherds.

Chapter 7

SOVEREIGNTY, SECULARISM, AND THE RULE OF LAW IN THE WEST

Henry V, Act IV, Scene III, St. Crispin's Day Speech
How did the West get from a sovereign Caesar, or Emperor, or Monarch to a sovereign government? How did the West get from there to the concept of ultimate sovereignty resting with the people, either directly or through elected representatives? While the concept of the sovereignty of God came to be a personal belief or choice in the secular West, it continues to be the cornerstone of Islamic Orthodoxy, at least in principle. Has this theocratic form of governance been an impediment to accepting and/or adjusting to "modernity" in the sense of "Westernization?" Can modernity be defined differently for Muslim orthodoxy?

How did the Seljuks begin to find a compromise that allowed for the distinction of rendering unto Caesar what is Caesar's, and unto God what is God's? How and why did Islam legitimize a distinction between Sultan and Caliph? How did Sultan Suleiman, the Lawgiver (*Kanuni*), expand that distinction through the development of a complex system of Administrative Law? Did the Byzantine system of governance, in some sense inherited by the Ottomans, create a framework conducive to the notion of having a Sultan and Caliph not necessarily being one and the same person... like the Emperor and the Pope or Patriarch?

Earlier Chapters offer some answers to these questions. In sum, the practical exigencies of rapid Muslim conquest probably fostered the usefulness of a distinction between Sultan and Caliph, between ruler and the clerical elite – the Sheik ul Islam (*Şeyhülislam*) and the Muslim legal scholars (*Ulema*). The case of Ottoman/Turkish acceptance or accommodation of, Western forms of secular governance is considered in a subsequent Chapter.

First, let us look at how Western Europe moved away from a Holy Roman Emperor and Papal authority to secular systems of governance, where a monarch and the Pope have been removed from the primary role of governance to more symbolic, spiritual, and titular function. This is not to suggest that their roles were, or are, not still significant. They are. So, let us examine a few of the more prominent stepping stones putting Western Europe on a path toward a separation of church and state – a path toward secularism and the notion of "popular sovereignty."

The story might begin with people thinking that they belong to a country, represented by a King in this case. The equivalent of this may be found throughout history anywhere. For the sake of discussion, some distinction begins to appear when one is asked to fight for King and country, not God and country. Certainly, God is invoked in support of the mission, but those being asked to face the ultimate sacrifice are being asked to do so first and foremost in the name of their king, the kingdom, and the homeland. The defenders are not defenders of the Faith. In the case of the Battle of Agincourt in 1415 CE, about which Shakespeare rhapsodizes in the speech of King Henry V nearly two centuries after the battle, the enemies are of the same Christian Faith. The English King's speech exhorts his men to take heart, disregard the unfavorable odds. Enter into the fray for glory, which will be preserved and heralded for time immemorial in the memory of a thankful country. One's family name will be honored in the annals of history.

The circumstances here are not intended to suggest that this situation is unique to the West. Rather, I use Shakespeare's dramatic writing to illustrate how a nation may begin to think of itself as a nation with a shared history, a shared sacrifice, the collective memory of which is self-perpetuating and self-reinforcing. In this case, the English, after three successive wars in a relatively short period of time, are coming to think of themselves as more than just a tribe fighting against another tribe, but rather a country or a nation fighting another country. Keep in mind, Shakespeare's audience included "commoners," not just the elites.

This sense of a shared history and the concept of Nation is a very gradual process, which one might argue, for the sake of discussion, begins with a change in the feudal relationship between the King and his Barons exactly two hundred years before the Battle of Agincourt at a place called Runnymede along the Thames River in England in the year 1215. That change is evidenced by the King's signing of The Magna Carta, a petition which begins to check the heretofore unlimited Divine Rights of the King. Before the onset of battle on "contested" French soil, hear the inspiring words of the King from the pen of Shakespeare. The scene begins with a lieutenant, Westmoreland, questioning the King about the apparently dismal prospects of the severely outnumbered English in this forthcoming contest.

St. Crispin's Day Speech, *William Shakespeare, 1599*
Enter the KING
"WESTMORELAND. O that we now had here
But one ten thousand of those men in England
That do no work to-day!
KING. What's he that wishes so? My cousin Westmoreland? No, my fair cousin; If we are mark'd to die, we are enow To do our country loss; and if to live, The fewer men, the greater share of honour. God's will! I pray thee, wish not one man more. By Jove, I am not covetous for gold, Nor care I who doth feed upon my cost; It yearns me not if men my garments wear; Such outward things dwell not in my desires. But if it be a sin to covet honour, I am the most offending soul alive. No, faith, my coz, wish not a man from England. God's peace! I would not lose so great

an honour. As one man more methinks would share from me For the best hope I have. O, do not wish one more! Rather proclaim it, Westmoreland, through my host, That he which hath no stomach to this fight, Let him depart; his passport shall be made, And crowns for convoy put into his purse; We would not die in that man's company That fears his fellowship to die with us. This day is call'd the feast of Crispian. He that outlives this day, and comes safe home, Will stand a tip-toe when this day is nam'd, And rouse him at the name of Crispian. He that shall live this day, and see old age, Will yearly on the vigil feast his neighbours, And say 'To-morrow is Saint Crispian.'

Then will he strip his sleeve and show his scars, And say 'These wounds I had on Crispian's day Old men forget; yet all shall be forgot, But he'll remember, with advantages, What feats he did that day. Then shall our names, Familiar in his mouth as household words- Harry the King, Bedford and Exeter, Warwick and Talbot, Salisbury and Gloucester- Be in their flowing cups freshly rememb'red. This story shall the good man teach his son; And Crispin Crispian shall ne'er go by, From this day to the ending of the world,

But we in it shall be remembered- We few, we happy few, we band of brothers; For he to-day that sheds his blood with me Shall be my brother; be he ne'er so vile, This day shall gentle his condition; And gentlemen in England now-a-bed Shall think themselves accurs'd they were not here,

And hold their manhoods cheap whiles any speaks that
fought with us upon Saint Crispin's day."

Magna Carta is Latin for Great Charter. It is sometimes referred as the "The Great Charter of Liberties in
England." It was first written in Latin (translated four
years later into Norman-French) and sealed by an oath
from a reluctant King John, whose Barons sought to limit
the King's Royal powers and protect their rights. One of
the key principles agreed to by the King follows.

"No Freeman shall be taken or imprisoned, or be disseised
of his Freehold, or Liberties, or free Customs, or be out-
lawed, or exiled, or any other wise destroyed; nor will
We not pass upon him, nor condemn him, but by lawful
judgment of his Peers, or by the Law of the Land."

In subsequent years, many of the rights of the Barons
were reconfirmed, usually in exchange for the payment
to the King of taxes, which were in arrears. For all the
significance of principles such as *habeas corpus*, much of
Magna Carta dealt with many more mundane matters
such as the King's exclusive Royal hunting and fishing
properties, guardianship of monasteries and taxes and
fees related to knights. The Magna Carta's importance as
a driving instrument of change may be said to come into
focus only later in the late 1500s and thereafter. From that
time forward, it might be argued that Magna Carta took
on a renewed life. It also came to be used, exaggerated, or
distorted, to suit the political purposes of those seeking to

change existing practices of governance. Nonetheless, its basic tenets gain currency in the 1600s.

Less than four centuries later, the famous English jurist, Edward Coke, commenting upon *Magna Carta*, wrote in 1606: *"no man be taken or imprisoned but per legem terrae, that is, by the common law, statute law, or custom of England."* It is thought that he wrote the Charter for the Jamestown Company, which gave the members of the Company (1607) these same liberties and rights in exchange for establishing a new colony. Similar assurances were granted the founders of the Massachusetts Bay Colony in their Royal Charter (1620).

The principles of judgment (trial) by one's peers and the Law of the Land (*Lex terrae*) found themselves, almost verbatim, in eight of the first constitutions of the new States of America at the time of the American Revolution. In 1787, the Continental Congress adopted the Northwest Ordinance for governance of areas in the United States outside of the individual states. Congress wrote: *"No man shall be deprived of his liberty or property, but by the judgment of his peers, or the law of the land."*

As we have now seen the beginnings of a chink in the armor of Royal prerogatives or the unchecked Rule by the Divine Right Kings in the West, we shall now again consider the significance of the advent of paper in Western Europe, compliments of the spreading of Muslim culture discussed earlier.

Introduction of Paper via Muslim Spain

The use of paper, as opposed to vellum, made the spreading of knowledge, the Wisdom of the Ancients, and technology more affordable in the West. Fresh ideas and principles governing the relationship between church and state in the late medieval period came from philosophers and scientists like Roger Bacon or Christian writers such as St. Thomas Aquinas. Their works were becoming more available and less expensive to produce. That would eventually include the Magna Carta and similar seminal documents of the period, even such things as Treaties between warring States.

Gutenberg, the Reformation and Democratization of the Written Word

Advancing the cause of the Protestant Reformation or the works of the Humanists, the invention and refinement of Gutenberg's printing press fostered a burst of learning and spreading of knowledge during the Renaissance. The copying and dissemination of government documents, books, publications, contracts, maps, scientific, political and dramatic works, and newspapers greatly broadened the scope of knowledge, and by extension, financial power in the hands of the beginnings of what came to be called a middle class. The equation of governance was being changed irreversibly in Europe. As the governance of larger and more densely populated States in Europe, compounded by the geographically increasingly far-flung empires became more complex, the role of the citizenry of a nation took on palpable significance. These physical and financial changes in the matrix of governance gave rise to one of two alternatives, greater tyranny, or a greater reliance on the Rule of Law. In the West, the genie was out of the bottle. The days of unfettered Royal privileges were numbered.

Humanism and Science, Erasmus and Galileo

Two of the leading lights of the Renaissance, Erasmus and Galileo, the former Dutch the latter Italian, both influenced the road toward rationalism stemming from ancient philosophy and science. Erasmus was a contemporary of Martin Luther, Galileo of William Shakespeare. Each was significant in moving the debate on the role of the Church and the State on the subject of governance. While their influence spanned well beyond their home principalities, each was a figure who States and Countries would later claim as their own in the process of building and reinforcing a sense of nationalism.

Known in his own time as "the Prince of the Humanists," Erasmus of Rotterdam preached and wrote in Holland, France, England, Italy, and Germany. He was truly cosmopolitan and an avowed Catholic. Using Greek and Latin sources, he revised the Latin and Greek editions of the New Testament. His versions were used by Luther to translate into German. It is believed that later editions of his New Testament were used by Tyndale in the writing of the first English translation of the New Testament and the

Geneva Bible (1579 CE) written by an English Protestant who had fled England, and finally, was used in the writing of the King James Version of the Bible in 1612. It is said that the Geneva Bible was used by William Shakespeare, John Donne, and John Knox and was carried to America, along with the King James Bible, on the Mayflower. It was the first mechanically printed, mass produced Bible and was offered to the public.

Erasmus' influence is more critical for our discussion because he was staunchly Catholic, but was at the same time critical of all the excesses and hypocrisy of the Catholic Church. However, he did split with the Protestants over the solution. His great virtue, though not sparing him the wrath of extremists on both sides, is his middle course appeal to reason and rationality with the benefit of incomparable scholarship. For example, while he challenged the corruption in many of the practices of the *Magisterium*, he also took issue with the belief in Pre-destination of the Protestant Calvinists. He argued in favor of "free will" in one's faith and that while the institution of Catholic Confession, for example, might be useful, it was not a substitute for the importance of a believer having a direct and personal relationship with God. Like Al Farabi and Imam Ghazali, who sought to legitimize Sufi Islam as being mainstream, Erasmus wanted Christianity to admit that the road to heaven was not *ipso facto* through a religious hierarchy, as important as the Catholic Church hierarchy was. The concept of "free will," while herein advocated within one's spiritual life, was a concept that fostered the notion that every man is significant and should have a voice, not just the political and religious elites. This became an important component in the evolution of the notion of popular sovereignty.

Galileo Galilei, mathematician, physicist, engineer, and astronomer spent the last years of his life under house arrest as a heretic. The Roman Inquisition, coming from the Catholic Counter-Reformation, found his further proofs of Copernicus' theory of the heliocentric nature of our universe to be heretical to conventional beliefs going back to Aristotle's geocentric theory. Galileo's was one more voice of the Renaissance, which took issue with the existing order of things. His science removed God's greatest creation, man, from the physical center of the universe. The revolutionary impact of such a notion was similar to the voyages of a century earlier demonstrating the earth to be round and not flat. Challenging the assumptions of the 'old order,' and arguing that man's reason and free will are an integral part of that reality, proved to be yet another broadside cannon shot threatening the sovereignty of God, the primacy of the Pope and Catholicism and, by extension, the earthly governance based upon the Divine Right of Kings.

Shakespeare and the King James Version of the Bible, Spreading English Culture

As already noted, The King James Bible was completed at the direction of James I, King of England, in 1612. Printed on paper, mass-produced, this Bible was ready to carry Christianity, Protestant Anglicanism, and the most elegant English of the time around the world. This was a time when London was becoming an enormous trading Metropole for what was fast becoming a globe-girdling Empire. The British Navy, not the English navy, as England, Wales, Scotland and Ireland were becoming one Nation, was beginning to become a dominant force on the world's oceans. As previously discussed, the Ottoman Navy had lost much of its dominance in the Mediterranean at the Battle of Lepanto (1577 CE) and the Spanish Armada had been defeated in 1588 CE by the English. Spain was still rich through its gold and silver mines in Central and South America. However, England, with the help of the Dutch, were fast developing the beginnings of dynamic financial and stock markets to support the rapidly growing world trade that was circumventing the old Silk Route trading axis. Also, England had its source of gold in Marrakesh, Morocco, a Barbary State which was never conquered by the Ottomans. While this growth and expansion were taking place, the Ottomans were largely preoccupied with battling the Safavid Persians for control of Mesopotamia.

Knox, Hobbes, Locke and the Scottish and English Enlightenment

John Knox is best remembered as the founder of Scottish Presbyterianism and breaking from Rome in 1560 CE. For our purposes, while this rupture continues to represent one more tear in the fabric of Ecclesiastical Sovereignty as part of the Protestant Reformation, it also presents a stark contrast with Anglican Protestantism. Having just noted that, the idea of the British Realm, a concept anticipated by Ibn Khaldun's "*asabiyya*" or "social solidarity" and taken on board by the Western Enlightenment, was becoming part of the conscience of the peoples of the British Isles. We see that geography can serve as both a centripetal as well as a centrifugal force in the making and breaking of a Society, Nation, and Civilization.

Geographical distance from France, Spain, and Austria, each under the spiritual rule of Rome and temporal rule of Catholic Monarchs, helped to incubate Protestantism in general. Similarly, distance between London and Edinburgh, distance between a people conquered and occupied by Romans as opposed to a people north of Hadrian's wall in Northern England continuing north on into the highlands of Scotland who were not, gave rise to conditions where distinctions in worship might help to make the political union of these two peoples more complicated. And to be sure, Catholicism was by no means totally defeated either in England or more particularly in Scotland. In fact, the Scots having an association with Catholic France would more often than not serve as a counter balance to English Protestant monarchs' attempts to control Scotland and Ireland.

All this is to note that nation building has always been a tenuous process. Religion may serve as much to divide as to unify in the process. In the face of cultural differences of the peoples involved, geography, like religion, will tend to serve to unify within and separate from without. Rivers, seas, oceans, and mountains would prove to foster the building of Nation States in Europe. Trade patterns and access to and development of strategic resources tended to sustain those geographic spaces. The absence of either or both seems to have made nation building more difficult to sustain – tending to leave coherence to linguistic, religious, or ideological underpinnings and the sword. The absence of trade and ready access to resources makes stability and prosperity harder to find and maintain.

Enter Thomas Hobbes, English political philosopher and proponent of a "Social Contract" theory seeking to more specifically define the relationship between the Ruler and the ruled as presented in his book, *The Leviathan*, published in 1651 during the Parliamentary Rule of the Commonwealth of England, Scotland, and Ireland, by Lord Protector, Oliver Cromwell during a nine-year period known as the Interregnum. Known as a Regicide, Cromwell was one of those who had signed King Charles I's death warrant. Not everyone in the Realm was convinced that the "radicalism" coming from this English Civil War between the Cromwell forces and the Royalists was good for the Country or the growing Empire.

As an aside, after the Stuart Restoration of King Charles II, the Crown sent sheriffs in search of the Regicides. Two of them had fled across the water to Boston. Hearing that sheriffs had arrived to seize and return them to justice in England, the two further fled to the Colony of New Haven in Connecticut where they quietly received "safe haven" and were hidden under the authority of the Governor of the New Haven colony, William Leete, who was born in Cambridge, England and came to America with other Separatist Puritans in 1638.

Hobbes was a supporter of the monarchy. He believed that "natural man," left to his own devices, would result in a "war of all, against all." He believed that a Leviathan, or King in the then contemporary English setting, is necessary to maintain order. But, the king does so in Hobbes' "moral science" by the consent of the people, directly or tacitly. In short, there is a social contract between the King and the representatives of the people, composed of an aristocracy, clergy, bourgeoisie, and the proletariat. In particular, the latter two classes, the bourgeoisie and the proletariat, had been given significance and status by the Protestant Reformation. This in itself was revolutionary, if one remembers that across the English Channel at this very time the Catholic King Louis XIV had proclaimed that *"L'Etat, c'est moi."* (I am the State).

Hobbes was a supporter of the need for an absolute monarchy. He qualified his support by stipulating that the sovereign is not so by virtue of a Divine Right of Kings, but by Right that comes via a contract where his absolute rule is granted in exchange for his agreement to protect the rights of his citizens. This is quite a step from the Magna Carta where the contract was between a Sovereign and his Barons and Clerical elites. Additional social-economic classes were admitted to the contract, and the notion that whatever right is not bestowed upon the King in the contract remains with the other classes and their representatives. It would be the better part of two more centuries before this concept would begin to take hold in the Ottoman world, and, arguably, not to this day in many Arab countries and Iran.

The next step in the evolution of the concept of a social contract came from John Locke, a physician and political thinker who was influenced by the Whig anti-absolute monarchy movement and John Milton, Cromwell's Latin (Foreign) Secretary and poet. In his *Two Treatises on Government*, probably written before the Glorious Revolution of 1688, but not appearing until immediately after, Locke takes issue with the notion of the Divine Right of Kings and adds to the equation of the social contract the importance of individual liberty, albeit circumscribed by laws.

He moves beyond Hobbes in contesting even the absolute supremacy of a monarch. He is known as the "Father of Classical Liberalism." In his system of political morality, individual freedom of conscience and religious tolerance, first so dramatically proclaimed by Martin Luther who refused to recant his beliefs in front of the Holy Roman Diet in Worms in 1521 CE, together with the European Wars of Religion of the preceding generations, led him to articulate a clear separation of Church and State.

Locke's influence on the Scottish and French Enlightenments cannot be underestimated. These include leading luminaries of the day in Edinburgh, known already then as the "Athens of the North," such as David Hume and his work based on empirical psychology titled, "An Inquiry Concerning the Principle of Morals" 1751. French luminaries and their works include: Diderot's French Encyclopedia, 1751-72, as well as Voltaire, Montesquieu, and Rousseau. The latter two and their strong philosophical connection to the American and French Revolutions later are discussed in a subsequent Chapter.

To conclude Locke's connection to the architects of the American Revolution, consider the words of Thomas Jefferson, *"Bacon, Locke and Newton... I consider them as the three greatest men that have ever lived, without any exception, and as having laid the foundation of those superstructures which have been raised in the Physical and Moral sciences".*

The Western Concept of Sovereignty
and the Treaty of Westphalia, 1648

At this point, we have seen how the concept of sovereignty had been evolving since the Magna Carta with the addition of more parties and classes of people, to a Social Contract and its impact on the previously unfettered Divine Right of Kings in England. Shifting back to the Continent, the European States had been at war for a long time on the questions of religion, the authority of the Church over the State, Imperial Rule over State Rule and the territories and assets of the States. After the Hundred Years' War, followed by the Thirty Years War, the Peace of Westphalia in 1648 provided a startling basis for a new international order. The sovereignty of States, as separate Nations, was deemed to be inviolable. Further, these States may choose the religion of the State. In the process, Protestants were recognized as equal before the law. This Peace was particularly favorable to the now independent of the Holy Roman Empire States and Duchies of Switzerland, Holland, Sweden and most of Germany – and, by extension, England. Of course, the Holy See and the Catholic *Magisterium* were furious with Pope Innocent X for agreeing to it and immediately sought to annul the provisions of the treaty. Now, sovereignty of these states referred to the people and territory of the state as well as its representatives abroad. Another provision, in an effort to fight piracy, Letters of Marque effectively authorizing individual citizens to raid the ships of other Nations in the name of patriotism and for the sake of shared profits with the state, was outlawed. We will see more of this issue later when discussing Piracy and Privateering in the American Revolution and during the Early American Republic.

From Magna Carta to The Glorious Revolution – 473 Years

On the centuries-old road to the notion of "sovereignty of the people," after 473 years since the signing of the Magna Carta, England managed to have a "bloodless revolution." This "Glorious Revolution" as it is known was led by a Parliament where both Whigs (Constitutional Monarchists) and Tories (Loyalists) made common cause. The issue, again the religion of the deposed King James II who was Catholic but by title was the head of the Anglican Protestant Church of England, was cause for concern about a Catholic restoration in England. When he came to the throne, he had daughters. But, within a couple of years he had a son who by hereditary succession became Prince of Wales and thus the presumptive heir apparent to the throne of England. James II had maintained very cordial relations with Louis XIV of Catholic France. This very King, the very year of James' accession to the English throne, revoked the Edict of Nantes of 1598 allowing French Protestants, Calvinists, to live in France with a reasonable degree of tolerance and peace. This revocation resulted in another exodus of French Protestants, also known as Huguenots, to Protestant or religiously tolerant states and colonies.

It may be of some interest to note that the colonies of New York (New Amsterdam), Virginia, and South Carolina played host to many of these religious refugees. In New York, the Huguenots established the town of New Paltz. In Virginia, they were settled on the old Monacan Indian site, Manakin-Sabot. And, Charleston, South Carolina remains the site of the only Huguenot church still in operation, operating since 1844. Some of their notable descendants were leaders in the American Revolution, including Paul Revere, Jack Jouett, and Francis Marion. Others, like Paul Masson of California wine fame, came to the New World via Scotland, also home to many Huguenot escapees.

Returning to the Glorious Revolution, with support from the then Protestant Dutch Republic, the Parliamentarians facilitated the arrival of a vast armada of Dutch ships, cavalry, and soldiers who crossed the English Channel and landed on the southern coast of England in the port of Torbay. They brought with them William and his wife Mary, Protestant royalty in the Netherlands. James II's government collapsed in short order and he fled to France. William and Mary were installed as King and Queen of England. Within a year, the English Parliament passed a Bill of Rights, which significantly restricted the Kings and Queens of England from acting on many fronts without Parliamentary approval, including not being able to maintain a standing army in peace time without the approval of Parliament. King William introduced a certain amount of religious tolerance in England. In 1693, he established the College of William and Mary in Williamsburg, Virginia. Some of its more famous students include Presidents Thomas Jefferson and James Monroe, 16 Signers of the Declaration of Independence, Chief Justice John Marshall, and Speaker of the House, Henry Clay, who first rose to prominence in the War of 1812.

The Rise of the Bourgeoisie and Global Trade

Bourgeois and petit bourgeois are terms well known around the world. As a class of people, which comes to be represented in the evolution of the social contract and the notion of liberty, it is important to understand how they became "stakeholders" in Western Europe. The Bourgeoisie arose in major trading cities as necessary participants in commerce between and among these cities, and later in the burgeoning global trade beginning in the 17th century. Etymologically, the word comes from Old French referring to a walled city. These early businessmen and traders banded together into guilds, both to protect their particular skills, such as masons, and to resist the aristocratic Feudal landholders who often sought to charge exorbitant rents. Over the centuries, through the Renaissance and into the world trade of the 17th century, these Bourgeois acquired capital, wealth, and property. They developed a vested interest in replacing the old Feudal system with a more democratic and predictable system of laws not subject to the whims of the upper classes or the King.

Though not as widely developed, their counterparts are found in the Ottoman Empire. Typically, they were non-Muslim communities (*millets*), which specialized in various business skills. They were technically second-class citizens. Their wealth and suspected divided loyalty left many of them all too often experiencing the brunt of harsh treatment by both the religious elites and the masses, which could be stirred to attack them, their property and possessions. The same was also true in Europe of the Middle Ages and the Renaissance.

Treatment of these *millets* could be similar, for example, to the expulsion of "money-lending" Jews who were accused of usury by King John in 1290. It was more convenient to expel them than to repay the royal debt to them which monies were often used to raise armies for the King's private purpose. Jews were only permitted to return

several hundred years later when Oliver Cromwell allowed them to return in 1657 in exchange for money.

The point to remember is that the merchant and artisanal classes had a vested interest in liberty and religious tolerance, including freedom to worship and the right to protection of property. I have included one of the most famous literary parodies in history of what might be called business moguls, fat cats (*tüccarlar*).

He is Monsieur Jourdain from Moliere's famous French Comedy, *"Le Bourgeois Gentilhomme"* of 1670 (here pictured). This class of people in Turkey, often Armenian, Greek, or Jewish, tended only to become franchised via the foreign imposition of "Capitulations" reluctantly approved by Sultans, especially in the 19th century. European aristocracy might have objected to the *'nouveau riche,'* even on religious grounds, but their political and financial enfranchisement was homegrown, not externally forced, as was the case in Ottoman Turkey.

Following on the subject of foreign influence on Turkey, we now will focus on the Ottoman response to the rise of industrial and military strength in the West – a strength propelled by science, the rule of law, rational thought, religious toleration, industrial innovation, financial markets, the protections of private property, and the political enfranchisement of the business classes.

Before doing so, one must consider one of those innovations in particular that proved to be critical to global trade and colonization. This innovation was the systematic development of the Joint Stock company. This was a company in which the ownership could be sold, in differential amounts, to investors in the form of stock. These investors were called "Adventurers." Of critical importance was the legal construction whereby one's risk was limited to the amount of one's investment. This allowed for merchants and the wealthy to engage in speculation that proved to be the vehicle through which large amounts of capital could be raised to undertake voyages in search of riches, spices, mineral resources, salt peter for gun powder, and gold and silver in particular. The value of shares could rise if the company made profits and the shares could be sold.

In 1600, in response to the defeat of the Spanish Armada twelve years earlier, Queen Elizabeth I authorized a Royal Charter for the establishment of the Joint Stock East India Trading Company. Seven years later, King James I chartered the Jamestown Company to establish a colony in North America between the 34th and 41st parallel – a full 5 degrees of latitude spreading West to who knew where. The limitation of liability for shareholders became the basis of the modern corporation. As the risks were great, ships and cargo could be lost at sea or seized by pirates, a company's debts could exceed the assets of the company. This risk gave rise to another critical invention. Legal instruments of insurance lent itself to the creation of an insurance market. This business innovation gave stockholders additional protections, at a price. Yet another business specialty, buyers, and sellers of insurance risk established that price. While there were, of course, winners and losers, the prospect of profit attracted ever-larger amounts of capital into the joint stock and insurance markets.

The next Chapter will focus on the Ottoman response to these systemic changes in governance, the rule of law, and the protection of private property in the West and the technological benefits following in their wake.

Chapter 8

THE OTTOMAN RESPONSE TO WESTERN INDUSTRIAL-MILITARY GROWTH

"I shall be satisfied if my narrative is favourably received by readers whose object is exact knowledge of facts which have not only actually occurred, but which are destined approximately to repeat themselves in all human probability."

—THUCYDIDES

"The policy of the emperors and the senate, as far as it concerned religion, was happily seconded by the reflections of the enlightened, and by the habits of the superstitious, part of their subjects. The various modes of worship, which prevailed in the Roman world, were all considered by the people, as equally true; by the philosopher, as equally false; and by the magistrate, as equally useful.

And thus toleration produced not only mutual indulgence, but even religious concord."

—EDWARD GIBBON, THE DECLINE AND
FALL OF THE ROMAN EMPIRE

Religion can play a significant role in the growth of a country or the expansion of an empire. It might also play a role in its contraction. Certainly, the Ottoman Empire had enjoyed explosive growth since its inception in the 12th century CE. This trend continued through the Reign of Suleyman the Magnificent, with two important exceptions. The first, after his success in Hungary, were the attempts to lay siege to the Hapsburg capital of Vienna in 1529 CE. Suleyman's forces were weakened due to extended logistic supply lines and bad weather, keeping his bogged down heavy artillery from ever reaching the front. The siege was abandoned by 1531. The myth of the invincibility of the Turks on land had been tested with satisfying results for the West. The second, Ottoman control of the Mediterranean was put to the test some 50 years later at the Battle of Lepanto (1571 CE). Again, the States of the Holy League (the Papal States, Spain, the Republics of Venice and Genoa, the Knights of Malta, and the Duchies of Tuscany and Savoy), with a stunning victory at sea, proved that the Ottomans could be defeated. However, the Ottomans were in no way finished. As Alan Palmer points out in his book, *Decline and Fall of the Ottoman Empire*, during the Reign

136 · TURKEY & AMERICA

of Mehmed IV (1649-1687), while the English were in the midst of a civil war,

> *"Sultan Mehmed IV was sovereign of more than 30 million subjects, twice as many as King Louis... In Europe alone his lands were greater in area than France and Spain together, while in Asia minor he was the direct ruler over a vast region which stretched as far south as the head waters of the Red Sea and the Persian Gulf, and he held as tributary states the Caucasian lands eastwards to the Caspian Sea. Rhodes, Crete and Cyprus acknowledged his sovereignty: so too did Egypt ... and he could claim vassal authority over Tripoli, Tunis and Algiers."*

In many respects, one might say the geographic East and West bookends of the Empire were set by the mid-1600s, the Safavids east of Baghdad and the Holy League in the West. Other boundaries would be the Sahara desert to the South, the Adriatic sea, the eastern reaches of the Alps in Europe.

The Decline of the Ottoman Empire

The Ottomans would return to Vienna, laying siege to the city in 1683. The Turks would find themselves in a series of wars far from home for the next fifteen years. At the Battle of Zenta (1697), Mustafa II's army was surprised at a river crossing in what is today Serbia and decimated by the Hapsburg Army. Estimates of up to 30,000 were killed or drowned. The Peace Treaty of Karlowitz (1699), though not decisive as far as the Ottoman Empire was concerned, resulted in a permanent removal of the Ottoman presence in the Danube River valley. This was a victory for the Holy Roman League and included not just a territorial reduction of the Ottoman Empire, but other more intrusive concessions. As Palmer observes, *"Clauses which offered trade concessions to Austrian merchants and confirmed the rights of Catholics to worship freely within the Sultan's lands might be imprecisely phrased, but appeared to give the Hapsburg Emperor a claim to intervene in the internal Ottoman affairs."*

Karlowitz also gave both sides the opportunity to focus on other threats, the French in the case of Austria and the Russians in the case of the Ottomans. It also allowed Grand Vizier Hüseyin to focus on internal reforms. Internal peace proved to be short lived. In 1703, a mutiny was organized by Jannissaries in Istanbul and spread. While it was put down in a month, unrest and corruption in the elite guard would continue to plague the Empire. Reform efforts and a publicity campaign were engineered by capable Grand Viziers like *Nevşehirli* Damat İbrahim Pasha, who directed the government from 1718 to 1730. European artistic and cultural influences resulted in greater exposure between the Turks and the Europeans. But, the Ottomans, still mired in the conservative influence of the *Ulema*, would miss opportunities to adequately modernize their army and their administrative systems. Even protecting Muslim pilgrims from the attacks of Bedouin horsemen became problematic. In one instance in 1757, some 20,000 of the Faithful were killed on their way to Mecca.

Ten years later, it is said because Mustafa III was convinced that the astrological signs favored him, he sent a badly equipped army and navy against Tsarina Catherine's Russian forces. It ended badly for the Turks. And by 1774, the Treaty of Küçük Kainardji, Catherine secured the Crimea and, more importantly, for the first time, the right for Russian merchant ships to pass through the Bosphorus and trade with ports on the Mediterranean.

By the end of the 18th century, America had gained Her independence, France had overthrown its monarchy, and the Ottoman Empire, engaged in wars around its periphery, found itself imploding. In the wake of continued military defeat, Western involvement increased in both the internal and external affairs of the Ottomans. With the final defeat of Napoleon, and a new international balance of power struck at the Congress of Vienna in 1815, concern over the fate of Christians and the Holy City of Jerusalem in Ottoman lands became a major preoccupation of the Western powers. European competition for control and influence was reduced to predictable religious and sectarian default lines. The Russians were sure that they were called to shepherd the interest of their fellow Orthodox cousins, from Greece to Georgia, and Eastern Anatolia to the Levant. Influence within the Ottoman territories also tended to bring with it commercial and strategic advantages. The same instincts and motivations also gripped the British and the West Europeans regarding geographic and strategic resources.

The Eastern Question and the Crimean War

Underlying all these considerations was the Western presumption that the Ottoman Empire would eventually fall apart of its own mismanagement. It was just a matter of time. However, as long as the Western powers could not agree who would pick up what pieces, it became more important to prop up Ottoman Turkey. The prospect of a chaotic dismemberment by interested powers, each seeking to carve out a sphere of influence, was frought with risk for all Parties. In the wake of the American Revolution, the newly developing principle of "nationalism" was probably more frightening to the kings of France, Germany, Austria, Hungary, and Italy than it was to the Ottomans. But, the Ottomans were in for a rude awakening on this subject.

The first great test of this new spirit of nationalism came shortly after the Congress of Vienna. The Greeks declared Independence from Ottoman rule in 1821. Immediately, on grounds of coming to the aid of a fellow Orthodox people, Tsar Alexander I considered invading through the Balkans to come to their defense. As this might also include gaining control of the Bosphorus, thereby giving military naval access to the Russians, the Austrians, French, and English became fearful of such a prospect. They immediately lined up to force the Russians to limit their intentions. England in particular, was moved by the Hellenophilic literature of the Romantic writers like Lord George Byron, who appealed to the notion of Greece having been the "Cradle of Western Civilization." He therefore supported the legitimacy of the impulse toward self-determination and a "restoration" of a Greek nation.

Within a decade, treaties were signed with Russia (Treaty of Adrianople, 1829), which acquired more rights vis à vis Ottoman Turkey, while Southern Greece (Treaty of Constantinople, 1832) was granted its independence. The bad news was that Ottoman Turkey lost both territorially and increasingly in the sovereignty of the remainder of its Empire. The good news was that Ottoman Turkey was still largely in tact.

No sooner was the Greek revolt settled than a revolt by the Sultan's Viceroy, Mehmet Ali, broke out in Egypt (1830). Mehmet Ali's forces, both ground and naval, were poised to possibly overthrow the Sultan. The Russians immediately seized upon this threat by offering to come to the aid of the Sultan. The Sultan agreed, in exchange for yet more of the increasingly hated "Capitulations" (special rules for the Russian millet). The French supported Mehmet Ali and the British supported the Sultan. The net result was another stalemate, more treaties, but the Ottoman Empire survived, now minus Egypt (1832).

By the 1840s, Nationalism and religion reared their disruptive heads in Prussia and other areas of Western Europe. This instability brought the French and English Governments into concert with one another, driving Russia and Austria into concert. Each of the two groups focused on the weakest link, Turkey and the "Eastern Question." That focus included the Suez and the Levant as well as the

Balkans, and related commercial interests. Both groups also manifested an increasing measure of sympathy for Ottoman-governed Christians, who's plight would also be seen through the eyes of newly arriving missionaries, including American missionaries.

The stage was set for a major contest between the two groups over the issue of control of the Ottoman lands. All sides wanted to expand their respective spheres of influence. Fulfilling the dream of Frederick and Catherine the Great of the 18th century, access to the Mediterranean for Russia's fleet through control of the Bosphorus and Dardenelles Straits, could now be achieved by Tsar Nicholas. Determined for that not to happen, the English and the French joined forces. The Austrians would largely sit out the upcoming war in hopes of picking up the pieces in the Balkans if the Russians were to lose. Again, religion and the protection of Christians in the Holy Lands would serve as the spark.

Noted English historian A.J.P. Taylor in his work, *The Struggle for Mastery in Europe, 1848-1918*, observed:

"...in some sense the Crimean war was predestined and had deep-seated causes. Neither Nicholas [of Russia] nor Napoleon [III of France] nor the British government could retreat in the conflict for prestige once it was launched. Nicholas needed a subservient Turkey for the sake of Russian security; Napoleon needed success for the sake of his domestic position; the British government needed an independent Turkey for the security of the Eastern

Mediterranean... Mutual fear, not mutual aggression, caused the Crimean war."

The conflict began in the Principalities of Wallachia and Moldavia between the Rusians and the Ottomans in what is today Romania. From there it spread to the Caucuses, where the British and Turks supported the Muslim communities to rebel against their Russian overlords. A year later, in 1854, the French and the British formally joined the Turkish side against the Russians. The Austrians were planning to join in the coalition with the Turks until the Russians withdrew from the Danubian provinces. At this point, the focus of the war shifted to the Crimea, the new sourthern home port of the Russian Navy.

The scope of this war was far larger than the term the Crimean War suggests. As Orlando Figes in his excellent book, *The Crimean War – A History*, states emphatically:

"The name of the Crimean War does not reflect its global scale and huge significance for Europe, Russia and that area of the world – stretching from the Balkans, to Jerusalem, from Constantinople to the Caucasus – that came to be defined by the Eastern Question, the great international problem posed by the disintegration of the Ottoman Empire."

The battle in the Crimea was horrendous. Arguably, the war was a harbinger of modern warfare to come. It was fought with, as Figes says, *"...industrial technologies, modern rifles, steamships and railways, novel forms of logistics and communication like the telegraph, important innovations in military medicine, and war reporters and photographers directly on the scene. Yet it was the last war to be conducted with old codes of chivalry....*" These technologies would be in great evidence five years later in the American Civil War.

The loss of life was enormous. At least three-quarters of a million soldiers died in battle or of disease of which, two-thirds were Russian, the next largest the French, the Ottomans, the British and the Sardinians. The eleven-and-a-half-month Siege of Sevastopol anticipated the trench warfare to come in the next century in Flanders Fields and Gallipoli. It is estimated that there are a quarter of a million soldiers, sailors, and marines buried in mass graves at Sevastopol.

In the end, the war offered a victory to the Turks and the European Allies. It left the Russian Empire in bad shape and the Ottoman in worse. One of the outcomes which has haunted the West to this day was, in the words of Figes,

> "*It opened up the Muslim world of the Ottoman Empire to Western Armies and technologies, accelerating its integration into the global capitalist economy, and sparked an Islamic reaction against the West which continues to this day.*"

The Charge of the Light Brigade, Florence Nightingale, and The Crimean Church

The Charge of the Light Brigade on Ocober 25, 1854, was a study in miscommunication and what can go terribly

wrong in war. During the Battle of
Balaklava, under the overall com-
mand of Lord Raglan, Lord Cardi-
gan's light calvalry, instead of chasing
a retreating artillery group, rode head
long into a well-fortified battery with fusillade fire. Cardi-
gan's men and horses were cut down mercilously. While
the charge reached its target, it was forced to beat a hasty
retreat with little effect on the enemy.

The charge as a military matter resulted in huge
controversy back in England with accusations between
and among commanders as to who was at fault. For
the survivors, for the *esprit* of the British Cavalry and
its respect even among the enemy, this disaster proved
to be anything but disastrous. While the folly of inept
command was patently obvious, these cavalrymen were
immortalized for their bravery and "derring do." Word of
their heroics reached the British troops back in Crimea
with much appreciation. Alfred Lord Tennyson's famous
poem recalling the bravey and the folly appeared within
six weeks of the battle. Three of six verses of Tennyson's
poem here follow:

I	II	VI
Half a league, half a league, Half a league onward, All in the valley of Death Rode the six hundred. "Forward, the Light Brigade! Charge for the guns!" he said: Into the valley of Death Rode the six hundred.	"Forward, the Light Brigade!" Was there a man dismay'd? No tho' the soldier knew Some on had blunder'd: Theirs not to make reply, Theirs not to reason why, Theirs but to do and die: Into the valey of Death Rode the six hundred.	When can their glory fade? O the wild charge they made! All the world wonder'd. Honour the charge they made! Honour the Light Brigade, Noble six hundred!

One cannot leave the Crimean War conflict without heralding the quiet work of an unsuspecting star, Florence Nightingale. Upon reading in the English press of the horrid conditions and the death rates of those in the British Hospital camps, she contacted her friend, the British Secretary of War, Sydney Herbert. As a trained nurse, she and her team were authorized to join the war with the objective of improving the hospital conditions. She arrived in October of 1854. She began her work on the Asian side of the Bosphorus in *Selimiye* Hospital in what the English called Scuturi (*Üsküdar*). She sent reports back to England decrying the unsanitary conditions and poor nutrition of the sick and wounded. Her dedication as a social reformer and skilled nurse earned her the sobriquet "Lady of the Lamp" as popularized in the "Times of London" article below written at that time.

"She is a 'ministering angel' without any exaggeration in these hospitals, and as her slender form glides quietly along each corridor, every poor fellow's face softens with gratitude at the sight of her. When all the medical officers have retired for the night and silence and darkness have settled down upon those miles of prostrate sick, she may be observed alone, with a little lamp in her hand, making her solitary round."

Florence Nightingale returned to London after the War and set up the first School of Nursing which carries her name and is part of Kings College London. She is recognized as the "Founder of Modern Nursing." Bernard Cohen wrote of her in "Scientific American,"

"Nightingale's achievements are all the more impressive when they are considered against the background of social restraints on women in Victorian England. Her father, William Edward Nightingale, was an extremely wealthy landowner, and the family moved in the highest circles of English society. In those days, women of Nightingale's class did not attend universities and did not pursue professional careers; their purpose in life was to marry and bear children. Nightingale was fortunate. Her father believed women should be educated, and he personally taught her Italian, Latin, Greek, philosophy, history and – most unusual of all for women of the time – writing and mathematics."

In conclusion, based on my own research and experience, I heartily concur with Orlando Figes when he notes that,

"Historians have tended to dismiss the religious motives of the war... Wars are caused by imperial rivalries, it is argued in these histories, by competition over markets, or the influence of nationalist opinions at home. While all this is true, it underestimates the importance of religion in the nineteenth century... All the powers used religion as a means of leverage in the Eastern Question, politics and faith were closely intertwined in this imperial rivalry, and every nation, none more so than Russia, went to war in the belief that God was on its side."

One is reminded of earlier discussions of the Crusades – especially the sacking of Constantinople in the Fourth Crusade, by Latin Catholic Christians at the expense of Orthodox Byzantine Christians. In this war, Latin Christians from West European countries were fighting and dying alongside Ottoman Muslims while fighting Orthodox Russians and Greeks. The irony should not be lost on anyone.

Before looking at the subject of Capitulations, when speaking of Westernizing influences and religion, Queen Elizabeth I sent a diplomatic delegation, together with an Anglican priest, to the Sublime Porte in 1582 during the Reign of Sultan Murat III. The degree of tolerance for other religions at the time might have been greater then as the Empire was still on the ascendant. Allowing Protestants to establish themselves alongside Byzantine Christians, both Catholic and Orthodox, would only demonstrate the multi-ethnic, multi-faiths, and multi-racial composition of a maturing Empire.

Fast forwarding to the 19th century, resentment had been building toward the overbearing foreign influence exacerbated by the side effects of the Crimean War as just noted. But in the case of the Crimean Church, reflecting on the shared fight against the Russians, Sultan Abdül-mecit donated land for this Anglican Church in Beyoğlu, located down the hill from the Swedish Embassy and the German High School in the direction of the Bosphorus. With donations from the British Regiments that served in Crimea, together with support from the English missionary group, the Society for the Propagation of the Gospel, between 1858-1868, the church (seen below) was constructed.

In its colorful history, the church provided a place of worship for White Russians after the Bolshevik Revolution and a safe haven for refugees of war, beginning with the First Gulf Crisis in 1991, and continues in this mission. This church has had a storied existence. For example, during the 2nd Energy Crisis of the late 1970s, the cost of heating the church, together with a declining member attendance, resulted in its being de-consecrated

and closed. Under the leadership of Father Ian Sherwood and a Vestry decision, the author was on that Vestry, the Crimean Church was "unofficially" reopened in the fall of 1990, with no heat, no electricity, and plenty of excitement. The heavy doors of this historic church swung open once more. *

The Crimean Church, like so many churches in Istanbul, perhaps beginning with Hagia Irene, established by Emperor Constantine, and completed in 360 CE, serves a variety of purposes, as places of worship, as well as offering architectural and artistic treasures and musical entertainment for the residents of and visitors to this grand city.

Capitulations, Westernizing
Influences, Tanzimat Reforms

Capitulations (*ahdames*) were extraterritorial rights and protections granted to the Christian States of Europe by a Sultan in favor of their communities in Ottoman lands. Special rights were initially extended on behalf of Christian Pilgrims traveling to the Levant to sites like the Church of the Holy Sepulcher in Jerusalem. The document here pictured is one such Capitulation agreed between the French King Charles IX and Sultan Selim II signed in 1569 CE.

In time, Capitulations came to be extended for a variety of reasons, absolving foreigners from the duty to serve in the Ottoman army in lieu of a tax, to provide certain property rights and commercial trading privileges, the latter coming more often in treaties at the end of various wars. Initially, they were extended out of a position of strength. Later, they were extended from a position of weakness.

Nineteenth century Capitulations were symbolic of unwarranted intrusions by "infidels" of the sovereignty of the Ottoman State. The negative memory of the Capitulations for many Turks remains, much like the failed Crusades, the fall of Constantinople and the sieges of Vienna are for many Christians of Western Europe. If there has been a salve for this pain, it has been the secularization of European, American, and Turkish society, fertilized by business and mutual security considerations. These considerations, as we have seen over time shift, resulting in ebbs and flows of trust between and among these societies. Having said this, it is useful to draw a distinction between often politically unstable government to government political relations and people to people personal relations. The latter tend to be steadier, more abiding, and tending to more consistently serve the cause of bolstering the foundations of "Where the Twain Meet."

Arguably, Westernizing influences have been both positive and negative for Turkey. On the positive side, they helped to facilitate a level of material, and cultural wealth, that sets it apart in the MENA (Middle East North Africa). And, just as it took changes over many centuries in European and then American societies to culturally take on board what is meant by the term "Western liberal democracy," it has taken, and is taking, time for Turkey to evolve and resolve the contradictions between its past, present, and where it is headed in the future. Societies are dynamic and Turkey and America, the East and the West, show periods of more and less stability over the decades and scores of years. At present, both countries, the East and the West, are exhibiting considerable instability adapting to changes and challenges in no small measure ocassioned by radical developments in technology in the 21st century.

For our purposes, it is more accurate to think of Western influence, at its inception, as being more properly described as European influence. And, it is important to remember that the influence was bi-directional, harkening back to the ancient Silk Road of ideas, goods, and services moving between the Orient and the Occident. Under Chinese leadership, these bi-directional trade routes are in the process of being reestablished. As amply demonstrated, there were centuries where influences may have been greater coming from the East than the West. On the West to East spectrum, influences in the modern era have been, and are, both accepted and rejected, or culturally altered to facilitate assimilation in Turkey and the East. If modern Turkey is the success story so many believe, it did not become so without accepting Western influence, however reluctantly and with however much pain. Let us now turn our attention to some of the various attempts to reform traditional Ottoman gorvernmental forms and institutions during the 19th century.

Experience is the best source of education. The most readily apparent education came in the form of battlefield experience. The lessons to be learned were not about bravery, but technology, engineering, and training. Once known and feared as "The scourge of the earth" and the "terrible Turks," the 1800s witnessed a falling away, on the periphery, one piece after another of the Ottoman Empire. Ethnic and local unrest, together with the strategic and commercial interests of Europe and Russia, placed the administratively and militarily over-stretched Ottomans in the line of fire. Successive wars, from the Levant to the Black Sea and the Balkans had shown, already by the late 1700s, that Ottoman Turkey was falling behind at a rate more apparent to the West than to the Ottomans. The net result of these losses gave rise to the recognition, even from within, that for the Ottoman Empire to have a chance to survive, it would need to be substantially transformed. Change increasingly came at the behest and under pressure from military victors, bankers, and Ottoman Government financial backers, such as the English and French in various conflicts and at the treaty negotiating tables. The reform process was halting and in many ways ineffectual. And, for whatever good it produced, foreign-imposed change certainly generated a spirit of resentment and xenophobia, in many, but importantly not all circles of Turkish society.

When Abdülmecid became Sultan at age sixteen in 1839, he was presented with unnerving facts. He had no navy in the Mediterranean and no army in the field with which to confront Muhammad Ali's forces who were nearing Istanbul. His father, Mahmud II had sought some Westernizing reforms. Beset by insurrections, his reforms had only superficial effects. Western dress did began to appear in the Court. Frock coat, dark trousers and the fez replaced the traditional robes and turban.

The young Sultan was not without two assets as noted by Palmer, *"...his mother, the Valide Sultana Bezmialem; and a promise of loyal support from the most skilled of his father's westernizing reformers, Mustafa Resid, who was a special envoy in London at the time.... She advised her son not to allow the Grand Vizier to put his appointees into office. He should wait until Resid returned from London to lead a reform effort. Resid was fluent in French and had served in the great courts of Europe. Sidestepping Grand Vizier Husrev, Resid persuaded the young Emperor to agree to Abdulmecid's first great act of office. The Noble Rescript (Hatt-i Şarif), pronounced by Resid in the Rose Chamber (Gülhane) of the Topkapi Palace before the assembled digntaries, Ottoman and foreign. The Edict proclaimed that a new era of reform would be ushered in protecting property rights of all citizens, Turkish and foreign (milletler) and that a new code of justice would be instituted that would give equal status to Jews and Christians with Muslims. The news, as calculated, was well-received in European capitals. The British Ambassador, Lord Ponsonby wrote in a dispatch to Lord Palmerston, 'A victorious answer to those who would say that this Empire cannot be saved by its ancient Government ...."*

In the succeeding years, many reforms were instituted including:

- the issuance of Ottoman Bank Notes and a Civil and Criminal Code (1840); a Ministry of Education (1845);
- the abolition of slavery and the slave trade (1847); railway and telegraph networks established (1847-1856);
- an Ottoman Central Bank and the *Hatt-i Humayun* Law establishing legal equality for all citizens (1856);
- founding of the Ottoman Imperial Lycée at Galatasaray; and,
- the Nationality Law making citizenship common to all irrespective of religion or ethnicity, culminating in the first Parliament on 1876.

The Constitution and Parliament were suspended less than three years later in 1878 by Sultan Abdülmecid II, who reasserted absolute rule, thereby ending the period of reform and reorganization known as the *Tanzimat*.

To be sure, the spirit of reform lived on in groups like the Young Ottomans who felt the reforms had not gone far enough. They were led by people like Namık Kemal and İbrahim Şinasi. From the Young Ottomans sprang the next generation of reformers and progressives known as the Young Turks. They were founded in Salonica (Thessaloniki), the home of the Third Army, in 1902. The young Mustafa Kemal, himself born in Salonica, was then 21 years old. He had already chosen a life in the military. He was imbued with a strong sense of the need for reform. By 1907, he had joined a secret society of military reformers, Motherland and Liberty (*Vatan ve Hürriyet*). Shortly thereafter, he joined the Committee for Union and Progress (C.U.P.) which engineered the Young Turk Revolution. The Third Army marched on Istanbul in 1908, forcing the Sultan to re-open the Parliament and re-establish the Constitution. Under the leadership of Talaat, Enver and Cemal, all Pashas, and under the banner of "Liberty, Equality, Justice" (*Hürriyet, Musavaat, Adalet*), C.U.P. seized virtual control of the Ottoman government.

The 19th century came and went with the Eastern Question still unresolved, horrible killing by the "*Hamidiye*" Kurds, and Government troops, of Armenians (as well as Orthodox, Catholic and Protestant believers) in the East and during Christian uprisings in Crete and Macedonia. Balkanization was about to hit full stride, as well as war with the Italians in Libya. In fact, resolution of the Eastern Question would only come in the wake of a world war, a War of Turkish Independence, the physical removal of the Sultan and Caliph from Istanbul and the establishment of a Republic in Ankara. And that resolution again proved to be temporary.

As the Ottoman Empire was in steady decline by the last quarter of the 18th century, a new country was in the making on the other side of the Atlantic. And, just as European spheres of influence were colliding with each other and the Ottoman world, so they were colliding in the Western hemisphere. Resulting in conflict between and among French, English, and Dutch colonies in the New World. In particular, conflict within one of the English colonies, America, had been brewing since 1763. The American Revolution would prove to be global in dimension, even more so than the Seven Years' War (The French and Indian War in America) concluded in 1763.

My wife arrived on the 20th to spend the last two weeks of the fall semester at Koç University where I was teaching. That entire fall, I attended church on Sundays with a low level of anxiety with heightened sensitivities to my surroundings in Beyoğlu. That anxiety, though unspoken, only increased when she arrived. We avoided the city, most days preferring to stay close to the university at the northern end of the Bosphorus. But, there would be Christmas Eve, Christmas Day and the last Sunday of the year, January 1st church services, before returning to the States together on the 3rd.

On a snowy Christmas Eve, we arrived at the Chapel of St. Helena's (named for Constantine's mother) which is located next to the British Consulate. The British Counsel General would be attending the service. The Turkish authorities, given the recent events, insisted, we soon discovered, on blocking off both ends of the street leading to the Consulate (site of a 2003 bombing which killed British Consul General Short, whom we had known from my banker days). In cooperation with the Turkish authorities, the British Consular security team set up a makeshift security check at the entrance to the chapel. We learned from Father Ian that evening that some group had taken the Church Facebook website, which contained the Holiday service dates, locations and times, and published them in a Turkish newspaper. The government wanted no more terrorist-related news in the press and had insisted on security measures both for the chapel that night, and the Crimean Church on Christmas Day and New Year's Day.

At this point, I had to explain to my wife what had been going on of late without overly alarming her. We returned on Christmas Day to the Crimean Church only to find four plain clothes policemen at the entrance gate to the church which is surrounded by high walls in the front, but only six feet in parts of the rear. During the service, ears were cocked for any unusual sounds during the service. Getting Marilyn safely back to the university later that day brought more relief than I let on.

On New Year's Day, a Sunday, I arose around 6:00 AM, checked my smart phone for the news only to discover that an AR-15-wielding Jihadist, around 1:00 AM, had killed thirty-nine revelers at a posh nightclub up the Bosphorus and wounded even more. It was decision time. Either abort the mission to go into town for our last service before leaving the country, or go, and tell myself we were not giving in to the threat of intimidation. I decided to do the latter, and not tell my wife the horrific news of that morning. Again, we made the trek in, by taxi, underground subway and then a 10-minute walk. Again we found plain clothes policemen.

After church, after a farewell lunch with a few friends and our beloved Anglican Priest, we said our goodbyes and made our way back to the university with a great sigh of relief. I might add, our Turkish friends had also been avoiding downtown Istanbul, and trying to keep their teenage children from the same, for two years at that point. I first learned this the preceding year when teaching the spring 2015 semester at Koç University.

<small>*</small>   This is perhaps a good place to share with the reader the anxiety I felt attending the Crimean Memorial church in downtown Istanbul in 2016. Churches had been declared targets by ISIS. In January, ten tourists were killed in a bomb attack near the Blue Mosque in Istanbul. A suicide bomber struck in March killing four and wounding others. June saw an ISIS-sponsored attack at the Istanbul Airport killing 41 and wounding others. On July 15th an attempted military coup had been put down. December 10th, Kurdish Separatists, the Falcons, targeted a large group of Turkish police, killing 44, including a Koç University student who was passing by the İnönü Soccer Stadium on his motorcycle. By early December, the families of American Consular officers in Istanbul had been evacuated to the States. On December 19th, the Russian Ambasador was assasinated in an Ankara art gallery by a young off-duty Turkish policeman protesting Russian support for Assad's forces in Syria.

Chapter 9

AMERICA'S FOUNDING

"Render unto Caesar what is Caesar's, and unto God what is God's"

—ATTRIBUTED TO JESUS IN THE SYNOPTIC GOSPELS

In 1783, the Americans sat a Peace Conference in Paris alongside representatives of the Great Powers of Europe – then the Great Powers of the Earth. How did this fledging Nation, which had sought Independence from England but seven years earlier, reach such a point in its infancy? Many of its Founders, their courage and tenacity notwithstanding, would attribute the outcome to Divine Providence. In today's parlance, one might say the American Rebels were "on the right side of history." Her Victory was the first fruit of the Age of Enlightenment, followed shortly by the French Revolution and similar popular struggles over much of the succeeding century.

The chances of America sitting in Paris at the Peace Table in 1783, where she had taken on the mightiest power on earth single handedly (initially), were slim to none. Let us now examine some of the key factors that indispensably contributed to America's Revolutionary War and near miraculous "escape" to freedom and independence.

The American Revolution is a story that begins midstream in a long and arduous history of man's reshaping of his relationship to society. It is a story of a yearning for individual freedom. It is the story of people and societies discovering that sovereignty need not rest in the Divine Right of King or Church – but in the Divine and Natural Right of people to freely govern themselves.

Sacrifice, courage, endurance, and death are hallmarks of the American Revolution writ large in the national memory of all the sides involved. Fact and "useful myths" of the key figures involved abound and abide. The American Revolution was a battle for the hearts and minds of people, waged in the context of the 18th century Enlightenment, and fought from the Indian Ocean to the Mediterranean, the Atlantic to the Caribbean, and along the Mississippi. It was fought in the halls of government in Philadelphia, in England, France, Spain, Russia, and the Netherlands. Pitched battles were fought from Canada to Bunker Hill, at Trenton, Brandywine and in the Ohio Valley, from Charleston to Guilford Court House. Naval engagements took place from the coasts of India to the Capes off the coast of Virginia, from Flamborough Head, England to the Caribbean, from the coast of Senegal to Manila, from Gibraltar to Yorktown. This was a war waged by Whigs and Tories, Rebels and Loyalists, kings, politicians, soldiers, sailors, mercenaries of many countries (some 30,000

Hessians alone), Native Americans, bankers, farmers, privateers, pamphleteers, slaves, men, women and children.

Philosophical Underpinning, the French Enlightenment Influences – Montesquieu, Rousseau

In an earlier Chapter on "Sovereignty, Secularism, and the Rule of Law," we considered the evolution of the concept of a social contract, which eventually challenged the principle of the Divine Right of Kings. The Glorious Revolution of 1688 in England resulted in the institution of a limited Constitutional Monarchy. Absolute monarchies continued in other States of Europe. The work of Hobbes, Locke, and Hume, leaders of the English and Scottish Enlightenment-carried over the English Channel to France.

That next wave of republican political thought came from the French in the 18th century. Montesquieu gave great insight into the rationale and mechanics of the principle of the separation of powers. In his work, *De L'Esprit de Lois,* published in 1748, he championed the achievements of the English and the Constitutional Monarchy achieved in 1688, and advocated for clearer distinctions of powers vested in the Executive, Legislative, and Judicial branches of government. His work was quickly banned by the Catholic Church of France. Research shows that the Baron de Montesquieu was the most frequently quoted authority on politics and government in pre-Revolutionary British Colonial America, cited more by the Founding Fathers than any other source except the Bible. His work was particularly influential on James Madison, the Father of the Constitution. It was Montesquieu who said, *"Republics end with luxury; monarchies with poverty."* With perhaps even greater perspicuity, he admonishes his fellow man with the observation that, *"If we only wanted to be happy, it would be easy. But, we want to be happier than other people, and that is almost always difficult, since we think them happier than they are."*

Jean-Jacques Rousseau was the next French (b. Geneva) Political Philosopher to contribute to ideas and words found in America's Founding Document, the Declaration of Independence. Appearing in 1762, near the close of the Seven Years War (the French and Indian War in America), Rousseau's, *The Social Contract*, began with the dramatic words, *"Man was born free, and he is everywhere in chains. Those who think themselves the masters of others are indeed greater slaves than they."* He also said, *"I prefer Liberty with danger than peace with slavery."* His work, perhaps unfairly, is more closely associated with the Jacobin phase of the French Revolution, but his insights on man in his natural state of freedom certainly added to the dismantling of feudal forms of government.

Taxation, Representation, The Rigors of Colonial Life

At the end of the Seven Years' War (1763), a treaty was signed in Paris. The British were the victors of this conflict, acquiring strategic and valuable land from Canada to Florida and the Caribbean, from Gibraltar to the West Coast of Africa and both coasts of India and Manila in the Philippines. The great losers were France and Spain. Both would be spoiling for a fight with the British in the future when the time seemed right. Of course, waging what was arguably the "First World War" was costly in terms of men and materiel. At least in England, King and Parliament both believed that their colonies reaped a variety of benefits and should be expected to share in the economic recovery and defense of Mother England via taxation.

England had one issue unique to her North American Colonies. Some of the Native American tribes fought with the English and others fought with the French. This presented a very delicate situation. The English wanted to reward their Indian allies with gifts and to protect their lands from further encroachment by American settlers moving west over the Appalachian Mountains in search of fresh land. They mistakenly chose not to also gift their Indian enemies, which would come to haunt them in  the case of some tribes who would later either remain neutral or join the American Rebels when the American Revolution broke out. The other objective was one of control. They did not want their American colonists venturing west where they could not be controlled or regulated by the Crown. With these differing considerations in mind,

King and Parliament passed the Royal Proclamation of 1763, precluding westward movement of the Colonists.

American colonists came to greatly resent this. They fought, bled, died, and suffered property damage during that war in the Colonies. They thought the land in the area of the Great Lakes, the Ohio River Valley and territory leading to the Mississippi River should be a kind of prize for their sacrifice. The Proclamation seemed like an indirect tax. By the following year, the British began to levy a series of taxes and offensive Acts: the Sugar Act (April 1764); the Stamp Tax (March 1765), and the Quartering Act (May 1765). Later that month in 1765, the Virginia Assembly voted to not comply with the Stamp duty. In the fall of that year, representatives of nine of the thirteen colonies gathered at what came to be known as the Stamp Act Congress. They voted to declare the Stamp Tax unconstitutional as the Colonists were being taxed without their consent. At the same time, in the Boston area, a group of tradesmen and artisans formed an organization called the Sons of Liberty. Their objective was to run the Stamp Tax collectors out of the Colonies and publish anti-British propaganda. Their ranks began to swell and spread to the other colonies. They were prepared to be violent and were on occasion.

As early as 1765, French Foreign Minister Vergennes had predicted that the loss of the French threat in North America would lead ultimately to the Americans "*striking off their chains.*" Ten years later, at the outbreak of the

Rebellion, Vergennes in an exchange with an English traveler as reported by John C. Bridge in his book, *From Island to Empire*, *"England will soon repent of the only check that could keep her enemies in awe. They stand no longer in need of her protection. She will call on them to contribute toward supporting the burdens which they have helped bring on her, and they will answer by striking off all dependence."*

In 1770, a snowball thrown in the face of one of the "Red Coats" resulted in a British soldier firing into the crowd killing five Colonists. Fanning the flames of anti-King and Parliament, the incident was immediately dubbed the "Boston Massacre." The next major event was an anti-tea tax response by a group of townspeople who in 1773 dressed up as Mohawk Indians, boarded a ship, and dumped a large cargo of tea into Boston Harbor. This event became known as the Boston Tea Party.

The following year, the outraged British passed the Intolerable Acts, stripping the Massachusetts Colony of self-government and judicial independence. The colony responded with a boycott on British goods. In September of that year, representatives from all the Colonies gathered in Philadelphia for the First Continental Congress to determine measures that might be taken against the Intolerable Acts.

It was outside Boston, in Lexington and Concord, mid-April of 1775 that Americans fired on British forces who were marching out to seize stores of gunpowder located in this area. Paul Revere was famously involved in warning his fellow Americans that the British were coming using a lantern in the bell tower of the Old North Church in Boston as a signal. This skirmish in which eight Colonists died, one British soldier was wounded, and the British were forced to retreat back to Boston signaled the beginning of open hostilities between Rebel Americans and the British. The incident was later made famous by Ralph Waldo Emerson, the poet (and Unitarian/Transcendentalist), in a poem called the "Concord Hymn" written in 1837.

"By the rude bridge that arched the flood, Their flag to April's breeze unfurled, Here once the embattled farmers stood, And fired the shot heard round the world."

On June 16, 1775, the Second Continental Congress appointed George Washington the Commander-in-Chief of the Continental Army. The next day, the first battle of the American Revolution took place in Boston, the Battle of Bunker Hill. The British succeeded in dislodging the American forces, but at a real cost in casualties, the British 1064, the Americans 357. In early July, the Congress sent an "Olive Branch" petition to King George III agreeing to a cease-fire in exchange for the repeal of the Intolerable Acts. The King rejected the proposal and declared the Colonies to be in open rebellion. The war was on. And again, this would become a world war fought round the globe, arguably, the "second world war."

Without wishing to appear too pro-American in this contest, I have noted that British efforts to recoup some of the costs of the previous war had a certain amount of logic to it, especially from the perspective of London. The issue really arose because the Colonists rightly claimed that they had no direct representatives in Parliament. The rallying cause was *"No taxation without representation."*

When standing before Parliament in London in 1766, then Colonial Agent Benjamin Franklin was questioned and tellingly answered as follows:

"Q. What was the temper of America toward Great Britain before the year 1763?

A. The best in the world. They submitted willingly to the government of the Crown, and paid, in their courts, obedience to acts of Parliament. Numerous as the people are in the several old provinces they cost you nothing in forts, citadels, garrisons, or armies, to keep them in subjection...

Q. And what is their temper now?

A. Oh, very much altered."

One must also keep in mind that the early Colonists had fought hard lives to settle America. They faced danger from Indians and starvation. Many died on the voyages before even reaching America. Many were Puritans who had fled religious persecution. Being five weeks or more by sail from England, the Colonists were a tough and self-reliant people, used to being independent and able to survive in very primitive circumstances. When England sought to impose its will on the Colonies, this was not comparable to a similar action on a small sugar-producing island in the Caribbean. America was part of a vast wilderness, a vast continent, waiting to be explored, exploited, and settled.

Authority tended to be very local. Loyalties tended to be very local. The farther one got from the large cities and towns, even abiding by the rules of individual Colonial Governments was seen as undesired, unneeded, and an unwelcomed intrusion.

Before looking at some of the foundation documents of the American Revolution, one may capture the spirit of the day by reading and imagine hearing of one of the most famous speeches ever given in history. This was a grandiloquent speech by Virginia Assemblyman Patrick Henry on March 13, 1775 at the South Church in Richmond, Virginia. The Assemblymen had met in Richmond, away from the Royal Governor's oversight in the capital of Williamsburg, a good half day's ride by horse. The Assembly was divided on the subject of raising a militia and putting the Colony on a war footing. Some felt that a diplomatic solution to the impasse on the subject of taxes and coming to the aid of their fellow Colonists in Massachusetts should continue to be sought. They felt that they were no match for the British Army. Others argued that they should consider the possibility of confronting the British and preparing accordingly. Below are a few excerpts from that speech as recorded in the minutes of the meeting and the recorded memories of many of the delegates who were present.

> *MR. PRESIDENT: No man thinks more highly than I do of the patriotism, as well as abilities, of the very worthy gentlemen who have just addressed the House. But different men often see the same subject in different lights;*

and, therefore, I hope it will not be thought disrespectful to those gentlemen if, entertaining as I do, opinions of a character very opposite to theirs, I shall speak forth my sentiments freely, and without reserve. This is no time for ceremony. The question before the House is one of awful moment to this country. For my own part, I consider it as nothing less than a question of freedom or slavery; and in proportion to the magnitude of the subject ought to be the freedom of the debate. It is only in this way that we can hope to arrive at truth, and fulfil the great responsibility which we hold to God and our country. Should I keep back my opinions at such a time, through fear of giving offence, I should consider myself as guilty of treason towards my country, and of an act of disloyalty toward the majesty of heaven. Which I revere above all earthly kings...

...I have but one lamp by which my feet are guided; and that is the lamp of experience I know of no way of judging of the future but by the past. And judging by the past, I wish to know what there has been inthe conduct of the British ministry for the last ten years, to justify those hopes with which gentlemen have been pleased to solace themselves, and the House?

...They tell us, sir, that we are weak; unable to cope with so formidable an adversary. But when shall we be stronger? Will it be the next week, or the next year? Will it be when we are totally disarmed, and when a British guard shall be stationed in every house? Shall we gather strength by irresolution and inaction? Shall we acquire the means of

effectual resistance, by lying supinely on our backs, and hugging the delusive phantom of hope, until our enemies shall have bound us hand and foot?

...It is in vain, sir, to extenuate the matter. Gentlemen may cry, Peace, Peace but there is no peace. The war is actually begun! The next gale that sweeps from the north will bring to our ears the clash of resounding arms! Our brethren are already in the field! Why stand we here idle? What is it that gentlemen wish? What would they have? Is life so dear, or peace so sweet, as to be purchased at theprice of chains and slavery? Forbid it, Almighty God! I know not what course others may take; but as forme, give me liberty or give me death!" History has passed down to posterity this impassioned appeal and flight of oratorical genius, rendered it was said, with dramatic cadence and from memory.

Founding Principles and Documents, Paine, Jefferson, and Madison

At the urging of Benjamin Franklin whom he met in London, Thomas Paine moved to America in late 1774. He arrived at a time when his talent and penchant for being an Essayist, Pamphleteer, and Propagandist would be fostered by a people losing patience with Colonial Rule from London. He would seize on this dissatisfaction and elevate it to a cause beyond just redressing the issue of hated taxation to the first open call for separation. Using the rhetoric of the Enlightenment, Paine wrote in plain language that appealed to the common man. His "Common Sense" was the clarion call to a war for independence.

"But where, say some, is the King of America? I'll tell you, friend, he reigns above, and doth not make havoc of mankind like the Royal Brute of Great Britain... so far as we approve of monarchy, that in America the law is king. We have every opportunity and every encouragement before us, to form the noblest purest constitution on the face of the earth. We have it in our power to begin the world over again." Common Sense, January 1776

"Common Sense" sold hundreds of thousands of copies within three months of its publication. Before becoming America's second President, John Adams is reported to have said, *"Without the pen of the author of Common Sense, the sword of Washington would have been raised in vain."*

Later that same year, with independence declared and the war raging, Paine again appealed to the common man to sacrifice for the cause of freedom and liberty in a second pamphlet, "The American Crisis" with these famous words:

"THESE are the times that try men's souls. The summer soldier and the sunshine patriot will, in this crisis, shrink from the service of their country; but he that stands it now, deserves the love and thanks of man and woman. Tyranny, like hell, is not easily conquered; yet we have this consolation with us, that the harder the conflict, the more glorious the triumph. What we obtain too cheap, we esteem too lightly: it is dearness only that gives everything its value." TheAmerican Crisis, December 1776

The Foundational document of the American Revolution, The Declaration of Independence, was a long list of specified grievances against King George III. What is best remembered of it is the Preamble, and its primary author, Thomas Jefferson. While the principles contained therein were not unique to Jefferson, the genius of his pen to put them in dramatic, edifying and elegant language has rendered this document a model for the just overthrow of tyranny ever since, beginning with the French Revolution two decades later.

THE DECLARATION OF INDEPENDENCE – July 4, 1776
"When in the Course of human events it becomes necessary for one people to dissolve the political bands which have connected them with another and to assume among the powers of the earth, the separate and equal station to which the Laws

of Nature and Nature's God entitles them, a decent respect to the opinions of mankind requires that they should declare the causes which impel them to that separation. We hold these truths to be self-evident, that all men are created equal, that they are endowed by their Creator with certain unalienable Rights, that among these are Life, Liberty and the pursuit of Happiness. ----That to secure these rights, Governments are instituted among Men, deriving their just power from the consent of the governed, ---- That whenever any Form of Government becomes destructive of these ends, it is the right of the People to alter or abolish it, and to institute new Government, laying its foundations on such principles and organizing its power in such form, as to them seems most likely to effect their Safety and Happiness..."* [The author has added the underlining.]

"One people", "Dissolving political bands", "separate and equal station", "Laws of Nature and Nature's God", "all men are created equal", "endowed by their Creator with unalienable rights", "Life, Liberty and the Pursuit Happiness" and "the right of People to alter or abolish, and to institute new Government" – these seminal aspirations did not just materialize in the heads of the Founders by Divine revelation in the summer of 1776. The "Spirit of '76," that new and great Experiment, came as the latest, and by no means, the last trial in the laboratory of human socio-political development. These aspirations had many antecedents.

Earlier antecedents include such "quantum leaps" in systems of governance in history as the bi-cameral legislature of the 3rd century BCE Lycian League of Patara, Magna Carta (1215), and the Glorious Revolution of (1688) in England. Without the English, Scottish, and French Enlightenment writers already noted, Jefferson could never have penned these words. The pitfalls of earlier failures of experiments in Republican forms, the City States of Ancient Greece and Imperial Rome, were poignantly chronicled by one of the greatest historians of any time, a member of the English Parliament and a contemporary of our Founding Fathers, Edward Gibbon. The first volume of his *History of the Rise and Fall of the Roman Empire*, from its zenith to the fall of the Byzantines, including Islamic and Mongol conquests, appeared in 1776. Its messages about overweening government and decadence were not lost on political leaders on both sides of the Atlantic.

The Separation of Church and State – Secularism and Thomas Jefferson

After the Revolution, in debates leading to the writing of the United States Constitution, Jefferson's pen again carried the day regarding one of the mainstays of the new Republic, the principle of the Separation of Church and State. Debates about Jefferson's religious beliefs, which certainly changed over time, and were in any case, a product of the European Enlightenment, which he found in heavy dose already at William and Mary College, Jefferson bridled against the authority of the Anglican, now Episcopal, Church. He and Madison were active proponents of religious toleration, believing that a man's right to worship or not worship God was a private matter – not subject to State jurisdiction. To that end, Jefferson authored the Virginia Statute for Religious Freedom during the Revolution and presented it to the Virginia Assembly in 1779. It was not adopted by the Assembly until 1786 at which time the Church of England was disestablished and freedom of religion was guaranteed. His words speak for themselves.

"Whereas, Almighty God hath created the mind free;

That all attempts to influence it by temporal punishments or burthens, or by civil incapacitations tend only to beget habits of hypocrisy and meanness, and therefore are a departure from the plan of the holy author of our religion, who being Lord, both of body and mind yet chose not to propagate it by coercions on either, as was in his Almighty power to do,

That the impious presumption of legislators and rulers, civil as well as ecclesiastical, who, being themselves but fallible and uninspired men have assumed dominion over the faith of others, setting up their own opinions and modes of thinking as the only true and infallible, and as such endeavouring to impose them on others, hath established and maintained false religions over the greatest part of the world and through all time;

That to compel a man to furnish contributions of money for the propagation of opinions, which he disbelieves is sinful and tyrannical; ..."

Jefferson's Statute became the basis of the Establishment and Free Exercise Clauses of the First Amendment of the American Constitution in the Bill of Rights.

It is worth noting that written on his gravestone, at his beloved home Monticello, his three most notable achievements, and three only, were authorized by him. They were: The Declaration of Independence; The Virginia Statute for Religious Freedom and, the University of Virginia. Not even the fact that he was President of the United States for two terms was an achievement that he classed with these three achievements of which he was most proud.

Jefferson's dear friend and neighbor, James Madison, was also a key contributor to the creation of the U.S. Constitution and the principle author of the Bill of Rights. Debates raged in the two to three years prior to the signing of the Constitution. The debates center on the role and limits of a National Government. Americans were very sensitive about centralized and concentrated power, having just thrown off the yoke of English rule. The issues in the debate were most forcefully presented by Founding Fathers Jay, Hamilton, Pinckney, and Madison in *The Federalist Papers*. Arguments were presented for and against a centralized government with taxing powers and the power to raise and direct an army. Many of the representatives of the former Colonies, now States, wanted a weaker Federal government with more rights devolving upon the States. Others were weary of too much government at any level and were strong advocates of Individual Rights hearkening back to Enlightenment precepts. One of those arguing most vociferously against a strong central government was Madison's fellow Virginian Patrick Henry, whose oratory in support of the Revolution was noted earlier.

Madison had long been seen as a legislative workhorse and a man who did his homework. He had spent considerable time not just reading books such as Gibbon's about earlier governmental republican experiments, but read about and studied then existing experiments in republican government, their pros and cons, those of the Swiss Federation and the Dutch Republic.

At the end of the debates, after many bitter compromises, the U.S. Constitution was signed into law on September 17, 1787. So heated remained the controversy surrounding the Constitution, that only 9 of the 13 States initially ratified it. It was not until 1790 that Rhode Island, the last to sign, and under some duress, ratified it. Near the close of the Philadelphia Convention, a committee was formed to write the following Preamble to express the spirit of the United States Constitution.

"We the People of the United States, in order to form a more perfect union,

establish justice, insure domestic tranquility, provide for the common defense, promote the general welfare, and secure the blessings of liberty to ourselves and our posterity, do ordain and establish this Constitution for the United States of America."

The Bill of Rights, a necessary corollary to constrain the inevitable overreach of a central government, was signed into law shortly thereafter in 1791. The Bill of Rights captured the essence of the Preamble to the Declaration of Independence, the "Spirit of '76" as it is sometimes referred, written thirteen years earlier, *"Life, Liberty and the Pursuit of Happiness."*

One should not fail to understand that the American Revolution was not just a war for independence. It was at the same time, America's first civil war. American Colonists had contributed significantly to a major victory for the British Empire in The French and Indian War. Imagine how traumatic it must have been to find oneself, one's family and one's fellow countrymen coming to be divided between Whigs and Tories, Rebels and "Scotchmen" as Jefferson often called them (not to be confused with the Scots Irish). What happened during this period to loyal British subjects who, as Americans all, would turn on each other? Many of His Majesty's subjects lived in fear of their neighbors, and each other. On January 30, 1776, the Middlesex Journal of New Jersey offered the following verse reminiscent of Shakespeare regarding the signing or not of the Rebel Petition in towns and at courthouses all over the Thirteen Colonies:

"To sign, or not to sign? That is the question, / Whether t'were better for an honest man/ To sign, and so be safe; or to...fly.../ And, by that flight, t'escape/ Feathers and tar..."

Some claimed, or feigned, to be indifferent or neutral in the contest. But the large majority of Colonists were faced with a frightening decision. Either way was fraught with risks and hazards. Sometimes voluntarily, sometimes under duress, families and communities made fateful and costly decisions. In the case of Tories, many chose to move to Tory-strongholds in East Florida, the Carolina coasts and New York City. Some chose to relocate to the British Caribbean, Canada, or England. In the case of Rebel supporters, many chose to relocate, lock, stock and barrel, to areas inland, closer to the Piedmont, the Alleghenys and the Shenandoah Valley. Neighboring towns in Connecticut, for example Danbury and the Eastern part of the State, were staunchly in the Rebel camp. Litchfield, in the center of the Colony, was a Tory stronghold. And, Stamford, Connecticut, being geographically closer still to British-occupied New York City, was a toss-up, with some families loyal to the Crown, some to the Rebel Cause. It is estimated that toward the end of the war, about 40% of the population was Patriot, 20% Loyalist and the remainder indifferent.

America would experience a second civil war during the War of 1812 during President Madison's term as President. The War Between the States during President Lincoln's term, though vastly more devastating and threatening to the fabric of the Union, was, I would argue, America's third civil war.

In order to have some appreciation of the military aspects of the Revolution, we shall focus on three key battles and one "strategic escape," two in the North and two in the South.

The Battles of Saratoga, Oriskany, Cowpens, and the Crossing of the Dan

The victory at Yorktown on October 19, 1781, when British General Lord Cornwallis surrendered to General Washington concluding the military conflict came after six long years of fighting. There were many times during those years when the rebellion looked like it would fail. Keeping the army together, paying and feeding the soldiers of the Continental Line, was always a nightmare for General Washington. The Militia, as important as they were, could disappear as fast as they appeared, returning home at harvest time or because they were worried that their families might be attacked by Indians or Loyalist Tories.

After some initial success in Boston, General Washington and his forces were forced out of Long Island and the City of New York – retreating to New Jersey. He wanted to hurt the British forces, but not in large, European-style, battles where he might put his entire Army, and the revolution, at risk. Back in Philadelphia, the Continental Congress was beset with conflict and disagreement as to how best to prosecute and pay for the war. Could the Americans find any allies in Europe who would support their cause, with money, military expertise, and military materiel? Did anyone believe that the American Rebels even had a chance to defeat the most formidable military in the world?

In fact, the British thought a significant show of force in a few strategic locations would break the spirit of the Americans in short order. They also assumed that Tory Loyalists in the Colonies would be able to help hold some of the strategically important areas and provide the necessary amount of food for the Red Coat army, their Hessian mercenaries, and their cavalry horses.

Washington desperately needed a strategic victory to keep the morale of his forces up, to stiffen the backs of the politicians in Philadelphia, and to convince potential allies, France in particular, that the Americans, with a little help, might just extract enough blood over enough time to sap the will and drain the treasury of the British, forcing them to abandon the effort to tame the Americans into submission. The Battle of Saratoga at Freeman's Farm and then at Bemis Heights in September and October of 1777 proved to be that victory so desperately needed.

Under the direction of General Burgoyne, the British had devised a plan to hive off the New England Colonies from New York and those Colonies farther south. If the British could do this and starve the New England Rebels in Connecticut, Rhode Island, Massachusetts, Vermont, and New Hampshire from political and military support, they could choke off the Rebellion. The strategy was based on a three-prong attack. One army under General Burgoyne would come from Canada down through Lake Champlain headed toward the Hudson River and New York. General Clinton and his army, already in control of New York City, would move forces north, up the Hudson River. And finally, British Forces from the Great Lakes and their Indian allies were to move east through the Mohawk River Valley and connect with Burgoyne and Clinton's forces in Albany, securing the Hudson River Valley. Seizing control of all of New York and the three river systems, the Hudson, the Delaware, and the Susquehanna, would be the key to their divide and conquer strategy.

Since time immemorial, rulers, in order to lessen the burden on their subjects, would raise taxes and borrow money to secure mercenaries. King George III initially tried to hire Russian mercenaries, fresh from a victory over the Ottoman Turks in 1773. Catherine the Great turned him down. Not so much because she did not sympathize with the policy of opposing any republican rebellion that might threaten monarchies, but because she thought King George was handling the American Rebels ineffectively. She recognized that distance from England was on the Rebels' side and thought he should be negotiating with them.

Having failed in his request of Catherine, King George III, also being Elector of Hanover, Germany, had ready access to soldiers in Prussia – his ancestral home (pictured here). Records indicate that to this end, during the course of the War, he hired 29,875 mercenaries for service in North America. They collectively were, and continue to be called, Hessians as most of them were from the area in Northern Germany called Hesse Kassel. Mercenaries were particularly hated by the Americans. Of this group, the 1st Division sailed on March 21, 1777 and the 2nd Division on June 1, bound for Portsmouth, England where they joined the British army and sailed for Montreal.

Gen. Burgoyne began to march south from Canada in the summer of 1777. Initially, he met with success in capturing the American Fort Ticonderoga. However, the 3-prong plan soon began to unravel. The Americans were determined to slow Burgoyne's movement down. They felled trees along the main path and surprised a detachment of British soldiers foraging into Vermont for food and supplies in Bennington where they achieved a decisive victory over the British detachment. Compounding the problems besetting the British plan, Gen. Clinton received his orders too late to move far enough north along the Hudson River to come to Burgoyne's aid. Finally, British forces coming from the West in the Great Lakes area and Fort Niagara were slowed by the logistical challenges of moving through the Mohawk River Valley while fighting New York Militiamen and American Indian allies. Adding to their challenges was a particularly intense summer heat.

Smelling a possibly major victory, Gen. Washington sent additional Continental Line forces to bolster General Horatio Gate's forces, the lead American general for this engagement. Additionally, Militiamen from Virginia, Pennsylvania, and Connecticut swarmed into the area giving the Americans a 3 to 1 advantage over Burgoyne's forces, British, Hessian, and Indian.

Burgoyne's army came to a point along the River where it would become exposed to the artillery set in a commanding position of high ground for the American forces. He knew British reinforcements would not arrive in time to come to his aid. He had to choose to either abandon the mission and retreat, after three hard months, or face the Americans. He chose the latter. The engagement at Freeman's Farm proved to be a tactical, but Pyrrhic, victory for the British, suffering much heavier casualties than the Americans.

Determined to follow the plan, and in hope that Clinton's force might arrive in time from New York City, he chose to engage the Americans again at Bemis Heights. Here, with the critical assistance of a Polish engineer and "freedom fighter," Colonel Thaddeus Kosciusko, who, with European training and battlefield experience, positioned the American artillery in a location which forced the British to have to take the heights if they were to be able to proceed south along the Hudson River down to Albany. In the ensuing battle, one of the heroes of the battle was Colonel Benedict Arnold, who was badly wounded in a flanking attack on a Hessian redoubt. He would later become the most infamous traitor to the American cause.

Burgoyne, outnumbered and eventually outflanked, surrendered his entire Army of 7,000 soldiers on October 17, 1777. This victory was a game changer and the French, Spanish, and Dutch bankers knew it. This was the evidence for which King Louis XVI and Foreign Secretary Vergennes had been waiting. This was further proof that with enough French support, the Rebels might send the British packing and would, in any case, leave the British with over-extended troop commitments and more vulnerable supply lines.

One of those serving in that Battle was a New Yorker, of French extraction, born in La Nouvelle France, otherwise known as Quebec, was one Christopher Joseph Delezenne. Here he received a battlefield promotion to Captain (serving with the New York Continental Line, Sappers and Miners, under the command of Col. Thaddeus Kosciusko. His service will be discussed further in due course.

Victory at the Battle of Saratoga in October of 1777 proved to be a mixed blessing. No doubt, it was a major turning point. While the French had actually been quietly preparing for war since 1775, they officially came into the war effort in support of the American Rebels and brought the Spanish with them. Both were aching to settle old scores, one the French and Indian War, the other the sinking of the Spanish Armada. Bad memories die hard.

One of the positive outcomes for the Americans was a changing perception and respect for the American soldier. As noted in Messrs. Victor and Hochwald in their book,

How America Fought Its Wars, one English Officer is said to have remarked, *"The courage and obstinacy with which the Americans fought were the astonishment of everyone, and we now became fully convinced that they are not that contemptible enemy we had hitherto imagined them, incapable of standing a regular engagement, and that they would only fight behind strong and powerful works."*

While the British appeared to bungle the war effort at times, regarding the issue of the quality of the wartime leadership in the contest, author Andrew O'Shaughnessy in his book, *The Men Who Lost America*, in his "warts and all" approach notes that, *"... that [the book] will consider their defects and their roles in contributing to the defeat, but it will also take issue with the popular misconception that they [the British generals] were simply incompetent and hidebound. The difference between success and failure is often a fine line."*

After the euphoria of defeating a British army of 7,000 and taking it captive had worn off, the business of how to deal with the prize became a challenge for Gen. Washington, the Continental Congress, King and Parliament, soldiers on both sides and citizens from New England to Virginia. They would come to be dubbed "the Convention Army", which would eventually be marched over six hundred miles south, there to be imprisoned at "The Barracks" in Charlottesville, Virginia, outside the combat zone during the War at that time.

The second battle to be considered took place along the East-West axis of the British strategy to separate

New York from the New England Colonies. The Battle of Oriskany, in August of 1777, was made famous to many Americans through Walter Edmonds' 1937 novel, *Drums Along the Mohawk,* and subsequent film adaptations.

The Mohawk River, what the Indians called *Tenonanatche,* flowed from East to West unlike the other rivers east of the Mississippi. The Native Americans who lived in the remote wilderness were tribes of the Iroquois Nation. It was an important trade route facilitating the movement of animal furs from the Great Lakes and northern New York east to Albany on the Hudson River. From there, joining with furs and other goods coming down from Canada, they could be moved down river for export to the world.

Settlement began in the first half of the 18th century. The Indians enjoyed the trade, but resented the westward moving settlement. Those arriving in this dense and dangerous wilderness included Germans (from the Palatine) and French (Huguenots) Protestant refugees, Highland Scots and Scots-Irish. They were followed by Christian missionaries to the Indians in the wake of the First Great Awakening discussed earlier. From their efforts, both Hamilton and Colgate colleges would be founded later that century and early the next, respectively.

The Battle fought that August summer day of 1777, while Gen. Burgoyne was moving his forces south along the Hudson, would prove to be the single bloodiest one-day battle of the Revolution. There were over 900 casualties.

The killing was savage, with muskets, bayonets, knives, tomahawks and war clubs. Notably, there were no British forces involved. Mercenaries, Indians, and Hessians fought with Loyalist New Yorkers. They fought against other New Yorkers, Rebels, Whigs, and Indians. As author of, *Bloody Mohawk*, Richard Berleth says of the New York warfare in his book, *"Nowhere else in the colonies did an array of antagonistic factions align themselves against each other with such ferocity. Beyond the politics of national and regional allegiances, upstate New Yorkers fought a war of cultural boundaries determined by ethnicity, religion, and tribe. At moments in the War for Independence, New York's strife coincided with the greater effort of the united colonies; at other moments, it was a blind and savage slugfest between family and neighbors."*

In the end, both sides claimed victory. The local fighting continued even after the Victory at Yorktown, with both sides, Tory and Rebel reluctant to put down arms for another year. Let us now turn our attention to the South, to the Southern Campaign. The years of 1779 and 1780 saw a kind of stalemate between Rebel forces and the British. The War gradually moved south to the Carolinas where it eventually concluded in Virginia at Yorktown.

Due to the stalemate in the North where Gen. Washington had been reluctant to engage the British until a French Army could join him, the British Army, under pressure for a major victory from King and Parliament, elected to move the focus of the fight to the Southern Colonies where it was believed that strong Loyalist support would ensure their success. General Lord Cornwallis was placed in command of British forces, additional units of which were coming from New York by ship. The British enjoyed success early on in their Southern Campaign, culminating in a humiliating surrender of the best part of the American army in the South, over 5,000 men, at the Siege of Charleston, South Carolina, in the spring of 1780.

By October of that year, the tide began to turn for the Americans. In the Battle of King's Mountain in early October (the 7th), Patriot forces surprised Loyalist forces to great effect. The Americans suffered fewer than 29 killed, the British, 290. The Americans captured 668 Loyalists. This victory was a great boost to Patriot morale. In an effort to capitalize on this minor success, Gen. Washington appointed one of his most able generals, Nathanael Greene, in October of 1780. He assumed command with reinforcements coming in Delaware, Maryland, Virginia, Over the Mountain men, Georgia, and the Carolinas.

The Battle of Cowpens on January 17, 1781, in a location just south of King's Mountain just over the border into South Carolina, one witnessed a signature strategy of Gen. Greene's. He split his limited forces and seasoned field commander Col. Daniel Morgan to rejoin the forces and move north. Meanwhile, with false intelligence, Cornwallis sent his dashing 26-year old Dragoon, Banastre Tarleton, to give pursuit to Greene's army, which they thought had gone to lay siege to Old Fort 96 farther south.

[Greene's men would lay siege to that Loyalist-manned fort later in the spring of that year. Under the strategic siege plan of Engineer General Kosciusko, Captain Delezenne, noted earlier, is mentioned in written accounts riding on horseback giving instruction to the Engineers and Sappers digging trenches and tunneling under the fort.]

Upon discovering that Greene's army was not at Fort 96, Tarleton gave chase to Greene's forces. With snow-melt-swollen rivers to ford to escape a major battle, Col. Morgan continued on until he found the right location to turn, stand and face the British. Tarleton marched his forces through the night to catch Morgan. By the time he arrived, his men exhausted and probably malnourished, Morgan was ready for him with a set of well-devised battle tactics. It was Greene's plan to inflict pain on the British, retreat and live to fight another day. Morgan's forces ended up shocking the British forces. While the Americans quit the field after a little more than an hour that morning, it proved to be a costly victory for the British. The Americans suffered light casualties, 25 killed and 124 wounded. Tarleton's losses were enormous by comparison, 110 killed, 229 wounded and well over 600 captured.

Of the many significant leaders in the Patriot Army was Gen. Washington's 2nd cousin, Lt. Col. William Washington, commander of the 1st and 3rd Light Dragoons seen here in a famous painting by William Ranney. Shown here is William Washington, per historical accounts, engaged with two British Dragoons, one of whom was Tarleton.

Washington is saved when his trumpeter, a black Patriot, shot the other Dragoon. Tarleton then shot Washington's horse out from under him and fled the field. Revolutionary War soldier and later Chief Justice of the Supreme Court, John Marshall observed that, *"Seldom has a battle, in which greater numbers were not engaged, been so important in its consequences as that of Cowpens."*

Nathanael Greene's army retreated north in an effort to get over the swollen Dan River to regroup and recoup. It was a forced march with Cornwallis and the British forces again in hot pursuit. Again, Greene divided his army with a diversion tactic to slow down and wear down the British, buying time for his larger force to reach and cross the Dan. Again, the British took the bait, gave chase to the diversionary forces. Upon discovering this, Tarleton, in a fit of pique, burned much of his baggage, tents (including those of his officers) and other non-essential supplies in order to lighten the load and allow his forces to move even faster.

The story is best told by Brigadier General Charles O'Hara in a letter to the Duke of Grafton dated April 20, 1781.

> *"...without baggage, necessaries, or provisions of any sort for officer or Soldier, in the most barren, inhospitable, unhealthy part of North America, opposed to the most savage, inveterate, perfidious, cruel enemy, with zeal and bayonets only, it was resolved to follow Greene's Army to the end of the world."*

In horrific winter conditions, with many of the American Army freezing and without boots, leaving trails of

blood in the snow, by some miracle, with British advance guards within hours of catching the Rebels with their backs against the Dan River, Greene (pictured on this equestrian statue) managed to get his army, horses, cannon, and men, in the late afternoon and in the fog of the night, over the river into Virginia.

When the fog cleared the morning of February 16, 1781, the British soldiers arrived. Looking across the swollen banks of the Dan River, they saw an American Army, cannons in place. In complete frustration, the British retired for the balance of the winter south near Guildford Court House (modern day Greensboro, NC) at Hillsborough, two days' march south. Assuming the Americans would need several months to regroup, refit, feed, and re-arm themselves, Gen. Nathanael Greene, but one month later, seized the moment. With fresh troops and tremendous support in the way of food and supplies from the residents of the surrounding Halifax County, he attacked the British at Guildford Court House. Again, the Americans quit the field, but not before seriously bloodying the British. British Whig Party leader of the opposition Charles Fox is said to have observed, "Another such victory would ruin the British Army."

At this point, Lord Cornwallis concluded that he had underestimated the will and skill of the Rebels and over-estimated the support of Carolina Tory Loyalists. He next made the fateful decision to concentrate all his forces at Yorktown on the east coast of Virginia from which he thought he could be easily supplied with troops and supplies. What he had not foreseen was a victory at sea by the French against a British fleet on September 6, 1781 at the Battle of the Capes, and a well-disguised combined march of Gen. Washington's army and the French army under the command of General Rochambeau down to Virginia. With Cornwallis' exit by sea now blocked, he faced the combined forces of the Americans and the French, outnumbering him 2 to 1. After a siege and fierce fighting in October 1781, Lord Cornwallis surrendered his beleaguered army – ending the main military conflict in the colonies.

It would be a troubled two more years before the British would finally be brought to the peace table, granting the Americans their independence. As we will see, the fighting may have largely ended in North America, but the British continued to face war around the world. We shall now turn our attention to the wider, global war, and to the critically important role of America's allies.

Allied and Other Country Contributions, the Roles of France and Spain, Holland, and Russia

In order to reach beyond an Anglo-centric focus and see this conflict through the wider lens of philosophic, political, economic, geographic, and military contexts, one must focus attention on America's most important ally, the French. A careful reading of the correspondence of men like Gen. Washington, Franklin, Robert Morris, Mason, Jay, Jefferson, Madison, John and Samuel Adams, Paine, Randolph, and the Marquis de Lafayette, to mention a few, clearly shows how keenly aware they all were that the war was being waged on many fronts – many of them well beyond the shores of the Thirteen Colonies.

Make no mistake. No American Rebels... No American Revolution. Other key actors notwithstanding, no General Washington... no successful Revolution... No American Revolution, no worldwide opportunity for America's Allies to redress the grievances and losses of the Seven Years' War.

Having said this, it is also true that without allies, without Old World countries jockeying for power, possessions, and resources, and, in particular, without the support of King Louis, his Foreign Minister, Charles Gravier, le Comte de Vergennes, the French navy, marines, soldiers, and military technology, weapons, munitions, uniform materiels, and bankers, there would have been no victory at Yorktown, and probably no nearly so successful a conclusion of the War for Independence as formalized by the Treaty of Paris in 1783.

There were many, many turning points in the conflict, moments when the fate of the Rebels hung ever so precariously in the balance. As was often observed by the Founding Fathers, theirs was surely a fate in the hands of what so many of them referred to as Divine Providence.

To this point, hear the words of Gen. Washington upon learning that Congress had ratified the Treaty of Alliance with France. The young, 21-year old Lafayette had ridden down Berwyn Road (Valley Forge), burst into the office, threw his arms about the startled General, planted a kiss on each cheek, and exuberantly advised His Excellency of the great news. After recovering his Anglo-Saxon composure, he joyously announced,

> *"It having pleased the Almighty Ruler of the Universe to defend the cause of the United States, and finally to raise up a powerful friend among the princes of the earth, to establish our liberty and independency upon a lasting foundation; it becomes us to set apart a day for gratefully acknowledging the divine goodness, and celebrating the important event, which we owe to his divine interposition."*

The American Rebels benefitted enormously from European powers seeking to settle old scores. Certainly, the Continental Congress and our diplomats, especially

Franklin, Adams, Jefferson, and Francis Dana, must be credited with seeking to draw England's enemies into supporting the American Cause. More significantly however, was Europe's reaction to Britain's overwhelming success and ensuing arrogance since its lopsided victories in the Seven Years' War, during which they acquired, by conquest or negotiation, French and Spanish territories from Manila to Havana, from India to Gibraltar, and from Canada to Florida, all confirmed by the Treaty of Paris in 1763.

The net result of this lopsided success, some 15 years later, was England's complete inability to persuade or buy a significant Sovereign ally in its war against the Rebel Colonists. Put simply, England's many enemies wanted revenge. As will be seen, even those countries that claimed Neutrality in the conflict were a great boon to the Americans in their effort to gain independence.

In particular, it is essential to examine the legacy of French contributions to the Revolution as an indispensable ingredient leading to the final outcome of the War and the Treaty of Peace.

This perspective in no way diminishes the prerequisite heroic and sacrificial efforts made by the American Patriots. Nor does it suggest that the French monarchy's motives were anything other than those intended to advance France's self-interest, leaving aside a very real sympathy for the American Cause in some quarters. Certainly, France's turn, and for that matter, England's turn, to be indebted to the American legacy in the history of their nations, would come soon enough. Nevertheless, as to the Founding of the American Republic, Americans must share credit where credit is due.

The French contribution to the American War of Independence began long before Amity and Peace treaties were signed on February 6, 1778. As early as March of 1776, on learning that a rebellion was in the making, Foreign Minister Vergennes offered his "Considerations" to the French King advising that now was the time to build up France's forces and quietly support the Americans. It was secretly agreed. Through the establishment of a dummy Portuguese trading company, munitions and other military supplies began to flow in the fall of that year to the Rebels on the hulls of Rebel Privateers' ships through "neutral" powers' Caribbean island colonies, in particular the Dutch islands.

French efforts accruing to the benefit of the Americans extended long after the victory at Yorktown on October 19, 1781. The major fighting may have stopped at that time in the Thirteen American Colonies, but war between America's allies, France and Spain, against the common enemy, England continued globally for another two years. All of these actions continued to sap the strength of His Majesty's realm, culminating in the Treaty of Peace signed at Versailles between and among the combatants, resulting, among other things, in the British recognition of American independence.

In addition to the philosophical input via the French luminaries of the Enlightenment and the pro-American diplomatic achievements, French military and materiel contribution can be summarized as follows:

- More than 100,000 combatants on land and sea
- Some 115 ships of the line and 107 frigates saw service against the English
- 5100 soldiers or sailors killed in action. 9,000 wounded
- Overall cost estimated at $22bn (2012) in current dollars. To the U.S. directly, $420 MM (35 MM Livres) in Loans were extended and $130 MM (11 MM Livres) in gifts

Some of the key diplomatic players included French Foreign Minister Vergennes (see here in Ottoman garb at the Sublime Porte where he was serving, 1775, becoming adept at "Old World intrigue) and war Minister Count St. Germain, Messrs. Beaumarchais and Bonvouloir.

On the military side, in addition to General Rochambeau, key players included Admiral de Grasse, the Marquis de Lafayette and Engineers Du Portail, Roche Fontaine and Pierre L'Enfant, and cavalry commander Le Duc de Lauzon among many others. Of all the key French figures in America, Lafayette became, and remains, the primary symbol of French support during the war. Part of this National remembrance is based on his well-known friendship with Washington, Jefferson, and other Fathers of the Revolution. His symbolic connection was further nurtured by triumphant returns to America where he made grand tours among the new States on two different occasions many years after the war.

Seeing the American Revolution, beyond the confines of a more traditional Anglo-centric perspective, adds critical dimension to a fuller understanding of the conflict. It affords one the global perspective, which America's Founding Fathers most assuredly had, and counted on. America owes a great debt of gratitude to the French. It also owes a debt to the Spanish, who helped not only with money, but also with supportive raids against British forts in West Florida and along the Mississippi. Additionally, together with the French, they tied up British soldiers, navy, and marines in the largest single battle of the Revolutionary period, the Siege of Gibraltar, for three years. The Dutch played a role as bankers to the American Rebels, and declared war on Britain in 1781. Catherine the Great, whom Gen. Washington referred to as "the great Potentate of the North," and the Russians also played a key, indirect, role.

While Catherine's refusal of King George's request for 20,000 Russian troops was helpful, it paled to insignificance compared with her seizing the opportunity to put England on its heels. Catherine resented British interference with Russian trade. The Anglo-Russian relationship was further exacerbated by England's trying to put the brakes on the Russians and their fleet from further capitalizing on their gains over the Turks in the Crimea and the Black Sea. Under the guise of Neutrality and the nascent

Law of the Seas, in February of 1780, Catherine announced that the Russian Navy would protect "Neutral" shippers. She encouraged other Neutrals, as did French Minister Vergennes, to join in a League of Armed Neutrality. First Denmark and Sweden joined, followed by the Netherlands, Prussia, the Holy Roman League, Portugal, the Kingdom of Sicily, and the Ottoman Empire. In the words of Jay Winik in his book, *The Great Upheaval*,

> *"In one bold stroke, the Doctrine of Neutrality redressed the balance of global sea power. More than that, the Tsarina had isolated Britain diplomatically – the first time that had happened in the 18th century – and curtailed Britain's vaunted maritime fleet while aiding France's. In so doing, she helped bolster the hopes of the beleaguered American rebels fighting for their lives and, in effect, almost inadvertently helped midwife America to independence."*

Before finishing with Catherine "the Great," it might interest one to know that in 1788 she gave America's most famous Naval Officer of the Revolutionary period, John Paul Jones, the very year the U.S. Constitution was promulgated into law, his first naval command as an admiral. In that year, he won a significant battle (the Battle of Liman) against the Turks in the Black Sea.

After eight long years of service, from Fort Ticonderoga in New York to Eutaw Springs in South Carolina where he was wounded in early September of 1781, the Frenchman, born in New France/Quebec, who became an American,

Christopher Joseph Delezenne, serving under Generals Lafayette, Kosciusko and Major Roche Fontaine, mustered out of the Engineer and Sapper Corps of the Continental Army at the Fort at West Point in 1783. He returned to his first-generation Dutch-American wife, Mary Dusenbury Delezenne, in Westchester, New York, whom he had married while on a fortnight's leave from Valley Forge in February of 1778. One of their offspring would marry a Baker in Philadelphia. And one of the Baker's children would marry a Sarah Phillips. And, Sarah would marry one William Hall Williams in 1880 in Detroit. He was the author's great grandfather.

Chapter 10

TURKEY'S FOUNDING – FROM SULTANATE TO A SECULAR REPUBLIC

Suleyman the Lawgiver

When one thinks of Suleyman in the West, one thinks of Suleyman the Magnificent (pictured here). A Venetian Ambassador, Bernardo Navagero, captures the essence of this magnificence when he wrote in 1553 CE.

> *"The Turkish Court is a superb sight, and most superb is the Sultan himself. One's eyes are dazzled by the gleam of gold and jewelry. Silk and brocade shimmer in flashing rays. What strikes one about Suleiman the Magnificent is not his flowing robes or his high turban. He is unique among the throng because his demeanor is that of a truly great emperor."*

Whether from the East or the West, whether a Muslim, Christian, or Jew, one recognizes the military prowess of

Suleyman's army, whether in his ruthless conquering of the Hungarians at the Battle of Mohacs in 1526 CE, or the success of his navy under the command of Hayreddin Barbarossa Pasha at the Battle of Preveza in the latter's victory over Andrea Doria and the Holy Roman League in 1538 CE.

While the wealth of Suleyman and the magnificence of the Sublime Porte are well-known, his importance in history, especially in the history of Islam, is largely based on his acheivements as Suleyman the Lawgiver (*Kanuni Süleyman*). Named for King Solomon in the Old testament and in the Koran, Suleyman would codify a set of administrative laws (*Kanun*) begun by his grandfather, Fatih Sultan Mehmed II, The Conquerer, and his father, Selim I.

While it is true that administrative laws, or dynastic laws, preceded the Ottomans and the Seljuks, arguably, the significance and shear volume of Administrive Law, as distinct from Sharia Law, expanded dramatically under the leadership of Suleyman and his Grand Mufti (Şeyhülislam), Ebussuud Effendi. As noted in Colon Imber's book, *The Ottoman Empire, 1300-1650*, the growing complexity of administering the Empire called out for the further development of a parallel sytem of Sharia and Administrative laws, so long as the latter were couched in the Koran and Sharia as interpreted under *hanefi* jurisprudence.

"From the fifteenth century and earlier, the sacred law – the shari'a – regulated most of the day to day affairs of Muslims in the Ottoman Empire, and many aspects too

of the lives of non-Muslims. It was not, however, the only legal system in force, but coexisted with Ottoman secular law or kanun.

Kanun regulated areas where the provisions of the sacred law were either missing or too much at odds with reality to be applicable. These were above all the spheres of criminal law, land tenure and taxation. The origins of the secular law lay in custom, and it was usage that in the first place gave it legitimacy. The late fifteenth and sixteenth centuries, however, saw the sultans enact written versions of the law, and modify it through decrees, giving it a dual character of customary and sultanic law. By the sixteenth century, consciousness of the disparity between the sacred and secular law led Kemalpshazade and later Ebu's-su'ud to redefine and systematize the ottoman laws of land and taxation in terms which they borrowed from Hanafi jurists. In doing this, they were following the tradition of their predecessors, who had also sought to explain the reality of feudal tenure and taxation using the terms and concepts of the classical law. Also like their mediaeval predesessors, what they produced were legal fictions which satisfied pious aspirations without upsetting legal reality."

How did any law other than Sharia law come to be accepted? What role did *Hanefi* jurisprudence have in facilitating the interpretation of the Koran and Sharia Law for the purposes of developing Adminstrative laws and Sultanic Decrees? How did *Kanun* law come to be promugated throughout the Ottoman Empire? Did the Seljuks lay some of the groundwork for a distinction between Administrative Law and Sharia Law, and with it a distinction between the roles and persons of a Sultan and Caliph? Were there fundamental and jurisprudential differences on this subject between the legal systems of Sunni and Shia Islam during the Ottoman era? Delving further into these questions, and discovering the doubtless varying scholarly opinions on the matter, however interesting, would take the author beyond both his ken and the purview of this book.

As we have discussed earlier, the business of expanding and conquering in the history of Islamic empires gave rise to the practical distinctions between the roles of a Ruler and that of a Spiritual Leader. Though it would take until 1924 to establish the "standard" version of the Koran, it can be said that in Sunni Islam the four Schools of Jurisprudence, *Hanefi, Hanbali, Şafi,* and *Maliki,* had largely been fixed, codified if you will, by the 10th century CE. Shia Islam compared to Sunni Islam accords a theoretically different role for the Grand Imam (Ayatollah) than the Sunni Caliph, as it is believed that he/they are descended from the bloodline of the Prophet through Ali, nephew and son-in-law of Muhammad, and the Prophet's nominated successor from his Ghadir Khumm sermon near the end of his life. Their role as the Shia spiritual leader is said to have permitted more latitude for a continuing evolution of the Shia *Jafari* interpretation of Sharia law than Sunni Caliphs.

Of the Sunni Schools of Jurisprudence, Hanefi is said to be the most "liberal" if you will, in the sense that by analogy (*fıkh*), the founder, Abu Hanafi (d. 767 CE) developed a method to derive Islamic law where the Koran and the Hadiths are silent or ambiguous in their guidance. I would suggest that this jurisprudential principle of legal reasoning by analogy would lend itself to the 16th and 17th century development of a growing body of *Kanun*, or Admistrative Law. It gave the Ottomans a framework of laws with which to govern a multi-racial, multi-ethnic, and multi-cultural Empire, including Muslims and non-Muslims. And because Suleyman gave such critical protection to Islam in the Empire, the Faithful recognized his legitimacy as both Sultan and Caliph – titles not always held by one and the same person. Murad I (1362-1389 CE) was the first Sultan to claim the title of Caliph. The Ottoman Caliphate is said to officially begin in 1517 (Selim I) and end in 1924, when abolished by the new Turkish Republic. Selim I actually took the title of Servant of the Two Holy Cities (*İki Kutsal Cami'nin Hizmetkârı*), a title used by all his successors.

Well-educated and a shrewd judge of men, *Kanuni* Suleyman surrounded himself with talented administrators, governors and military leaders. I would argue thathis success in administering his Empire by *Kanun* administrative laws, a system of laws and decrees operating derivatively in parallel with Sharia, was key to much of his success as a Ruler. I would further argue that this dual system of laws, one religious, the other, quasi-secular if you will, culturally helped to pave the way for secularizing reforms in the 19th century, even if the reforms did not sit well with much of the religious elite (Ulema). These complimentary legal systems were the beginning of a process which reduced over time the lock that the religious elites had enjoyed over the governance of the people.

Westernizers and Reformers

We have already discussed the reforms begun under the Tanzimat culminating in a short-lived Constitution in the mid-1870s. One of the more lasting outcomes of these reforms was the establishment of secular Government schools as opposed to religious schools (*medresse*). Many of the sons of reformers, Government bureaucrats and sons of military officers, including Mustafa Kemal, were educated in these schools. They were exposed to foreign languages, French in particular, and European culture. Given the weakening state of the Empire, especially in the battlefield, it was not surprising that young people coming out of these schools, as well as other schools established by missionaries like Robert College, would be more receptive to reform, even imitating the West and Western practices.

Of course, Newtonian laws of physics called for a reaction by the religious elites whose influence was slowly being eroded under the direction of foreigners and reformers. Reaction from some Sufi groups and the religious establishment was strong, if disparate. This dichotomy in the direction that Turkey needed to take to regain its strength and importance in the world produced a concommitant tension in Ottoman society. Preferential treatment of Christians did not sit well with the average Turk or Kurd – especially those living in communities near to Armenian Christians in the east of Turkey. This situation would worsen later in the 19th century just as the reform movement was gaining support in ever wider circles in Turkey. This will be discussed in more detail in a subsequent chapter.

"The Sick Man of Europe," Tsar Nicholas I

"Capitulations", under the pressure and direction of European States, were one manifestation of the Ottoman response to the Western issue of dealing with the "Eastern Question" discussed earlier. Just prior to the outbreak of the Crimean War, fear of the Ottoman Empire crumbling in a rapid and chaotic manner was a prospect that went beyond the initial question of who would, and who should, protect Orthodox, Catholic and Protestant Christians and Christian Pilgrims in the Ottoman Empire, and in the Holy Lands in particular. The prospect of European States going to war over the pieces and who might be the winner and in what parts of the Empire, the Balkans, the Levant, and North Africa, was enough to keep the European States busy trying to prop up the Empire, while gaining special advantages for their respective States. The prospect of this feared chaos was further exacerbated and complicated by Suzerain Provinces of the Empire seizing local control as had just happened in Egypt in the 1830s and 1840s.

It was in that environment in 1853 that a conversation has been reported between Tsar Nicholas I and the British Ambassador to Russia in which various words uttered by the Tsar likened Turkey to a sick man. Ambassador Seymour is reported to have agreed with the diagnosis, but differed from the Tsar in the treatment of the patient. Regardless of the veracity of this exchange, now etched in stone by convention, European government's concern for the risks associated with managing a Turkey in decline were palpable. The fact that this diagnosis was again rendered only seven years later about the risk of collapse of the Hapsburg Empire only served to refocus the geographic

epicenter of the Eastern Question to the area of the Balkans. Ironically, it was precisely there that, like Lexington and Concord in the American Revolution, another shot was fired that was heard around the world in July of 1914 (The assasination of the Arch Duke Franz Ferdinand pictured here.).

Young Turks, the C.U.P. Government, and The Balkan War

So let us take the fruits of the 19th century reforms and move them into the first quarter of the 20th century. Now add to them the, by then, well-accepted, if feared by European absolute monarchies, principles of "self-determination" and "nationalism." Beginning in Greece in the 1820s and sweeping through Western Europe in the 1840s, these new norms were gaining currency. Of course, these norms were selectively accepted/applied by various States. More often than not, the now increasingly secular Atlantic-bordering States of Europe were more accepting of these norms than the Russians and Hapsburgs.

As these norms came to be rapped in indigenous movements in the Balkans, The Levant, the Caucasus and in the Borderlands of Turkey and Russia, they could no longer be ignored. How to deal with centrifigal ethnic and religious forces would vary from State to State, empire to empire. In any case, the various policies used to remedy these yearnings proved to be largely inadequate. As so aptly stated by Michael Reynolds in his book, *Shattering Empires*, *"If empire means the domination of one "nation" over other "nations" and the denial of the inherent right of the latter to self-determination, then the destruction of empire becomes a moral necessity, and its occurrence a cause for celebration".*

The Russo-Turkish War of 1877-78 was as much an ethnicity driven conflict over control of the Balkans as a religiously motivated war. Just as pan-Italian and pan-Germanic sentiments had precipitated the unification of those two countries, a pan-Slav rationale motivated the Russsians to join forces with the Bulgarians and slavs in Macedonia against their Turkish overlords. The Russians were too successful. Accordingly, European powers, led by Otto Von Bismarck, stepped in at The Congress of Berlin in June of 1878 and returned the area of Eastern Rumelia and Macedonia to the Turks, reduced Greater Bulgaria to a smaller Principality, established an independent Romania, Serbia, and Herzegovina, and the British acquired Crete. For all intents and purposes, three new States and a Principality were just then created. The net result of these new state creations was that the Ottoman control in the Balkans had been reduced and further pressure for reform and religious freedom for the Orthodox in Macedonia were part of the agreement.

Turkey's sovereign borders had now further shrunk. Unrest in the Balkans continued unabated, especially in Northern Greece and Macedonia, whose borders were fluid, whose peoples were both Slav, Turk, and Greek, Orthodox and Muslim. In short, with empires weakening about them, and ethnic and religious homogeneity a new normative rationale for the just creation of a new nation states, the Balkans remained a tinder box. The effective means for fighting or adapting to these tendencies gave further impetus to revolutionary groups within these new inchoate states, and within the Empires trying to hang on to their borderlands.

By the 1890s, unrest extended from one end of the Ottoman Empire to the other. To be discussed in more detail later, but anti-progressive, anti-ethnic, anti-Christian responses, countenanced by Abdülhamid II and the Islamic clerics, led to horrific slaughtering of Armenians, both in Istanbul by Medresse students calling for absolute implementation of Sharia Law and in Eastern Turkey using Kurdish proxies (*Hamidiye*).

Secret, and not so secret, societies arose seeking both to nurture the tendency toward "national homogeneity," whether it be Serbian, Montenegrin, Greek, Georgian, Armenian, Maronite, Druze, or Jew, and societies to either counter or accommodate these tendencies.

Salonika *(Thessaloniki)*, home to the Ottoman Third Army (now Northern Greece), is a good place to pick up the story of reform in the context of nationalism. The secret officers' reform group, The Committee on Union and Progress (İttahat ve Terakki) was based in Salonika. Their objective was the restoration of the 1876 Constitution and progressive reform. Leadership of this organization was assumed by a 26-year old officer, Enver, a Balkan Turk. He would eventually lead this army to Istanbul in 1908, and within a year, replaced Abdülhamid with his brother, Muhammad V, declaring as translated by Reynolds from S. S. Aydemir's *Makedonya'dan Orta Asya'ya Enver Paşa*, *"Now by working together with all citizens, Muslim and non-Muslim, we raise our people free, our homeland higher. Long live the people! Long live the homeland."* Reynolds goes on to say that people of different religious and ethnic backgrounds joined hands and rejoiced. Enver was dubbed the "Hero of the Revolution." The euphoria was short-lived. War broke out with the Italians in Libya, followed by rebellion in Albania and Macedonia leading to two Balkan Wars between 1911 and 1913.

After half a millenium of subjugation, now independent Southern Greece was focused on regaining Salonika, a city whose primary urban residents were Ladino-speaking Jews who had turned the city into a commercial hub, now centuries after their earlier initial arrival going back to their expulsion from Spain during The Inquisition. The area surrounding the city was populated by Turks, Greeks, and Slavs. One of those Turks was Mustafa Kemal, born in 1881 and educated in a government school, and then, in military schools. As a young officer, he had joined the ranks of the Young Turks and the Unionists. He may have questioned the usefulness of preserving the Sultanate, but he, like Enver, was thrown into the breach from Istanbul, to Libya, and Albania as soldiers tasked with putting down insurrection and rebellion.

As Robert Kaplan points out in his book, *Balkan Ghosts*, where Greece was concerned, *"For British Prime Minister and romantic philhellene, Lloyd George, had encouraged them to believe that, whatever Greece did, the Western Allies would certainly support a Christian nation and the heir to ancient Greece against Muslim Turks."* While not wanting to get ahead of the story, Kaplan goes onto to say, *"This naïve trust, fortified by a spreading anarchy in Turkey following the collapse of the Sultanate, caused the Greeks to embark upon their Megali Idea, the "great Idea": the return of every inch of historic Greece to the Motherland."* It would only be a matter of time before irredentist claims by different ethnic and religious groups, supported by the Western Powers, would precipitate war in the Balkans. Again, in the course of local rebellion on the preiphery, Ottoman Turkey would lose more territory.

Turkey's Civil War in the Midst of a the Great War

Conflict continued to spread from the Balkans, east and west, north and south. Large alliances between various European Powers were formed as the ensuing contest was looking to go beyond the Eastern Question and become a global race for power. As Christopher Clark notes in the introduction to his book, *The Sleepwalker – How Europe Went to war in 1914*:

> *"The European continent was at peace on the morning of Sunday 28 June 1914, when Arch Duke Franz Ferdinand and his wife Sophie Chotek arrived at Sarajevo railway station. Thirty-seven days later, it was at war. The conflict that began that summer mobilized 65 million troops, claimed three empires, 20 million military and civilian deaths, and 21 million wounded... The debate over why it happened began before the first shots were fired and has been running ever since."*

By the outbreak of WWI, a triumvirate of the three Unionist Pashas, Talat, Enver, and Kemal, were in complete control of the Ottoman Government. It would be their job to determine with whom to ally and then fight to their best advantage, hoping that they had chosen the winning side. With Enver Pasha having studied military science in Germany and having become conversant in German and believing that the Germans would finance the rebuilding of the Ottoman military, in weighing the pros and cons of the Great Power alliances shaping up, a dilemma in any case, Enver and the CUP leadership cast their lot with the German-led alliance against the French, English, and Russians.

The Turks almost immediately found themselves fighting the English and Sherif Hussein's Arab forces (remember Lawrence of Arabia), meeting with some success finally in Baghdad where they stemmed the British advance for a time. They also met with some success, again moving troops around on the newly built German-designed rail system from Mesopotamia to Eastern Turkey, where they managed to hold off Russian advances on approach through Iran.

Mustafa Kemal was gaining more and more battefield experience, from Libya to Baghdad. He would need it a year later when the Western Allies, under the military direction of Lord Kitchener and his second in command, young Winston Churchill conceived and launched a joint attack on the Dardanelles and the Gallipoli Peninsula in an effort to break the German back by attacking what Churchill called "the Soft Underbelly of Europe".

We will briefly consider the Gallipoli Campaign later. I want to return to what I will call a civil war within the larger war, involving the Turkish army and its proxy forces. The chaos of the larger war was seen as the exact right moment to reassert indigenous efforts to establish autonomous states based on ethnic and religious identity.

This involved seeking support from the Triple Entente enemies of Turkey, more or less happy to disrupt Turkey behind the lines.

The internal fighting/civil war was especially brutal in Eastern Turkey with Ottoman and Kurdish forces fighting Armenian forces, and at times, Russian-backed Armenian forces. Atrocities on both sides were rampant, exacerbated by dislocation, disease, and starvation. Resentment had been growing between nomadic Kurds against increasingly city-and town-dwelling Armenians who were seen to be more educated and economically more successful. At the end of the day, whether with the Unionist Government explicit written direction, or its tacit compliance, the wholesale slaughter of many hundreds of thousands of Armenians, including civilians, together with the forced relocation of Armenians in Eastern Turkey, attested to by diplomats and missionaries serving in the area, biased or not, was horrific and undeniable. Death by killing or by starvation and exposure, either way, the Ottoman and Kurdish treatment of the Armenians, from the 1890s through the fateful year of 1915, remains perhaps the most shameful of all the many episodes of brutality perpetrated by all sides, including the Armenians, during the run-up and including the Great War. Having said that, and not by way of a justification, it must be remembered that the Turks were fighting for their lives on all fronts, knowing that losing in this titanic conflict would result in the complete dismemberment not just of the Empire, but of the

Anatolian heartland itself. Of all the combattant States and Empires in this conflict, such a prospect was alone faced by the Ottomans.

Sykes-Picot, and the Treaty of Sèvres

If there were any doubt about the high stakes of the war for Turkey, the revelation of a secret agreement between the British and the French, signed in March of 1916, and after a consultation with the Russians the previous month, removed it. In this document, "spheres of influence" were assigned to the Entente Powers. The British were to receive control of the ports of Haifa and Acre on the Mediterranean, and inland to the River Jordan and the southern part of Iraq. The French were to receive the lebanon, Syria, southeastern Turkey, and Northern Iraq. The Russians

were to receive Istanbul, control of the Bosphorus Straits, and the Armenia Provinces of Northeastern Turkey. The agreement shamelessly ignored promises in exchange for support that had been made to Sharif Hussein and the Arab Tribes which he had placed at the service of the British against the Ottomans. (see map above).

From the outset of the war, then British Chancellor of the Exchequer David Lloyd George had given assurances to Zionist leader Herbert Samuel that he was keen to establish a Jewish state in Palestine. From the following report in May of 1917, by Member of Parliament W. Ormsby–Gore, details of the agreement had been leaking out, suggesting that the right hand of the British Government might not know what the left hand was doing at that time.

In May 1917, W. Ormsby-Gore wrote, *"French intentions in Syria are surely incompatible with the war aims of the Allies as defined to the Russian Government. If the self-determination of nationalities is to be the principle, the interference of France in the selection of advisers by the Arab Government and the suggestion by France of the Emirs to be selected by the Arabs in Mosul, Aleppo, and Damascus would seem utterly incompatible with our ideas of liberating the Arab nation and of establishing a free and independent Arab State. The British Government, in authorising the letters dispatched to King Hussein [Sharif of Mecca] before the outbreak of the revolt by Sir Henry McMahon, would seem to raise a doubt as to whether our pledges to King Hussein as head of the Arab nation are consistent with French intentions to make not only Syria but Upper Mesopotamia another Tunis. If our support of King Hussein and the other Arabian leaders of less distinguished origin and prestige means anything it means that we are prepared to recognise the full sovereign independence of the Arabs of Arabia and Syria. It would seem time to acquaint the French Government with our detailed pledges to King Hussein, and to make it clear to the latter whether he or someone else is to be the ruler of Damascus, which is the one possible capital for an Arab State, which could command the obedience of the other Arabian Emirs."*

The degree of mistrust was further aggravated with the publication of a letter from UK Foreign Secretary Lord Balfour to Baron Rothschild stating the following:

"His Majesty's government view with favour the establishment in Palestine of a national home for the Jewish people, and will use their best endeavours to facilitate the achievement of this object, it being clearly understood that nothing shall be done which may prejudice the civil and religious rights of existing non-Jewish communities in Palestine, or the rights and political status enjoyed by Jews in any other country."

With the collapse of the Tsarist Government and the establishment of a Bolshevik Government, the new Government of Russia declared that all prior international agreements were null and void. They immediately published, in November of 1917, the details of the Sykes-Picot-Sasanov Agreement. The British were greatly embarrassed, the Arabs felt betrayed, and the Turks felt vindicated.

In response, on November 7, 1918, just days before the Armistice ending the Great War, an effort was made to reconcile the conflicting promises with the joint Anglo-French Declaration stating in part the following:

"The goal envisaged by France and Great Britain in prosecuting in the East the War let loose by German ambition

is the complete and final liberation of the peoples who have for so long been oppressed by the Turks, and the setting up of national governments and administrations deriving their authority from the free exercise of the initiative and choice of the indigenous populations.

In pursuit of those intentions, France and Great Britain agree to further and assist in the establishment of indigenous Governments and administrations in Syria and Mesopotamia which have already been liberated by the Allies, as well as in those territories which they are engaged in securing and recognising these as soon as they are actually established..."

The conflicting promises made during the war by France and England in particular resulted in Arab distrust of the West continuing down to our time. In a 2002 interview with the publication, *The New Statesman*, British Foreign Secretary Jack Straw observed, *"A lot of the problems we are having to deal with now, I have to deal with now, are a consequence of our colonial past. ... The Balfour Declaration and the contradictory assurances which were being given to Palestinians in private at the same time as they were being given to the Israelis—again, an interesting history for us but not an entirely honourable one."*

In July of 2014 in an IS (ISIS) You Tube video, the newly proclaimed Caliph of the Islamic State, Abu Bakr al-Baghdadi at the Great Mosque of Al-Nuri in Mosul declared, *"...this blessed advance will not stop until we hit the last nail in the coffin of the Sykes–Picot conspiracy"*. Again, bad memories die hard.

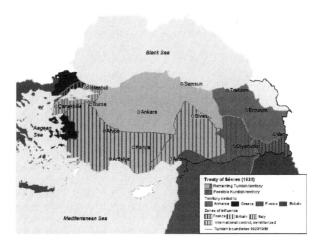

At the conclusion of hostilities with the Ottomans, the Ottoman Government on October 30, 1918, on board a British Warship, signed the Mudros Armistice, which was essentially an unconditional surrender, including the demobilization of the army and a British occupation of Istanbul. The Great War Armistice was followed by a series of negotiations lasting fifteen months leading to the Treaty of Sèvres. It fulfilled all the pre-war goals of France and England. It gave territory in the Southwest, including the area from Antalya to Konya, to the Italians. Much of the Northwestern part of Anatolia, from Smyrna east and north toward the Dardanelles was given to the Greeks. Under the direction of American President Woodrow

Wilson, an autonomous Armenia area was granted. Russian pre-war designs were largely moot, as the Bolsheviks had already signed a less aggrandizing treaty with the Ottoman Government and was itself pre-occupied with fighting the White Russians. By the terms of this agreement, the Kurdish population was hived off into three separate countries, Turkey, Syria, and Iraq.

On August 20, 1920, the Treaty was signed in the town of Sèvres in France. As reported by Llewellyn Smith, *Ionian Vision*, and quoted by Andrew Mango in his book, *From the Sultan to Ataturk*, in the words of Andrew Ryan, the Dragoman at the British Embassy in Istanbul, the Treaty died "'intact, though dead, whole though unratified.'" Of all the signatories, the fact that it was only ratified by the Greek Government, made the Sèvres Treaty all the more humiliating, culturally emasculating, and excessive. The harshness of Treaty has never been forgotten by Turkey. As aptly observed by Mango, *"If to this day it is a criminal offence in Turkey to denigrate 'Turkishness,' the reason should be sought in the memory of the Treaty of Sevres."*

The Turkish War of Independence, Wilsonian Principles, and the Treaty of Lausanne

The Treaty of Sèvres was "dead on arrival." The ink had not dried before the Nationalists were gathering in Eastern Turkey, pledged to push back the "foreign" spheres of influence in every direction. Mustafa Kemal, as both an Aide de Camp to the Sultan and the hero of the Anafartalar Battle in the Gallipoli Campaign, was dispatched from Istanbul to Central Anatolia to oversee the disarmament of what remained of the Ottoman Army. He sailed on the *Bandırma*, landing in Samsun on the Black Sea on May 19, 1919. The anniversary of this event remains a National Holiday.

At the same time, with the urging of Lloyd George and the British, the Greek army had landed on Aegean Turkish shores (Ayvalık) and were moving east in Thrace. With the British in control of Istanbul, Kemal would not return before Turkey had won a War of Independence that would last three years. By June of 1919, he had met with the remaining military leaders of the Army, Ali Fuad Cebesoy, Kazim Karabekir, and Husein Rauf Orbay, all friends from the War Ministry. On June 19th in Amasya, a meeting was held which outlined the basis for a Nationalist Movement. In short, it was agreed that the Ottoman Government was incapable of salvaging Turkey from foreign control, and that only the Turkish people could save the nation.

In July, representatives of the Eastern Provinces met in Erzurum, elected Mustafa Kemal the Chairman of the Congress, and proclaimed that the Ottoman state could not be governed under a foreign Mandate or Protectorate and that special privileges (Capitulations) could not be given Greek and Armenian Christians. Further, it established a Pact which proclaimed the sovereignty, indivisibility, and independence of Ottoman lands as defined by the "armistice lines" of November 1918.

Having rounded up all the Nationalists in Istanbul, the Sultan ordered Kemal Pasha to return to Istanbul. He refused. A larger Congress was convened in early September in Sivas. The British sent a contingent of soldiers to stir up the Kurds against the new Nationalists, but to no avail. By now, in the words of Michael Reynolds, *"Fear of the dismal fate for Muslims portended by foreign rule motivated most of Anatolia's Muslim Turks, Kurds, Circassians, and multiple other ethnicities to support Mustafa Kemal's forces"*.

By November of 1919, plans were made for a new National Assembly. In March of 1920, the Nationalists claimed that the Ottoman Parliament had been illegally dissolved and that a new government and parliament had been formed in Ankara. On April 23rd, the Assembly elected Mustafa Kemal as President and İsmet İnönü, the representative from Edirne, Chief of the General Staff. The process of legitimizing the new government in Ankara, step by step, and de-legitimizing the government in Istanbul was carefully planned by the Nationalists. Of course, being a legitimate government on paper and an actual government in practice would require a strategy to assume control of the country from the various foreign interests occupying it.

The Nationalists quickly made peace with the Bolsheviks, recognizing their interests in the Caucasus, much to the chagrin of the Azeri Turks and other Muslim Turkic groups in that area. The Bolsheviks were keen on keeping the Nationalist Movement in Turkey alive, thereby diverting allied support for Danilov and the White Russians. Most importantly, the Nationalists received in the bargain very substantial financial and military support in the form of weapons and munitions with which to wage war against the Armenians in the East, and the British and French in the South East. With this assistance, the Nationalists proved to be very successful in relatively short order.

With the Eastern rear guard secure in 1921, the Nationalists turned their focus on the West, where General Venizelos and the Greek Army had pushed from the Aegean coast deep into the heartland of Anatolia. İsmet İnönü Pasha had been outflanked by the Greeks at Eskişehir. They pushed within 30 miles of Ankara. These were dark days for the Nationalist forces. Morale in the Army was low with desertions increasing. It is at this point that Mustafa Kemal adressed the Assembly saying, *"We are not defending a line, but an area that encompasses the whole of the fatherland. Not an inch of it is to be surendered until it is drenched with the blood of our citizens."* With Kemal Pasha now in command of the troops, and the Greeks having overextended supply lines, the Turkish Army launched a counter-attack at what came to be known as the 2nd Battle of Sakaria the second week of September. By the third week, it was clear that the Greek offensive had been checked and was in retreat mode. He returned triumphantly to Ankara to advise the Assembly of the victory, for which he was duly made Field Marshall of all

Nationalist forces and awarded the title of *Gazi,* Warrior for Islam.

The fighting and brutal retribution on both sides prompted King Constantine, himself in the battle zone, as Mango writes, *"...to admit to himself, both sides fought each other with the greatest cruelty. The term 'ethnic cleansing' had not been invented at the time, but the reality was practiced by both sides."* Mango goes on to quote the Greek Royalist, German-trained , General Metaxas who offered a balanced explanation for the Greek military reversal observing:

> *"It is only superficially a question of the Treaty of Sevres. It is really a question of the dissolution of Turkey and the establishment of our state on Turkish soil...And the Turks realise what we want. If they had no national feeling, perhaps such a policy would be possible. But they have proved that they have, not a religious, but a national feeling. And they mean to fight for their freedom and independence."*

By October, the French had signed a separate Treaty with the new Nationalist government establishing the border between Turkey and Syria. The Italians quit the field. And the English would not support a Greek plan to march directly on Istanbul. Almost a year after the victory at Sakarya, the Nationalist forces amassed a refreshed and resupplied army at Kocatepe. The Greek line after the first day did not hold and their retreat from Anatolia began in September of 1922. Later in that month, Allied ships arrived at the port of Smyrna (İzmir) and began an extraordinary evacuation of Greeks, Armenians and others, men women and children, totalling some 213,000. It is said that there were at that time more Greeks in Smyrna than in Athens itself. By any measure, without assigning blame, the burning and fear was a trauma the memory of which lives on, if less intensively today, as it did when the author lived in Salonika in the early 1970s.

As if to recall the victory at Gallipoli, Mustafa Kemal then sent forces to the perimeter of British troops then occupying the fort at Çanakkale on the Asian side of the Dardanelles. Kemal was making a statement. The initial response by the British was to beef up the navy and army presence in the area. Appeals to the New Zealanders and Australians to enlist, or re-inlist, fell on deaf ears. In the end, the "Chanak Crisis" proved to be the undoing of the wartime governments in London and Athens. No one wanted to return to fight "Johnny Turk." War weary, the French saw the handwriting on the wall and they offered no support to the British. Peacetime governments had come to power, and it was clear, using the new and persuasive logic of "self-determination" and national identity, that the Western Allies would need to return to the negotiating table to redo the failed Treaty of Sèvres. On October 11th, an Armistice with the Turks was signed at Mudanya.

On the 1st of November, the Assembly in Ankara abolished the Sultanate. On the 17th, the last Ottoman Sultan, Mehmed VI Vahdettin, fled Istanbul on a British warship. The Assembly officially deposed him as Caliph and chose a successor. On the 21st, new treaty negotiations commenced in Lausanne, Switzerland and a new treaty was signed in July of 1923. Turkey regained its October 1918 Armistice borders. Provisions were made for the fair and equal treatment of all religions and nationalities of Turkey. There would be no "Capitulations," but no reparations to be paid by the Greeks to Turkey. The job now was to change the direction of the new State of Turkey. It began on October 29, 1923, with the Capital being moved to Ankara in the heartland, when the National Assembly declared the Turkish Republic and declared Mustafa Kemal its President and İsmet İnönü the Prime Minister.

Chapter 11

LEADERSHIP TRAITS – GEORGE WASHINGTON, FT. NESSESITY TO AMERICAN PRESIDENT

There is virtually no disagreement that George Washington and Mustafa Kemal were great leaders, among the greatest in modern recorded history. The fact that they both had shortcomings makes them human, making their achievements all the more remarkable. In this and the next chapter, we will examine some critical events in the lives of both men by which one might measure their greatness – the right man for their respective moments in history. The fact that popular imagination is prone to mythologize their achievements should in no way diminish their extraordinary contributions to their respective nations. Rather, it is a reflection of the essential need for a people to have an image of their highest aspirations around which they might bind, inspite of sometimes significant differences as individual and constituent parts of the common entity.

The American Revolution, the American Experiment, is based on an idea, a set of principles, which was a first in world history. All such experiments, from the Republic of

Rome to the Republic of Turkey, can not be disembodied ideas. They require special individuals who, for all their human frailties, emerge as the personification of those ideas and the ideals which sustain them. Both America and Turkey were blessed and dependent on having "legends in their own time" as Founders. Each was also blessed with a band of brothers, military and political, on whom they could rely to realize the grand visions of their new Republics.

While these two Patriots were born a century and a half apart, in different circumstances, there is ample evidence that they faced similar challenges. They both met with some failure along the way, but shared a number of attributes that proved to distinguish them from their peers. Both became worthy icons around which their respective social, legal and political nation-building experiments could form a Union. Both Unions have been tested many times since. Neither would have happened without these two extraordinary figures, George Washington and Mustafa Kemal.

When the Chips Were Down, Trenton and Valley Forge

George Washington was born into a life of privilege. Both his father and his older brother died early in his life. He was taken under the wing of Lord Fairfax and began a life of training as a soldier and a surveyor. By all accounts, Washington grew to be a giant by the standards of his time – perhaps 6 ft. 3in. and between 175 and 200 pounds.

He had a muscular body and a rugged constitution, capable of surviving the physical hardships that he endured for most of his life.

Militarily, he cut his teeth as a Provincial Officer, Lt. Colonel, during the French and Indian War (1754-1763) serving under the authority of the British Governor of Virginia, Lord Dinwiddie. In his first experience with command, at the age of 26, he was defeated in Western Pennsylvania at the Battle of Ft. Necessity by the French and their Indian Allies.

Upon returning to Virginia, he accepted responsibility for the loss. He did not blame anyone else. The Governor exonerated him on grounds that he had done the best he could under the circumstances of inadequate supplies and the failure of friendly Indian forces to arrive as expected. This explanantion notwithstanding, it had long been argued  that his inexperience led to tactical errors in the field, both in preparing for battle and in the prosecution thereof. This characterization suggests that as a military tactician, he was likely to never be more than average. In response to this characterization, it would be fair to note that his military training was never remotely comparable to his counterparts in Europe.

After some initial success during the American Revo-lution in Boston, there followed a string of tactical defeats and strategic retreats beginning with the Battle of Long Island and New York. In fairness, the brothers, General Howe and Admiral Howe had arrived in New York har-bor with an armada of war ships (427) with cannon and an invasion force of 32,000 trained British and Hessian troops. Nevertheless, the fact remains that Washington (with 20,000 troops) was out-generaled, and, more impor-tantly, was slow to realize the extent of his disadvantage. Washington did manage to organize a clever and arguably miraculous strategic retreat over the Hudson River to New York State and New Jersey. He learned an important lesson. As long as he could keep his Army intact, the British could not supress the rebellion. And, with large areas of the Colo-nies held and controlled by American rebels unavailable to supply food to the British Forces and their horses, the Brit-ish Fleet would be preoccupied with an enormous logistical and supply problem that would plague them throughout the war. It has been estimated that the British required 32 tons of supplies coming in by sea a month to sustain their forces. With so many war ships tied up in escorting these supply convoys, it left the British blockade of American Naval and Privateer ships with relative freedom of move-ment – free to attack smaller unescorted British supply ships – and free to sail to neutral islands in the Caribbean to obtain military supplies for Washington's forces as well as various of the Colonial Militias.

So how did Washington react in the face of his first significant military defeat of the war – losing the strategically significant port of New York? Author J. T. Flexner writes the following in his book, *Washington – The Indispensable Man*:

"Washington, of all historical Americans, is still alive. A fallible human being made of flesh and blood and spirit, not a statue of wood. And inevitably, we as Americans believe, and those of us who study closely, know, we have here a great man and good man. In all history, who possessed unassailable power have used that power so gently, so calmly, so self-effacingly for what their best instincts told them was the welfare of their neighbors and all mankind. It was as if he – calmly on that horse at the Battle of New York, tears streaming down his face as the mercenary Germans bayonetted the wounded, yet maintaining his perfectly upright posture, quietly giving orders for an orderly retreat – knew we today, in the 21st century, would desperately need him to model the composure and confidence to guide us through the slings and arrows of our fortune."

By all accounts, Washington was a gifted leader of men, leading by example. A man of courage and self-awareness of the importance of setting an example for others. Knowing that after the losses of the fall of 1776, with political leadership in Philadelphia unsteady, low troop morale with pay in arrears, knowing therefore that many of his soldiers would not re-enlist come the end of that year, he desperately needed a victory. In the midst of deep winter, with the odds of success heavily stacked against him, he launched a bold and unexpected raid on Trenton and Princeton in New Jersey where there were large groups of wintering Hessians.

Washington's risky attack, crossing the Delaware River at night in freezing rain and snow, was exactly what the Americans needed. He was on this occasion, decisive, bold and effective.

Arguably, a year later, the winter of 1777-1778, Washington's reputation as the Commander of the American Forces was being questioned. A cabal of officers secretly planned to have him demoted. Their plot was discovered and foiled. In similar circumstances, others might have either quit or done something wreckless. After all, the British were comfortably ensconsed below in the city of Philadelphia. Washington's forces were encamped on the Heights at Valley Forge eighteen miles away. Disease and starvation wracked his army. Many deserted in order to improve their chances of surviving the harsh winter conditions.

On Dealing with the French Allies

Fortune began to turn for Washington in February of 1778. He learned from his Aide de Camp, Lt. General Marquis de Lafayette, that the French had agreed to openly ally themselves with the Americans. In due course, the French would be sending an Army to the Colonies as well as money, and military supplies in large quantities. On learning of Congress's ratification of the Treaty with the French a few months later, mark the response of General Washington. The young, 21-year old Lafayette had ridden down Berwyn Road, burst into the office, threw his arms about the startled General, planted a kiss on each cheek, and exuberantly advised His Excellency of the great news. After recovering his Anglo-Saxon composure, he joyously announced,

"It having pleased the Almighty Ruler of the Universe to defend the cause of the United States, and finally to raise up a powerful friend among the princes of the earth, to establish our liberty and independency upon a lasting foundation; it becomes us to set apart a day for gratefully acknowledging the divine goodness, and celebrating the important event, which we owe to his divine interposition."

Washington was also blessed with another European "freedom fighter" who joined his camp, Baron Freidrich Von Steuban. He, together with Lafayette, drilled and trained Washington's Continental Line troops through the spring of 1778 with great effect. In the summer campaigns against the British troops, the Americans proved to be able to stand and fight admirably against the enemy. All that improvement in their effectiveness would not, however, be a substitute for Washington's leadership, under fire, at the Battle of Monmouth in New Jersey that June. His natural leadership abilities, in the midst of battle, would again be on display.

The British and the Hessians had successfully stemmed an American attack and counter-attacked the Americans, who were poorly lead by Major General Charles Lee, whose forces fell into a chaotic retreat. Seeing this, General Washington rode to the front of the battle line, rallied the soldiers and took command, fighting the British to a standstill. One of his Lieutenants and a Founding Father, Alexander Hamilton, who also distinguished himself in that battle, later wrote:

> "As we approached the ... place of action we heard some frightening rumors of what had happened, in consequence of which the General [Washington] rode forward and found the troops retiring in the greatest disorder and the enemy pressing upon their rear. I never saw the general to so much advantage. His coolness and firmness were admirable. He instantly took measures for checking the enemy...

The sequel is, we beat the enemy and killed and wounded a thousand of their best troops. America owes a great deal to General Washington for this day's work; a general rout; dismay and disgrace would have attended the whole army in any other hands but his. By his own good sense and fortitude he turned the day. He did not lead from a distance but by his own presence he brought order out of confusion, animated his troops, stood tall and led to success."

From his early years, Washington, read and reread a handbook on etiquette and good behavior, *Rules of Civility*. It is clear that he modeled his behavior and deportment on those virtues. It is apparent that his discipline and self-awareness predisposed him to realize that others would take their cues from him. He was said to be quiet, reserved, unboastful, even-tempered and courteous. He knew there were others smarter, better educated and more skilled in various disciplines. He was very respectful of others, beginning with his wife, Martha.

The General knew when to be forceful and when to delegate responsibility, especially to his field commanders. He knew that in battle, time is of the essence. Accordingly, he was careful to select subordinates who proved to be capable of acting independently, creatively, and decisively. With the notable exception of Benedict Arnold, whose military talents were never in question though he would betray Washington and the Rebel Cause, going over to the British side, Washington has been credited with being a shrewd judge of men, character, and talent.

King George III on President George Washington

It is appropriate here to recall the words of King George III, Washington's arch-nemesis during the war, who, when advised by Benjamin West, an American court painter, that when the war was over General Washington plans to step down as Commander of the Army and return home a private citizen, the King is said to have remarked, or words to this effect, *"If he does that, he will be the greatest man in the world".*

Though finally having reconciled to defeat by the Americans, as reported in O'Shaughnessy's book, *The Men Who Lost an Empire, "During an emotional meeting with John Adams in 1785, King George III gave a fitting epitaph to his own role in the American Revolution:*

I wish you sir, sir, to believe, and that it may be understood in America, that I have done nothing in the late contest but what I thought myself indispensibly bound to do, by the duty which I owed to my people. I will be frank with you. I was the last to consent to the separation; but the separation having been made, and having become inevitable, I have always said, as I say now, that I would be the first to meet the friendship of the United States as an independent power."

General Washington's "Farewell Orders" – West Point

Washington's grace, humility, and devotion to his Country were never more obvious when, upon disbanding the army in 1783 at a time when the new Republic was weak and there were those who wanted him to become King, he chose to step down. In response to one such suggestion the year before, he replied,

"Be assured, Sir, no occurrence in the course of the War, has given me more painful sensations than your information of there being such ideas existing in the army as you have expressed [which] I must view with abhorrence, and reprehend with severity. If I am not deceived in the knowledge of myself, you could not have found a person to whom your schemes are more disagreeable... Let me conjure you then, if you have any regard for your Country, concern for yourself or posterity, or respect for me, to banish these thoughts from your Mind..."

At the disbanding of the Army in November of 1783 at West Point, Washington, in what he calls his "Farewell Orders," takes no credit for himself. Rather, he extolls the virtues of his officers and soldiers and exhorts them to become exemplary citizens of the new Republic. A paragraph from that speech follows.

"In order to effect this desirable purpose and to remove the prejudices which may have taken possession of the minds of any of the good people of the States, it is earnestly recommended to all the Troops that with strong attachments to the Union, they should carry with them into civil society the most conciliating dispositions; and that they should prove themselves not less virtuous and useful as Citizens, than they have been persevering and victorious as Soldiers. What tho, there should be some envious individuals who are unwilling to pay the debt the

public has contracted, or to yield the tribute due to merit;
yet, let such unworthy treatment produce no invective or
any instance of intemperate conduct; let it be remembered
that the unbiassed voice of the free Citizens of the United
States has promised the just reward, and given the mer-
ited applause; let it be known and remembered, that the
reputation of the federal Armies is established beyond the
reach of malevolence; and let a conscientiousness of their
achievements and fame still unitethe men, who composed
them to honourable actions; under the persuasion that the
private virtues of oeconomy, prudence, and industry, will
not be less amiable in civil life, than the more splendid
qualities of valour, perseverance, and enterprise were in
the Field. Every one may rest assured that much, very
much of the future happiness of the Officers and Men will
depend upon the wise and manly conduct which shall be
adopted by them when they are mingled with the great
body of the community. And, altho the General has so
frequently given it as his opinion, in the most public and
explicit manner, that, unless the principles of the federal
government were properly supported and the powers of
the union increased, the honour, dignity, and justice of the
nation would be lost forever. Yet he cannot help repeating,
on this occasion, so interesting a sentiment, and leaving
it as his last injunction to every Officer and every Soldier,
who may view the subject in the same serious point of
light, to add his best endeavours to those of his worthy
fellow Citizens towards effecting these great and valuable

purposes on which our very existence as a nation so mate-rially depends."

A month later, at Fraunces Tavern, which exists to this day at the foot of Wall Street in New York City, in a teary farewell to his top officers, he concluded by saying, *"With a heart full of love and gratitude, I now take leave of you. I most devoutly wish that your latter days may be as prosperous and happy as your former ones have been glorious and honorable."*

Washington then retired and returned to Mt. Vernon, his beloved home to which he returned only twice, and briefly, during six years of war fighting. Knowing that so many of his fellow colonists were poor and struggled for their very existence, he had refused pay for his service as Commander of the Army for all those years. His generosity to those many visitors to Mt. Vernon after the war was legion. Against his wishes, when called by his Country to serve, knowing that there was much dissension between and among the new States of the Union after contentious debate at the Constitutional Convention, he came out of retirement to become America's first President, unani-mously elected. Again, he asked not to be paid but was persuaded that it would establish a bad precedent requir-ing that all future candidates for the office would need to be independently wealthy as a prerequiste for office.

Time and again, with the knowledge that people would look to his example, George Washington would, when friends and opponents would both seek to use him, he remained *au dessus de la melée*. He knew his legacy needed to be as much, as humanly possible, above reproach. Of the many Founding Fathers who had slaves, it is noteworthy that he alone granted them their freedom, freeing many in his lifetime. While Washington never received the accolade of a Parliamentary Resolution naming him Father of his country, as did Mustafa Kemal during his lifetime, George Washington was, and remains, quintessentially the Father of his Country. The fact that he never had children of his own certainly added to his own sense of being Father of a new Nation.

Chapter 12

LEADERSHIP TRAITS – MUSTAFA KEMAL, GALLIPOLI TO ATATÜRK

"Mustafa Kemal Pasha will have a pedestal in the heart of every true Turk, even among those who have irretrievably been wronged by him."

—HALIDE EDIB ADIVAR (1884-1964)

Early Military Career and Gallipoli

Born in 1881, the young Mustafa, later Mustafa Kemal (the Perfect One), in the words of American General Wesley Clark (ret.),

"...grew up in a difficult and poten-
tially insecure environment under
constant challenge and threat, in
the cauldron of a "clash of civi-
lizations". At the time Salonika
was a cosmopolitan seaport under
Ottoman rule but threatened

by Greek revanchism, pan-Slav nationalism, guerilla conflict and great power competition between Russia,

*Austria-Hungary, Germany and Britain... Young Mustafa
would have felt the pull and tug of all these cultural and
political forces in his daily life."*

Mustafa's father, Ali Rıza, died when he was only seven.
Washington lost his father and older brother when he was
young as well. Albeit with different means, both were setting goals early in life. Both proved to be ambitious, hard
working. Both seem to have developed a sense of purpose
and direction early on. Mustafa's mother, Zübeyde, wanted
her son to follow the traditional route of a religious education. His father wanted him to be a soldier. He lived in
a cosmopoltitan port city, teeming with life, commerce,
Muslims, Sephardic Jews, Christians, Bulgarians, Greeks,
Slavs, Vlachs. European influence was palpable. Mustafa
was excited by what he saw in Salonika, especially military
cadets and officers in dashing uniforms. After all, the Ottoman Third Army was based nearby in Monastir. Before he
died, his father saw to it that the young man would attend
a government school where he would be exposed to science,
math, and foreign language. By the time he was twelve, he
had entered a military preparatory school, embarking on a
military career. As noted by his classmate, Cebesoy in *Sınıf
Arkadaşım Atatürk, 9*, as reported by Gawrych in *The Young
Ataturk*, "I owe a debt of gratitude to Tevfik Bey. He opened
a new horizon for me." Gawrych goes on to note another
friend, Ali Fethi, who is said to have introduced him to the
writings of Voltaire and Rousseau, and to French Enlightenment luminaries also familiar to Washington and his

peers 150 years earlier. Like many of his generation, he was moved by the poetry and the revolutionary message of Namık Kemal, whose writings were officially banned in the early 20th century as being subversive. But his message was also patriotic, stirring, and spoke to the glory of defending one's Fatherland, not as an Ottoman, but as a Turk in his "Poem of the Fatherland" (*Vatan Şiiri*):

> *"Wounds are medals on the brave's body; The grave [martyrdom] is the soldiers highest rank; The earth is the same, above and beneath; March, you brave ones, to defend the fatherland."*

Mustafa Kemal went on to distinguish himself academically at the War College in Istanbul. From there, he moved onto the elite Military Staff College, graduating near the top in class. Clearly the depth of his military training surpassed that of the young Washington. Mustafa Kemal knew that education and the military would be the means to his advancement in life.

One of the predictable consequences of Mustafa Kemal's exposure to a secular education, with Westernizing and modernizing influences, was an early sense of the need for reform, and not just in the military. He also felt a keen need for political reform and joined with the secret Young Turk movement. Unlike Washington, Mustafa could be outspoken, sometimes even alienating his friends. His preoccupation with the desire for radical change landed him in prison for a brief term, followed by a short side-tracking of his military career when posted off to the Middle East. But, the dangers were too great, and the needs too pressing for the government not to use one of their brightest stars in a more central theater.

Opportunities for military action came quickly in those turbulent times. He served in the Turco-Italian and then Balkan Wars from 1911-1913. Just two years later, in August of 1914, all of Europe, its Colonies, and the Ottoman Empire were at war. The First World War erupted, spreading like wildfire. The carnage from the beginning, in the face of the technological lethality of 20th century fire arms and chemical warfare, was massive. A generation of young men would be more than decimated over the next four years. And millions more would die within two years of the 1919 Armistice from a plague of Spanish Influenza.

One of those survivors, one who had been engaged in battle from 1911 to 1923, twelve long years, was Mustafa Kemal. He survived by his training, his keen mind, his extraordinary battlefield instincts, and an abundance of moral and physical courage. These attributes he put on display in spades at the Battle of Gallipoli/Çanakkale. His bravery in the face of physical danger, swift analysis of the tactical situation on the ground, a strategic sense of the significance of defeat or victory in the moment, and the leadership to inspire the often confused and frightened men about him, is reminscent of General Washington at the Battles of Trenton and Monmouth discussed earlier.

With the Australian-New Zealand Commonwealth (ANZACs) soldiers nearing the tops of steep ravines in the early dawn of April 25, 1915, and soldiers of the Turkish 9th Army on the run, Kemal ran to the top of Chunuk Bair, and while exposed to the enemy, he scanned the scene with his binoculars, made an assessment of the situation, returned to the fleeing soldiers and issued the following orders, set in stone for all time.

"Men, I am not ordering you to attack. I am ordering you to die. In the time that it takes us to die, other forces and commanders can come and take our place. If you don't have ammunition, you have bayonets! FIX BAYONETS! GET DOWN!"

In the words of Austin Bay in his book, *Ataturk – Lessons in Leadership from the Greatest General of theOttoman Empire,*

"To borrow Kemal's own trenchant metaphor for military insight and foresight, he fought Gallipoli's first hours with binoculars, not a sword...His insight pierces the immediate present's chaos and confusion and identifies military, political, social, and even psychological opportunities that others cannot see; his foresight anticipates future circumstances, which he will shape and create by actions (operations, in military jargon)".

Though only 33 years old at the time of the Gallipoli Campaign, we see certain principles which will guide the young officer in both his military and later political careers. Through an exhaustive examination of Mustafa Kemal's own reports, military publications, correspondence and speeches, Gawrych summarizes the man's *modus operandi* as follows:

> *"Together, sentiment [his], mind [dimağ], and conscience [vicdan] helped shape Atatürk's character and purpose-driven life, and after the War of Independence, Atatürk led the Turkish Revolution along these axes."*

From this point on, Mustafa Kemal gradually became an icon which he and his supporteres burnished with every future success.

There was another arrow in his quiver. His exposure as a military diplomat, first in Sophia, Bulgaria and later as an Aide-de-Camp to the Crown Prince and future Sultan Vaheddedin on a wartime trip to visit allies Austria and Germany, would add an important dimension to his personna, adding some finishing touches to the future President of Turkey. While born an aristocrat, Washington never enjoyed such exposure.

Outcome for the Allies – Churchill
Personally, Australia and New Zealand

The Western Allies would win the war. But, the loss at Gallipoli had several important and lasting effects. Colonel Mustafa Kemal's success was mirrored by Winston Churchill's failure as First Lord of the Admiralty. As the Gallipoli campaign had been championed by Churchill, he was saddled with the failure. There were others, Lord Kitchner in particular, who share blame. But, the disaster at Gallipoli, with a quarter of a million men dead, nearly half from disease, or wounded, with nothing to show for it, left Churchill in disgrace. His star would be diminished for twenty years, when it would again rise in connection with the Nazi threat.

For the Australian and New Zealand soldiers, a sense of "nationhood," separate and above membership in the British Commonwealth, was born in the blood and sacrifice of their fighting men and tragic losses. To this day, April 15th is a national Day of Remembrance in both countries. Their newly forged sense of independence would be clear six years later when the British sought to raise ANZAC troops to return to fight the Turks. Their answer was, with all due respect, "no."

The Turks came away from Gallipoli, largely fought and commanded by Turkish soldiers and officers, albeit with German support, with a sense of pride not regained until victory in the War of Independence, 1919-1923. As noted in a talk given by Prof. Dr. Feroz Ahmad at Koç University on March 27, 2015, in addition, the Unionist Government enjoyed a feeling of some success not felt since before the Balkan Wars. And furthermore, he made the point that this victory raised Turkey in the eyes of their ally Germany as having made an important contribution to the war effort. In fact, the Kaiser would come in the spring of 1917 and call on the Sultan and the Government. He would have it all recorded, German warships, horse-drawn carriages, parades and all, in a propaganda film to be shared with the other german allies and the German people as evidence of the strength of the alliance. [An extraordinary restoration of that film resides in the Koç family collection, which the author saw while on public display.]

Strategically, one might only speculate on the various outcomes if the Gallipoli Campaign had succeeded. Had the British secured the Peninsula and Dardanelles: had its fleet and troop transports been able to pass through the Bosphrus to the Black Sea; had Istanbul fallen; had supply lines to the Russians been opened; had the Turks surrendered Istanbul and European, if not Anatolian Turkey, might the Germans have been compelled to surrender earlier. Would an earlier culmination to the Great War have forestalled the Russian Revolution, at least for a time? Would an Turkish independence war ever have ever have broken out? America's entrance into the war might have been precluded. Certainly, a plausible case can be made for such a scenario. While congratulations in holding Gallipoli largely went to Enver Pasha and the Unionist Government in the immediate aftermath, *Gazi* (warrior) Mustafa Kemal, the "hero" of Gallipoli, would survive the fall of the Ottoman government. His reputation and his charisma, would later serve as the nucleus of the appeal for a "nationalist" War of Independence.

During the war, Mustafa Kemal's star would continue to slowly rise while serving on the Eastern front against the Russians in August of 1916, where he enjoyed some short-lived success as XVI Corps Commander in retaking Muş and Bitlis from the advancing Tsarist army. For this, he was promoted to Brigadier General. He was now Mustafa Kemal Pasha.

By the spring of 1917, the Bolshevik Revolution in March resulted in an immediate withdrawal of Russian forces from Anatolia. That good news was offset by British and Indian forces taking Baghdad. Kemal Pasha again argued with his German superior (Falkenhayn) and with his own government about objectives in the Mesopotamian theater. He came to some important realizations and conclusions before resigning his command and retuning to Istanbul. As noted by Austin Bay, quoted from Volkan and Itzkowitz in *The Immortal Ataturk*, Mustafa Kemal observes,

> "... if the war continues, the greatest danger we face is the possibility that the great dynasty of sultans, rotten in all its parts, may collapse suddenly from within. [Regarding the Germans], we are losing our country, which is likely to become a German colony soon. For this purpose, General

Falkenhayn is using the gold he brought from Germany and the blood of the last remaining Turkish sons from Anatolia. Leaving any corner of our country to the influence and administration of a foreigner would mean the complete abandonment of our sovereignty at a time when it is all about the defense of the motherland."

By Christmas of 1917, British General Allenby had taken Jerusalem. Kemal was no longer asociated with that theater. By then, he was preparing for a diplomatic trip to Austria and Germany with the Ottoman Crown Prince. Failure in the Eastern theater would not attach to Kemal.

The Bandırma and Rescuing the Remains of the Ottoman State

The Ottoman Government sued for and signed an Armistice with the Allies on October 30, 1918. Twelve days later, on the 11th day of the 11th month at 11:00 AM, an Armistice with the Germans was signed ending hostilities. A disillusioned Kemal began plotting with fellow officers the rescue of Turkey from the ashes of the Great War.

In the spring of 1919, Kemal Pasha's prestige was sufficient to name him as Inspector, with the support of the British occupying Istanbul, to be sent to Central Anatolia with the job of disarming and disbanding the remains of the Ottoman Ninth Army gathered there at the conclusion of the war. It might have been also assumed that it would be good to get him out of Istanbul where he could likely scheme against the government. This would prove to be a fateful decision which the Sultan, the acting government, and the British would live to regret. Their grave error in judgment would be Kemal's opportunity to break away and lead a fight to save his country.

The more suspect Mustafa Kemal Pasha became in the eyes of the Sultan and the Unionist Government, the more he distanced himself from them. Once loose in Anatolia, with the support of some key military commanders, while the Greek Army was invading Western Anatolia, a Nationalist cause and a Nationalist Army was being reconstituted in Eastern Anatolia.

Kemal Pasha, some officers and men embarked on the Bandırma, a cargo ship originally built in the Scottish boatyard of Paisley in 1878. They landedin a storm, on May 19, 1919 at the Black Sea port of Sampson. This ship carried an important cargo, the seeds of a "nationalist movement" and the future leader of a war for survival, and then, independence. The odds of their succeeding, as with the case of Washington and the Rebels at the outset of the American War for Independence, were daunting to say the least. As far as the government in Istanbul and the Western Allies were concerned, Mustafa Kemal and his co-conspirators were soon to be deemed outlaws. It would not be long before he was ordered to return to the capital, probably to be stripped of his rank, if not imprisoned.

Nationalist Turkish Identity in the
Aftermath of the 2nd Battle of Sakarya

Mustafa Kemal, the great communicator, and his fellow Nationalist leaders and commanders began this improbable cause with two critical advantages, one the modern telegraph and two the patrimonial emotional reaction to Allied support of a Greek invasion of Western Anatolia. Adding insult to injury, the Armenian, French and British forces, looking to secure their respective spheres of influence in the Anatolian heartland of the Turkish people, trophies of the Sykes-Picot Agreement and its realization via the Treaty of Sèvres, gave the Nationalists the high moral ground of being saviors of the Turkish state and people.

The Nationalist forces met with success against the Greek forces in March of 1921 under the leadership of İsmet Pasha. As reported in Mango's book, *Ataturk: The Biograpghy of the Founder of Modern Turkey*, Mustafa Kemal sent a congratulatory message to his friend, with the additional value of bolstering the spirit of the Grand National Assembly, *"Few commanders in the whole history of the world have faced a task as difficult as that which you undertook in the pitched battles of Inonu... It was not only the enemy you have defeated, but fate itself – the ill-starred fate of our nation."* With these magnanimous words, Mustafa Kemal showed signs of not just an accomplished politician, but of a statesman. While characteristically laudatory of his officers when appropriate, Washington preferred to have others do his political bidding, preferring to stay, or appear to be staying, above the messy business of politics. Whereas, Mustafa Kemal, in due course, showed clear signs of relishing the politics of high office.

The war with the Greek army continued. Mustafa Kemal could see that they were bringing in reinforcements in preparation for an all-out assault on Ankara, the Grand National Assembly and its leaders. He called for a map, determined the location, the area east of the Sakarya River, which would extend the enemy supply lines the furthest. His strategy would seek to lure the Greek Army into an expansive area difficult to secure, supply and, in the process, achieve an all-out victory. He had learned the value of a strategic retreat leading to a plan for ultimate victory, a lesson well-learned and use by General Washington. Using all his prestige and political capital as President of the Assembly, he asked for special authority to simultaneously serve as Assembly President and Commander of the Armed Forces. He argued that in order to execute a seamless military strategy, he could not be bound by the delays and deliberations of a political approval process. Certainly, General Washington was plagued time and again by similar political deliberations and machinations of the Continental Congress in Philadelphia.

Desperate times call for desperate measures. On August 5, 1921, the Assembly granted Kemal total military command for three months. As he predicted, an exhausted and over-extended Greek Army began to attack his hardened positions. He sent skirmishers to attack the flanks of the

Greek Army, further sapping their energy and momentum. Almost miraculously, he received his first shipments of Bolshevik Russian arms and ammunition. The time to strike back approached. He waited until September 8th and then began a 3-day counterattack which left the Greek Army in dissarray and retreat. The tide had been turned, the Greek offensive stalled on lines which remained static for another year. Mustafa Kemal's comrade in arms, Rauf Orbay, as quoted in, *Quotations about Atatürk – Turkey*, praised the Commander saying,

"He took this duty and vanquished the enemy at the line he drew. He returned from Sakarya with a childish smile. By his personal effort, he had won a battle, which would have been the absolute end of the Turkish independency, if he had lost it."

By October of 1921, the French had signed a Peace Agreement with the Nationalists. The Allies had been split. By March of 1922, the Allies were prepared to accept Nationalist sovereign control of Anatolia. Now in the position of growing stronger by the month, the Nationalists were no longer in a compromising mode. There was still the European part of Turkey.

Greek army morale was ebbing by the summer of 1922. Kemal devised a plan to drive them to the sea, the Mediterranean as he termed the objective. Kemal quietly slipped out of Ankara at night arriving at his command post on a high promontary, *Koca Tepe*, from where he launched a major attack beginning on August 28th.

Benefitting from lessons learned in Allensby's great use of the cavalry in his 1918 Palestine Offensive against the Turks and Germans, his horsemen swept through the Greek Army front lines at key points. They succeeded in cutting telegraph lines and causing general mayhem in the rear. With news of a Turkish victory, by September 7th, the waterfront in Smyrna, modern day İzmir, was lined with officials and others seeking a ship, any boat by which to escape. Two days later, some 400 of the Turkish calvalry arrived and on the night of the 12th, fires decimated the Greek and Armenian sections of town. We have earlier discussed the miraculous evacuation of a huge number of those fleeing on British warships and other vessels.

Mustafa Kemal's reputation rose again. The Treaty of Lausanne was signed the following year. The "Sick Man of Europe," was now neither sick, nor Ottoman, but now the Republic of Turkey. Gawrych aptly describes Mustafa Kemal's genius in his article *"Kemal Ataturk's Politico-Military strategy in the Turkish War of Independence, 1919-1923: From Guerrilla Warfare to Decisive Battle"* when he says, *"Ataturk deserves recognition in the West as one of the great military strategists and commanders of the twentieth century, a soldier who understood well the relationship between politics and war, between national will and military power, and between strategy and tactics."*

Impact on and Popular Perception of Mustafa Kemal in Turkey and the West

One can hardly overestimate the prestige President Mustafa Kemal Pasha garnered at home and abroad with his success in leading a Nationalist Movement from which  was born a Republic modelled on Western governmental forms – a President, Prime Minister, Parliament and a Judiciary – all secular. His fame was already unrivalled within his own country, dissident forces notwithstanding. In the fourth weekly addition, in the first month of its founding, the March 23rd edition of *Time* magazine featured this man on its cover.

Forty years later, in commemoration of Atatürk's passing, twelve days before he was assassinated, President John F. Kennedy eulogized him saying,

"The name of Atatürk brings to mind the historic accomplishments of one of the great men of this century, his inspired leadership of the Turkish People, his perceptive understanding of the modern world and his boldness as a military leader."

Kemal's military victory was but a necessary means to a larger end. The military victory created an opportunity to implement dramatic changes that were meant to secure the basis for a permanent recasting of the Ottoman world into a new mold, that of a secular state seeking to emulate the pragmatic successes of Western civilization and culture. That would mean starting from the ground up with the education of a people 90 percent illiterate at that time. Here, it would be illustrative to report a story, as reported in Bay's book, as told by Dr. Yürük İyriboz, the son of a teacher, Nihat İyriboz, who offered to join in the fight against the Greek army and bring his students with him. After listening to the teacher, Kemal replied, *"No, we are going to beat them anyway. But we will need your students after our victory. I need you for what comes next."*

The Secularizing Iconoclasts – No Turning Back

Mustafa Kemal would enjoy a realtively short time window in which to introduce changes and reforms which were radical. One by one, he and his supporters would dismantle the architecture of Ottoman society and rule where sovereignty had rested with the Sultan, his army, and the religious elite, for centuries. He began with secularizing changes called for in the 1921 Constitution.

The last Sultan had been sent packing in 1922. A more radical reform was countenanced by Kemal and the core, if not all, of his Nationalist supporters. Such reforms he knew would be controversial with implications that would reverberate beyond Turkish shores, east into the heartland of Islam. But the die was cast. Preservation of the new state, the revolution and its leaders required a symbolic, and actual, severing of the ties of church and state. It would require the political disestablishment of the religious elite

(*Ulema*). In March of 1924, the new Parliament passed a bill which deposed the last Caliph, abolished the institution of the Caliphate and banished from Turkey all members of the Ottoman dynasty. On March 4th, the last Caliph was spirited away to the West in a special coach attached to the Orient Express train. [He remained in exile in Paris where he died late in the Second World War]. Kemal Pasha proclaimed that,

> *"Those who use religion for their own benefit are detestable. We are against such a situation and will not allow it. Those who use religion in such a manner have fooled our people; it is against just such people that we have fought and will continue to fight."*

Within weeks of the Caliph's exile, Sharia Law was abolished and religious schools were closed. In April of 1924, the Constitution of the new Republic was adopted.

While Kemal began the process of protecting the revolution with the disestablisment of religion and its officials, he was quick to realize that women and their contributions to the war effort had served in roles traditionally reserved to men and could not be left behind in the recrafting of the new Turkish society. He spoke of the weaknesses of the future of a society which would fail to fully incorporate women into positions of educational and political leadership. To this end, he boldly sought to cajole the people into a changed mindset based on the following question and rationale:

"Human kind is made up of two sexes, women and men. Is it possible that a mass is improved by the improvement of only one part and the other part is ignored? Is it possible that if half of a mass is tied to earth with chains and the other half can soar into skies?"

The great communicator completely understood the value of symbols, those which reinforced the old ways and those which might serve to open minds and hearts to new ways. Nineteen-twenty-five saw a spate of new laws seeking to undermine religious institutions, while outwardly encouraging a new look for the dress of the citizens of a Republic, as distinguished from the subjects of an empire. Sufi Dervish orders were abolished. The Western, or Gregorian, calendar was adopted. The wearing of the Fez hat, symbolic of the *ancien régime*, was outlawed. While preferring to have fashion, rather than law, be the basis for change in ladies' attire, he encouraged Western dress for both men and women and went to considerable lengths to model that form of dress. After all, military men had already accepted western uniforms, pants and tunics some 75 years earlier.

Nieteen-twenty-six brought even more radical forms of legal engineering with the wholesale importation of Western Law Codes whose principles were based on Roman Law and Judeo-Christian practice and custom as codified by university jurisprudents going back to the Napoleonic Code (1803). On these matters, the author wrote his Masters thesis and Doctoral dissertation. To say the least, these changes were anathema for traditional Islamic law and Turkic laws, customs, norms. The new Codes are discussed in more detail in a subsequent Chapter.

In 1927, Islam, as the religion of the State, was removed from the 1924 Constitution. In 1928, the Latin alphabet replaced Ottoman script. In 1933, the Arabic call to prayer and public readings of the Koran were to be rendered in Turkish, unlike the linguistic changes to vernacular languages of Europe in the 15th and 16th centuries seen in religious and humanist writings appearing in the vernacular languages of the Europeans, rather than the written and spoken Latin understood by only the smallest of elites. In 1934, women were given the right to vote and to hold public office. The people were required to adopt surnames. Mustafa Kemal was given the honorific, "Father of the Turks," Mustafa Kemal Atatürk, by act of Parliament. He, like George Washington, both without natural children of their own, were recognized as Fathers of their respective countries, Kemal by law in his lifetime, Washington, by popular convention, beginning as early as the Revolution in his capacity as Commander-in-Chief. Both men had their detractors, then and since. Revisionist historians are having their say about both, some of it sensational, some of it valid. Both men having been deified, iconoclasts are inevitable.

In 1925, no sooner than the Caliphate was abolished, the Sufi order of Nahkshibendi in Diyarbekir sought to overthrow the "godless" work of the new order and restore it. Others within his own party thought his personal dominance was excessive and tried to form a second party, the Progressive Party. A plot was uncovered to assassinate him in 1926 over the issue of the Caliphate. And not all his reforms lasted. Muslim Prayer reverted back to Arabic for example.

The risks were there and President Kemal knew they would be. He dealt with them head on, sometimes quietly, often in a draconian fashion when and where he thought he could get away with it. If he and his closest associates gave in to revanchist sentiment, they knew that the entire experiment could, and probably would, unravel. In fear for his own neck and all that he believed his Nationalist leaders had achieved through the War of Independence, he forged ahead, armed with his "Six Arrows" or principles underlying the revolution: Republicanism, Populism, Secularism, Reformism, Nationalism, and Statism. Consideration of these principles will be further examined as we continue to consider his works and his legacy. Here one is reminded of the trepidation of the Founders at the Signing of the Declaration of Independence so aptly described by Benjamin Franklin, " *If we do not all hang together, we will surely hang separately*".

Influence of Benjamin Franklin and
Thomas Jefferson on Mustafa Kemal

Setting standards by which to live were set for George Washington with the little book which informed his training as a young man, *The Rules of Civility*. American Founding Father, inventor and diplomat Benjamin Franklin famously crafted "13 Virtues" by which to order his life at the age of twenty. These were: Temperance, Silence,  Order, Resolution, Frugality, Industry, Sincerity, Justice, Moderation, Cleanliness, Tranquility, Chastity, and Humility. Each Virtue was accompanied by the briefest of descriptions. Curiously, Gawriych tells us that while reading widely, from early Islamic battles, the Waterloo campaign, Schiller, Shakespeare, and Rousseau, in four languages, he discovered a 79-page translation on Benjamin Franklin noted in Kemal's personal journal dated November 1907. He refers to Franklin as *"the great individual"* and the "inventor of the lightening rod." The notebook also contains all Thirteen of Franklin's "Virtues," twelve of which have his own marginal annotation. Gawrych goes on to say, "

> *"For Mustafa Kemal, Franklin provided a compelling example of the best of the Enlightenment. His broad-ranging mind achieved much in science and technology, and his service as a diplomat helped advance the cause of America's independence. Moreover, Franklin was clearly committed to his own personal virtues, as Mustafa Kemal also was consciously committed to his own character development."*

While there appears to be no evidence of Kemal's study of Thomas Jefferson directly, noted Jefferson scholar Garrett Ward Sheldon has carefully illustrated the many political principles enshrined in Jefferson's work which liken their respective contributions to their respective wars of independence.

"At first glance, Thomas Jefferson and Kemal Atatürk seem to be unusual compatriots. Jefferson, the eighteenth-century North American philosopher and a Founder of the United States; and Atatürk, the twentieth century soldier of the Ottoman Empire and Founder of the modern Republic of Turkey, seem separated by history, culture, and temperament. Yet a closer examination of these two historic figures reveals striking similarities in background, interests, and ideals. From their growing up in vast, of these two historic political but decaying, empires to their leading national independence movements, to their shared ideals of representative democracy, economic equality and progress, religious freedom and liberty, and love of the country side, Thomas Jefferson (an icon of American civilization) and Kemal Atatürk (the hero of Modern Turkey) show remarkable kinship across cultural and historical landscapes. This book examines these common characteristics and ideals in Jefferson and Atatürk, showing that distance and culture are not barriers to shared sacred ideals and practices. Although many specific differences exist between these two leaders, the extent of similarity, given their contrasting

environment and times, is an encouragement to all who believe in the commonality of humanity, wherever and whenever found on the globe...

Both, Jefferson and Atatürk insisted that the battle for national independence was not for a restoration of the past but for an entirely new political system in America and Turkey: a democratic republic. Each authored a "Declaration of Independence" extolling principles of republican government by the consent of the people. Both became outlaws to the old Empires... A key component of a modern republic, for Jefferson and Atatürk, was freedom of religion. Each had grown up in a society with a state religion: The official Church of England for Jefferson and the official Islamic state for Atatürk. Both saw the legal involvement of religion in politics as corrupting both religion and politics... Likewise, both Jefferson and Atatürk saw education as essential to self-government. Each inherited a society in which education was only for the privileged few; and each helped establish a public education system that elevated the average citizen to literacy and intelligence..."

1934 Çankaya Pavillion Speech,
Allied Deaths at Gallipoli

At the age of 52, showcasing his development as a magnanimous statesman, Atatürk grandiloquently observed,

"Heroes who shed their blood and lost their lives! You are now lying in the soil of a friendly country. Therefore rest in peace. There is no difference to the Johnnies and the Mehmets to us where they lie here side by side in this country of ours. You, the mothers, who sent their sons from far away countries wipe your tears; your sons are now lying in our bosom and are in peace. After having lost their lives on this land, they have become our sons as well."

"Biz Bize Benzeriz" and Nation Building

Mustafa Kemal witnessed a lifetime of Ottoman attempts to administer, tax and the resulting strain in the business of the governance of a vast empire of diverse peoples and religions. Instinctively, he knew that countenancing differences among citizens by race and ethnicity was likely to result in a "no-win" cycle of popular frustration and antagonism, bringing back the fractious culture of the past. His Reforms were designed to simplify and streamline the business of governing. The assumption was that if all are seen as Turkish citizens, equal before a secular system of laws, that tension should be lessened in the governance of one people. At the time, it seemed to be working well for Western countries.

One might say Kemal set out to homogenize the people of the new Republic of Turkey in the image of pure Turks. One way to do this was to imagine all citizens are just different strains of Turks, be they Black Sea Turks, Mountain Turks, or European Turks. And as such, he professed that all resemble each other more than they resembled anyone else (*"Biz bize benzeris."*). For example, the fact that Arab Turks more resemble their non-Turkish cousins over the Southeastern border was ignored. In 1927, Kemal said, *"We must delve into our roots and reconstruct what history had divided."*

The fact that Kurds more resemble their cousins across the Eastern and Southern borders was not the point. The fact that they may speak a different language needed to be set aside in this new Republic. The fact that Alevi and Sunni Turks worship very differently could be minimized. Christian and Jewish Turks are not part of millets (sub-constituencies of the Ottoman State) now, they are Turkish citizens. In principle, this is an ideal to which all nations aspire. But it is an ideal that sits more comfortably with the *Staatsvolk*, in this case of those people who consider themeselves Turk, first and last. For understandable reasons, significant other constituencies do not start with that assumption. Time, political, and economic enfranchisement may produce the desired effect, but not in the breakneck timeframe that Kemal sought to engineer these changes. American geography was more favorable to such a result, at least before the advent of 21st century commmunications technology. Within the borders of modern Turkey, many non-Turks long preceded the arrival of the Turks. Following his death, by the early 1950s, it was clear that homogenization of the people in a secular framework probably worked inside the military, but was not wholly acceptable to various constituencies around the country, especially as one moved farther away from Ankara, the center of political power.

The "Kemalist" separation of church and state was reinforced by the notion that Islam and the Clerical Elites, was said by the reformers to have, in current parlance, been part of the problem and not part of the solution. Islam in the public arena was to be subordinated to a secular Rule of Law. About Islam Kemal said, " *Know that whatever conforms to reason and logic and the advantages of our people conforms equally to Islam. If our religion did not conform to reason and logic, it would not be the perfect religion, the final religion.*" If the logic does not necessarily hold, clearly the idea is a clever conflation of competing ideologies.

In order to incubate the Kemalist experiment, and to avoid exposing it to the entangling intrigues of its neighbors, Kemal announced a foreign policy based on a proclaimed message of "Peace at home. Peace abroad." Here again, his instincts for survival of the new Republic were similar to those of George Washington.

Isolationism – Xenophobia vs. Fear of Foreign Entanglements, Turkey and America

We might begin by stating that isolationism is not the same as xenopobia, though the latter may be a symptom of the former. Like George Washington, Mustafa Kemal and his reformers had a revolution to protect and nurture. Without the benefit of vast oceans providing a buffer zone,

Kemal had to work with exhausted peoples who had been at war with others and with themselves for a long time. Xenophobia was more the product of ever-increasing subversion of Ottoman sovereignty over its subjects. While Nineteenth Century Reformers found the Capitulations galling, they nevertheless admired the technical achievements of a more secular West. Others, especially the Ottoman Ruling religious elites, grew bitter about intrusions into the socio-religious basis of their authority and power. Kemal knew by bitter experience that these elites had to be totally disenfranchised. He also recognized that the emerging new secular elite would understand that their future and necks were dependent upon a thorough-going and radical departure from the past – no going back. Between those on the trailing edge and those on the leading edge was the vast majority of a poor people desperate for peace, food, and economic sustainability. If secularist reformers would give them that, they would abide by reforms where necessary and quietly disregard them when and where possible. Further, both Washington and Kemal would seek to nuture their revolutions with a concerted attempt to avoid foreign interference and foreign entanglement.

George Washington, who had wished to serve only one term as President, found that conflict between his Secretary of the Treasury, Alexander Hamilton, and his Secretary of State, Thomas Jefferson and their respective followers had become so inflamed that, for the sake of the

Union, he put away his first Farewell Address, and reluctantly served a second term.

During that second term, war broke out between England and France. Controversies, sparked by representative agents of both countries, together with their sympathetic American constituencies, largely drawn on regional lines, further threatened the stability of the Union. Worn down and frustrated by the domestic political strife between and among former friends and comrades in arms, Washington declined the offer of a third term as President, first and foremost, in principle. Political office should be a temporary honor and necessity, after which one should return to private life.

He declined the offer in fear and trepidation for the future of the United States of America. In September 1796, his Farewell Address was published. I have excerpted portions of the letter as they reveal much about the dignity, experience and foresight of the man King George III extolled as the greatest man of the world. He begins with an apology that his strength, after the ravages of decades of public military and civil service, will no longer allow him to adequately serve his people. He wanted no more than an opportunity to return to his beloved home at Mt. Vernon, where he might spend his final years in peace.

"The acceptance of and continuance hitherto in the office to which your suffrages have twice called me have been a uniform sacrifice of inclination to the opinion of duty and to a deference for what appeared to be your desire. I

constantly hoped that it would have been much earlier in my power, consistently with motives which I was not at liberty to disregard, to return to that retirement from which I had been reluctantly drawn. The strength of my inclination to do this previous to the last election had even led to the preparation of an address to declare it to you; but mature reflection on the then perplexed and critical posture of our affairs with foreign nations and the unanimous advice of persons entitled to my confidence impelled me to abandon the idea. I rejoice that the state of your concerns, external as well as internal, no longer renders the pursuit of inclination incompatible with the sentiment of duty or propriety, and am persuaded, whatever partiality may be retained for my services, that in the present circumstances of our country you will not disapprove my determination to retire."

He goes on to caution his people to be wary of those who would seek to divide them as a nation.

"In contemplating the causes which may disturb our union it occurs as matter of serious concern that any ground should have been furnished for characterizing parties by geographical discriminations--Northern and Southern, Atlantic and Western-- whence designing men may endeavor to excite a belief that there is a real difference of local interests and views. One of the expedients of party to acquire influence within particular districts is to misrepresent the opinions and aims of other districts. You can not shield yourselves too much against the jealousies

and heartburnings which spring from these misrepresen-
tations; they tend to render alien to each other those who
ought to be bound together by fraternal affection..."

Moving beyond the borders of the country, Washington seeks to establish a sense of respect for all nations, and
avoid being drawn into their conflicts with other nations.
Clearly Kemal similarly sought to maintain neutrality with
other nations, allowing the revolution at home to husband
its resources for the furtherance of the New Republic of
Turkey. Certainly, the memory of having chosen the losing
side in the First World War was at the forefront of his
mind. Washington waxes on this same point.

"In the execution of such a plan nothing is more essen-
tial than that permanent, inveterate antipathies against
particular nations and passionate attachments for others
should be excluded, and that in place of them just and
amicable feelings toward all should be cultivated. The
nation which indulges toward another an habitual hatred
or an habitual fondness is in some degree a slave."

"So, likewise, a passionate attachment of one nation for
another produces a variety of evils. Sympathy for the
favorite nation, facilitating the illusion of an imaginary
common interest in cases where no real common interest
exists, and infusing into one the enmities of the other,
betrays the former into a participation in the quarrels
and wars of the latter without adequate inducement
or justification."

In the following passage, he explicitly calls attention to the importance of time without either internal dissension or engagement in the conflicts of other nations.

"The inducements of interest for observing that conduct will best be referred to your own reflections and experience. With me a predominant motive has been to endeavor to gain time to our country to settle and mature its yet recent institutions, and to progress without interruption to that degree of strength and consistency which is necessary to give it, humanly speaking, the command of its own fortunes." "

He concludes in a self-deprecating tone, asking that he be forgiven actions and policies which may be seen then and in the future, to have been in error.

"Though in reviewing the incidents of my Administration I am unconscious of intentional error, I am nevertheless too sensible of my defects not to think it probable that I may have committed many errors. Whatever they may be, I fervently beseech the Almighty to avert or mitigate the evils to which they may tend. I shall also carry with me the hope that my country will never cease to view them with indulgence, and that, after forty-five years of my life dedicated to

its service with an upright zeal, the faults of incompetent abilities will be consigned to oblivion, as myself must soon be to the mansions of rest.

With the fate of both revolutions in the balance, Washington and Kemal Atatürk believed in isolationism in the sense of avoiding long-term political-military alliances which might endanger their survival. Neutrality was the key. Both Nations remained so for some time after the Founders had passed away, a testament to the wisdom of both leaders and to the durability of their legacies. Both were deified by adoring peoples who took solace in their common admiration of their iconic leaders, the shared memory of whom was often their only bond.

Here the words of General Richard Henry Lee in his eulogy of his Commander and Chief and President stated the following words which have come down to our school children to this day, when he aptly observed, George Washington was, "First in War, First in Peace, First in the Hearts of his Countrymen."

Monuments to both great men (seen below, The Washinton Monument and the Ataturk Mausoleum) will not spare them the pens of revisionist historians. Both men made and revised history in their lifetimes by sheer force of will. The thinking of both men suggests that they would be open to such modern revision where fairly rendered. Both would also reconcile to the reality that "fairness" might be in the eyes of the beholder and that in any case, the criteria for judgments would no doubt change, and change again, as time wore on.

The following tributes to Mustfa Kemal Atatürk and his legacy are perhaps best rendered by those outside of Turkey who watched with careful admiration what he was able to achieve in his lifetime against all odds.

"The death of Atatürk, who saved Turkey during the war and revived the Turkish nation, is not only a loss for his country, but it is also a great loss for Europe. The sincere tears that people from all classes have shed, are nothing more than the true reflection of this great man – the Father of the modern Turkey." Winston Churchill

"Atatürk has left Turkey without a single enemy. This is something that no other state leader of our time has succeeded in doing." German Volkischer Beobachter Journal

"We meet genius people very rarely in centuries. It is so unlucky that, in this century that great genius person belongs to the Turkish Nation. The centuries rarely produce a genius. Look at this bad luck of ours, that great genius of our era was granted to the Turkish nation." D. Lloyd George, Prime Minister of the United Kingdom

"England salutes the great man, that England has known first as a brave and noble enemy, then as a faithful friend." Sunday Times of London.

Chapter 13

NATIONALISM EXPRESSED IN AMERICA

Nationalism in America is the result of a long Colonial experience eventually leading to a war of independence from the Mother country, England. It has been a process which has seen many challenges and obstacles which have changed over the course time. The process begins with a growing sense of independence from the Mother Country born of the vast distance between England and her North American Colonies separated by an ocean. Others of her colonies were even further away, from the islands in the Caribbean to the West coast of Africa and India. Why it took, if one thinks of Hong Kong, one hundred and fifty to two hundred years longer for her other colonies to become independent, the answer might initially be attributed to geography, demographics, and the relative homogeneity of race and ethnicity in the American Colonies.

The geography factor is the fact of a large land mass, in the temperate zone, and the blessings of an abundance of water, forest, mineral deposits and farmable land. Unlike the French experience in North America with its small, resource-extraction oriented, and widely dispersed, population, the sheer numbers of British Colonists, all white and largely Christian, aiming at settling the new continent, made for a different outlook in the Thirteen Colonies. It was not many decades after the colonists first arrived that they began to outnumber the Native Americans living East of the Mississippi. The white population was growing to meet the challenges of survival, permanent establishment, and later conquest. The Native American population decreased at an accelated rate largely due to diseases spread by the Colonists from which they had no immunity. It should be noted that many of the same diseases, coming from Asia it is thought, had afflicted the English and European populations (the Black Plagues) in the centuries prior to the colonization, with survivors developing immunities.

Having noted the natural advantages leading to sustainability of a growing white population, it must be recognized that a nation was forged over some two centuries. Colonists originally saw themselves just as that. Some were religious Separatists like the Puritans of Massachusetts. Others came for economic reward as part of trading companies, Catholic-oriented as in the case of Maryland and Anglican Protestant in the case of the Virginia colony. Early on, affinity was very local with a larger tie to England. In time, the tie to England would weaken and attachment to their respective colonies would strengthen. Commercial and trading ties, especially along the Eastern seaboard increased a sense of interconnectedness with the other American colonies. But due to the mercantilist system of trade instituted by England, primary external loyalty and affinity remained with the Mother Country. Conflict with the Native American tribes and the war against the French and its Indian Allies brought different colonies into alliance with each other. British taxation policies beginning in the mid-1760s, in part to pay for the war in the colonies in North America and in her other colonies around the world, brought the American colonists into an increasingly common cause against the Mother Country. This led to a war of independence. Like the Turkish case, Americans in general came reluctantly to the fight. The purpose, direction and ultimate objectives of the war and its aftermath were not completely clear at the beginning – just as they were not for Kemal and the Nationalist cause in Turkey. One has a Congress, the other, a Parliament. While the notion of popular consent through elected representatives was more fully established in America, both had deliberative bodies with no king.

Some important concepts had to be shaped from scratch in the American experience. The Nationalists in Turkey, by their very name, had benefited from earlier revolutions that had been based on the notions of Nationalism, the "right of self-determination," and some form of popular sovereignty. With these wars of independence, based on the ideals and purposes of these struggles, both called for new republican governments to be created and sustained.

In 1783 at the Paris Peace Treaty, America gained her independence. The United States of America became a fact on paper. Turning that fact into one Nation with a common set of principles and governing bodies at both the State and Federal levels was every much as challenging as the War itself. It is a process which never ends in any Nation State. Part of the American process of national integration would require another additional wars, the War of 1812, and the Civil War of 1861-1865, in an effort to "strive for a more perfect Union." Let us now turn our attention to the early years of the "Great American Experiment." Those Patriots who had been allies in war would not always be allies in peace.

Federalism versus States' Rights – Federalists and Republican-Democrats

On September 5, 1774, at the first Continental Congress, Delegates, still professing a Loyalty to the King, authored and signed the Articles of Association. Its primary purpose was to unite the colonies into a boycott of British Goods in response to the various taxes imposed by the Crown on the Colonies for which the Colonies had no direct representation in the English Parliament. From this Congress came Committees of Correspondence, under the leadership of John Adams in Boston. Through these Committees, matters of political interest were communicated, thereby increasing the sense of mutual awareness throughout the Colonies as a whole. The bonds were increased during the

Revolution with the creation of the Articles of Confederation in 1777. This document was ratified by all Thirteen Colonies early in 1781. These Articles conferred almost all powers to the participating Colonies, now States. The Federal Government was largely powerless do much of anything, including the growing need after the war to intervene in interstate commerce where interstate trade tariffs were inhibiting trade growth. By 1786, rifts between the States and between the States and the Federal Government began to surface. In particular, Shay's Rebellion in Western Massachusetts, was precipitated by economic pressure on the common man, harsh policies for the collection of taxes, and anger against the elites and their cronyism. These sentiments held by many in the rural areas, many of whom were former Revolutionary soldiers, are perhaps best expressed by one such rural farmer, Plough Jogger, as reported in Howard Zinn's book, *A People's History of the United States*:

> "I have been greatly abused, have been obliged to do more than my part in the war, been loaded with class rates, town rates, province rates, Continental rates and all rates ... been pulled and hauled by sheriffs, constables and collectors, and had my cattle sold for less than they were worth ... The great men are going to get all we have and I think it is time for us to rise and put a stop to it, and have no more courts, nor sheriffs, nor collectors nor lawyers."

His sentiment was widespread in the back country of many of the States. While Shay's Rebellion was put down by a local militia, the fact that the Federal Government did not have the money to even raise a small force to deal with such situations gave support to advocates of a stronger Federal Government. That weakness would change by 1791, after the promulgation of the new U.S. Constitution, when a similar rebellion broke out in Western Pennsylvania. Then President George Washington was able to dispatch Federal forces to put the Whiskey Rebellion down. However, rancor between States' Rights advocates and Federalists had already been apparent in 1787 in Philadelphia at the Constitutional Convention.

Shay's Rebellion, and similar occurrences since the end of the War, prompted proponents of a stronger Federal Government to come together, though often reluctant political bedfellows. A campaign to convince those on the fence on the subject in favor of a stronger National Government appeared in serial form in the newspapers of the time. Collectively, they became known as the *Federalist Papers* that were discussed earlier. Concern for the inadequacies of the Government based on the Articles of Confederation for people like Alexander Hamilton, a former military man and diehard proponent of a strong Federal Government, together with other leaders like James Madison of Virginia, whose natural instincts had always been on the States' Rights side, brought them to ally with one another during the Constitutional debates. He would later have some misgivings about a strong Federal Government, that he thought had become overweening during the Presidencies of Washington and Adams. He would later rediscover, when he was President and the Country was attacked by the British in the War of 1812, the importance of having a strong army at the ready. When war broke out, Madison found himself and the Federal Government forces totally inadequate to the task of defending the new Republic.

Another significant factor in swaying people into the Federalist camp was the treatment of American merchantmen trading on the Mediterranean. In fact, negotiating with representatives of the Barbary States, to ransom back ships, men and sometimes women, was a major occupation of Thomas Jefferson in his time as America's Minister to France. Even before American Independence, men like John Adams had been engaged in the same effort, both while he was in France and later when he was in England. The European powers had been paying ransom for years, and they were not about to use their navies to help protect American shipping after her independence.

During the debates at the Constitutional Convention, stories were told of American sailors, their ships and cargoes being seized/captured off the coasts of Morocco, Algiers, and Tripoli. It was both humiliating for the new Country and expensive. Piracy gave fuel to the Federalist position that if America were going to be treated as a proper Nation, worthy of sitting at the table with European powers, it must have a Navy and marines to protect American commercial interests. The importance of Piracy on the shaping of the American Constitution and the early Republic will be discussed in more detail in a subsequent Chapter concerning the various circumstances under which Americans and Turks came to know each other.

Hamiltonians versus Jeffersonians – Federalizing the American Debt

"It's not worth a Continental" is an expression which comes down to us today. It refers to the paper money issued by the United States Government during and after the American Revolution. The expression came to mean that a Continental was scarcely worth the paper it was printed on. This money was not redeemable for gold or silver. After the War, the new Country experienced rampant inflation leading to further devaluing of the currency. The situation was aggravated by the burden of a large debt carried by the Government and by the States occasioned by borrowing and printing more money needed to prosecute War. It has been estimated that the National debt was approximately $5 million and the States' combined debt was $25 million. For a sense of the size of these debts, multiply the numbers by a factor of 22 times, or $660 million. The Louisiana Purchase, which doubled the size of the United States, was $15,000,000. In short, the debt burden was monumental, with little taxing authority available to the States and less for the Federal Government

One of the Founders, Alexander Hamilton, being the son of a ship merchant in the Caribbean, gained experience in business and trading as a young man. He was later educated at the College of New York, which later became Columbia University. He proved to be a capable military officer during the Revolution. He was a man of action and soon became an *Aide de Camp* to General Washington during the War. As early as 1781, he said, *"Most commercial Nations have found it necessary to establish banks; and they have proved the happiest engines for advancing trade."*

Ten years later, as the first Secretary of the Treasury in Washington's government, he sought to address the continuing weakness and vulnerability of the American economy. He began to study banks in other countries, France, Holland, and England in particular. He came to believe in the role of Public Finance and the importance of a National Bank. According to Ron Chernow in his book, *Alexander Hamilton*, *"He kept a copy of it [the charter of the Bank of England] on his desk as a handy reference as he wrote his banking report..."* on the problem. Noting the popular adversity to banks in general, he was committed in his report to present the advantages that a bank may bring. Chernow goes on to say, *"Echoing Adam Smith, he showed how gold and silver, if locked up in a merchant's chest, were sterile. Deposit them in a bank, however, these dead metals sprang to life as 'nurseries of national wealth,' forming a credit supply several times larger than the coins heaped in the bank's vault."*

Opposition was swift, coming especially from the agrarian States of the South. The opposition was led by Jefferson and Madison of Virginia. They believed that a National Bank was unconstitutional and if created would give the Federal Government a level of power never intended by the new Constitution. Continuing to defend the value of a National Bank that would assume the combined Federal and State debts, Chernow quotes Hamilton as saying in an official quarterly Treasury Report, *"If banks, in spite of every precaution are sometimes betrayed into giving a false credit to the persons described, they more frequently enable honest and industrious men of small or perhaps no capital to undertake and prosecute business with advantage to themselves and the community."*

Washington found himself in the middle of the debate. Jefferson and Edmund Randolph advised that he veto the proposed bill. They smelled a tyranny in the scheme reminiscent of the powers of a king. They sent a laundry list of objections to it which Washington promptly forwarded to Hamilton. He asked that a rebuttal to these objections be sent him within a week. He complied in a powerfully argued dissertation on what came to be described as the concept of "implied powers," an expansive interpretation of the Constitution. Chernow goes on to say, *"If Jefferson's and Randolph's views were upheld,* [in Hamilton's words] *'the United States would furnish the singular spectacle of a political society without sovereignty or of a people governed without government.'"*

After reviewing Hamilton's arguments for two days, Washington signed the Bill into law. And with that, polarization in American Politics morphed into the formation of two competing parties, the Federalists, led by Hamilton, and the Republican-Democrats led by Jefferson and Madison. The alliance between Hamilton and Madison in their joint defense of a strong central government, just three years earlier in the Constitutional debates in Philadelphia, was now irrevocably severed. Washington despaired of the break-down of friends and comrades in arms barely a decade after achieving independence. The two parties largely split on regional lines, as they had in the Constitutional debates, North and South. War between England and Revolutionary France, recently commenced, would find supporters and detractors of each country, again along party factional and geographic lines.

As noted earlier, Washington sought to steer a middle course between the two parties. He chose to be neutral between the two European antagonists as well, supporting a Treaty with England calling for Neutrality. The terms of the Treaty were largely crafted by Hamilton, negotiated by John Jay, and backed by President Washington. It was ratified in 1796 by both governments, for a term of ten years, to the profound dismay of the Jeffersonian-Democrats. They saw it as a Treaty with the former enemy that would redound to the exclusive benefit of Federalist strongholds in the Northern States. The Federalists carried the day, but the tide would begin to turn against them in four short years when Jefferson would become President.

The Monroe Doctrine, Manifest Destiny – Native Americans and The Trail of Tears

During Jefferson's Presidency, now in power and now under the scrutiny of public opinion, he found some of his anti-Federalist inclinations to be harder to maintain when confronted with the challenges facing the Country at that time. For example, the exigencies of time led him to exceed his Presidential authority in authorizing a borrowing from Dutch Bankers to purchase Louisiana from a Napoleon desperate to raise money to support his war with the English. The fact that the $15 million purchase of the Louisiana Territory, virtually doubling the size of the United States overnight notwithstanding, and was a deal not equaled since the Dutch purchase of the island of Manhattan in 1626 for the sum of some $24, President Jefferson did not have the Constitutional authority for such an undertaking. In principle, he needed Congressional approval. Another example came when his friend and now Vice President, James Madison, also convinced him of the need to build a Navy that could stop the continuing depredations of the Barbary Pirates on American shipping in the Mediterranean. This was contrary to the general tendency to avoid a strong central Navy and Army held by the Jeffersonian Democrats.

Military weakness, combined with a failure to renew the Federal Bank Charter, would leave the United States grossly outgunned when the British attacked America in the War of 1812.

America faced the darkest hour of its then short history in August of 1814 when British forces burned the White House. The Country's fourth President, James Madison, came to understand the importance of a Federal Bank and a standing Army and Navy. America's fortunes would, however, rise late in the war with the defense of the harbor at Baltimore. Mid-September of 1814, the British began an enormous bombardment of Fort McHenry. The next day, above the Fort at reveille in the early morning of September 14, 1814, a giant American Flag was hoisted indicating that the Fort was still standing. On a neutral ship in the harbor, an American lawyer and poet, Francis Scott Key, penned words to this defense of Fort McHenry which were then set to a British tune and became known as the Star-Spangled Banner. It was not until 1931 that the song became the official National Anthem of the United States.

With the war beginning to go against them, the British signed a Treaty in Ghent in December of that year. Before the news of the Treaty could reach the warring parties, the

Americans scored another victory under the direction of Major General Andrew Jackson in early January, 1815, in the Battle of New Orleans. As one of his last acts as President, now with a battle-tested fleet, President Madison sent a sortie of American war ships to settle old scores with the Barbary Pirates. The bottom line was that America was on the way to becoming a world power. The prospects for growth and prosperity seemed ripe. Madison would hand the government over to the last of the Revolutionary War generation, James Monroe.

James Monroe was wounded in the Revolutionary War at the Battle of Trenton. He studied law under Jefferson and became an Anti-Federalist. He gained executive experience as the Governor of Virginia and went on to distinguish himself as a diplomat in France during the negotiations for the Louisiana Purchase. Later, under President Madison, he served as both Secretary of State and Secretary of War.

With the Federalist Party severely weakened, Monroe easily won election in 1816, becoming the Fifth President, and the Third Founder to die on Independence Day, July Fourth, in his case, 1831.

Toward the end of the 1700s, even before the Revolutionary War, Americans had begun moving west through the Cumberland Gap (Virginia), an old buffalo and Indian trail, and began to settle West of the Appalachian Mountains in Indian Territory. Famous explorers and pioneers in this process included men like Dr. Thomas Walker and Joseph Martin of Charlottesville, Virginia and Daniel Boone, originally from Pennsylvania. It has been estimated that by 1800 some 200,000 Americans had travelled through the gap into what would become West Virginia, Kentucky, and Tennessee. This was dangerous business. The British had used Cherokee and other Native Americans against the Americans during the Revolution. In spite of the risks, in search of new land, Americans burst forth into the Ohio and Mississippi River valleys. These Americans were a hardy and independent lot. They had successfully fought for Liberty and Freedom from the British and thought they were entitled to move into Indian Territory, treaties and proclamations to the contrary notwithstanding. By the end of the War of 1812, Americans began to see themselves as a Nation with a God-given right to settle the land, eventually coast to coast.

Looking back, through the long lens of a century, Frederick Jackson Turner reminds one of the inexorable flow of pioneers from his vantage point of the late 1800s. Poetically, he proclaimed the yearning to conquer the continent, beginning with the first mass movement of Americans through the Gap and across the plains to the Rocky Mountains, with new States coming into the Union with each passing decade.

"Stand at Cumberland Gap and watch the procession of civilization pass, marching single file – the buffalo following the trail to the salt springs, the Indian, the fur-trader and hunter, the cattle-raiser, the pioneer farmer – and the frontier passed by. Stand at South Pass by the Rockies a century later and see the same procession with wider intervals in between."

President Monroe's term as President, from 1817 to 1825, became known as the "Era of Good Feelings." During this period, treaties with Spain were negotiated to acquire Florida, and with the English, to establish the northern boundary of America at the 42nd parallel, literally extending America to the Pacific Northwest. In fact, this Westward expansion was self-righteously seen as America's "Manifest Destiny." America's sense of its proper sphere of influence extended beyond its shores, to its hemisphere. Authored with the assistance of his Secretary of State, John Quincy Adams (the next U.S. President), Monroe proclaimed this vision in the form of a doctrine in 1923, becoming known as the Monroe Doctrine in 1823. It essentially promised that America would not involve itself in the internal affairs of Europe or their Latin American Colonies, but admonished that any attempts to further colonize in South America would be met with American intervention. In fact, many Portuguese and Spanish colonies were at that time in the process of attaining their independence, following the American example.

This freedom and prosperity, with seemingly endless resources to absorb the American population growing both internally and by mass emigration from "Old Europe," for reasons ranging from famine to political disaffection, initially brought Irish, Germans and Southern Europeans to the American Shore. The Statue of Liberty, opened to the public in 1886, was a gift from the French Nation to the American Nation and bore the following inscription at the base:

"Keep, ancient lands, your storied pomp!" cries she
With silent lips. "Give me your tired, your poor,
Your huddled masses yearning to breathe free,
The wretched refuse of your teeming shore.
Send these, the homeless, tempest-tost to me,
I lift my lamp beside the golden door!"

Freedom and Liberty were not experienced by all Americans during this expansion. The plight of African American slaves is discussed later.

Another such population in America, Native Americans, also did not enjoy the rights proclaimed in the Declaration of Independence. Treaties giving them land were routinely broken. One case, symptomatic of this shameful period in America's expansion, involved the Choctaw, Cherokee, Chickasaw, Creek, and Seminole Indians living primarily in Georgia, Alabama, Mississippi, and Florida. With the support of President Andrew Jackson (of Battle of New Orleans fame), the Indian Removal Act was passed in 1830. Tribes which refused to assimilate with the white settlers and become American citizens, in order to preserve their autonomy, would be forcibly removed to new Indian Territory West of the Mississippi to an area which later became Oklahoma. Several thousand of these Indians, especially the Cherokee, died of disease and starvation between 1831 and 1835. These forced relocations came to be known as "The Trail of Tears." Many of these Indian tribes had become economically integrated with the economy, but the White-American desire for their land was inescapable. Discovering gold on some of their land only increased the temptation. The position with which these Indians were faced is perhaps best described in a "Farewell to the American People" letter written in 1932 by a Choctaw Chief and educated lawyer, George W. Harkins, who painfully wrote the following:

> "... We were hedged in by two evils, and we chose that which we thought the least. Yet we could not recognize the right that the state of Mississippi had assumed, to legislate for us. Although the legislature of the state were qualified to make laws for their own citizens, that did not qualify them to become law makers to a people that were so dissimilar in manners and customs as the Choctaws are to the Mississippians... We as Choctaws rather chose to suffer and be free, than live under the degrading influence of laws, which our voice could not be heard in their formation.

Much as the state of Mississippi has wronged us, I cannot find in my heart any other sentiment than an ardent wish for her prosperity and happiness.

I could cheerfully hope, that those of another age and generation may not feel the effects of those oppressive measures that have been so illiberally dealt out to us; and that peace and happiness may be their reward. Amid the gloom and horrors of the present separation, we are cheered with a hope that ere long we shall reach our destined land, and that nothing short of the basest acts of treachery will ever be able to wrest it from us, and that we may live free. Although your ancestors won freedom on the field of danger and glory, our ancestors owned it as their birthright, and we have had to purchase it from you as the vilest slaves buy their freedom."

French Philosopher and traveler Alexis de Tocqueville witnessed this tragedy first hand in Memphis, Tennessee, observing in his book, *Democracy in America*, the following:

"In the whole scene there was an air of ruin and destruction, something which betrayed a final and irrevocable adieu; one couldn't watch without feeling one's heart wrung. The Indians were tranquil, but sombre and taciturn. There was one who could speak English and of whom I asked why the Chactas were leaving their country. "To be free," he answered, could never get any other reason out of him. We ... watch the expulsion ... of one of the most celebrated and ancient American peoples."

The issue of their sovereignty and limited autonomy went for adjudication to the Supreme Court. The first decision went against the Indians in 1831. In 1832, a decision in favor of limited autonomy and against forcible removal went in favor of the Indians. Already entangled over issues of States' Rights verses Federal power, President Jackson did not want any part of the Supreme Court ruling in favor of the Indians. He allowed the removal to take place in spite of the Court's ruling in favor of the Indians. He repudiated Chief Justice John C. Marshall, a cousin of Thomas Jefferson and an able soldier in the Revolutionary War, and his court's decision, saying the following, *"John Marshall has made his decision; now let him enforce it! ... Build a fire under them. When it gets hot enough, they'll go."* Native Americans were also removed in the New York area. Those that remained behind to become American citizens were often exposed to degrading treatment by the white population. As Americans moved farther west, this story would be repeated with the Apache, Comanche, Ute, and Navaho in the years just following the American Civil War.

Manifest Destiny, like the German concept in the 20th Century of *"Lebensraum" ("living space"),* became a rationale for racism and unbridled territorial expansion. It should be remembered that Native Americans also fought courageously to protect their hunting grounds in the face of overwhelming demographic pressure from the new Americans. Since well before even the French and Indian War, these Native Americans, not without their own intra-tribal violence and conflicts, had been pawns of European civilization seeking treasure and then space in North America, the English and French from the East and the Spanish from the South and West.

> "American Democracy was born of no theorist's dream; it was not carried in the Susan Constant to Virginia [the largest of the 3 ships that arrived in Jamestown, captained by Christopher Newport], nor in the Mayflower to Plymouth. It came stark and strong and full of life out of the American Forest, and it gained new life each time it touched a new frontier."

These words were spoken by the famous American Historian Frederick Jackson Turner in 1893 on the occasion of the opening of the Columbian Exposition at the Quadra-Centennial of Columbus' arrival on the shores of America. This was more commonly known as the Chicago World's Fair and it symbolized so extraordinarily the bold, resourceful, frontier-blazing spirit of Americans who had moved across this country in fulfillment of its "manifest destiny." The raw, crude, sometimes violent and can-do spirit of the people came to define the notion of "American Exceptionalism."

To have some appreciation of the extent to which many of the leaders of these Tribes had integrated into American society, a photograph of the Principal Chief of the Cherokee, John Ross, is shown here shortly before his death in 1866.

For whatever their sins and shortcomings, between The Revolutionary War and the First World War, America became a Nation with a sense of being part of a large Union. Not all the constituencies were treated equally and many struggled. Native Americans and foreigners from places like China might be heathen, but the civilizing of them and turning them into Christians if they were not already, was once presumed a passport to what became the "American Dream." After all, from America's first colony in Virginia, in the same year African slaves were first brought to America, Virginia planter John Rolfe famously married an Indian princess, Pocahontas in 1619. Before white Americans became missionaries abroad, in their sense of cultural and racial superiority, white Englishmen had sought to civilize and Christianize "heathen savages." The spirit of Manifest Destiny combined with Nationalism and Christian religiosity provided spiritual food to the 19th century missionaries, first at home and then abroad. The paradoxes of these patriotic and humanitarian causes are elegantly laid open in John Demos' book, *The Heathen School – A Story of Hope and Betrayal in the Age of the Early Republic.* As worthy, and at the same time cynical, as these American forces were, they were an important part of the fabric of America becoming a Nation in the 19th century, warts and all.

In conclusion, Nationalism in America has been a process of coming together and staying together. America begins as an idea, an experiment. That great idea is based on two concepts, liberty and freedom. These concepts underlie the Founding Documents of America. They are the ideational aspirations which have served to make the American experience unique. To these ideas, in the fleshing out of this experience, the sinews of the American Union are masterfully laid out by Simon Winchester in his book, *The Men Who United The States – America's Explorers, Inventors, Eccentrics, and Mavericks, and the Creation of One Nation Indivisible*. Winchester refers to this as the, *"physiology and the physics of the country, the strands of connective tissue that have allowed it to achieve all it has, and yet keep itself together."* He cites in particular *"innumerable real, visible, tangible connections – by survey lines and marks; by roads; by canals; by railways, telephone lines, power grids; ..."* as examples.

Colonial settlements initially followed the Eastern Seaboard and the major rivers, all of which, like the Seaboard itself, followed a North-South flow, including the Hudson, Delaware, Allegheny, Potomac, Ohio and Mississippi rivers. As noted earlier, by the middle 1700s, the first significant East-West movement of the Americans, like the traditional axis of the old Silk Routes from China to Europe, was initiated in the Mohawk River Valley of New York connecting the Great Lakes and the Midwest to the East, and from there, the connection north and south to the shipping harbors of Quebec and New York City. These arteries and the trade they promoted gave colonists of one area, or one's "country" as it was known at the time, an association with another area independent of the Mother Country of England.

By 1804, President Jefferson arranged for the Government to underwrite the Lewis and Clark Expedition, both friends of his, in search of a water route from the Mississippi to the Pacific. Following their route and developing others, beginning in the 1820s, wagon trains of settlers would travel to St. Louis on the Mississippi River. From there, they would take a boat up the Missouri River and be outfitted and join a wagon train in Independence, Missouri. Settlers, homesteaders, would then travel on one of three Westerly routes, Northwest, West, and Southwest. Wagon train travel would be replaced by train travel to the West in the 1870s. It is interesting to note that Samuel Morris,  inventor of the Morris telegraph code, sent his first public telegraph in 1844. Ten years later, it received its first military application in the course of the Crimean War.

Alexander Graham Bell officially opened the first long-distance telephone line from New York to Chicago in 1892 (pictured here). One advertisement for his company read, "Making a Neighborhood of a Nation." Leveraging the inventions in wireless telegraphy by European inventors like Branly, Hertz, and Marconi, Canadian-born Reginald Fessenden, from his station in Brant Rock, Massachusetts, with his further invention, was able to hear the voicing of the letter "s" being spoken in Cornwall, England and by Christmas Eve, in 1906, he was able to broadcast music by Handel to ships at sea.

Travel by automobile was in its infancy, but already, on poor or non-existent roads, occasioned the "Great Race" of 1908. The Americans raced against French, Italian, and German teams in a trip from New York, across the Bering Strait,  through Siberia and Europe to Paris. The Americans won in what became the famous "Thomas Flyer" automobile (pictured here).

Cross-country travel by air had begun in the late 1930s. Train travel was then supplanted by highways whose design was completed prior to WWII and executed in earnest after the war. Winchester goes on to make the point that..."*Without an engaged and functioning federal government, the development of the country's connective tissue would probably have been either delayed or never achieved at all.*"

Film and the television would further tie the Nation together, and America to the world. However, in the words of Simon Winchester, "*The moment instant communication was within the grasp of all – banker, baker, merchant, soldier, doctor, farmer, and yes, even a hesitant Indian chief – America was bonded and annealed into an almost unbreakable and indivisible one."*

The next chapter looks at Nationalism in Turkey which was born of both civil war and war against foreign powers, much of the time at one and the same time in the first quarter of the 20th century.

Chapter 14

NATIONALISM EXPRESSED
IN TURKEY

As duly noted in the previous Chapter, Nationalism as it developed in the 18th and early 19th centuries was a concept in search of an application. The United States of America was perhaps the first large, non-racially (Black Americans, Native Americans), non-ethnically (English, Scots, Irish, Dutch, French, German) homogenous example of "the Birth of a Nation." In the case of Turkey, using the same analogy, the birthing of modern Turkey required the disintegration of an empire. In any case, all such creations seem to be attended by a certain amount of civil war at their founding and during subsequent trials along the path of sustaining the revolutionary principles that sparked the engines of change.

One may look at the English Civil War, which began during an interregnum of the Stuart monarchy, and concluded in an essentially peaceful revolution in 1688 with a revitalized Parliament and ended with a Dutch Protestant King and Queen, William and Mary. In the American Revolution, serious fighting went on between Colonists who supported the Crown, the Loyalists/Tories and the Rebels/

Whigs. Civil war continued in the American experiment both in the War of 1812 and the more horrific Civil War of 1861-1865. The French Revolution witnessed its revolution, overthrow of a monarchy, followed by a civil war and a bloody Reign of Terror. Revolutions in Italy and Germany experienced a similar process. Each of these revolutions sought to unify a nation around a more liberal or democratic system of government. Each was yet another building block in the formation of a nation as distinct from a Principality, Monarchy, or Empire. Each offered natural geographic borders within which a nation state could distinguish itself from neighboring states. Each offered a common demotic language spoken by its overwhelming majority of inhabitants.

In the case of Turkey, as discussed before, the concepts of nationalism and the right of self-determination had gained currency in the late 18th and early 19thcenturies. Nationalism as a concept certainly informed the Unionist Movement in Turkey. It began with the C.U.P Government in 1908 with its focus on uniting of the geographic core of the Ottoman Empire. It ended with an Independence War and the creation of a new nation-state in 1923 from the ruins of a collapsed empire. As distinct from the Ottoman Empire, the new Turkish Republic linguistically enjoyed an overwhelming majority of Turkish speakers as either their native or their second language. Culturally however, it might be argued that compared to some of the other cases noted, Turkey was less homogenous.

In Turkey's case, racial (Turk, Arab), ethnic and religious (Muslim – Sunni/Alevi, non-Muslim) factors played a primary role in its path to nation-statehood. Religion played varying roles in each of the earlier cases noted above as well. In the Turkish Revolution, it started in the early years of the Unionist Government as being in principle, all encompassing of the religions of its various constituent elements. The exigencies of war and state survival, however, inflamed centuries of distrust between the Sunni government and its millets (minorities), which led to increasingly intolerant policies during WWI, especially toward the Orthodox and Armenian Christians.

During the Independence War, the Nationalists continued the same practices for largely the same reasons. The Greek and Armenian Christians were seen as threats ranging from enemy combatants to threatening internal forces and influences. Both groups were in league with European co-conspirators. Together, these groups and European powers fought against the survival of an emerging Turkish State. Additionally, others, like some Kurdish and Arab groups who fought with the British in Eastern Turkey during the Great War, were also seen as threats to the emerging State. These conflicts with the former Christian millets, Kurds and Arab constituents of the Ottoman Empire were examples of internecine civil war.

In the process of the demise and dissolution of the Ottoman State, the civil strife included tension between those Turks who wished to retain some form of the Ottoman

State and Sultanate and those who wished to completely dismantle any vestiges of the *ancien régime.* This did not happen overnight. When the Sultanate was abolished by the Nationalists, as being nothing more than a pawn of the victorious powers, the pace of iconoclastic reform quickened. At this point, an individual person's confession of his or her religious preferences was tolerated, but officially, the new religion, or ideology, by which to bind the citizens of the Turkish Republic was secularism. Unofficially, while Islam was still the religion of the people, if not the State by 1927, for reasons of homogeneity, increasingly, and to this day, the traditional confession of the majority, one may call them the *Staatsvolk,* was not just Islam. More to the point, it was Sunni Islam. Any deviation from that norm presented an undesirable complication to the "unity" message of the Kemalist Reformers.

While Islamic sectarian factors have divided Turks since the Founding of the Republic, their open wounds have been voiced and are more readily apparent since the 1990s. Another wound of more tragic and lasting import is Turkish Nationalism as expressed before WWI, and more egregiously during that War, is related to the story of the treatment of the Armenians during WWI. It remains a shameful episode that cannot be blamed on the Turkish people as a whole. Like America's treatment of the Native Americans (President Andrew Jackson's administration) discussed in the previous chapter and slavery in a subsequent Chapter, responsibility for what many authorities characterize as genocide must, in varying degrees be laid at the door of stated, or tacit, C.U.P. government policy. Each of these tragedies represents an indelible stain on the birthing of both the American Turkish nations.

Ethnic cleansing, death by violence, starvation and related disease in the context of forced migrations of peoples is not unique to America and Turkey. Its approximate equivalents go back to biblical times and have continued into modern history to the present time. The lethality of ethnic cleansing has only increased since the 1930s. Sadly, the brutality and efficiency of such events is not necessarily related to advanced technology. Large-scale slaughter has continued, from Stalin's time to the situation in Rwanda in the early 1990s, where primitive weapons were the means, machetes and guns.

Wars within Wars, the Armenian Conflict

The relationship between Armenian subjects of the Ottoman Empire and the Muslim Ottomans went from tolerable to intolerable over the course of the 19th century. The Armenian millet had enjoyed relative autonomy for centuries. They paid their taxes and kept their self-government, church, customs and practices. For long stretches of history, they had been termed the "loyal millet" by Ottoman authorities. As described by Ronald Grigor Suny in his book, *Looking toward Ararat: Armenia in Modern History*, the Armenians and Turks enjoyed what might be described as *"benign symbiosis."*

The stories and causes of how the relationship deteriorated are numerous. The results came to be tragic, but not just for the Armenians, especially if one looks at the hundred years leading up to Turkish Independence. The focus here will be on the civil war that transpired between the Turks and Armenians during the Great War and the War of Independence – 1914 to 1923. This period of time must, however, be seen in a larger and longer context in order to more fully understand the hellish circumstances of a succession of wars, killing, and dislocation of the religious and ethnic groups comprising the patchwork quilt of the once strong Ottoman Empire. As noted by author Justin McCarthy in his book, *Death and Exile – the Ethnic Cleansing of Ottoman Muslims, 1821-1922*,

> "Between 1821 and 1922, more than five million Muslims were driven from their lands. Five and one-half million Muslims died, some of them killed in wars, others perishing as refugees from starvation and disease... The contemporary map of the Balkans and the southern Caucasus displays countries with fairly homogenous populations, countries that were created in the wars and revolutions that separated them from the Ottoman Empire. Their ethnic and religious unity was accomplished through the expulsion of their Muslim population."

The tone was set for this hundred-year period with the Greek War of Independence beginning in 1821. As in all subsequent "nationalist movements," outside patron states, Christian powers, aided and abetted these movements in the name of addressing the Eastern Question, which we have discussed in considerable detail. European imperial ambitions, though un-trumpeted, proved to be as, or more important in the rationales, overt or tacit, for interference in the internal affairs of the Ottoman State. Christian missionaries played a role in destabilizing the Empire as noted by McCarthy, *"Missionaries and others taught them a sense of superiority and of community with the European Imperial powers."* He goes on to observe that, "As Christians advanced economically, *Christian pride met traditional Muslim pride, which also presumed superiority based on religion and centuries of dominance."*

In 1861, as quoted in McCarthy's book, historian George Finlay wrote,

"In the month of April 1821, a Muslim population amounting to upwards of twenty thousand souls was living dispersed in Greece, employed in agriculture. Before two months had elapsed, the greater part was slain – men, women, and children were murdered without mercy or remorse... The crime was a nation's crime, and whatever perturbations it may produce must be a nation's conscience, as the deeds by which it can be expiated must be the acts of a nation."

Findlay goes on to note that similar events had taken place in Greek Orthodox Romania, where Greek rebels under Alexander Ypsilantis attempted a revolt in the Balkans with the expectation that Russia would come to their aid. Ypsilantis and his rebels seized Galatz and Iasi in Romania. He describes the results as follows, *"Turks of every rank, merchants, sailors, soldiers were surprised and massacred in cold blood."*

Throughout the balance of the 1800s, as the Ottoman Empire shrank, millions of refugees from the Balkans, the Circassians, Abkhazians, Laz from the Caucasus, and Tatars from the Crimea were set adrift, most of this the result of Russian territorial expansion at the expense of the Ottoman Empire. The cost to the Ottoman Government of maintaining an army engaged in protecting its subjects, with war and rebellion from Egypt to Eastern Turkey, the borderlands north of the Black Sea and the Balkans, left few resources with which to absorb the millions of Muslim refugees.

It is against this tragic backdrop that one must look at the Armenian story. While there is no justification for the harsh treatment these Ottoman subjects received, particularly in the early 1890s and during WWI and the War of Independence, these were traumatic times in the Empire. For much of the 19th century, the Kurds of Eastern Turkey had assisted Ottoman tax collectors in extracting payment from the Armenians, largely peasantry. The Kurds had traditionally put what one might call a surcharge on the taxes as "protection money." As noted by Guenter Lewy, *The Armenian Massacres in Ottoman Turkey – a Disputed Genocide*, *"Large numbers of Armenian peasants existed in a kind of feudal servitude under the rule of Kurdish Chieftains. The settled Armenians provided winter quarters to the nomadic Kurds and paid them part of their crop for protection."* When these people could not bear increasing taxes plus tribute, the Kurds, *"never very benevolent – engaged in savage attacks upon the largely defenseless Armenian villagers that led to deaths, the abduction of girls and women, and the seizure of cattle."*

During this same time, with Nationalism being the new rallying cry, and the success of the Greeks and Bulgarians in their revolutions, Armenian intellectuals began to organize parties (Hanchuks and Dashnaks) for independence. This movement began in the European Diaspora and spread from there into Anatolia. Before the Treaty of Berlin in 1878, by which the Sultan had agreed among many other European dictates, to reform the Armenian areas but had failed to do so, as quoted in Lewy, Lord James Bryce, a friend of the Armenians wrote:

> *"If there had been no Treaty of Berlin...the Armenians would doubtless have continued to be oppressed, as they had for centuries. But they would have been spared the*
> *storm of fire, famine, and slaughter which descended upon them in 1895... Before the Treaty of Berlin the Sultan had no special enmity to the Armenians, nor had the Armenian nation any political aspirations."*

As the Europeans kept leaning on Sultan Abdul Hamid II about the Armenian situation, as quoted in Lewy, the Sultan told the German Ambassador in November of 1894 that he would rather die than submit to *"... unjust pressure and grant the Armenians political autonomy."* To make matters worse, his paranoia regarding Russian and Armenian objectives in the East, modeled after the Russian usage of Cossacks, led him to form regiments totaling some 50,000 Kurdish soldiers known as the *"Hamidiye* Regiments" to police the border areas. As reported by Taner Akçam in his book, *A Shameful Act: the Armenian Genocide and the Question of Turkish Responsibility,* the numbers killed range between 80,000 and 300,000. Looking at various commentaries on the subject, one might safely assume that over 100,000 Armenians and 25,000 Syrian Christians were killed, another 100,000 probably died of disease and starvation, hundreds of churches were converted to mosques and hundreds of Christians were forcibly converted to Islam. With the telegraph in wide use by then, stories of these atrocities reached the Europeans quickly. Even if they were exaggerated, the anti-Turk propaganda publications, in France and England especially, were fast portraying the Sultan as a butcher and the Turks as cruel.

It is also true that there were Armenian reprisals. Muslims died as well, but not in remotely comparable numbers. International sympathy in the West helped the Armenian independence movements. In spite of this sympathy, within the Armenian community, as reported in Lewy, Armenian historian Vahakn N. Dadrian noted that, *"the Revolutionaries were not only opposed by the bulk of the*

Armenian population and of its ecclesiastical leadership, but comprised a very small segment of the population." Lewy goes on to note that the Armenian revolutionaries terrorized their own people if they did not contribute sufficiently to the cause. He quotes American Author George Hepworth in his book, *Through Armenia on Horseback* (1898), *"...the revolutionists are doing what they can to make fresh outrages possible. That is their avowed purpose. They reason that if they can induce the Turks to kill more of the Armenians, themselves excepted, Europe will be forced to intervene."*

Initially, The Young Turks in the Unionist Government that came to power in 1908 tried to ameliorate the situation. In 1909, they even tried and hanged some of those responsible for the murder of Armenians and those responsible for inciting popular riots against them. While the number executed may have been a token, it was the first time Turks had been hanged for murdering Christians. The situation continued to fester in spite of Russian-led efforts in the European community to initiate reforms which would provide relief to the Armenians in the Eastern provinces. Those negotiations and related initiatives died with the assassination of the Hapsburg Arch Duke in June of 1914 and the onslaught of world war by August of that year. By 1915, Russian Armies were invading Northeastern Turkey. With the prospect of Armenian independence in sight, Lewy notes that, *"...when many Armenians manifested open sympathy for the Russian invaders of the eastern provinces, the Young Turks became convinced that only a radical measure such as the wholesale displacement of the Armenian population would provide a permanent solution to the recurring treasonous conduct of the Armenian minority."*

The situation from the outset of WWI was dire in Turkey for Muslim and non-Muslim alike. Lewy quotes the American Ambassador Henry Morgenthau, who described the situation in Turkey in the spring of 1915, as being, *"... deplorable: all over Turkey thousands of the populace were dying daily of starvation."* Conditions were so bad the last two years of the war that, Lewy quoting and Armenian Pastor in Urfa said, *"Starving Armenians and Turks were begging side by side in front of the same market and were together gathering grass from the fields."* In various areas on the Eastern front, by 1918, thousands of Turkish troops were dying of starvation. These dire conditions on both sides notwithstanding, the C.U.P. Government must be held accountable for the ethnic cleansing that took place. The facts of confiscation of Armenian property, mass killing of Armenians, death marches, starvation and forced relocation are undeniable. Estimates of Armenian death murder or starvation vary from 850,000 to 1.5 million, much of it occurring in 1915 but continuing throughout the Great War.

During the War of Independence that followed, with the Bolsheviks having taken the Russian armies out of the field, the post WWI Armenian Government found itself on its own. Support from British and French troops was limited as they were preoccupied by fighting with

Nationalist forces. In the process of taking back land lost in the east by the Treaty of Sèvres, the Nationalist forces, under the command of Kazım Karabekir, Armenian civilians in the area again paid a heavy price with a death toll in the range of 200,000.

To say that the losses on both sides during the eight years of war, while true and must be countenanced when seeking to pass judgment as to culpability. Whether or not the extermination and removal of Armenians was governmentally sponsored and systematically organized to the level of the Nazi extermination of the Jews or not, one must allow for differences of opinion on the applicability and appropriateness of the term genocide. Genocide as a term was coined during the Second World War to describe the Nazi holocaust. Not all scholars find justification for the use of the term genocide in connection with the Armenian tragedy. For just such a view, one might read British historian Norman Stone's article, "There is no Armenian Genocide", who finds it especially repugnant that the French Government could make it a crime to deny that the Armenian tragedy was a holocaust.

Suffice it to say, for decades after these tragic events, official doctrine and explanation left succeeding generations of Turks in many ways either ignorant of the facts, in denial, or a combination of both. In more recent years, a willingness to revisit the history of that period on a professional and academic basis augurs well for a day when admissions on both sides will permit more balanced judgments of the issues and the facts leading, it is hoped, to some measure of healing. Holding recent generations responsible for the excesses of their distant forbears, in the end, provides little redemption for either side. However, some redemption, some attempt to clean the slate is better than continuing to circumvent the rigors of a useful healing process. No side is without some responsibility. The same may be said for Americans today regarding the practice and tragedies related to the institution of slavery a century and a half and more after the fact. Being remorseful for those sins need not run to perpetual condemnation for succeeding generations. The Biblical injunction comes to mind, "let he who is without sin cast the first stone".

When looking at the underlying causes of the Armenian tragedy, one is well-served to look at the intellectual and cultural bases of nationalist policies from the Young Turk period forward as a means of better understanding the principles guiding the Unionist Government and its successor, the Republic of Turkey, under Kemalist one-party rule. Here it is useful to look at the work and influence of one of the leading luminaries of the period, Ziya Gökalp.

Ziya Gökalp and the Homogenization of Ethnicities, Kurds and Others

Imagine you are born in the Province of Diyarbakir in the last decades of 19th century Ottoman Turkey. You grow up in a borderland area of a diminishing empire. Your neighbors are Turks, Armenians, and Kurds. In order to pursue veterinary studies, you leave for Istanbul the very year that Armenian Revolutionaries held up the Ottoman bank in Istanbul. Constantinople, as it continued to be known by many, is a seething hot bed of revolutionary activity inspired by nationalist movements which are eating away at empires, most notably the Ottoman Empire. As an educated person, you have access to European literature where you discover the concepts of "national identity," representative government, and popular sovereignty. You see defeat and chaos around you and learn of the same around the borderlands of the Ottoman Empire. You learn that the Sultan, Abdulhamid, is governing in the face of strong head winds for change, and he is resisting them at every turn. You sense that change is inevitable from forces both within and outside the Empire. You are anxious for the future of your country as you know it. You know that Russians and other Christian nations are propping up the current regime for fear of the chaos that would ensue were it to collapse suddenly. This is the environment that young Mehmed Ziya found when he arrived in Istanbul. In search of meaning and purpose in his life, he would join revolutionary groups, abandon his veterinary studies and throw himself into the revolutionary fray of Constantinople at the turn of the 20th century. He would spend a number of months in the Sultan's prison for his "subversive" activities. Through a friend, he would discover the works of Emile Durkheim and Friedrich Nietzsche. Through their concepts of nationalism and a super race, Mehmed Ziya began to craft his concept of reform and survival for a modernized, notably not specifically westernized, Turkey.

Ziya's synthesis of the idea for the future of Turkey would be a nationalism based upon the model of Japan after the Meiji Reform that had during that time period produced radical and Westernizing reforms without compromising the traditional culture of Japan. It was this latter attribute that most appealed to Ziya. Moreover, the Japanese had just defeated a European power, the Russians, in war in 1905. He joined the Young Turk leaders who were grappling for a set of reforms that could work. He began to write of that future and took the pen name and sir name of Gökalp, meaning "sky hero." He became a well-known journalist and political figure. His concept of nationalism, perhaps a little out of step with his contemporary Unionists, focused on a "social solidarity" that would lead to "cultural unity." Geography was not the defining characteristic. Common language, common culture, common religion, these were to be the cornerstones of the future of Turkey if it were to survive.

After World War I, Ziya was arrested as a member of the Committee of Union and Progress, the defeated government, and was briefly exiled. There he continued to refine his principles of nationalism which were published in 1923 and titled "The Principles of Turkism." Jacob Landau in his book, *Pan-Turkism, from Irredentism to Cooperation*, summarizes Zia's concept of nationalism as, *"a nation [that] is not a racial or ethnic or geographic or political or volitional group but one composed of individuals who share a common language, religion, morality and aesthetics, that is to say, who received the same religion."* I think it is fair to say that Gökalp's Pan-Turanism was not territorially expansionist as much as it was intended to keep alive the kinship connectedness of all Turkic peoples. He has been accused of providing a rationale for ethnic cleansing – specifically of the Armenians. He has also been taken to task for denying the existence of Kurds. Quite possibly actually being part Kurd, I think his take on the matter was that they, the Kurds, were Turks culturally, by virtue of a common language (as educated Kurds spoke Turkish), a common religion and a common culture in the larger sense of the term.

In the end, Gökalp's concept of "Turkishness" (*türkçülük*) appealed to the Kemalist reformers. In their zeal to find cultural commonality among the various ethnic components of post-war Turkey, the revolution and reform they lead brought in its wake, for many, a forced sublimation of factually differing identities. The new Turkey was made up of cultural Turks. Kurds were cavalierly dubbed "Mountain Turks." In retrospect, these policies were draconian, repressive of the various religious, ethnic and even racial differences of a "mixing bowl" of peoples who, Turk or otherwise, found themselves within the diminished borders of the New Republic of Turkey. If the revolution were to succeed, the Kemalists believed, and probably with good reason, it had to be iconoclastic, rigid, persuasive and not seen to be vacillating between the Ottoman world and the new world of a modernizing Turkey.

As to the age-old Eastern Question, it had finally been resolved. The sovereignty of the new Republic was readily accepted by the European powers. These Allies got what they wanted. Christian territories were hived off and substantially ethnically cleansed of Muslims. But for "The Sick Man of Europe," not only were its people pushed beyond human endurance, the loss of human life from 1911-1923 being massive, but Turkey had to absorb hundreds of thousands of Muslim refugees (the Exchange of Populations agreement with Greece and Bulgaria) with precious few resources left for the modernizing task at hand. The mistakes of the previous one hundred years were not lost on the reformers. Leaving the door open to the past was laden with potentially paralyzing risks. It was necessary that the citizens of the New Republic subordinate their religious identity, Muslim and non-Muslim, in favor of a "Turkish" identity, a Turkish Muslim cultural and linguistic identity.

"How Happy I am to Call Myself a Turk"
"Ne mutlu Türküm diyene" was easier for Atatürk to say than it was for many to swallow. If one were a member of the Ottoman elite, that person might feel superior to that particular identity. If one were Kurd, Arab, or Christian, accepting such an identity might have been problematic. Curiously, complicating the future, many Turks born after

WWII, learned this famous saying in elementary school and found it to be a source of pride, grew up thinking Kemal's assertion perfectly accepted and otherwise unremarkable. What may have been lost on later generations of Turks, not to mention people from other countries who hear this obviously patriotic statement, is the fact that at the time Atatürk said it, calling someone a Turk, had different implications. In elite quarters at that time, the word Turk may have referred to simple people, country people, poor and uneducated. Elites might have been thinking "commoner" when they used the term, reserving Ottoman to define their more elevated status. This is why when Mustafa Kemal, a Pasha and a member of the military elite, made a point of saying how happy he was to be a Turk, he was making a statement that was "loaded." It was a message about the pride that citizens of the Turkish Republic in particular, and Turkic peoples in general, who had once ruled, not just Ottomans, over large areas of the earth, from India to Spain, should feel. In fact, it was the common Turk, including the soldiers who had fought alongside and under him from Libya, to Aleppo to Çanakkale, whose identity as a Turk, was being elevated. The foot soldiers of the Nationalist forces in Anatolia, the heartland of Turkey, were those who carried the fight to enemies which had literally surrounded them when the movement began in 1919. And finally, this was a message the Kemalist reformers used, even manipulated, to reinforce the notion that they were all, as Turks, engaged, side by side shoulder to shoulder, in the monumental task of radically transforming Ottoman society to the benefit of all Turks, not just the elites. It was a tactically, sociologically, and philosophically brilliant message, even if some segments of the population were anxious about its implications.

It is more than reasonable to speculate that without such draconian reforms, modern Turkey as we know it today, modern Turkey as distinct from its neighboring countries, Muslim and non-Muslim, would not have materialized. If the country was ready to assume a functionally more democratic government, devoid of ubiquitous military oversight and safe guards, it was not demonstrably obvious. Corruption and cronyism had plagued a Turkey and Turks not accustomed to functioning in a non-hierarchical society in the post WWII era. For some observers today, with the benefit of hindsight, standing in judgment of Kemalist notions of "nationalism" and "statism," might now conjecture that Kemalist policies were doomed to failure from the beginning. The distinction this author would make is the fact that while one might argue that their iconoclastic policies were entirely appropriate for the initial emergence of the Turkish Republic, one might also maintain that they need not have been dogmatically rendered for time immemorial, otherwise offering the possibility in time for a more culturally sensitive application in some areas.

The hallmark of the revolution, Kemalist secularism, has yet to be called into question openly by Turkish leaders.

Here changes in international orientation by the Turkish State, not inappropriately rationalized and fueled by business diversification, opportunity, and success, have exposed secular Turkey to the temptation to reactivate a more Ottoman-like vision of its role in the MENA, more imperially motivated. Turkey is undergoing a traumatic and cathartic struggle to redefine itself in the twenty-first century. It is a titanic struggle, fraught with change and fraught with risks, as the July 15, 2016 military coup revealed. It is sophomoric to dismiss the Ottoman analogy by countering that the times are incomparably different. What seemed to be unthinkable fifteen years ago in Turkey has happened. When ISIS leaders can reference the righting of wrongs which date to the Sykes-Picot Agreement, when Sunni and Shia counter-claims along historic geographic fault lines, one cannot assume that Turkey is immune to the possibility of "backsliding" regarding the spirit of Kemalist secularism. The army is no longer there as a Kemalist guarantor. Too many people in the MENA are animated by beliefs, events and the long memories of history to cavalierly dismiss the possibility that Turkey can be transformed by oil-fueled political-Islam back into something unforeseen by its revolutionary founders. While it is for the Turkish people to sort out the country's future orientation, political Islamist tendencies will be countered by those who value Turkey's commitment to traditional Republican values and the rule of secular law. Regarding this future, the Turkish people may currently never have been so polarized since the late 19th century. The biggest difference between the two eras is the people now are literate and can vote, and it is the Islamists that are holding sway, but only by the thinnest of margins. In the absence of democratic checks and balances, it would appear that the country is largely run by its President alone.

In retrospect, it is easy today to conclude that the suppression of Ottoman religious institutions, by relegating them to a status subordinate to secular law, in the end has never satisfied some pious Sunni elements of Turkish society. Also, some of those same elements may have been satisfied in earlier generations, and their sons and granddaughters may not be today. It may be easy for some to criticize the "excesses" of Kemalism, including the military serving as the guarantor of Kemalist secularism. When doing so, one must ask what the alternatives were that would insure the safe birthing of the Republic, free from the real possibility of civil war(s).

The author was living in Turkey in the late 1970s, when the politicians had made a mess of the country. There were sugar shortages, electric shortages, political murders, and near chaos compounded by a worldwide energy crisis. Both economic and political instability were feeding off each other, leaving the country vulnerable to civil war and possible external intervention from the Soviet Union. Was it wrong for the military to step in, again, in 1980? Did they return power to civilian hands within three years and give room for Turgut Özal to launch Turkey's first economic boom? Yes, the role of the military needed to be curbed. However, that is easier to say after a potential civil war and economic chaos had been averted.

Certainly, the American Union was severely tested by a horrible war in the 1860s. Fortunately, those fearing the Balkanization of Armenia along regional lines concluded that the preservation of the Union was somehow more important than the lives that were shed to keep it. For Turkey and America, the whole was, and is, greater than the sum of the parts. Imagine a Turkey at the end of WWI, in the absence of a unifying secular authority, was governed by some entity, which sought to accommodate all the minorities. The Balkanization of Turkey into Alevi, Sunni, Kurdish, Armenian, Jewish, Anatolian Turkish, and European Turkish zones, would have left an ungovernable patchwork of political factions similar to Lebanon. That is a prospect that Atatürk and the Reformers believed could not be hazarded. Multiculturalism of that kind smacked of Ottoman governance using a "Millet system," with a Ruling class of Sunnis, with the minorities being called citizens, but citizens of second-class legal status. For different reasons, such a prospect Turkey could not then, and Turkey cannot now, sustain indefinitely.

To Atatürk's lasting credit, he knew what had to be done and the risks associated with the compromising of end goals. A leader other than Gazi Mustafa Kemal Atatürk might have been lured on by glory in 1923 to retake some of the borderland territory that was given up in 1922 and 1923, an irredentist urge that continues in some quarters in Turkey today. Part of his greatness, like General Washington's, was to know when and why to avoid the temptation to overreach, to become overextended, tactically or strategically, exposed. It was clear to him that the primary requirement for survival and success was to nurture the new Turkey. What precious energy remained in the Country needed to be spent on making the revolution work. "Peace at home. Peace abroad" was the watchword. "Statism" was not so much a response to years of foreign manipulation and intrusion as it was an economic argument for self-reliance – complete with tariffs – to develop and protect an "infant industry" and a new country for a period of time. Yet, one piece of former Ottoman territory Kemal did think was strategically worth an exception to his otherwise non-expansionary rule.

The 1939 Plebiscite in The Hatay – The Issue of Minorities

Originally settled by the Akkadians in the early Bronze Age, and subsequently controlled by Hittites, Assyrians, Persians, and Greeks, the city of Antioch (*Antakya*) became a regionally significant city under Roman rule. By 638 CE, it had been conquered by the Umayyad Muslims, then the Byzantines, then Seljuks, Crusaders, Mamluks and finally, under Sultan Selim I, the Ottomans in 1516. It was then defined as the Sanjak of Alexandretta, the site of the Mediterranean port city in the area. Writer, Middle

East traveler, archeologist, cartographer, and spy in the employ of the British, Gertrude Bell, in her book, *Syria the Desert and the Sown,* published in 1907, commented on the substantial mix of Arabs and Turks in the area. A demographic map of the area published in 1911 showed a majority of Arabs, with smaller areas of Turks and Armenians.

There are maps dating back to the 18th century showing Alexandretta and the area as being part of Syria. At the end of WWI, the area was occupied by the British. By treaty between the French and the Turkish Governments, the area became autonomous. Under the Treaty of Lausanne, signed and ratified by the Republic of Turkey, responding to French preference, Alexandretta was placed within Syria. By 1925, under the authority of the League of Nations, Syria, including the Hatay area, came under the French Mandate, attached to the State of Aleppo. A census at the time showed that in addition to Arabs, the area contained Sunni Muslims, Alawites, Greek Orthodox, Greek Catholics, Syriac-Maronites, Jews, Syriacs, Kurds, and Armenians. The Hatay was a microcosm of the Middle East. Bashar al Assad's grandfather was an Alawite (*Nusayri's*) living in the mountains of the Hatay at that time. The area continued to be contested in the 1930s. The question arose, should the area be under the control of Turkey or French-mandated Syria?

The reason for dwelling on this story is that the question of State control, official language and cultural sphere of influence squarely placed the question of the Hatay within the geographic province of Atatürk's brand of homogenized nationalism. His interest in the Hatay was not just strategic. Given the recent history in the Levant, Atatürk may well have feared for the safety of the Turkish population by Syrian Arabs when the French would leave. With WWII looming, the French wanted the Turks to remain neutral, if war broke out. With that in mind, they began negotiations with the prospect of handing over the area to the Turkish Republic. In 1938, the Hatay Assembly declared itself a Republic, and with French and Turkish agreement, a plebiscite was to be held to determine the wishes of the inhabitants. "Self-Determination" of the inhabitants would determine the state to which it would be attached.

Atatürk secured this agreement less than three months before he died. To increase the chances of obtaining the desired outcome, he had sent Turkish forces to the Hatay in June of that year. He also had his Ministry of Education announce that the ancient Hittites were actually Turkic people. In fact, the Ministry declared that modern science confirmed that the Hatay had been named for that connection. Of course, the explanation was more than a reach. A year after the Turkish forces arrived, the referendum was held. The outcome of the vote favored Turkish association. It has been suggested by many that the vote was rigged. It may well have been. Certainly, this was a case of fanciful and contrived ethnic and racial homogenization, albeit predicated importantly on strategic considerations.

In any case, for a variety of reasons, this was the only case of an irredentist claim put forth by the New Government. And, the Republic remained true to Kemal Pasha's wish, "Peace at home. Peace abroad." Turkey remained neutral during WWII, husbanding its resources and sustaining its secular government.

As for the Hatay today, Turkey was close to an agreement with Assad's government for Syria to drop its claim in 2010. What a difference a few years can make. Doubtless, the situation will remain officially unresolved as far as the current Syrian Government is concerned. While the Hatay remains on Syrian maps of Syria, it is officially recognized as part of Turkey by the rest of the world. On this matter, the situation is analogous to Turkish Cyprus – a sovereign country only recognized by Turkey.

In the next chapter, further consideration will be given government structural and systematic legal reforms brought forth in the formative years of the Turkish Republic.

Chapter 15

TURKISH GOVERNMENTAL STRUCTURES – EUROPEAN MODELS

Secularization of Governance in Turkey, The *Fez* (Hat) Law and Fashion

With the War of Independence behind them, the President of the new Turkish Republic began the war to end Ottoman forms of government and the institutions that sustained them. Like the War of Independence, it was a battle waged on many fronts. The methods and tools used to wage the war were both draconian and stealthy. The legal reforms were radical, iconoclastic, requiring the abolition of centuries of Islamic institutions, Sharia, and custom. These included the end of the Sultanate (1921) and Caliphate (1923), and the marginalization of the religious elites. What remained of the Islamic Institutions, including *Medresse* Schools and Mosques, were placed under a secular Ministry of Education. More recent research by people like Amit Bein in his book, *Ottoman Ulema – Turkish Republic: Agents of Change and Guardians of Tradition*, indicates that although the secular reformers sought to peripheralize the Ottoman religious architecture, the New Ministry (*Diyanet İşleri Başkanlığı*) was, in the end, staffed by many officials of the pre-revolutionary religious establishment. The same was true of The Directorate of Pious Foundations members of which, according to this author, were at some pains to quietly preserve pieces of the old religious culture. However, Sharia Law and the judges who administered it were summarily replaced by secular courts and judges under the administration of the Judicial Branch of the government. While Islam was removed as the official religion of the State (1927), significantly, it was not politically severed from government. For reasons of cultural sensitivities and so the Reformers could maintain oversight of the Imams and the Mosques, their expenses, wages, and maintenance were covered under the state budget.

Using the French Model of government structure, the new Republic of Turkey, founded in 1923, established a parliamentary system, with three branches, Executive, Legislative, and Judicial. Until a Constitutional Change in the law in 2015, The Executive was headed by a popularly elected Prime Minister under a proportional representation formula. And, with that Constitutional change, the President is also popularly elected. By June 24, 2018, with the passing into law of a referendum held in 2016, the role of Parliament was diminished, the Office of Prime Minister was abolished, and the powers of the President were greatly enhanced, a model loosely patterned after the

American Government, albeit without the same checks and balances. This subject is treated in more detail later in the book.

While the Ottomans had experimented with the institution of a Parliament (*Meclis, 1878*) during the 19th century reforms (*Tanzimat*), it was prorogued in less than three years by the Sultan. The Parliament was brought back in the 1908 revolt, after which the Sultan functioned with newly more limited sovereignty.

As with the case of England in the 17th century, popular sovereignty as expressed through a representative parliament, would also take time and bloodshed to establish. One important difference from early Western experiments with parliamentary democracy in America and France is that the Kemalist Reformers had the benefit of various models of democracy from which to choose. Additionally, they had the benefit of the work of the leading sociologists of the time, Emile Durkheim, whose works we know were influential on Mustafa Kemal, and Max Weber. Kemal and the other Reformers were not wandering in the dark when it came to appreciating the complexities of the task of transforming Turkish society. Only a decade earlier, another famous "Founder of a Nation", the Republic of China in 1912, Sun Yat-sen, had launched a similarly ambitious revolution. In 1904, Max Weber wrote in an article titled "Objectivity,"

> *"There is no absolutely "objective" scientific analysis of culture... All knowledge of cultural reality... is always*

knowledge from particular points of view. ... an "objective" analysis of cultural events, which proceeds according to the thesis that the ideal of science is the reduction of empirical reality to "laws," is meaningless... [because]... the knowledge of social laws is not knowledge of social reality but is rather one of the various aids used by our minds for attaining this end."

Weber's observation points to the challenges and limitations of changing law on the books. These limitations remain operative until, and unless, the source and spirit of the law are accepted and inculcated, and become a functional attribute of the legal culture and practice of a people and nation. In order for this to happen, the historic legal cultural norms of Turkic custom and Sharia Law needed to substantially retreat in the hearts, minds, and practice of the people, and, in turn, be replaced by the new legal norms in the consciousness of significant constituencies of the Turkish people. This was a process requiring ultimate "buy-in" over many decades and succeeding generations of secular education and secular governance. Before looking at the wholesale importation of systems of laws designed to regulate the commercial, penal, and civil systems of law and legal practice, it is instructive to look at the Hat Law of 1925 as an eminent example of iconoclastic change that treaded perilously toward the objective of altering mindsets by outlawing a cultural symbol that was part and parcel of Turkish identity. The Hat Law also shows the limits of change at a point in time. It was one thing to require a change in dress and hat attire for civil servants, and quite another to mandate change, for example, in women's traditional dress codes.

What's in a hat? Especially coming from a military background, Kemal knew that outward appearances were important. The fez symbolized the Ottoman past. Brimmed hats he deemed would result in Turkish citizens looking like "civilized" Europeans. As noted in Yasemin Doğaner's, "The Law on Headdress and Regulations on Dressing in the Turkish Modernization" article, *"While the fez replacement of the wadded turban was considered as a symbol of progress during the reign of Mahmut II, it became the sign of conservatism during the era of Atatürk."*

A fine line had to be drawn. Something as public and visible as customary dress had to be dealt with carefully. Recognizing that any attempt to outlaw anything like a head covering (*başörtüsü*) for women could only backfire, as head covering was and remains a sign of modesty and respect in the "traditional" eyes of both religion and custom. Shortly after passing the Hat Law, some of Kemal's political associates suggested he do the same regarding women's veils. As noted in *Turkey in My Time*, A. E. Yalman reported that Kemal responded to such a suggestion as follows:

> *"You can't catch me doing that. When religious prejudices and men's jealousy over their women's faces being seen in public are coupled in this problem, it becomes most difficult to cope with. No legislation about veils! There is*

a natural law, which will take care of it more easily than any written law. It is called fashion".

While the Koran stipulates no particular head dress, Kemal's own mother wore a head covering. But his adopted daughters would, with his encouragement, lead the way by sporting western dress. When promoting the new Hat Law, Mustafa Kemal chose a bastion of conservatism in the Black Sea area of Turkey, *Kastamonu*, to make the announcement. Between 1925 and 1934, a series of laws were passed regarding dress codes, including for schoolchildren – all fashioned after Western dress.

Resistance to the Hat Law was immediate. While many wore no hat, or wore Western-style hats with brims, others continued to where the *fez*. Records indicate that over 800 people were arrested for violating the new law. Fifty-seven were executed including the famous case of İskilipli Atif Hoca, a Muslim cleric, and Madresse teacher. In his trial, he claimed that Muslims wore the *fez* to distinguish themselves from "infidels." Aping the Western dress, he went on to observe, was a tacit acceptance of the immoral practices of Westerners, including alcohol, prostitution, theater, and dance.

To meet the practical objection of brimmed hats for Muslim prayer, Atatürk suggested that the English tweed sports cap would be ideal in that it could be worn backwards for prayer. Train car loads of these hats were shipped to Turkey during those years. Not surprisingly, negative reaction to the secular reforms continued in many quarters and parts of Turkey.

Disenfranchisement of the Religious Institutions and Elites, Closing Tekkes

The new government received a shock in December of 1930, the *Menemen* incident. It was believed that the secular reforms were beginning to settle into the hearts and minds of the people. A Nakshibendi Sufi Dervish, Mehmet Efendi, rallied an armed crowd calling for the restoration of the Caliphate and Sharia Law. A squad of local garrison troops arrived under the command of Lt. Mustafa Fehmi Kubilay. One of the soldiers fired a bullet, apparently wooden, into the crowd. The crowd then rioted, beheading the Lieutenant and killed two municipal watchmen. Several of the rioters were also killed in the incident. Clearly, the road to secularism would be loaded with pitfalls.

The closing of the Tekkes (Sufi centers of worship) and the confiscation of their property in 1925 did not destroy the influence and practice of Sufism. One is reminded of the great Persian mystic and poet Saadi in his poem Gülistan,

"*Of what avail is frock, or rosary,*
 Or clouted garment? Keep thyself but free
 From evil deeds, it will not need for thee

To wear the cap of felt: a darwesh be
In heart, and wear the cap of Tartary."

The Reformers reacted to the *Menemen* incident by further clamping down on vestiges of the Ottoman past by expanding the secularizing school programs, translating the Koran into Turkish and converting the Muslim call to prayer from Arabic into Turkish. These new rules were couched in the reformist rationale of nationalism, continuing the effort to create a Turkish identity common to all. President Mustafa Kemal had made this perfectly clear in his speech in Kastamonu in 1925.

> *"In the face of knowledge, science, and of the whole extent of radiant civilization, I cannot accept the presence in Turkey's civilized community of people primitive enough to seek material and spiritual benefits in the guidance of sheiks. The Turkish republic cannot be a country of sheiks, dervishes, and disciples. The best, the truest order is the order of civilization. To be a man it is enough to carry out the requirements of civilization. The leaders of dervish orders will understand the truth of my words, and will themselves close down their lodges [tekke] and admit that their disciplines have grown up."*

In retrospect, as noted in a Turkish Review article, "A History of the Headscarf Ban in Turkey" from October 1, 2012, opposition to the reforms quietly continued, especially in rural areas.

"By extending their secularization drive beyond the formal, institutionalized Islam, the Kemalists now touched such vital elements of popular religion as dress, amulets, soothsayers, holy sheikhs, saints' shrines, pilgrimages and festivals [sic]. The resentment caused by these measures, and the resistance put up against them was far greater than, for instance, in the case of the abolition of the caliphate [...] While the government succeeded in suppressing most expressions of popular religion, at least in the towns, this did not, of course, disappear. To a large extent, the *tarikat* went underground. But through the simultaneous imposition of an authoritarian and -- especially during the 1940s -- increasingly unpopular regime and suppression of popular Islam the Kemalists politicized Islam and turned it into a vehicle for opposition."

Turkic Custom, Sharia Law in the Face of Wolesale Importation of European Law Codes

Turkish legal culture, custom in the general area of dispute resolution was in practice an amalgam of ancient Turkic custom with centuries of Islamic, Byzantine, and Persian customs, practices, laws, and institutions. At the top of the pyramid was the Caliph, the Grand Mufti, the Imams, and moving down to the Village headmen (*muhtar*), and the Councils of the Elderly (İhtiyarlar). However successful in so many ways over the decades that Kemalist reforms proved to be, its limitations are squarely addressed in the excerpt below taken from the October 1, 2012 Turkish Review article, "A History of the Headscarf Ban in Turkey."

"In contrast, in the towns and cities the push towards a secular state helped create a new secular elite consisting of bureaucrats, officers, teachers, doctors, lawyers and entrepreneurs of larger commercial enterprises" -- a group that would grow and dominate Turkish politics into the 21st century and become known as the "secular bloc." This group became vested in the new reforms, which gave them a privileged edge over the pious masses, and created a secular-Islamic split in Turkey that survives to this day. In summary, outwardly religious people retreated from the public sphere at this time -- but while they took a low profile, they did not disappear."

With a secular system of government established in 1923 at the founding of the Turkish Republic, it was only a matter of time before the Reformers turned their attention to a replacement of the Sharia and Sharia courts. The primary issue at the time was a determination of which Codes to import. As stated by the Chief Reformer in his 1925 Kastamonu speech, President Mustafa Kemal stridently offered the following:

"We must liberate our concepts of justice, our laws and our legal institutions from the bonds which, even though they are incompatible with the needs of our century, still hold a tight grip on us."

Ottoman reforms, designed to be acceptable to Europeans in hopes of and in exchange for dropping the special laws and rules, known as Capitulations, for the non-Turkish millets (nationalities) included a new Commercial Code introduced in 1850. Most of the 19th century legal reforms were inspired by French law Codes. With the apparent success of the transplantation of the Prussian/German Commercial Code used in Japan during the Meiji Reformation, and an increased familiarity with their German as wartime allies, the German Commercial Code was translated into Ottoman Turkish and adopted in 1925. Culturally, this area of law was easier to absorb. It had two advantages. It enhanced the prospects of trade with the West and affected only the commercial area of life in Turkey, outside and beyond the home.

Turkey also did not want to put all its legal eggs in one basket. The socio-religious rigor underlying the Italian Penal Code had a certain appeal and created another connection with another country, and one with which they had not just been at war. The impartial application of any law is always a different matter, regardless of how modern and scientifically crafted. Penal laws are perhaps especially susceptible to abuse. They were used to enforce compliance with the goals of nationalism and the policies of Kemal and the Reformers. The same or similar penal laws may again be used to manage outcomes desired by new Turkish leaders with a different agenda. The Rule of Law can be subverted as noted by Journalist Mustafa Akyol, who wrote the following on January 10, 2014 in the Op Ed section of the *New York Times* in an article titled "Turkey Needs Justice for All":

"For the past month, Turkey has been plagued by an all-out political war between the government of Prime Minister Recep Tayyip Erdoğan and certain elements within the judiciary and the police. No one knows how it will end, but its meaning for Turkey's troubled democracy is already clear: There is little rule of law here, and "justice" easily falls victim to power.

This is a problem with deep historical roots. When Mustafa Kemal Atatürk founded the modern Turkish Republic in 1923, he devised the legal system as the protector of his "revolution" — rather than citizens' rights. His politically motivated "Independence Courts" executed or imprisoned many dissidents. Soon, Turkey imported its penal code from Mussolini's Fascist Italy, where the law simply served the state, not the citizens."

The point made above about the application of the Penal Law, is not applicable to the Civil Law. Yes, change was being enforced, but here the "rights of the people" were better balanced in the sense of "human rights" as we use the term today than was the case under Sharia law, as will be discussed below.

The most controversial, the most iconoclastic, the most ambitious of the legal reforms was in the area of Family Law. This body of law is contained in the Civil Code which governs the Law of Persons, Marriage and Divorce and Inheritance. This was the reform which would strike most deeply, most uncomfortably, at the Turkish and Islamic legal culture of Turkey and its people. The Code concerned interpersonal and familial relations that were now to be governed by a European law code the organizing principles of which were based on Roman Law, Judeo-Christian norms, and produced in the universities of an "infidel" Europe.

The Swiss Civil Code Becomes the Turkish Civil Code

The selection of which European Civil Code to adopt was more challenging than the choice of Commercial and Penal Codes. The French, or Napoleonic Code, dated to 1804 and was considered old. The decision to go with Europe's newest code offered a number of obvious advantages. Switzerland was a "neutral" country – not engaged in Europe's wars for centuries. Its code was thought to be the most scientific. It had been written in 1907 and only promulgated into law in 1912. As such, it was thought to be an amalgam of the best features the various European Codes which had preceded it. As Switzerland had Cantons, or provinces, with four different linguistic and cultural groups, the Swiss Code gave more "judicial discretion" (*takdir hakkı*) in applying the law to the facts of a case. In short, it was a law that countenanced the equal importance of its French-, Italian-, German- and Romanche- speaking populations. The Code in Switzerland was actually translated into three of its prominent linguistic groups and deemed equally applicable. It was specifically designed to accommodate the multi-cultural nature of Switzerland. The Turkish legal reformers thought that such a code would lend itself to the multi-cultural aspects of Turkish society, without pandering to Turkey's Sharia norms and practices. The added advantage of allowing the judge some room to interpret the law led them to believe that new law and its underlying norms would settle more comfortably, over time, geographically, across the various socio-economic groups. It was assumed that the educated elites, clustered more in the Western part of the country, would gravitate to the law relatively more quickly. They did.

To more thoroughly understand the theory and intent of the law, the new government expended considerable time and effort studying Swiss commentaries on the law. Of course, the increased judicial discretion could be a two-edged sword. For reasons noted above, those who joined the new government, joined in the spirit of modernization and Westernization. Once on board, they were reluctant to back-peddle. The author's own Doctoral Research looked carefully into the subject of the question of the degree to which the interpretation and implementation of the Code faithfully followed the spirit and letter of the Law. To this end, randomappellate level, the Court of Cassation (*Yargıtay, Aile Hukkuku Dairesi*)), decisions in Divorce Cases from 1926 to 1976 were examined. The Latin Alphabet Reform came two years after the adoption of the Code which made the cases easier to read. By a stroke of great fortune, my Turkish language teacher in Ankara in the late 1970s was a lawyer by training. The cases were therefore reviewed with the benefit of one trained in Turkish law assisting interpreting the different rulings and judgments.

Cases from the first two years (1926-1927), in Ottoman Script (*Osmanlıca*), were translated by a then recently retired Pasha (Corps General) whose early years of education began with Ottoman Script. Back to the totality of the review, in short, looking at the lower court rulings, which were very largely upheld at the Appellate level, allowed for the conclusion that the law was, at least within the author's sample, being strictly and uniformly applied by the Lower Courts (*Mahkemeler*). Additionally, having looked at a small sample of the Swiss appellate cases, in French, it certainly appeared that the Turkish courts were, on the whole, interpreting and applying the law consistently with Swiss practice.

The Swiss Civil Law was so progressive when it was written that among the six grounds for divorce, the sixth ground was "incompatibility" (*geçimsizlik*). In 1926, that concept had not been introduced into the other European Codes. Somewhat surprisingly, in the late 1970s when doing my research, "incompatibility" had only been introduced under New York law earlier in that same decade. One of the other aspects of the Swiss Law that appealed to the Reformers is that the law was designed to give the benefit of the doubt to the presumed weaker party. In divorce cases, under normal circumstances, the weaker party was usually deemed the woman.

Needless to say, a woman having an equal right to divorce, and to have a divorce settlement that might favor her, was, in a world of divorce having been a unilateral male right (*talaq*), was considered anathema in many quarters in Turkey in the early decades of its application. Having said this, Islamic Law did allow, however rarely used, divorce by mutual consent with the involvement of Sharia Courts (*khul*/forfeiture of woman's dower and *mubaraa*/a mutual release). Equally clearly, this was a law that sat "on the books" for a long time in many quarters and parts of Turkey. Furthermore, one had to have a civil marriage (*resmi nikah*) in order to seek a divorce in a Civil Law court. The husband and wife had to be registered citizens. Civil marriages required the man to be at least 18 and the woman 17. By contrast, Islamic Law on this subject stipulated only the need to have reached puberty. The Civil Code required Birth certificates as proof of age. In practice, males were often only registered several years after they were born in order to postpone military service and road tax. The man and the woman were supposed to have health certificates. Men might object to the idea of a male doctor examining the woman. Doctors were often as far away as the courts. In short, there were many practical hurdles to the Civil Code's acceptance. In fact, some civil laws had to be suspended or amended from time to time. For example, in 1938 the law was amended to lower the marriageable ages to 17 and 15, male and female respectively. In addition, the issue of polygamous marriage was legitimized by special laws in 1932, 1934, 1945, and 1950.

The people more often than not continued to recognize the sanctity of marriage only when it was performed by an Imam (*imam nikahı*). To this day, no matter how secular, even the well-educated still observe the traditional practice a civil marriage made culturally legitimate with Imam wedding, usually right the civil ceremony. Nevertheless, divorce cases did come to the Civil Courts from the beginning, and not exclusively brought only by the wealthy and educated. Other factors tended to combine to create incentives to have a civil marriage, even if socially and culturally, the Imam marriage remained the norm. Interestingly, one of the incentives came in the course of the Korean War. If a woman's husband was either wounded or killed in action, the Government paid some benefits to the spouse. Even the less educated people whose sons were going to be drafted into the army or whose daughters were going to marry someone who would be called up to serve under the laws of a compulsory draft, soon came to the ready conclusion that it made little sense not to take out such an "insurance policy."

After Turkey joined NATO and entered into the Korean War effort, the practice of having "dual" marriages began to become the norm. More educated and wealthier people found the civil marriage, in the possible event that a marriage could fail, especially the woman's family, found the Civil Law an enlightened and sensible practice. If parties to a dispute chose not to register their marriages, and the Government was unaware for whatever reason, marital disputes could be and were resolved using Islamic practices. Certainly, this was for some decades after the civil marriage laws went into effect, the practice among the poor and rural in particular. Even where a marriage was registered, the families might agree to allow the parties to divorce on grounds of incompatibility and sort out any financial implications privately, using customary practice guided by relatives, the Headman, or the Village Elders. Variations on the usefulness of Civil Law Divorce practice ranged. Where both parties, or the families of both parties, agreed that a divorce was warranted, the civil courts were often seen to be of marginal value, costing money and time. But where one party/family felt that the grounds for divorce were unfair, and especially when there were young children involved, fathers/families of the aggrieved party, typically the wife, would avail themselves of the more equitable justice they could expect to find in a civil court proceeding. Under *Hanefi* law formulas, the accepted Turkish Sunni School of Jurisprudence, the institution of *talaq,* or the unilateral male right of divorce, was given its most inequitable license. The new Civil laws, however inconvenient, offered an opportunity to resolve a marital dispute more equitably, and certainly from the woman's point of view. If these new laws flew in the face of custom, they certainly worked together with other reforms, to enhance the status of women as partners to the institution of marriage in Turkey.

In the course of research, instances were found where the Court of Cassation judges tended to read into the Swiss Law an interest to establish the details of the basis of the breakdown of the marriage – a practice not strictly called for by the Code. The result of this could have the counter effect of discouraging parties from entering into the civil law process. Although my research did not support such a general characterization, others may have different conclusions. As K. Lipstein noted in his article, "Reception of Foreign Law in Turkey", in *International Social Science Bulletin*,

> *"It would seem, however, that the Turkish Court of Cassation has discarded the purely objective approach of Swiss law and requires evidence of the respondent's guilt for the breakdown of the marriage before a decree of divorce can be granted. This practice discloses a deliberate or unconscious desire to curb the number of divorces where the law itself does not show such a tendency."*

Inheritance laws historically had been highly developed in Islamic Jurisprudence. The Prophet Muhammad himself famously said in reference to the laws of inheritance, understanding them is *"half the sum of all useful knowledge."* One might begin by saying that Koranic Inheritance Law, as laid out in the "Verse of Bequests," differed from strict agnatic rules of succession in the Arab tribal custom. Women and daughters, while receiving smaller shares than husbands and sons, were entitled to some shares. It is also true that Turkic custom and practice vis à vis Sharia inheritance law did not usually follow the letter of the law. What is critical to understand is that in intestate succession under Sharia and Turkish practice, parents of the deceased were entitled to a share. In certain cases, male collaterals, uncles would also inherit. Such practices insured that the elders, fathers in particular, would inherit from their married children, especially sons. The institution of polygamy potentially compounded this by virtue of the practice of marrying widows to their agnatic cousins by marriage. There are two notable results of this system. One, it tended to support the preservation of the patrilineal extended family. Two, it tended to result in shares that could easily be become miniscule. In an agrarian society, the principal object of inheritance is land, especially before an economy becomes thoroughly monetized. In general, succession was usually handled informally, away from the courts even before the imposition of Swiss Law in Turkey.

Without going into details, the new Civil Inheritance Laws were particularly repugnant to many people, again especially those still living in extended families. The Western Codes were predicated on the maintenance of the nuclear family. The Swiss Civil code introduced the notion of equality of the sexes and the notion of excluding the parents of the deceased where there are descendants. Popular acceptance of the first notion came more easily and sooner than the second. As Paul Stirling notes in his book, *Turkish Village*, written in the 1960s:

> *"Occasionally, when the stake is high or when the parties are more interested in victory over the enemies than economic advantage, villagers do go to the law, and cases of this kind are sufficient to clog the national machine and keep it permanently in arrears. But in most cases, the threats are idle, and only a tiny percentage of land disputes actually reach the courts."*

In conclusion, the Civil Courts are now used extensively in Turkey to resolve disputes. Marriages are civilly registered. Anecdotally speaking, it is probably safe to say that Imam religious ceremonies continue as much as ever, both in Istanbul and in the hinterlands. The pace of change during Atatürk's Presidency was dizzying and often resented and disregarded where possible. All the religious and cultural disruption caused by the Revolution notwithstanding, without the Independence War and iconoclastic reform, modern Turkey would likely have become a mere shadow of its current state. Had the kinds of incremental reform that had plagued the 19th century Ottoman Empire continued, while less shocking to the traditional legal culture, arguably Turkey might have been largely dismantled, Balkanized at best. It helps if one keeps in mind that the Kemalists were in the main frustrated Young Turks. From their perspective, the risks of moving too slowly were greater than the risks of moving too fast. As I. E. Postacıoğlu stated in his article, "The Technique of Reception of a Foreign Code," regarding Kemal's revolutionary tactics, *"It was the typical Atatürk method of acting quickly and almost by surprise, without leaving the cantankerous and the captious the time to riposte."*

It must also be remembered that during the negotiations for the Treaty of Lausanne in 1923, a number of the signatories were hesitant to remove the demand to maintain the Capitulations. Representing Turkey in those discussions was İsmet İnönü, later President of Turkey after the death of Atatürk, who at the bargaining table implied that Turkey would in due course adopt a European form of law. This expectation resulted in a willingness of the Christian Allies to drop the retention of the system of Capitulations. Atatürk and his fellow reformers did not disappoint in this regard. As political developments unfolded, the Democrat Party, and again in the 1990s with Necmettin Erbakan's Islamist Party (*Refah Partisi*), and currently with the appeal of the current Ruling Islamist party (*Ak Parti),* Turkey did not forget its Ottoman and Islamic past. The battle between Secularists and Islamists and the future direction of the country continues.

We will now turn our attention to how and when Americans met Turks in history.

Chapter 16

PERCEPTIONS AND EXPERIENCE – HOW AND WHEN AMERICANS MET TURKS

If one were to ask young Americans and young Turks when they thought their countries first had any real contact, you might hear the Cyprus Intervention / Invasion (1974). If one is an American above the age of forty, one might remember President Nixon's anti-drug war policies and the implications of that policy from the movie *Midnight Express*. Certainly, Turks of that same age, whose name might be "Barış" ("Peace") would have learned from their parents when they got older that the name became popular for babies born in the late 1970s in the aftermath of the Cyprus debacle. Their parents might have told them that the American Government, under the influence of the Greek-American lobby, sided with Greece and the Greek Cypriots and/or that the British had abdicated their responsibility as a Guarantor under the Tri-Partite Agreement (1960) governing Cyprus. Only much later would some Americans learn, mostly only those who follow International Relations in that part of the world, that the attempted annexation of Cyprus by mainland Greece was based on a military plot supported by the American CIA. If they were older, in their 80s in the 21st century, you might hear that soldiers met during the Korean War. Certainly, young people today in both countries might think, that the Second Gulf War and the Turkish Parliamentary decision (a very close vote) to not make the İncirlik Air base available to America and its Coalition forces, was the first substantive intercourse between these countries.

Turks today, young and old, will remember many things about U.S. Turkish relations that might include, from the Turkish Perspective, the infamous Hood event (*Cavuş olayı*) in 2003, President Barack Obama's address at in the Turkish Parliament in 2009, the American Diplomatic and Foreign Affairs establishment support of the rise of Recep Tayyip Erdoğan and his current Ruling Party, indirect American support of the Kurdish PKK terrorists in the Syrian debacle, the American harboring of the Fethullah Gülen, the Muslim Cleric alleged to have lead the attempted coup against the Turkish Government and President Erdogan in 2016, and a raft of largely U.S.-Turkey relations since in the most negative in the history of the relationship.

Americans in general, due to America's geographic relative isolation from the other Continents, tend to have relatively little concept, let alone understanding, of U.S.-Turkey relations. This is true of U.S. International Relations in general. Exceptions to these generalizations arise due to various segments of the population that have familial, artistic, professional, commercial, military, and government ties which bring a Turkey-specific focus to those relations. There are, however, issues and subjects, which have captured the attention of Americans in general. Some of this attention is seen in a negative light, some in a positive light. Personal, and business to business, experiences tend to fair better than government to government relations.

Further, one might postulate that perceptions and experiences tend to be limited to a time span of three generations. Children and grandchildren often learn from their grandparents. Unless one is a student of history, foreign relations, anthropology, linguistics, and similar disciplines, the average person is therefore likely to have impressions and perceptions that are carried along a time frame of plus or minus seventy-five years. Of course, the history, both positive and negative memories, of any one group may be passed down through many generations. That is a history particular to that group. One might be descended from those who fought for the South in the American Civil War. One might be descended from an Asia Minor Greek whose forebears fled from Smyrna at the end of the Turkish War of Independence. One might be descended from someone who fought "Johnny Turk" at Gallipoli. One might be a Turk whose parents were "Gastarbeiter" (Guest Worker) in Germany. And one might be of African slave or immigrant Irish extraction. In these particular cases, one's perceptions, related to that particular history, may be carried down for hundreds of years. This reality and these exceptions notwithstanding, for the average person, one may say that for that person, history starts when one's grandparents were born, if not more recently.

Of course, general perceptions, interpretations, and stereotypes are in the eyes of the beholder and may come down through the ages in the lore, if not the facts, of racial, ethnic, and tribal group memory. America's history with the Turks starts with its European ancestors whose collective memories might be said to date from the time of the Crusades and Moorish Spain. Turks'history with America, as America is a younger country, begins more significantly in the 19th century. In any case, the history of relations between the two countries goes back well beyond the post-World War II era.

European Images of Turks Reach the New World, from Jamestown Forward

American Colonists' oldest perceptions of Turkey may be dated to Jamestown Settlement Governor, Captain John Smith, in the early 1600s. Before coming to America, John Smith had served as a mercenary against the Ottoman Turks, was captured, imprisoned and escaped. Smith's opinion/bias, as reported by author Michael Oren in his book, *Power, Faith, and Fantasy – America in the Middle East 1776 to the Present*, was shared by the Colonial Treasurer of the Virginia Colony, George Sandys, who had traveled to the Middle East in 1610 and concluded, *"I think there is not in the world an object that promises so much...to the beholders, and entered, so deceiveth the expectation."* Massachusetts Bay Colony's leading minister, John Cotton Mather and Harvard's first president, Samuel Langdon (early 1700s), both called for the destruction of the Ottoman Empire to make way for the Jews to return to their ancestral lands. Arguably, the Bible was Colonial Americans' original source of conception of the Middle East, including images of temples, hanging gardens, oases, and deserts. To this was later added the allure of the Persian story of, *A Thousand and One Arabian Nights*, which appeared in English in the early 1700s and was very popular in Colonial America. At this point, the image Americans had was indirect, if any, coming through such stories and the writings of some European travelers to the Middle East. In sum, the perceptions may be thought to have been based on the fantasies of Ali Baba, Sinbad, and Scheherazade, tempered by images of a barbarous people dating from the Crusades onward.

The first real contacts with the Turks and Arabs came via shipping commerce that had grown to some significance by the 1770s. As reported by Oren, it is estimated that, by the time of the American Revolution, one-fifth of American colonial export was bound for the Mediterranean in some 100 American ships. American merchantmen were carrying timber, tobacco, sugar, and rum, "Boston Particular," in particular, in exchange for Oriental delicacies and Turkish opium.

By the end of the 1700s, America's first Middle East explorer, a Connecticut Yankee by the name of John Ledyard, landed in Alexandria in 1788. Earlier, during the American Revolution, he had sailed with Captain Cook on an expedition (1779) to the Pacific, jumped ship in Oregon and wrote of his travels in what became America's first adventure book, a best seller. Later, in Paris, he befriended Franklin, Jefferson, Tom Paine, and John Paul Jones. From Egypt, Ledyard wrote his new friend Thomas Jefferson, as quoted in Oren's book, describing Alexandria as being gripped by, *"Poverty, rapine, murder, tumult, blind bigotry, cruel persecution, [and] pestilence!"* Ledyard traveled down the Nile to Cairo where he learned from the Venetian Counsel that while Westerners referred to Middle Easterners as Orientals, they referred to Europeans and Americans by the term "Franks," in the context, a pejorative term dating to the Crusades. Ledyard continued to write about the area and, according to Oren, with some fondness for the liberty enjoyed by a nomadic people who traveled across deserts on camels, irrespective of borders and governments, which image would in the West, be conflated with the image of colonial frontiersmen and later Western cowboys. Ledyard even fought with the Mamluks in a civil war on the side of the Ottomans.

Other more positive and alluring images came with Mozart's comic opera, *The Abduction from the Seraglio,* about a Spanish woman rescued from an Ottoman harem. Others followed like Joel Roberts Poinsett, who explored

Persia in 1806, discovered a plant, later named for him (Poinsettia), and a pool of oil which he speculated could be used as a fuel. He would later go on to become Secretary of War under President Martin Van Buren.

Thomas Jefferson served as Minister Plenipotentiary to France from 1785 to 1788. Like John Adams before him, Jefferson spent much of his time trying to negotiate the release of crews of American merchant ships captured by the Arabs of the Barbary Coast of North Africa. They sailed out of the ports of Morocco, Algiers, Tunis, and Tripoli, ruled by Beys and Deys who, with the exception of Morocco, paid tribute monies to the Ottoman Sublime Port. The system of bribery to have safe passage, or for the return of ships, had been the practice of European powers for at least four centuries at that point.

**Adams and Jefferson, Paying Tribute
Money and Ransom to Barbary States**
Jefferson tells of an encounter he and Adams had in London with the Representative of the Dey of Algiers, Abd al-Rahman who, in response to an American offer of a small tribute and a Treaty of Friendship, repeated his demand for a million dollars reputedly saying,

> "It was written in the Koran, that all Nations who should not recognize Moslem authority were sinners, that it was their right and duty to make war upon and slaves of all they could take as prisoners, and that every Mussulman who should be slain in battle was sure to go to Paradise."

The Barbary Pirates and the Threat
to American Sovereignty

While it is true American colonists and their ships had been illegally seized from time to time for more than 100 years, the vulnerability to piracy dramatically increased when in 1776, the New Republic declared its independence and found itself no longer under the mantle of the British Navy. Women were especially prized for harems. Sailors were enslaved and often brutalized, dying in far off prisons or sometimes ransomed. Even European navies would forcibly impress American sailors. As noted above, two of America's diplomats, Jefferson in Paris and Adams in London, spent a great deal of time trying to rescue ships and sailors, generally with inadequate ransom monies authorized by the new American Government, which preferred to pay the pirates than to build a Navy and fight them. Every time a ransom was paid, another ship would be seized and more ransom money sought. The American Government at the time operating under the Articles of Confederation, could not even raise national taxes to meet the ransoms sought.

America was groaning under a mountain of debt and weary of entangling "old world" alliances. With no friends in Europe, Ben Franklin quipped, *"If there were no Algiers, it would be worth England's while to build one."*

One example of piracy is the 1784 capture by Algerian raiders of the Betsy, a 300-ton brig out of Boston. With the aid of a double bank of oars, the Algerines aligned their ship's gunwales with the Betsy and according to one sailor's account, bare-chested in turbans and wearing pantaloons, they boarded with *"sabers grasped in their teeth and their loaded pistols in their belts."* Richard Henry Lee remarked, *"Curse and doubly curse the Algerines for these pirates I fear have certainly made war on our commerce."*

While there were many other critical factors and issues in the Constitutional debates, it can certainly be argued that the Barbary threat was of great significance in shifting the balance of opinion in favor of the Federalists and a stronger Central government as noted in an earlier chapter. The Constitution, officially adopted on the 4th of March 1789, empowered Congress to declare war and *"to provide and maintain a navy."* Adopting the Constitution and enforcing its provisions proved to be easier said than done.

Jefferson was recalled from Paris in 1789 to assume the role of Secretary of State during George Washington's first term as President. Pirate depredations continued. With mixed emotions on the subject, Jefferson on the one hand argued in favor of Congressional input on the determination of foreign policy, fearing as he said, a President acting like an *"Algerine."* On the other hand, he observed, *"...the liberation of citizens has an intimate connection with the liberation of our commerce in the Mediterranean,"* he explained to Congress. He continued to try to find a joint solution to the Barbary problem with various European nations. But, with war looming between France and England, no country was interested in supporting American interests in the Mediterranean. Which European country would wish to foster Yankee competition in its own backyard? In the end, political and economic factors aside, by March of 1794, on a narrow vote, Washington signed into law a bill authorizing an outlay of $688,888.82 for the building of six frigates *"adequate for the protection of the commerce of the United States against Algerian corsairs."*

While the government hemmed and hawed about disbursing the money, diplomatic efforts, ransom, and tribute continued to be authorized. It has been estimated that as much as 20% of U.S. Government revenues annually were being diverted to the Barbary States in the form of gold, precious stones, and perversely, cannon powder and gunboats.

Adding insult to injury, by the late 1790s, America, during what came to be known as the Phony Wars, found its ships being captured and sailors impressed into both the French and English navies. By 1799, America finally launched three of the six frigates commissioned by Congress, ships with a complement of 124 guns (the United States, the Constitution, and the Constellation) and strengthened by a newly created Marine Corps. These small but potent forces went on to successful battle against the French in the Caribbean who had sought to interrupt "neutral" trade with British colonies.

From 1800 to 1807, a time known in American History as the Tripolitan Wars, under the authority of President Thomas Jefferson, a Captain William Bainbridge received orders to sail the new frigate George Washington to the Middle East, the first U.S. Navy ship to enter the Mediterranean. In its hold was some $500,000 worth of tribute with goods all destined for Algiers. Upon arrival, Cpt. Bainbridge was apparently expecting a show of respect. As reported by Oren, the Ruler, Hassan Dey, scoffed at the Captain and said *"you pay me tribute, by which you become my slaves."* He ordered Bainbridge to transport the tribute to Istanbul, as a gift from Hassan Dey to the Sultan. Bainbridge refused. He was then reminded that his new ship sat directly under the guns of the city and within cannon range of the Crescent, the 32-gun frigate that President Adams had earlier given them as tribute. To the tribute already on the ship, the Captain was forced to take on board livestock, tigers and lions, parrots, and ostriches, the Algerian Ambassador and some 100 slaves. The American Flag was lowered; the pennant of Algiers raised and, the Captain departed for Istanbul. Records show that the U.S. Flag was raised for the ship's entrance into the Bosphorus at the Sublime Porte.

The situation had become so humiliating that now President Jefferson, fearing ambivalence in Congress, decided to side step the Constitution and ordered a *"police action,"* in keeping with various treaties that had been made and breeched by the Barbary States, allowing the Navy to *"chastise"* any pirate aggression,*"by sinking, burning or destroying their ships."* In so doing, Jefferson set a precedent for future presidents. Shortly thereafter, in May of 1801, the Dey of Tripoli, Karamanlı, declared war on the United States, claiming that the U.S. was late in its payments. This marks the first formal declaration of war against the United States since declaring its independence.

In response, America dispatched a squadron to the Middle East, and in February of 1802, passed the Act for the Protection of Commerce and Seamen of the United States – a de facto declaration of war where provoked. The Tripolitan War was now in full swing.

The young Navy was hard put to find success in the early years. But, by 1804-1805, the first truly uplifting events occurred, around which the American people rallied with pride. In October of 1803, the luckless Cpt. Bainbridge, while chasing a shallower draft Tripolitan ship, struck a reef and his ship, the Philadelphia, foundered. With his guns now pointed in useless directions, he was forced to surrender along with 307 crewmen. Using several ships and cables, the pirates were able to pull the Philadelphia off the reef and tow it into the port of Tripoli. Bainbridge managed to get a message to fleet Commodore Edward Preble, saying that some plan should be hatched to deny the Pirates their prize.

Preble conceived a plan that involved sailing a recently seized Tripolitan ketch with Americans aboard that would sail into the harbor at night. He chose a young naval officer by the name of Stephen Decatur, aged 25, to lead. On the night of February 16, 1804, Decatur, together with 67 volunteers dressed as Maltese sailors, sailed the newly christened Intrepid into the harbor and came in alongside the Philadelphia. They were successful in surprising the Tripolitan crew, killing them all, setting the frigate aflame and escaping. Britain's Lord Nelson pronounced it *"the most bold and daring act of the age."* At the end of the day, the Dey still held Captain Bainbridge and the sailors, and continued to beat, starve, and humiliate them.

In March of 1805, an American Agent, and former Consul to Tunis, William Eaton, overstepping his bounds but distraught with the fecklessness of the U.S. government ever ready to continue to pay ransom and bribes, organized an Army in March of 1805. The army consisted of nine American marines, ninety Tripolitans (led by the brother of the Dey) opposed to the Dey of Tripoli and 250 Bedouins... bent on *"regime change"* (lead by the brother of the then current ruler). Eaton pronounced himself "General" and started out to cross 500 miles of desert. The trek proved to be daunting on many accounts. They arrived on the coast on April 25th, 30 miles west of Tobruk. Miraculously, by prior arrangement, the USS Argus arrived in the harbor with water and supplies. The Army continued westward to Darna (in Libya today), an excellent city from which to launch a final assault on Tripoli. With three American ships bombarding the city by sea, Eaton and his army stormed the city. After four hours of close combat, the American Flag flew over the city of Darna. Now, threatened by a nearby enemy force, the Dey of Tripoli eagerly accepted Jefferson's latest deal. In exchange for Eaton withdrawing his army, the U.S. return of 100 Tripolitan prisoners, plus $60,000, the USS Constitution was allowed to sail into the harbor of Tripoli, receiving a 21-gun salute and the opportunity to rescue Captain Bainbridge and 296 of his men. (Note, it was the modern USS Bainbridge that rescued the U. S. Captain of the Maersk Alabama in April of 2009 off the coast of Somalia).

Eaton's battle was the first American victory on foreign soil and is commemorated in one verse of the U. S. Marine Corps anthem hymn "... from the Halls of Montezuma to the shores of Tripoli." A year later, America's oldest military monument to this battle was commissioned, carved in Italy of Carrara marble, and brought back as ballast by "Old Ironsides" (the USS Constitution) and was placed in the U.S. Navy Yard in Washington, and later moved to Annapolis in 1860.

In many ways, success on the Mediterranean was short-lived. By 1812, President James Madison found himself at the helm of an ill-prepared and under-financed America embarked on a war with the British. At the outset of the war, in the face of the superior British Navy, no American ships could be spared for service in the Mediterranean. This war not only threatened America's security, but after the burning of the White House by the British in 1814, New Englanders who were opposed to the war, contemplated secession. In the end, America acquitted itself well against the British at sea (and on the Great Lakes), and with the success of Andrew Jackson in New Orleans (this victory not then yet known to the negotiators), America was able to secure a peace with Britain on the eve of Christmas 1814 with the Treaty of Ghent.

With victory came a public outcry to settle the Barbary problem once and for all. President Madison, now 64 and frail, under public pressure, went to Congress seeking a declaration of war and got it. The man chosen to command the expedition, Stephen Decatur, was given orders to achieve nothing less than *"a just and lasting peace."* On May 15, a squadron of 10 warships, including the captured British ship Guerrière, departed for the Mediterranean. This time, America exacted revenge and dictated terms along the Barbary Coast. Decatur is reputed to have said to the Ruler of Algiers, *"If you insist in receiving powder as tribute, you must expect to receive balls with it".*

America authorized a permanent squadron to remain on station in the Mediterranean. After the war, and now a Commissioner of the Navy, Stephen Decatur uttered what became his famous toast at a social gathering in Washington, *"Our Country! In her intercourse with foreign nations may she always be in the right, but, right or wrong, our country!"* In the words of author Michael Oren, *"The Pirates of Barbary who had captured a total of thirty-five American vessels and seven hundred sailors, and who had threatened America's survival and tarnished its pride, were crushed."*

While many forces were at work, American reaction to the depredations of the Barbary pirates was a critically important force behind the forging of a strong Constitution that anticipated the need to raise taxes to support a military force to defend the new Republic against external threats. The costs and indignities borne by its people served to bring unity to the New Republic. It also left the United States with a first class, battle-hardened, Navy, capable of projecting power anywhere in the world – ushering in the Era of "Good Feelings" and expansion of the Country's "National interest" via the Monroe Doctrine.

"Admiral" Porter and the Opening of the U.S. Diplomatic Mission, 1831

Levi Parsons, in Boston's Old South Church, spoke, in 1819, of restoring ("restorationist") their Jewish brethren to their ancestral and biblical home. He and Pliny Fisk obtained letters from then Secretary of State, John Quincy Adams, vouchsafing their credibility and proceeded to begin exporting evangelical Protestantism. The Old Testament was in. Missionary activity was not to be limited to the Native American Indians. President Monroe's Manifest Destiny was not to be confined to the Western Hemisphere. Sympathetic to Christian evangelization, John Quincy thought that missionary work could work hand in hand with commercial expansion into the Muslim Middle East.

Others like a Massachusetts-born George Bethune English, and member of the Harvard Class of 1807 majoring in Divinity and Hebrew, joined the Marines and disembarked, in Egypt. He converted to Islam, became fluent in Arabic and Turkish, becoming Mahmud Efendi. He became an advisor to the Egyptian military and led an expedition up the White Nile, resulting in the claiming of the Sudan by Egypt. He eventually returned to America, wrote a book about his harrowing travels, and was invited by John Quincy Adams to secure from Egypt a treaty, which would be America's first treaty with Egypt.

Jealous of America's growing commercial and military influence, the Europeans put pressure on the Sublime Porte not to engage with the Americans. They were said to be insignificant. In 1820, as noted by Oren, an official report was prepared for Sultan Mahmud II concluding that, *"There is no benefit for the Porte to make a treaty with the* [American] *republic because such a treaty would irritate Great Britain."* Complicating the Ottoman decision was the fact that much of England and America were on the same page in their sympathy for the Greek Independence movement. Philhellenic sentiments were being expressed not only by poet George Byron in England, but also famous Statesmen such as John Adams and Thomas Jefferson, the second and third Presidents of the new Nation, as well as leaders from the North and the South such as Daniel Webster and Henry Clay.

In the end, fearing European reaction to American involvement in the affairs of Europe and its implications for the Monroe Doctrine in the Western Hemisphere, President Monroe decided to withhold aid to the Greeks. As a result, in the eyes of the Sublime Porte, the American star rose and that of the Europeans who were supporting the Greeks diminished. However, President John Quincy Adams' pro-Greek sentiments undermined any prospect of a treaty with the Porte. It would wait for the new President Andrew Jackson, "Old Hickory," who wanted a commercial deal with the Ottomans and was not bothered by "romantic" sentiments about the Cradle of Western Democracy. As for the Sublime Porte, following the success of the Greek independence movement, it found itself knee-deep in insurrectionist movements, from Egypt to the Balkans. With no sympathy on these issues from European governments, the Turks were anxious to strike a deal with the Americans.

President Jackson got his treaty in 1830. It was a Capitulation like the ones European countries had in the form of a Treaty of Navigation and Commerce with the Ottoman Empire. America was given trading privileges on the Black Sea. Importantly, in exchange, America pledged gunboats and arms including Harpers Ferry rifles, colt revolvers, and

cannon, all at discount. American Naval Officers were engaged in Ottoman naval training as well. The precedent of America selling arms into the Middle East had begun.

America now needed and wanted a diplomatic presence in Constantinople/Istanbul with the Sublime Porte.

President Jackson appointed David "Sinbad" Porter, potentially said by some to be a *"loose cannon on the deck,"* who was once court martialed and drummed out of the Navy, to represent America at the Sublime Porte. He was a swashbuckling and talented Naval Officer who had distinguished himself during the War of 1812 and the Second Barbary War. Never really an Admiral in the American Navy, like John Paul Jones in the service of Catherine the Great after the American Revolution, both received their highest rank, their rank as Admirals, in the service of foreign governments, Porter from Mexico.

Porter was named Chargé d'Affaires in 1831 and took up residence in Istanbul. He began to revamp America's diplomatic presence on the Mediterranean, replacing "foreign" Consuls with Americans. Sultan Mahmud II later elevated him, with American approval, to Ambassador. Other areas in which Porter excelled were in establishing protection for Jews in the Ottoman Empire, reminding the Sultan that in America Jews, Muslims, and Christians are all equal before the law. One of Porter's most vexing problems however was dealing with missionaries working in the Levant who were trying to convert Oriental Christians, Maronites in particular, to Protestantism. He was not unsympathetic, but chastised the missionaries as acting in violation of the American – Ottoman Treaty, reminding them that if they persisted, they would not be protected under the terms of the Treaty.

With a change of Administration in Washington, Daniel Webster became Secretary of State. He was an active Congregationalist and was also an honorary member of the American Board of Missions. He promoted a policy that missionaries should be protected at all times. Porter locked swords with Webster on the subject but died soon after in Istanbul in 1842. Perhaps his greatest legacy was to enhance America's influence in that part of the world precisely because, unlike the European powers, he convinced the Ottomans that America had no territorial designs on Ottoman lands.

Missionaries and the Near East College Foundation – Robert College

European intervention in Egypt in support of Ottoman authority resulted in a thankful Sultan who issued a decree that all peoples of the Levant, regardless of their religious affiliation, were to be treated equally. This opened the gates for what Oren terms "manifest Middle Eastern destiny." With improved health conditions and less interference from Ottoman authorities, American missionaries in particular stepped up their presence. Cyrus Hamlin, one of those future missionaries, was an orphaned boy from Maine who won a scholarship to Bowdoin College where he graduated in the top of his class. He prepared for a career in missionary work, with the addition of training young people in the sciences and manufacturing. He arrived in Istanbul in 1940 and opened a school where Science and

English grammar were emphasized, and in the afternoon, the students went to work in a flour mill or building various products such as "Franklin stoves" – all very practical, very American. By the 1850s, Oren notes that, *"Hundreds of Muslims, Christians, and Jews were studying in missionary institutions throughout the Ottoman Empire, reading American textbooks produced by American religious presses and absorbing American ideas."*

By 1860, Hamlin was convinced that his mission was to open a larger secular school. He immediately met resistance from the Catholic and Orthodox churches. Sympathetic to Hamlin's mission, Admiral Farragut, the adopted son of former Ambassador David Porter, arrived with a fleet in Istanbul and managed to secure the permission of the Sultan to build such a school up the Bosphorus in *Bebek.* Hamlin was disowned by the Missionary Board back in the States who would give him no money for a secular school. He left for America in hopes of raising money. With the American Civil War looming, he found no philanthropists willing to gamble on a school in the Middle East. Dejected, he left, returning to Istanbul by way of Paris. There he met Christopher Rhinelander Robert, a philanthropist from New York who agreed to advance an initial amount of $30,000 which would later grow into hundreds of thousands of dollars. With this initial grant, he returned to Istanbul to begin work on what would become Robert College (pictured below) and later *Boğaziçi* University. The college opened in 1863 in the middle of the American Civil War. Because Hamlin's mission was to educate young people, first non-Turk, then Turks as well, in a secular curriculum, it survived, unlike mission schools which retained the proselytizing Christian mission. Western civilization, with its Hebrew, Greek, and Roman origins, was transmitted to generations of youth who were taught to respect the dignity of one another's religion and culture. Among the many accomplished graduates of the school, Robert College has yielded five Prime Ministers, including Tansu Çiller, Turkey's first female PM.

In the 1860s another American Missionary Pioneer in the Middle East, Daniel Bliss opened The University of Beirut. Oren quotes Bliss and the challenge he faced. *"Their faces are so entirely devoid of expression"* Bliss said of the Arabs, Armenians and Jews in 1855. Bliss went on to say, *"It is hard to realize that some of them have souls."* What many of the missionaries had learned by this time is aptly characterized by Bliss' opening remarks as the cornerstone was laid for the Syrian Protestant College, later Beirut University, *"...a man white, black or yellow, Christian, Jew, Mohammedan or heathen, may enter and enjoy all the advantages of this institution...and go on believing in one God, or in many Gods, or in no God."*

One of the legacies of Christian missionaries in the Middle East was an abiding belief that the Jews should be returned to Palestine. Their sentiments on the subject came back with them to the West, to France, England and especially America, that Zion should be restored to the

Jews. Mordecai Manuel Noah, an American Jew, served as an Emissary of the United States in Tunis and elsewhere in the 1830s and 1840s in the Middle East, establishing an American tradition of using Jews as intermediaries with the Muslims of the Middle East. He was an early advocate of Jews returning to their Biblical homeland.

Public reaction in the later 1800s against anti-Semitism, pogroms in Russia, and the Dreyfus Affair in France lent support to Theodore Hertz and the Zionist Movement. Such sympathies would lead to the Balfour Declaration in 1917 during World War I. And, as we have seen, a return of the Holy Lands into the hands of Christians and Jews, is an idea in America that traces back to the Pilgrims of New England.

The Treaty of Versailles and the Principle of Self-Determination

The first American President to think seriously about the peoples and the geography of the Ottoman Empire, Turkey, and the Middle East, was Woodrow Wilson (former President of Princeton University). He was President from 1913 to 1921. While preferring to keep America neutral during the first three years of The Great War, his primary consideration of the area was focused on the plight of the Armenians. During the period of America's neutrality, and because of her neutrality, the American Embassy became a clearing house for information of all kinds – especially that of the circumstances of the Armenians. In 1915, the

American Committee for Armenian and Syrian Relief was formed as a charitable organization. With the support of America's State Department and its Ambassador in Istanbul at the time, Henry Morgenthau, Sr., Committee funds were used to purchase food, clothing and supplies, and to set up clinics and refugee camps. By act of Congress in 1919, this organization became the Near East Relief organization and continued a massive aid program until 1930.

At war's end, with America never having engaged in hostilities against the Ottoman Turks, she enjoyed a high moral authority in the Near East. In the postwar negotiations, David Lloyd George had proposed that a new Armenia become a U.S. mandate. Wilson appointed a Commission, the King-Trane Commission, with General James Harbord at its head, to go and study the Armenian claims to see if, under the right of self-determination, Armenia would qualify under Wilson's Fourteen Points. The Commission returned and the 12th Point follows:

"The Turkish portion of the present Ottoman Empire should be assured a secure sovereignty, but the other nationalities which are now under Turkish rule should be assured an undoubted security of life and an absolutely unmolested opportunity of autonomous development, and the Dardanelles should be permanently opened as a free passage to the ships and commerce of all nations under international guarantees."

By terms of the Treaty of Sèvres in 1920, Wilson and the Americans were given the task of drawing the boundaries for an independent Armenian Republic. His map included the Provinces of Van, Bitlis, Erzurum, and Trabzon. In May of 1920, Wilson asked Congress for authority to accept Armenia as a mandate. It was soundly defeated by the Republicans in the Senate.

In the meantime, the Turkish War of Independence had begun before the Treaty of Sèvres could be ratified by the parties. The Nationalist Movement immediately set its sights on the fledging Armenian Republic which it defeated quickly. The Armenians signed a Treaty in Alexandropol in November of 1920, and a year later again signed at the Treaty of Kars. Separately, the Armenians signed a Treaty that same year with Russia. These treaties fixed the borders of the Armenian Republic and were confirmed by the Treaty of Lausanne in 1923. Although Stalin tried to annul the Treaty of Kars, and reclaim those Eastern provinces on behalf of his satellite Armenian Republic, Winston Churchill and the U. S. State Department would not support the Soviets on this. These borders have remained fixed to this day.

There is a little-known story of rather some import in the history of Turkish American relations. This is the story of Asa K. Jennings, during the evacuation of some 350,000 Asia Minor Greek refugees in the burning and war-torn city of Smyrna (Izmir), who is largely responsible for their rescue. Subsequently, he organized the rescue of some 1,250,000 Greeks, from the Black Sea to Syria, in the exchange of populations agreement between and among

Turkey, Greece, and Bulgaria. He met with Ghazi Musta-
pha Kemal on September 20, 1922, in Smyrna where he
was at the time, Director of the YMCA, and obtained permission to try to arrange their rescue, with the primary
condition that Greeks and Turks be exchanged one for
one, giving rise to the Population Exchange Agreement.
Asa Jennings was later recognized by Mustafa Kemal,
the Greek Government, and the Ecumenical Orthodox
Patriarch in Istanbul for his humanity services. This is
the story of one American, not an American official, who
made a significant impression on the President of the new
Republic of Turkey.

From Marshall Plan to the Korean War and NATO

America's fascination with the Middle East continued
alongside the political issues being dealt with by the American Government. In 1921, Rudolf Valentino starred in the
Sheik of Araby. Khalil Gibran's, *The Prophet*, came out to
wide public acclaim. America joined with the Europeans
in the oil business and signed an agreement to become a
partner in the Iraq Petroleum Company in 1924. In 1938,
American oil explorers struck oil in Saudi Arabia. In the
middle of World War II, Humphrey Bogart and Ingrid
Berman starred in a block buster anti-Nazi propaganda
film *Casablanca*, set in French-controlled Morocco. In 1945,
President Roosevelt met with King Ibn Saud, sealing the
U.S.-Saudi relationship. Two years later, America's involvement in the Middle East rose to another level with its

1947 vote in the newly formed United Nations in favor of Resolution 181, which partitioned Palestine into two States, one Arab and one Jewish.

Franklin Roosevelt had passed away before the end of WWII and was succeeded by his Vice President, Harry Truman. With the foresight of those such as Winston Churchill, notably in his "Iron Curtain" speech of 1946, together with the influence of career U.S. Foreign Service officer George F. Kennan, the Western Allies were coming to believe that they had replaced one enemy for another, Russia for Germany. Kennan, in his capacity as Deputy Chief of Mission in Moscow under Ambassador W. Averill Harriman, had authored a secret document known as the "X" article, which subsequently was published in the journal of Foreign Affairs in 1947 under the title, "The Sources of Soviet Conduct." Its significance follows in the official U. S. State Department Official History:

> *Kennan's ideas, which became the basis of the Truman administration's foreign policy, first came to public attention in 1947 in the form of an anonymous contribution to the journal of Foreign Affairs, the so-called "X-Article." "The main element of any United States policy toward the Soviet Union," Kennan wrote, "must be that of a long-term, patient but firm and vigilant containment of Russian expansive tendencies." To that end, he called for countering "Soviet pressure against the free institutions of the Western world" through the "adroit and vigilant application of counter-force at a series of constantly shifting*

geographical and political points, corresponding to the shifts and maneuvers of Soviet policy." Such a policy, Kennan predicted, would "promote tendencies which must eventually find their outlet in either the break-up or the gradual mellowing of Soviet power."

In short, a policy of "Containment" of the Soviet Union became known as the Truman Doctrine. The doctrine sparked enormous controversy in America with some, like well-known journalist and commentator Walter Lippmann, who coined the term "Cold War," arguing against the doctrine as being unsupportable grounds for U.S. imperialism. Others like Dean Acheson and John Foster Dulles, Secretaries of State under Presidents Truman and Eisenhower, argued for a more aggressive roll-back of Soviet expansionism.

Under the auspices of the Truman Doctrine, the Marshall Plan was developed as the greatest antidote to Russian expansion. The idea was to rebuild the economies of Western Europe, including Greece and Turkey. This policy was also good for American industry. At the end of WWII Stalin, who had wanted control of the Dardanelles for years, put pressure on the weak government of Turkey at the end of the war to gain control of the Straits. In February of 1947, Great Britain, spent from two world wars, asked the United States to pick up the mantle with aid to Greece and Turkey. Understanding that both countries represented the front line of Soviet expansionist influence, and recognizing that if they fell into the Russian sphere that it could result in what Foreign Secretary Dean Acheson called the "Domino effect," the U.S. Congress approved a $400,000,000 emergency aid package in order to prop up the governments of both countries.

America's involvement in the area steadily grew, first with the C.I.A. support of Nasser in Egypt in 1952 and then the overthrow of Mossadegh in Iran in 1953 and the installation of the Shah Reza Pahlavi. During the Suez Crisis of 1956, America intervened, with Russia and the UN, in support of ousting Israel, France, and England from Egypt, and then forestalled Russian efforts to gain control of Libya.

America's involvement in the Middle East deepened further in connection with the "Six-Day War" and the 1973 Arab-Israeli Wars. After the second war, Henry Kissinger launched his famous "shuttle diplomacy" in an effort to bring calm to the area. In 1983, as part of a Multi-Lateral Peace Keeping force in Lebanon, 299 American and French soldiers and marines were blown up in their "barracks" by two suicide car-bombers. The bombing was claimed by then obscure group called "the Islamic Jihad." Of those killed, 241 were Americans, mostly marines. America had not lost military men in the Middle East since the Barbary Wars of the early 1800s. By the 1980s, based on economic and political interests, America found itself inextricably engaged in the Middle East and the rest of the world. While not an empire of conquest, "Manifest Destiny" and commercial interests had led the U.S. into a global network of commitments, replacing in influence, if not by occupation, the Colonial Empires of all of Europe combined.

Under the aegis of Western Democracy, Turkey took sides at the end of WWII, joining the Allies in the last months of the war. Seeing the Soviet Union as a clear and present danger, and not for the first time, Turkey formally joined the North Atlantic Treaty Organization in 1952. Turkey immediately sent soldiers to fight alongside the Americans in Korea. American perception of Turks as fighting men grew as they observed how tough and disciplined they were. When ordered to dig a foxhole, for example, the Turkish soldiers dug holes deep enough to adequately cover themselves. The Americans, it had been noted, had a tendency to dig shallow holes and paid the price in shrapnel wounds and death. After the Korean War, Turks' survival instincts and skills were formally studied by the American psychological-medical community.

In 1963, Turkey became an Associate member of the European Union. In 1999, Turkey was declared a Candidate for membership. In 2002, Turkey signed the European Convention on Human Rights. In 2005, while riding high economically, Turkey was invited to begin the "Acquis" process to become a full member. This was a high point in Euro-Turkish relations. America "officially" supported Turkey's entrance. Polls indicated that well over half the population of Turkey believed that joining the EU would be advantageous for Turks and for their country. As noted by David L. Phillips in the 2004 September/October issue of *Foreign Affairs* titled, "Turkey Dreams of Accession,"

"Meanwhile, joining the EU has become an obsession for many Turks. Liberals and the business community want membership because it will promote their basic freedoms and accelerate economic reform. Minorities, including the Kurds, see it as the best way to secure greater human rights. Islamists think that such a move will reduce the chances of a military takeover; military officers believe that it will ensure Turkey's territorial integrity."

Phillips goes on to note, *"Still, some Turks believe that no matter how much the country reforms, the EU will ultimately reject a Muslim candidate. Christian Democrats in Europe, who are already uneasy about Muslim minorities in their home countries, argue that bringing Turkey into the union would mean importing problems from the Middle East."* Certainly, relations between the EU and Turkey have been strained since the ham-fisted response to the Gezi Park protests (2013), abridgement of rights of free speech during the 2014 Municipal elections when Google and Twitter were temporarily shut down by the Government. Signs of the same interference were reported in the Parliamentary election of June 7, 2015, the results of which, namely the success of the HDP Party (Kurdish supported among others), significantly angered the Ruling elite AKP party. In the process, the number of journalists sitting in jail on dubious charges, only increasing after Prime Minister Erdoğan became President Erdoğan, served to call into question the agreements Turkey made in the Copenhagen Accords of 2002 regarding the Rule of Law and Human Rights. Even the Turkish cartoonists (Baruter and Aydoğan, 2013, Kurtcebe, 2015) who were jailed for "offensive" imaging of President Erdoğan, serve as an example of the increasing politicization of alleged offenses against "Turkishness" (*Türkçülük*) in Turkey.

Turkish Image of America Falls in the Wake of Conflict in Cyprus

If Turkish and American perceptions of the policies of each other's countries appear to have been on a roller coaster, it is a reality that goes back more than a half century. The halcyon days of the late 1940s and 1950s and the Marshall Plan era image gave way to some degree of mistrust dating back to tension over the island of Cyprus beginning in 1964 and the subsequent Turkish intervention/invasion of the island in 1974. The fact that at that time, a significant Greek-American lobby weighed in on Washington perceptions, when Turkish-Americans were few in number and were decades away from even having a lobby, has typically been overlooked. Also, the fact that the CIA was supporting the Greek Junta and the Greek Cypriot guerilla forces who were in the process of staging a coup on the island was unknown to the American public and most of the Government, skewed American perceptions against the Turks. For Turks, the heretofore impartial and supportive Americans appeared to be blind as to what was actually happening, as was England, a Tri-Partite Guarantor of the Cyprus Government. When the Arms Embargo was implemented, opinion in Turkey of America hit bottom. In a word, the Turks felt betrayed. The West/NATO was unfairly taking sides with one member versus another NATO member.

Changing Turkish and American Perceptions, the Gulf Wars

In retrospect, foreign policy considerations for NATO members during the Cold War, seemed comparatively clear, unambiguous. But, with the fall of Communism, policy choices for NATO members in an increasingly multi-polar world became more problematic. Differences between and among members on any given American or NATO policy initiative have revealed divergence coming from the NATO Capitals regarding differing perceptions of "shared risk." Examples include: Germany's position on the Afghan war; France's position on the war in Syria and the halting entrance of America and then Turkey into the England-France-Italy-led war on Gadhafi's Libya; Turkey's later preoccupation with the toppling of Assad's regime in Syria in which the American President was undecisive regarding U.S. intervention; targeting deconfliction strategies between Turkey and America in the Syrian civil war, and finally, "targeting priority" differences in Syria regarding ISIS and the PKK. It is clear that NATO policy formulation has become cloudy at best. Accordingly, this division of political sensitivities and goals has strained relations between the governments of America and Turkey. Relations with EU members are scarcely better. President Erdoğan's policies, both on domestic and foreign matters, have alienated many States of Europe as well.

To focus on one of these issues, America, not unlike Turkey's feeling when a NATO arms embargo was placed on it in the wake of the Cyprus affair, when the Turkish Parliament voted in the new Justice and Development Party (*Adalet ve Kalkınma Partisi*)-controlled Turkish Parliament, denying the use of Incirlik air force base for Coalition purposes in the 2nd Gulf War was seen in America as a slap in the face of a country which had benefitted enormously from America's security umbrella and financial aid. It was seen in America as a sign of bad faith on the one hand, and rationalized on the other hand as having been a democratically arrived at decision by the Turkish Parliament and therefore a sign of the growing maturity of Western Liberal values. The Defense Establishment saw it as an open rebuke of America's foreign policy. It was clear that NATO Alliance ties with Turkey were beginning to grow weaker. Similarly, Turkey's trust of the West, America in particular, was showing early signs of strains. However, Turkey's economic miracle seemed to be the rising tide that would float all boats.

The so-called "peace dividend" heralded by George Bush the Elder with the fall of the Berlin Wall, proved to be all too ephemeral, in America, Turkey, the Middle East and around the world. Coordinating the military objectives of NATO countries beyond the world of the Cold War has proven agonizingly difficult for all the members. Muslim refugees, political and economic, from war-torn areas from Afghanistan west, flooding into Europe via Turkey and North Africa, has only exacerbated the relations. Tensions have further risen as Putin's Russia has seized upon Western discord to reinsert itself into the Middle Eastern vortex, after an absence since the mid-1950s. Turkey's attempt to offset some of the decline in relations with its NATO and EU Partners, by engaging with Putin's overtures of transactional opportunities in trade, energy, tourism, and defense. President Erdoğan's proclivity to play the Sunni Caliph with the Muslim Brotherhood and the Palestinian cause, using Qatari money, have combined in recent years to further aggravate the trust gap between Turkey and its Western Allies.

Tourism and the Arts, a Counterbalance to Government to Government Relations

It is important to note that "official" relations between countries, not least of all Turkey and America, do not necessarily move in lock step with "people to people" perceptions. If the internal situation of a country is bleak enough, disaffected peoples can, and have been throughout history, cajoled by failing rulers to focus their frustrations on a "devil," or scapegoat. The devil can be local or foreign, or both. Counter-balancing "official" portrayals of hostile governments, are business to business and, individuals and individual, relations. In the B2B world, the players tend to take longer term views on the potential advantages of weathering more seasonal political storms. On the individual level, whether they are Turks and Americans fighting side by side in Korea and Afghanistan, Turks visiting America, musicians and artists collaborating, students on exchange programs, or Americans visiting Turkey, these relationships, where positive, tend to transcend "official" relations which ebb and flow.

Based on an anecdotal observation over decades of experience in many different arena's, it is the author's view that Turks traveling to America in the last half century have come with high, if sometimes vague expectations. The obvious limitations of my experience notwithstanding, I feel more confident in observing that Americans, businessmen, tourists, and military personnel, probably have tended to come to Turkey with lower expectations, if any. Experience has shown that Americans are typically stunned and pleasantly surprised to discover a country and a people that can be appealing in so many ways. While there are exceptions to any rule, and obvious limitations to my personal observations about Americans' and Turks' expectations, the vast majority of what I have witnessed, and heard from others, is that Americans had no idea of how charming the people could be. They are surprised by the level of their development as evidenced by spectacular 5-Star hotels and resorts. They have typically been amazed to discover the architectural remnants of so many civilizations that have called Anatolia home. Whether it is the hustle and bustle of Istanbul, its mesmerizing beauty with ships and ferries plying the Bosphorus, or the serenity of Turkey's Aegean and Mediterranean beaches, or its extraordinary cuisine, Americans almost unanimously are taken with the country. Having lived and worked in Greece and Italy as well, the author has witnessed very different levels of expectation versus revelation where Turkey is concerned. The moral of this story is best captured in the phrase, "seeing is believing." While such an observation is not exclusive to Turkey, it may be as good an example of this saying as can be found around the world.

Hollywood and the Impact of Midnight Express

With the world at the brink of war in the Cuban Missile Crisis in 1962, possibly nuclear war, Hollywood again captured the fancy of the American public in Peter O'Toole's epoch portrayal of T. E. Lawrence in the movie Lawrence of Arabia. The historic details of the period were lost on the American viewing public. The scenes were cinematographically stunning, the story compelling, but the message was unfavorable toward the Turks, who were seen as the oppressors and the "bad guys." Audiences enjoyed the appeal of Omar Sharif, and the Arabs and the British combining to overthrow the Turks inquest of the "right of self-determination" set at the conclusion of the Great War. The exotica of the "Orient," the Levant, was preserved but at the expense of the image of the Germans and the Turks. The unsympathetic view of the Turks, following an old British tendency dating back to the Greek War of Independence, subliminally, left a message of Turkish brutality for the American audience to absorb.

The various movies on Gallipoli, including the Mel Gibson 1981 film, from an image standpoint, have romanticized the Australia and New Zealand forces, panned the British generalship and senseless loss of life, with little focus on the heroics and losses on the Turkish side. Two thousand fifteen was the centennial of this battle. In anticipation of that, Russell Crowe directed and starred in the 2015 movie titled Water Diviner. It is set two years after the Great War and is based on a father coming from Australia in search of the graves of his three sons who died during the battle. It is said to be a love story set in the aftermath of that war. Three of the co-stars are Turkish film actors. The movie flashes back to scenes of the Battle, with the net intended effect that a more sympathetic and realistic presentation of the Turkish soldiers and their sacrifices and losses, be seen for the first time in Western film. The movie was shot in Turkey on the Gallipoli Peninsula and offers a more balanced view of all the Parties to the conflict.

To date, however, the single most unfavorable picture of Turkey and the Turks is the 1978 movie Midnight Express. If most Americans at that time had little or no impression of Turkey, this movie, shot in Malta, cast the Turkish people in a brutish light. The movie followed in the wake of the negative "PR" in America of the Turks following their "invasion" (intervention the Turks would say on behalf of the 20% Turkish minority on the island) of Cyprus just a few years earlier. Since the turn of this century, when the author has asked young people if they have seen or heard of the movie, the answer is invariably "no." It is just as well. American author, Mary Lee Settle, in her book *Turkish Reflections*, wrote, *"The Turks I saw in Lawrence of Arabia and Midnight Express were like cartoon caricatures, compared to the people I had known and lived among for three of the happiest years of my life."* The author was living in Turkey at that time and remembers the reaction of Turkish friends who saw it as anti-Turkey propaganda of the worst kind. Upon returning to America in 1979, for many years the author was asked if Turkey was really like what they had seen in the film. A picture is worth a thousand words. The Greek-American lobby could not have asked for more. My impression during those years was that Turkey was "in denial" about its image abroad. It was not until President Turgut Özal's administration when the Government learned it had to play the "image game" and spend real money crafting a positive image abroad. This meant hiring top flight International Public Relations firms to counter negative imaging coming from other groups. Özal's image on CNN during the first Gulf War was the beginning of a commitment to "positive" imaging in the world of media.

From American Jazz to Nobel Laureate Orhan Pamuk

One scarcely knows where to begin on the people to people artistic and cultural exchanges between Turkey and the United States. As good a place as any to start is the Istanbul Music Festival launched on the 50th Anniversary of the Founding of the Republic in 1973. With a top drawer cast of international music talent and what has become an international audience, growing larger by the year, is emblematic of Turkey putting on an appealing face for world consumption. Growing out of this festival sprang the International Jazz and Pop-Music Festival which now runs in parallel with the music festival. These events are just the tip of the iceberg of cultural, historic, and gastronomic tourism that has paralleled the dramatic growth of the Turkish economy.

Turkish Americans and their friends are now adding to the positive imaging of Turkey as well, especially in large cities around America. Perhaps the most compelling story is that of Ahmet Ertegün. The great grandson of Sheik İbrahim Edhem Effendi, Ahmet and his older brother Nesuhi were born into an aristocratic family. Ahmet's father was posted to Washington D.C. in the mid-1930s where he was elevated to the rank of Ambassador. His mother was a musician, and she purchased records at the time by virtue of which the boys were introduced to music of all kinds. But it was jazz which first captured the fancy of Ahmet who, with his older brother, used to secretly attend the "black" night clubs in the Washington area to hear the bands of Cab Calloway and Duke Ellington, and the voices of Louis Armstrong and Billie Holliday. As reported in a *Rolling Stone* article by Robert Greenfield in 2012, Ahmet felt a kinship to black people, saying, *"I began to discover a little bit about the situation of black people in America and experienced immediate empathy with the victims of such senseless discrimination, because, although Turks were never slaves, they were regarded as enemies within Europe because of their Muslim beliefs."*

Ertegun went on to become a legend in his own time, starting the Atlantic Record label and signing artists from Aretha Franklin to Ray Charles to the Rolling Stones and Led Zeppelin. The author does not know the exact origin of the affinity for Western music and Jazz in particular coming out of Turkey, especially Istanbul, since the 1920s, but the author can attest to an extraordinary and abiding fascination with American Jazz, regardless of whatever other music forms were the current rage in popular music coming out of Europe, America, England, or Australia. The author had the privilege of meeting Ahmet Ertegün at a benefit concert in 2007 hosted by The American Friends of Turkey.

If the sounds and rhythms of Dede Effendi (famous early 19th century composer of Ottoman classical music) are in the DNA of Turks, perhaps American Jazz strikes a similar chord. Ahmet Ertegün died in 2012, but his legend and philanthropy live on in the spirit of his many fans. At the very least, his impact on music coming out of America had a positive influence in Turkey and America, in spite of the political ups and downs of the official relationship between the two countries over the years.

Of the many Turkish artists to break onto the world stage, Nobel Prize-winning author Orhan Pamuk is among the best known. A graduate of Robert College, his books, *The Black Book*, *My Name is Red* and *Snow*, among others, have captured the interest of world audiences. His works are translated into 62 languages. For those who have lived in Istanbul, his *Istanbul: Memories of the City* is a particular treasure. Others of his works, such as *Snow*, take up the controversial issues of secularists versus Islamists. Another author with international appeal, Elif Şafak, has come on the world scene. Her book, *40 Rules of Love*, (*Aşkin Turkish*) was discussed earlier in the context of the subject of mysticism and Sufism in an earlier chapter. Both authors are examples of literary figures who have increased American understanding of Turks.

Of course, there are many American authors writing today on all aspects of Turkey, both as residents of Turkey and America. Of those long resident Americans in Turkey, one of the more influential and enduring authors has been Professor John Freely, whose book, *Strolling through Istanbul*, has been a must read classic for decades for those wanting to feel the rhythms of the Great City. Others include Andrew Finkel and Hugh Pope, both of whom write for news organizations, journals, magazines as well as books. Turkish students have been coming to America by the thousands for many, many years. Until the unrest in Turkey in 2016, one had begun to see American students increasingly coming to study in Turkey. And finally, the numbers of researchers and teachers from America coming to Turkey to study and teach has, or had until 2016, been on the increase.

Finally, and significantly, American business has been investing since the early 1950s, beginning with the Hilton Hotel group. Investment Banking is what brought the author to Turkey in 1988 for a second stay of four years in Turkey. Privatization sales by the government as well as direct foreign investment, whole or in Joint-Venture, began to take off during the Özal years, the 1980s and early '90s. This will be discussed in more detail later. The significance of U.S.-Turkey, Turkey-U.S. business development is exemplified by the American Turkish Council and its many corporate members from both countries, together with participation from TUSIAD, TOBB and other Turkish business organizations. The story of Muhtar Kent, Chairman and CEO of Coca Cola, is one the compelling examples of cross-cultural business development and opportunity that is important to profile and emulate. His story is famous, of course, in Turkey. In fact, his story is well-known in business circles all around the world, not least of all in America.

Proximity to Turkey and being a part of the EU Customs Union has favored European investment in Turkey and from Turkey into Europe. To a somewhat lesser degree, U.S. investment continues to grow in Turkey, as does Turkey in America. In conclusion, when one thinks of the history of business between America and Turkey countries in the modern era, one should remember the licensing agreement between Vehbi Koç and Henry Ford, signed in 1925 in Ankara, to export Ford Model T's at that time for sale in Turkey. Ford and Koç is certainly one of Turkey's oldest continuously running business partnerships. There are many world class businesses in Turkey today, not least of which is THY, the Turkish Airlines, which has been voted the best European airline for years of late.

Chapter 17

SLAVERY, CIVIL RIGHTS AND MINORITIES – INTOLERANCE IN BOTH COUNTRIES

"I am a Jew. Hath not a Jew eyes? Hath not a Jew hands, organs, dimensions, senses, affections, passions? fed with the same food, hurt with the same weapons, subject to the same diseases, healed by the same means, warmed and cooled by the same winter and summer, as a Christian is? If you prick us, do we not bleed? if you tickle us, do we not laugh? if you poison us, do we not die? and if you wrong us, shall we not revenge? If we are like you in the rest, we will resemble you in that. If a Jew wrong a Christian, what is his humility? Revenge. If a Christian wrong a Jew, what should his sufferance be by Christian example? Why, revenge. The villany you teach me I will execute, and it shall go hard but I will better the instruction."

—WILLIAM SHAKESPEARE, *THE MERCHANT OF VENICE*, ACT I, III – SHYLOCK

> *"Why, sir, I trust I may have leave to speak; And speak I will; I am no child, no babe: Your betters have endured me say my mind, And if you cannot, best you stop your ears. My tongue will tell the anger of my heart, Or else my heart concealing it will break, And rather than it shall, I will be free. Even to the uttermost, as I please, in words."*
>
> —WILLIAM SHAKESPEARE, *THE TAMING OF THE SHREW*, ACT IV, SCENE III – KATHARINA

The institution of slavery and bondage is recorded in the Hammurabi Code of 1760 BCE, from the Egyptian and Babylonian captivity of the Jews to slavery in America. Every civilization and society has engaged in the practice, including the Greeks, the Romans, and the Byzantines, the Arabs, the Mongols, the Vikings, the Ottomans, Barbary Pirates, and one African tribe of another, the Incas et. al. Slaves are/were chattels, personal property that can/could be traded for other chattels or to satisfy debts. Slavery is today illegal everywhere but flourishes in parts of Sub-Sahelian Africa and South East Asia. Trafficking in children, both as servants and in the sex trade, is alive and well in spite of world organizations, public and private, striving to eradicate the practice.

The Hymn "Amazing Grace", Slavery in America and the Civil War

The English, followed by other European powers, were instrumental in making slavery a transoceanic business. The arrival of African slaves in the early 1600s in America was not the first instance of slavery in America. Native Americans enslaved other Native Americans. Parts of South America, the Caribbean and the Southern Colonies in America were the prime destinations for slaves who became the backbone and the muscle of mining and agricultural development. In the Southern Colonies, wealthy land owners with large land grants built an economy based on the clearing of large land tracts, followed by the planting of tobacco, wheat, corn, and subsequently cotton. Eli Whitney, a Massachusetts born Yale Phi Beta Kappa graduate of the class of 1792, perhaps ironically being a Northerner, reinvigorated the cotton industry with his invention of the cotton gin in 1793. His invention renewed the South's commitment to slavery, even as it seemed to be otherwise dying out for economic reasons. This new process and mechanization, counterintuitively, did not reduce the demand for labor. It permitted the economic harvesting of Upland cotton which simply grew the whole industry.

It has been estimated that at the time of the American Civil War, when cotton was "King." four out of every five jobs in England were directly or indirectly tied to cotton. Cotton was then further processed and transported on English ships around the globe. Opposition to the trade and to slavery in principle had its proponents going back to King Charles I of Spain, a contemporary of Suleyman the Lawgiver, who had proposed its abolition, both the African and the Indian slave trade, in the middle of the 15th century CE. By the late 1600s, Quakers and other Evangelical Christian groups began to denounce slavery as being un-Christian and inhumane. Their voices were strengthened by the religious "Great Awakening" in America and by the authors of the Enlightenment in England and France.

James Oglethorpe, who founded the Colony of Georgia in 1732, arranged to have slavery outlawed there, for both humanitarian and security reasons. As a buffer colony separating the English colonies from the Spanish colonies in Florida, it was argued that slave loyalty could be compromised by the Spanish, possibly promoting escape. Better to require that land holding be limited to 50 acres and that families farm this acreage themselves. After Oglethorpe died, under pressure to compete with its economically thriving neighbor South Carolina, which employed slave labor, Georgia instituted slavery.

The Abolition Movement gained traction in England when a Member of Parliament, James Wilberforce, had a religious conversion and became an Evangelical Christian. He joined the movement, became a philanthropist, and took up the cause for the rest of his life. He railed against the horrendous conditions of the slaves in the "Triangular Trade." In this trade, British goods were carried to and sold in Africa. The proceeds were used to purchase slaves who were then placed in the holds of ships for the dreaded and inhumane "Middle Voyage" by which they were transported to the Caribbean, where some were sold there for sugar. The rest would be largely, though not exclusively, sold in the Southern Colonies, and some in the Northern Colonies, the proceeds from which were then used to buy rum, made with Caribbean sugar, timber and wood products, which were then sold back in Mother England.

One of those who joined with Wilberforce and the Abolitionists was a former captain of an English slave trading ship by the name of John Newton. After surviving a terrible storm at sea where one of his sailors was washed overboard, Newton began to rethink his involvement with this inhuman trade in slaves. He eventually became an evangelical minister and penned the words to what has become the most famous hymn in history. Possibly based on the Biblical story of the Prodigal Son, it is a hymn which speaks of redemption from a life of sin by the Grace of God. It was set to a familiar tune in England at the time and the words speak volumes about the possibility of turning one's life around and becoming good by the grace of the Creator. The words of the first verse follow.

"Amazing grace! / how sweet the sound/, who sav'd a wretch like me! / I once was lost but now am found, / Was blind but now I see".

The story is told here in the context of slavery for obvious reasons where Newton is concerned. More importantly, while it never became particularly popular in England, it swept into the American Protestant hymnody during the Second Great Awakening and became a song whose message resonated with Christians and Abolitionists leading up to the Civil War, a musical hallmark of the anti-slavery forces in America. It was sung in churches, including Black churches, and is said to be the most often sung hymn of all time.

While the Slave Trade was outlawed in America in 1808, American ships remained busily employed in the trade with other countries. It would not be until 1833, within a month of Wilberforce's death, that slavery was outlawed in England and most of her Colonies. The institution of slavery continued in America after the external trade was abolished, but increasingly, in the North, Abolitionists gained strength – especially in the Quaker State of Pennsylvania. In 1780, following a similar act in Vermont, Pennsylvania passed the Abolition Act, a gradual program as follows:

"That all Persons, as well Negroes, and Mulattos, as others, who shall be born within this State, from and after the Passing of this Act, shall not be deemed and considered as Servants for Life or Slaves; and that all Servitude for Life or Slavery of Children in Consequence of the Slavery of their Mothers, in the Case of all Children born within this State from and after the passing of this Act as aforesaid, shall be, an hereby is, utterly taken away, extinguished and forever abolished."

In the 1790 census, there were 3,700 slaves in Pennsylvania, which later outlawed slavery in 1857. By 1860, the population of Black Africans registered in the Pennsylvania State census was almost 60,000, none were slaves any longer.

It is interesting that in Virginia, where the slave trade had flourished for more than 150 years, plantation farms had been profligate in their farming techniques and soil-management both in the Piedmont and the Tidewater areas. As a result, the land began to fail to support a profitable tobacco crop, so the business began to move to Colonies deeper in the South. Cotton moved even farther south. Along with these labor-intensive industries went the slaves. The Founding Fathers had been conflicted on the subject of slavery from the beginning, even as the Declaration of Independence proclaimed that "...All men were created equal...."

Due to the nature of plantation farming in the South, the slave population was large and growing. As a result, forces aligned against the Abolitionists were strong and vocal, the more so in the Southern Colonies. Interestingly, the need for large amounts of slavery in Virginia had actually declined substantially by the 1820s, especially in the Valley and in the Western part of the State. The issue of male suffrage voting requirements and slavery became heated in Virginia and a Convention was organized to come to some conclusion regarding these issues. In the 1820s, Virginia was one of only two States which required property ownership to vote. In the end, property rights of white males to be eligible to vote were reduced from the ownership of at least 100 acres of land, or 25 acres of land with a home on it, to a much lower threshold of property ownership. Slaves were deemed to be 3/5's of a person in calculating the number of representatives allocated to a political district within the State. These rules were hated by the largely white population in the mountainous area of West Virginia where the majority of the people tended to be poor and farmed for themselves. They felt under-represented and at the mercy of large landowners in the Piedmont and Tidewater areas of the Central and Eastern parts of the Commonwealth. Slavery came within one vote to being abolished at the Virginia Convention of 1830.

By the time the Civil War broke out in 1861, Virginians found themselves in a real quandary. They knew that, being a border State between the North and the South, much of the fighting and the blood spilled would come from a State whose economy and a people which was actually no longer dependent on slavery. The decision to secede from the Union and join the South, where the maintenance of slavery was thought to be essential to its economic survival, came reluctantly to Virginians. In fact, it can be argued that Virginia was not in the war until they were in it, in battle, with fellow Virginians dying in the early months of the conflict. Western Virginia separated from Virginia on the matter, joined the North in the fight and soon created a new State, the State of West Virginia.

Slavery, and a war fought largely over the business and institution of slavery, is a stain on the history of America, but the victory of the North and the preservation of the Union produced in principle, if not always in law or practice, a result which fulfilled the promise of 1776 and the Declaration of Independence in recognizing that all men are created equal.

The Emancipation Proclamation and the Gettysburg Address

The American Civil War, which the author counts as America's third civil war, broke out five years after the Crimean War. Several Slave States in the South seceded from the Union, forming the Confederate States of America. The reasons are complicated, born of generations of suspicion and resentment, and born of different styles of life. There was plantation farming versus smaller scale individual farming. The south was a slave-based economy versus the North's industry-based economy. All of these factors contributed to a mistrust that could, and would, be largely geographically defined between the Northern and Southern States. Four of the slave States, Kentucky, Maryland, Missouri, and Delaware did not join the Confederacy with its capital in Montgomery, Alabama. Of the first six States to secede, nearly 50% of their population was slave. These States argued that they were exercising their States' Rights, a principle and source of friction from the very Founding. After seceding at the end of 1860, Confederate States began to seize Federal property in the South. President Lincoln had been elected and assumed office in March of 1861. Six weeks later, Confederate forces began a bombardment and siege of the Federal Fort Sumter in Charleston South Carolina. Lincoln sent the United States Navy to relieve the fort. Whether the war might have been avoided with different or better leadership, the die had been cast.

The North began the War fighting to preserve the Union. The Abolitionists had used pictures depicting the cruelty of slavery to promote their cause. As noted two years into the War in response to a letter from Abolitionist Leader Horace Greeley, President Lincoln said,

"If there be those who would not save the Union, unless they could at the same time save slavery, I do not agree with them. If there be those who would not save the Union unless they could at the same time destroy slavery, I do not agree with them. My paramount object in this struggle is to save the Union, and is not either to save or to destroy slavery. If I could save the Union without freeing any slave I would do it, and if I could save it by freeing all the slaves I would do it; and if I could save it by freeing some and leaving others alone I would also do that. What I do about slavery, and the colored race, I do because I believe it helps to save the Union; and what I forbear, I

forbear because I do not believe it would help to save the Union... I have here stated my purpose according to my view of official duty; and I intend no modification of my oft-expressed personal wish that all men everywhere could be free."

The South fought to preserve its slave-based economy and in response to what it saw were unfair terms of trade. It was believed that too much of the profit of their agricultural industry ending up in the hands of Northern Bankers and Shippers. As new Territories to the West became States, the Southern States insisted that those which chose to employ slave labor should be allowed to do so. The Missouri Compromise (1819) whereby new states would be admitted two at a time, one being a slave State and the other being slave free, would only last so long.

Three years into the War, the President made Slavery a *casus bello* – a rationale for war in addition to preserving the Union, when in January of 1863 Lincoln issued the Emancipation Proclamation.

The Proclamation freed the slaves in those 10 States that were in rebellion, the Confederacy. It affected three to four million slaves. The Proclamation infuriated White

Southerners, angered Northern Democrats, energized Abolitionists and gave hope to Blacks and Black slaves alike. As expected, it spurred more slaves to seek to escape to Northern-controlled areas.

Importantly, the Proclamation did not outlaw Slavery. However, the Northern Cause, from that point on, did take on an air of moral superiority. But it would take two plus additional years to bring the war to a conclusion. Confederate General Robert E. Lee surrendered to Union Army Lt. General Ulysses S. Grant at Appomattox, Virginia on the 11th of April, 1865. Five days later, President Lincoln was assassinated. 620,000 soldiers died in the War, two-thirds from disease.

Four months after the Battle of Gettysburg, on November 19, 1863, President Lincoln arrived with an entourage to mark the graves of this hallowed site. Following a two-hour eulogy by Senior American Statesman Edward Everett as had become the custom at such events, President Lincoln delivered a speech of only a few minutes. It has come down in the annals of English public oratory and American history as one of the greatest speeches ever given. It reads as follows.

"Four score and seven years ago our fathers brought forth on this continent a new nation, conceived in liberty, and dedicated to the proposition that all men are created equal.

Now we are engaged in a great civil war, testing whether that nation, or any nation so conceived and so dedicated, can long endure. We are met on a great battlefield of that war. We have come to dedicate a portion of that field, as a final resting place for those who here gave their lives that that nation might live. It is altogether fitting and proper that we should do this.

But, in a larger sense, we can not dedicate, we can not consecrate, we can not hallow this ground. The brave men, living and dead, who struggled here, have consecrated it, far above our poor power to add or detract. The world will little note, nor long remember what we say here, but it can never forget what they did here. It is for us the living, rather, to be dedicated here to the unfinished work which they who fought here have thus far so nobly advanced. It is rather for us to be here dedicated to the great task remaining before us—that from these honored dead we take increased devotion to that cause for which they gave the last full measure of devotion—that we here highly resolve that these dead shall not have died in vain—that this nation, under God, shall have a new birth of freedom—and that government of the people, by the people, for the people, shall not perish from the earth."

I quote it in its entirety as a seminal encapsulation of the "Spirit of 1776," the Declaration of Independence, and the work yet unfinished to realize its lofty goals. It speaks to the divisions in the fabric of the American Society that were then so gaping and the risks hazarded to heal those divisions in quest of a stronger Union. And finally, the Gettysburg Address, along with the Declaration, are and remain, the foundational documents of the Civil Rights Movement which began during Reconstruction after the Civil War and continued down to the Civil Rights Movement of the 1960s. The Thirteenth Amendment to the United States Constitution outlawing slavery was adopted into law in December of 1865. The work of Black African civil rights and women's rights in their infancy then. The Civil Rights struggle continues as one tracks more recent incidents in places like Tahrir Square in Cairo (2011), Gezi Park in Istanbul (2013), Baltimore Riots (2017) and everywhere around the world.

Women's Rights, the Suffragette Movement and the 19th Amendment (1920)

It would not be an exaggeration to say that women in Colonial America had few rights if any outside the home. The road to Women's Suffrage was a long one in both Europe and America. Ironically, women's involvement in the Anti-Slavery Abolitionist Movement brought to home their own lack of rights, including the right to vote. The struggle also exposed them to the mechanics of organizing and fighting for a cause. The first Convention specifically called to address Women's Rights was organized by two pillars of the movement, Elizabeth Cady Stanton and the Quaker Abolitionist Lucretia Mott at Seneca Falls, New York, 1844. The Delegates to the Convention adopted a

"Declaration of Sentiments, Grievances and Resolutions" which echoed the Declaration of Independence by putting forth the proposition that "All men *and women* are created equal" [Author's underline].

The first States to grant women the vote were States West of the Mississippi River beginning with Wyoming in 1869. Illinois was the first State east of the Mississippi to grant women the vote in 1913. The First World War, as wars tend to do,  engaged women in all sorts of work normally relegated to men. This engagement included women involved in the "Progressive Causes" of the period. One of those "causes" was the Woman's Suffrage Movement led by the indefatigable Susan B. Anthony. With the support of recent convert to this cause President Woodrow Wilson, the State of Montana elected the first National Congresswoman in history, Jeanette Rankin, in 1917. In 1919, as the Turkish War of Independence began, American-born Nancy Langhorne Astor, Lady Astor, was elected Britain's first female Member of Parliament. In 1920, the 19th Amendment to the Constitution was finally passed into law giving women the right to vote.

Women's Rights in the Spirit of The Turkish Civil Code (1926)

While not germane to this topic, it is interesting to note that some women, during the Sultanates of women in the 16th and 17th centuries, certain women of the harem, often slaves, exerted a significant influence in the making of State decisions. A number of these women were  the mothers of very young Sultan's known as *Velide* Sultanas. During the period of Tanzimat Reforms in the 19th century, some Ottoman women began to demand certain rights, including access to education, paid work, and an end to polygamy. The first Women's Rights organization in Turkey was formed in 1908. Among its members was author and political activist Halide Edip Adıvar, who lamented the fact that Turkish women seemed to be uninterested in improving their low social status. After the establishment of the Republic in Turkey, the Women's Rights effort worked in tandem with Kemalist Reforms. Women's Rights advocates were swept along by the secularizing reforms beginning with the new Civil Code in which women gained equitable divorce and inheritance rights and an end to polygamy. Women gained the right to be elected to local office in 1930 and to national office in 1934. In the 1935 elections, 18 women entered Parliament. The author's own inquiries in the late 1970s revealed that Sharia Law and Turkish custom continued to be practiced for decades, unofficially, by the Village Headman and the

Elders in the course of dispute resolution in rural areas, especially in the East and South Eastern parts of Turkey, long after the law on the books had been changed.

In 1993, Turkey elected its first woman Prime Minister, Tansu Çiller. As noteworthy an accomplishment as that was, domestic violence as reported in the press and in studies, not just among the rural poor, and "honor killings" continue to illustrate the need for more education and more effective implementation of the laws protecting women in Turkey. While the percentage of women in the workforce had been increasing, especially in the early years of the AKP Party rule, a disturbing downward trend, matched by a decrease in the number of women in Parliament, has begun to show in recent years.

At a women's Justice Summit on November 24, 2014 in Istanbul, President Erdoğan stated that women are unequal to men and that certain work goes against women's "delicate nature," and *"their characters, habits, and physiques are different from men's... Our religion [Islam] has defined a position for women: motherhood."* He had previously announced that Turkish women should have *"at least three children and preferably five."* A related phenomenon that seems to be spreading across the Islamic world is a growing number of those women choosing or being "encouraged" to wear the veil. It would appear that current trends in gender equality are moving away from the secular goals of the Founders of the modern Republic of Turkey. If such trends are cast as being "democratically"-inspired, clearly then the political-social norms of some segments of the population are moving away from the Western secular model.

As an aside, the daughter of one Naci Pasha who was a close friend of Kemal Atatürk, Perihan Arıburun, was one of the first women admitted to the new Law School. She went on to become a Member of Parliament representing the Democrat Party. She and her husband, Commander of the Turkish Air Force and later President of the Senate in the 1970s, Tekin Pasha, were put into prison during the Coup over-throwing Prime Minister Adnan Menderes. In 1977, shortly after arriving to begin Doctoral research, my wife and I were introduced to them and became friends. They were both very well-educated, refined and multi-lingual. It was she who first introduced me to the tales of *Nasrettin Hoca.* They were a particularly interesting couple for us to meet. They were part of a cross-over generation who had gone through the radical transition from the Ottoman State to the Turkish Republic. Their manners were "old world" elegant (*çok Effendi*) and worldly. Another gentleman comes to mind here as well. One of our dearest and oldest friends, then recently retired Corps General Adnan Orel, helped me translate early Appellate Court case decisions still written in Ottoman Script between the Civil Law's adoption in 1926 and the "Latinization" of the alphabet two years later. Like Tekin Pasha, Adnan Pasha had served in Paris and London and spoke a beautiful, almost Victorian English. He had begun his military career in the cavalry on horseback in Eastern Turkey in Atatürk's lifetime. It was an education, and an honor, to know them.

The American Civil Rights Movement

As proved to be the case in the Kemalist Reforms, changing the law on the books does not mean that the practice changes. The Emancipation Proclamation and the 13th Amendment were slow to change the practice in many areas of the South and "Copper Head" areas in the Mississippi and Ohio River Valleys of the Mid-West. From 1865 to 1875, during Reconstruction, the Federal Government stationed troops in the South to ensure that Black Americans were not re-enslaved. When the troops left, many found a way to effectively "re-enslave" many of the Blacks. Douglas Blackmon, in his Pulitzer Prize winning book, *Slavery by Another Name*, published in 2008 recounts the practice of leasing Blacks, said to be guilty of some crime, often insignificant, to plantations and corporations who would then become virtual slaves. This practice continued up to World War II. Jim Crow laws passed in Southern States legalized the segregation of the races, in schools and public places, from restaurants to bathrooms, and from busses to movie theaters.

Civil Rights continued to be slow in coming to Blacks and other minorities. Public schools, for example, were segregated in much of the South. In 1954, a landmark ruling by the U.S. Supreme Court in the *Brown v. the Board of Education* case clearly ruled that segregation of the races in public schools was against the law. In 1957, then President Dwight Eisenhower sent the National Guard into Little Rock, Arkansas to enforce the desegregation of a public high school.

On grounds of States' Rights to organize the public education of its citizens, many State Governors and officials continued to defy the Federal law. By the late 1950s, fewer than 10% of Black children attended integrated schools. Civil Rights leader Martin Luther King, Jr. led a boycott that ended segregated bussing in Montgomery, Alabama. Just weeks before the 1960 Presidential election, King was arrested while leading a protest in Atlanta. Significantly, Jack Kennedy called Martin Luther King, Jr.'s father to express concern while his brother, Robert Kennedy, called the local judge to get King out of jail. These acts of concern and kindness put the Kennedys on a permanent pedestal with the Blacks and the Civil Rights movement. In the 1960 election, 70% of Blacks voted for Jack Kennedy. In a National Election settled by slightly more than 500,000 votes, the Black vote helped carry a few critical States in to the Kennedy/Democrat win column.

Earlier that year, four Black college students were refused service at a lunch counter in Greensboro, North Carolina. They refused to leave and staged a "sit-in." They were relieved by volunteers and sit-ins swept across 12 States in the South and in 65 cities with some 50,000 young people joining in the protests. Kennedy placed his Vice President, Lyndon Johnson, as the head of the Committee on Equal Employment Opportunity. His brother, the Attorney General Robert Kennedy, turned his attention to Voting Rights abuses of Blacks.

Kennedy's victory margin was slim and was interpreted to mean that he would need to go slowly on the Civil Rights bandwagon. But the genie was out of the bottle. Some interstate bus lines organized "freedom rides" on integrated buses. Freedom Riders were taken off buses and arrested in North Carolina and beaten in South Carolina. In Alabama, a bus was stopped, over-turned and burned with many of the riders beaten with baseball bats and tire irons. Attorney General Kennedy sent in 400 Federal Marshalls to protect the Freedom Riders.

In 1962, an Air Force veteran, James Meredith, Jr., applied and tried to register at the University of Mississippi State. Four times he was turned down. President Kennedy and Attorney General Kennedy spoke by phone with Mississippi Governor Ross Barnett to no avail. When Federal Marshalls accompanied Meredith to "Ole Miss" to register, a riot broke out. The President mobilized the Mississippi National Guard and sent Marshalls to the campus to restore order. Dozens of people were injured and two died.

In the spring of 1963, Martin Luther King, Jr. called for a city-wide protest of Birmingham, Alabama – a city which he proclaimed to be the most segregated in the South. King was put into jail on Good Friday and his supporters immediately organized a protest march. The Commissioner of

Birmingham, Eugene "Bull" Conner turned the fire hoses and police dogs on the protestors. A thousand protestors were arrested. Significantly, the entire incident was seen on public television, changing public awareness, especially in the North. In response, the President sent several thousand troops to an air base in Alabama. In June of 1963, Governor Wallace "stood in the doorway" to prevent two black students from entering the University of Alabama. Jack Kennedy "federalized" the National Guard of Alabama and went on television to explain to the American people that segregation was immoral, unconstitutional, and illegal. He went on to say that major Civil Rights legislation would follow shortly, guaranteeing equal access to public education and an end to segregation as well as Federal protection of Voting Rights.

"I Have a Dream" Speech, Martin Luther King, Jr.

In August of 1963, a march was organized to celebrate the Centennial of the Emancipation Proclamation in Washington D.C. It was estimated that a crowd of 200,000 of mixed races and ages gathered in support of the commemoration. It was here that Martin Luther King, Jr. delivered his most passionate and eloquent appeal for a future free of racial discrimination. Part of the speech follows:

> "I am happy to join with you today in what will go down in history as the greatest demonstration for freedom in the history of our nation. Five score years ago, a great American, in whose symbolic shadow we stand today, signed

the Emancipation Proclamation. This momentous decree came as a great beacon light of hope to millions of Negro slaves who had been seared in the flames of withering injustice. It came as a joyous daybreak to end the long night of their captivity.

But one hundred years later, the Negro still is not free. One hundred years later, the life of the Negro is still sadly crippled by the manacles of segregation and the chains of discrimination. One hundred years later, the Negro lives on a lonely island of poverty in the midst of a vast ocean of material prosperity. One hundred years later, the Negro is still languishing in the corners of American society and finds himself an exile in his own land. So we have come here today to dramatize a shameful condition.

In a sense we have come to our nation's capital to cash a check. When the architects of our republic wrote the magnificent words of the Constitution and the Declaration of Independence, they were signing a promissory note to which every American was to fall heir. This note was a promise that all men, yes, black men as well as white men, would be guaranteed the unalienable rights of life, liberty, and the pursuit of happiness.

It is obvious today that America has defaulted on this promissory note insofar as her citizens of color are concerned. Instead of honoring this sacred obligation, America has given the Negro people a bad check, a check which has come back marked "insufficient funds." But we refuse to believe that the bank of justice is bankrupt. We refuse to believe that there are insufficient funds in the great vaults of opportunity of this nation. So we have come to cash this check -- a check that will give us upon demand the riches of freedom and the security of justice. We have also come to this hallowed spot to remind America of the fierce urgency of now. This is no time to engage in the luxury of cooling off or to take the tranquilizing drug of gradualism. Now is the time to make real the promises of democracy. Now is the time to rise from the dark and desolate valley of segregation to the sunlit path of racial justice. Now is the time to lift our nation from the quick sands of racial injustice to the solid rock of brotherhood. Now is the time to make justice a reality for all of God's children.... I say to you today, my friends, so even though we face the difficulties of today and tomorrow, I still have a dream. It is a dream deeply rooted in the American dream. I have a dream that one day this nation will rise up and live out the true meaning of its creed: 'We hold these truths to be self-evident: that all men are created equal'... This will be the day when all of God's children will be able to sing with a new meaning, "My country, 'tis of thee, sweet land of liberty, of thee I sing. Land where my fathers died, land of the pilgrim's pride, from every mountainside, let freedom ring.

And when this happens, when we allow freedom to ring, when we let it ring from every village and every hamlet, from every state and every city, we will be able to speed up that day when all of God's children, black men and white men, Jews and Gentiles, Protestants and Catholics, will be able to join *hands and sing in the words of the old Negro spiritual, "Free at last! free at last! thank God Almighty, we are free at* last!"

President Kennedy would not live to see the passage of the Civil Rights Act. He was assassinated on November 22nd of that year, 1963. His successor, President Lyndon Johnson, former Senator from Texas would use his political connections in the South, moved by Kennedy's untimely death, to persuade enough Southern Congressmen to vote for its passage that, together with Republican Congressional leadership, the Civil Rights Act would be passed the following year. In the process, the Jim Crow laws were deemed null and void. Legal equality for the Blacks had been achieved, but much remained, and much remains to heal racial rifts in American Society.

While much progress has been achieved, facts on the ground, and perhaps more crucially, "perceptions," continue to call for more work and better understanding. And tragically, key players in the process were gunned down in April and June of 1968, Martin Luther King, Jr. and Attorney General Bobby Kennedy, respectively.

The need and the work on healing the racial divide in America continues as evidenced by developments in Ferguson, Missouri in 2014. After three months of investigation of physical evidence and 60 witnesses, on November 24th, the Grand Jury, a jury of three Black and 9 White men and women, decided that grounds to indict did not exist. Police Officer Darren Wilson would face no charges in the shooting death of Michael Brown. The Public Prosecutor announced the Jury finding at 9:00 at night. As authorities were expecting rioting and looting regardless of the decision, the Governor had readied the National Guard and the police were prepared for the worst. President Obama immediately came on National television calling for calm. Ferguson protestors, many from outside Ferguson, erupted in protest, burning cars and 25 businesses. The police struggled to contain the violence with tear gas. Sympathetic protests took place in New York, Seattle, Los Angeles, and Oakland.

A year later, in the late spring of 2015, a black man, Freddie Gray, died while in police custody in Baltimore, Maryland. Further protests were organized after Gray's death became public knowledge, amid the police department's continuing inability to adequately or consistently explain the events following the arrest and the injuries. Spontaneous protests started after the funeral service, although several included violent elements. Civil unrest continued with at least twenty police officers injured, at least 250 people arrested, 285 to 350 businesses damaged (many specifically directed by black rioters against Korean-, Chinese- and Arab-owned businesses), 150 vehicle fires, 60 structure fires, 27 drugstores looted, thousands of police and Maryland National Guard troops deployed, and with a State of Emergency declared in the city limits of Baltimore.

The complexity and the danger of social unrest are aptly described in the following two quotations. On April 28, President Barack Obama strongly condemned the violence during a White House press conference, saying,

> *"There's no excuse for the kind of violence that we saw yesterday. It is counterproductive. ... When individuals get crowbars and start prying open doors to loot, they're not protesting. They're not making a statement. They're stealing. When they burn down a building, they're committing arson. And they're destroying and undermining businesses and opportunities in their own communities. That robs jobs and opportunity from people in that area." Obama went on to applaud the actions of peaceful protesters whom he felt were being undermined by the violence, and called upon the nation to take meaningful action to collectively solve poverty and law enforcement issues fueling what he described as "a crisis."*

John P. Angelos, Chief Operation Officer of The Baltimore Orioles Baseball Team, said in connection with the postponing of a game at that time for security reasons,

> *"My greater source of personal concern, outrage and sympathy ... is focused neither upon one night's property*

damage nor upon the acts, but is focused rather upon the past four-decade period during which an American political elite have shipped middle class and working class jobs away from Baltimore and cities and towns around the U.S. to third-world dictatorships ... plunged tens of millions of good hard working Americans into economic devastation and then followed that action around the nation by diminishing every American's civil rights protections in order to control an unfairly impoverished population living under an ever-declining standard of living and suffering at the butt end of an ever-more militarized and aggressive surveillance state. The innocent working families of all backgrounds whose lives and dreams have been cut short by excessive violence, surveillance, and other abuses of the Bill of Rights by government pay the true price, an ultimate price, and one that far exceeds the importance of any kids' game played tonight, or ever..."

The media is too often the handmaiden of the tendency to magnify such events beyond their due proportion, or before the facts are established. Events and incidents which may happen very infrequently, with motives and facts often overlooked or unknown, are sometimes cast in the context of larger "political" agendas, rather than just a presentation of the news. In the absence of facts, and well prior to any judicial rulings on such events, the "court of public opinion," shaped by the actions and statements, or notable inactions, on the part of public officials and political leaders, not infrequently results in an unconstructive contribution to civil unrest. Using alleged injustices as a rationale for burning, looting, stealing, destroying private property, and injuring police officials was not in Martin Luther King, Jr.'s playbook of remedies for the redress of social, legal and political inequality. Violent behavior bullying and intimidation are not a Civil Right. For all its progress, Civil Rights in America continues to struggle in search of viable solutions. Recognizing that there are groups and forces that thrive on social and political unrest must be part of any amelioration of the underlying causes.

Chapter 18

IMMIGRATION AND IDENTITY POLITICS

The following chapter seeks to explore the role of immigration, changing demographics, and communication technology in changing the political landscape of America and Turkey.

The Statue of Liberty and Immigration in America

From the beginning, America was a Promised Land. People came for many reasons, mostly economic, to escape religious intolerance, and often a combination of the two. The Native Americans were soon dwarfed in population size and technology by the immigrants, who also brought with them diseases for which the Native population had no natural immunities. Europeans had earlier experienced the Bubonic Plague, coming it is said from the Far East, with the survivors tending to develop immunities. Immigrants came largely from Europe. The English and Dutch came to the Eastern seaboard. The French largely came to Canada and the Great Lakes. The Spanish came to Florida, New Mexico, and Southern California. The original European settlements in North America are: St. Augustine, Florida

(1565); Jamestown, Virginia (1607); Quebec City, Canada; Santa Fe, New Mexico (1608); and Plymouth Colony, Massachusetts (1620).

The next wave of immigrants coming in large numbers were African slaves, beginning in 1620. They were followed by Scots-Irish, more English and Germans. Many of these Europeans came as indentured servants. Indentures were typically from 5-7 years, after which they would become "freemen." By the early 1700s, regional differences began to widen. The Northern colonies settled around towns and were populated by small farmers, fishermen, and tradesmen. There, education was important, even if narrow in scope and religious in orientation. Harvard, for example, was founded in 1635 to train ministers. The North also enjoyed a preferable climate in terms of disease control, winters tending to kill off mosquitos for example, resulting in low infant mortality rates. As many hands were needed, families were large, with 6, 8, 10 children or more by one mother common. They were largely Separatist Protestants of one denomination or another.

The Middle Colonies, New York, Pennsylvania, Delaware, and Maryland were more heavily populated by the Dutch, Quakers, Germans, and some Swedes. They were similarly employed as the New Englanders. In religion, in addition to Quakers, the Middle Colonies also had German Lutheran Protestants and, in Maryland in particular, Catholics.

By contrast, in the South, whose founders in many cases had large land grants from the King, people lived farther apart from one another. Families were a little smaller and the labor was largely supplied by Africans, and again, white indentured servants. By descent, the Southerners were approximately 55% British, 38% Black, and 7% German by the mid-1700s. Religious worship was Anglican Protestant officially, with Methodists, Presbyterians, and Quakers practicing more discreetly further inland as one got closer to the Appalachian Mountains or further into the Shenandoah Valley.

Connecting all three of these areas was the Atlantic on one side, the Eastern Sea Board, and the Appalachian Mountains on the western edge. From the Alleghenies, to the Blue Ridge, to the Smokey Mountains, these frontier inhabitants were largely Scots-Irish Presbyterian Protestants with German Lutherans in the Shenandoah Valley.

Native Americans by choice, and Africans (but later and mostly in the North) by requirement, were both schooled in English and Christianity. Dartmouth College in New Hampshire (then a part of Massachusetts) was founded in 1769 by a Congregational Minister expressly to educate Mohicans and other native tribes in the area.

In the Colonial period, beyond or west of the Appalachians, in the Great Lakes and the Ohio and Mississippi River Valleys, the inhabitants were largely made up of traders, voyageurs and Native Americans. When the French lost the French and Indian War (1754-1763), a mass migration of French left Canada, Arcadia (Nova Scotia) in particular, and came down the Mississippi and settled in the New Orleans area. They flourished in the area and are to this day known as Cajuns, people from Arcadia. They were largely Huguenots or French Protestants. Well prior to the American Revolution, French Huguenots, as discussed earlier, had settled in Pfalz and New Rochelle, New York and Manakin-Sabot in Virginia. Population in the American Colonies was approaching 4,000,000 by the end of the 18th century.

The Spanish had their Colonies in Florida and New Mexico where they lived alongside Native Americans, the Seminoles in Florida and the Pueblo in New Mexico. In between, was yet undiscovered, unknown until President Jefferson sent the explorers Lewis and Clark to map and describe the interior of the Country (1804-1807), in search of a Northwest Passage to the Pacific. These were the Great Plains and what became known as the Rocky Mountains, which they crossed reaching the Pacific Ocean in the area of what became Oregon.

The immigrant population growth subsided dramatically in the first two decades of the 1800s. But, beginning in the latter 1830s, it began to explode, especially with the Irish Potato Famine in the 1840s. Upwards of 2,000,000 Irish immigrated to America between 1840 and 1860. By the 1850s, due to nationalism and unification movements in Europe, large numbers of Italians and even more Germans began to come to America. Between 1850 and 1930, approximately 5,000,000 Germans immigrated to America, including my paternal grandmother's family. As many as 300,000 of the Union Army troops in the American Civil War were made up of German and Irish immigrants.

By 1886, immigrants coming into New York, on their way to processing at Ellis Island before being allowed to land in New York City, all passed by that icon of welcome, the Statue of Liberty. The total numbers between 1840 and 1930 is a number in the range of 25,000,000. They came from Poland, Italy, Greece, Hungary, China, and Jews escaping Russian Pogroms. They largely settled in the industrial cities of the North. To gain some perspective, Turkey's total population today is about 80,000,000.

Of course, earlier immigrants, very largely Protestant, found this newer wave of immigrants, often with lower literacy levels. Catholics and Chinese were typically seen as potentially threatening to the status quo. A political party formed in the mid-1850s, the Know Nothing or Nativist Party, formed in response to a fear of Irish and German Catholics getting political control in various parts of America and being ruled by the Pope by extension. A century later, the same fear was expressed about John F. Kennedy first when he ran for Massachusetts Senator, and more so later, when he ran against Richard Nixon for President in 1960.

In 1875, America passed its first immigration law, the Page Act or Asian Exclusion Act. The Chinese were being brought in large numbers to build the transcontinental railroad. The Irish and Germans provided much of the labor building the rails from the east, while Chinese "Cooley" labor was used to build the rail from California in the west. Beginning in 1882, quotas were set for Chinese immigrants. Just prior to the outbreak of World War I, upwards of 1.5 million Swedes and Norwegians, fleeing political oppression and poverty, came to America. By 1924, quotas were being placed on Southern Europeans, Lebanese, and Syrian Christians. Of those who did come, many found their way to Detroit, providing labor in the steel mills and the burgeoning automotive industry.

Many of the longer-established Americans worried about strains on the social and political fabric of America. The question then raised was, given the low skill level of many of the immigrants, was America still a "melting pot" or a "dumping ground?" In 1921, and again in 1924, additional quotas were established attempting to stabilize the ethnic and religious landscape of America set according to census figures from the turn of the century. This led to a curbing of "extra" immigration, including Jews fleeing from Nazi Germany.

After WWII, immigration preferences were made for displaced persons, wives or fiancées of American servicemen from countries in which they had served, refugees from the Hungarian Revolution, those fleeing Fidel Castro's Cuba, and Vietnamese loyal to the American war effort there.

Clearly, by the 1960s, the demographic make-up of America had radically changed since the Civil War. Setting aside the special and protracted plight of African Americans, it should be remembered that immigrants to America's shores, from the beginning in the 1600s, each succeeding wave were exposed to disease, starvation, danger, and violent death. No group was handed an easy life. From the early Venturers and Separatists of Jamestown and Plymouth Bay, to the Irish and Germans, to Jews and Catholics, all struggled against enormous odds in the process of assimilating into their new country. The Native Americans struggled against smallpox from even before significant colonization, as well as an often heroic but a losing battle to European technology, immigration and birth rates. Certainly, many Native Americans and colonists paid with their scalps and their lives in a contest for control for land and resources, and not infrequently at the hands of their own races.

Between 1781 and 1917, a period of 136 years, peace in America was interrupted for only eight years total, the War of 1812 and the Civil War years. During this time, the American population exploded and spread across a large land mass, eventually connected by barge, rail, electricity, telegraph, and telephone. During that same period of time, Turkey was wracked with almost continuous war, forced migration and social dislocation.

In conclusion, one should note that after hundreds of years of survival and adaptation, complete with tension, conflict, and sacrifice, the American Experiment has survived. *E Pluribus Unum* was an aspiration which, against all odds, and over the obstacles of many anti-immigration political movements and quota bills, saw its fulfillment in the "American Dream." While the process was messy and often uninspiring, the promise of America as a "melting pot" continued to function. Identity politics was culturally and racially alive and well, but exercised more on State and local levels.

I would argue that the Vietnam War, Social Protest, Birth Control, the mainstreaming of recreational drugs, Water Gate, aided and propelled by technological advances in television, profoundly changed America and how Americans perceived themselves and their country. Televisions in the 1960s had become as ubiquitous as cell phones in the 1990s, and smart phones in more recent years. Previously established mores, taboos, and institutions of authority were called into question by many, eventually even within the establishment.

Arguably, all technology has presented mankind with a two-edged sword. It may serve to bind the Nation, where one thinks of electricity, the rails, baseball on radio, Franklin Delano Roosevelt's "fireside chats" to a frightened anxious and underemployed population, U.S. War Bonds, and later a lunar landing. While bronze, iron, and gun powder had lent themselves to both constructive and destructive uses, and modern communication technology has been no exception. But with the advent of television and its ability to bring live, and taped, images into the homes of millions of people, such as its coverage of Civil Rights marches, race riots in Detroit and Watts, the Kent State protest shootings by National Guardsmen, and nightly newscasts of the death toll in Vietnam, the temptation to shape the news, rather than just report it, increased the risk that the TV medium could control images and related perceptions across an entire population could be Orwellian. Radical anti-establishment movements, from SDS to the Black Panthers, spread across academia and urban centers from coast to coast, aided by this new medium, amplified by this new medium. Kennedy's "New Frontier" and Johnson's "Great Society" were "anti-status quo" official government policies, sometimes leading, sometimes following, the sea-changes taking place in American Society broadcast into the homes of all Americans.

Mixing Bowl to Salad Bowl – Centrifugal Racial, Religious, and Cultural Forces

Joyce Millet in her article, "From Melting Pot to Mixing Bowl", succinctly defines the trend of recent decades noting, *"Today the trend is toward multiculturalism, not assimilation. The old "melting pot" metaphor is giving way to new metaphors such as "salad bowl" and "mosaic," mixtures of various ingredients that keep their individual characteristics. Immigrant populations within the United States are not being blended together in one "pot," but rather they are transforming American Society into a truly multicultural mosaic."*

Given the seismic social and political shifts that have gripped "post-Sputnik" America, with external pressures adding heat to the process, from the Energy Crises of the 1970s to unrest in the Middle East, Latin, and Central America, the Cold War, producing new waves of immigration, from Mexico in particular, multiculturalism became increasingly seen as inevitable, desirable and "politically correct." American confidence in its "traditional values" as the basis for a healthy and prosperous society came under attack from the Liberal and progressive end of the political spectrum, compounded by anti-establishment students of the Vietnam and Watergate eras who called into question the legitimacy of traditional norms and institutional authority.

The era of President Ronald Reagan restored much of America's sense of confidence. This was especially evident with the fall of the Berlin Wall and the triumph of the Capitalist model over the Communist model of society. The end of the Cold War brought with it a very short-lived peace dividend. In the absence of the titanic struggle with the Soviets, and the concomitant common cause that had made foreign policy choices relatively less complicated for "Allies," old alliances began to show signs of stress. Countries and populations around the world found themselves caught up in the process of reexamining and redefining themselves. This phenomenon began already in the early 1990s, both at the National and sub-group levels regarding their national and group-interests, including NATO allies.

Sub groups, with the benefit of the internet, began to see themselves as a collective, with potential political power. Some of these groups began to identify themselves first by racial, ethnic, or issue descriptors, and secondarily as Americans. At the risk of oversimplifying vastly complicated social transformations, one might look at the net results of these processes as culminating in a "crowning" of the concept of multiculturalism as the quintessential embodiment of the American Experience. In the process, the quintessentially American ideal of the "melting pot" gave way to what Joyce Millet described as a *"mixing bowl."* With these developments in mind, one might view migration to America as a kind of transplantation of migrant groups into an American culture prone to celebrate, and accommodate, difference rather than to encourage assimilation. These thoughts do not represent a judgment, rather an observation of changing patterns of citizen identification.

Immigration in America – From Ellis Island to the Mexican Border

America is a nation of immigrants, historically, very largely legal immigrants. If the Statue of Liberty is the symbol of freedom and welcome, Ellis Island was also the legal gateway to that promise. Between 1892 and 1954 when it was closed, it is estimated that some 12 million people, entered America through Ellis Island. Since the last Amnesty of some three million illegal aliens, mostly Mexican, during President Reagan's second term in the late 1980s, America has become home to an additional estimated 12 million illegal aliens, or as they are now more benignly described, "undocumented" persons.

The largest number of immigrants to arrive at Ellis Island was in 1907, slightly over one million. The largest number to arrive in a day was over 11,000, also in 1907. Over its history, about 2% were detained, either dying there in hospital or were returned to their home country as suspected criminals or afflicted with potentially contagious disease. There was an area on Ellis island where family members already in America would wait to welcome them. After WWI, increasingly some were held as political subversives and then deported. During WWII, suspected subversives, primarily German and Italian, and those already living here in the case of the Japanese, were interned for the balance of the war. Other than the sick and the suspect, most were admitted after four or five hours of physical/ medical examination and inspection. Country of origin and name were the primary questions asked. The official request was that immigrants arrive with a minimum of somewhere between $18 and $25 it is said, enough money to get to their relatives and/or a place of work. Some were deported due to their lack of skills, with concern that they would become indigent and then wards of the State.

Illegal immigration over the Mexican border is a complex issue, but at the very least, it begs the question of the significance of borders. There are proponents of "open borders," bringing with it the risk of an inability to guard against the entrance of the medically contagious, "radicals" of one stripe or another, criminals, the poor, and the unskilled. Each of these prospects is a potential danger to America and Americans. To say that these same risks exist in America irrespective of illegal immigrant is not an argument for adding to existing risks. Not being able to control a country's border also calls into question the Sovereignty of a country, and by extension, its Sovereign borders. All others from around the world looking to come to America, even genuine political refugees, enter, and have always entered, by a legal process. Having said this, clearly America is groping for an equitable solution to an immigration problem. Turkey is dealing with a massive immigration problem in the wake of the Syrian war. And by extension, the EU is dealing with the largest migration of peoples to its shores since WWII. It is similarly conflicted on the best course of action. Jordan and Libya are two other countries dealing with migration issues. In fact, all over the globe, where there is interminable political strife and violence, one sees large, and often uncontrollable, migration.

The legal Mexican immigrant population was estimated at 2.1 million in 1980, 4.3 million in 1990 (including the Amnestied of 1986) and 7.8 million in 2000. Add to this number, another 9 + million undocumented residents, the Mexican-American population probably numbers something like 16 million. A large portion of Mexico's 122 million people have emigrated to America. In an effort to stem the tide of this migration, the 1986 Immigration Control Act instituted fines against American businesses which hire illegal aliens. This is a law which has never been seriously implemented. The argument has been that these workers help keep the cost of goods and services down in some industries and that they are willing to do work that Americans are no longer willing to do. If the first rationale is probably true, the second assertion is harder to prove. It might be true that Americans are hard to find who will do hard labor for minimum wage, especially when various taxpayer subsidies tend to dull both the appetite for such work and the incentive to move to where such work may be offered. If some Latino laborers are exploited, they work here voluntarily in the face of apparently worse alternatives in their own countries. Such an observation might be hazarded about all immigrant groups until they can establish themselves, first economically and then politically.

When and where the mechanization of agriculture takes place, even hard-working labor can be displaced causing migration to urban areas in search of jobs, driving the price of labor, unskilled in particular, down. This phenomenon results in over-crowded urban areas and a tendency to movement across borders, legally and illegally, into other countries in search of work. Certainly, this is a familiar story in Turkey beginning in the 1970s down to the present. Beginning in the late 1960s, the German *Gastarbeiter* (Guest Worker) program occasioned onward migration from rural Turks to Ankara and Istanbul and, with overcrowding and depressed wages, onward movement to Germany. There they were given jobs Germans no longer wanted to, or felt the need to, do themselves. A similar migration from the South, especially the Blacks, to the Northern Industrial States during and after WWII in America took place in search of better pay, and an escape from the bane of Jim Crow laws in some areas of the South.

Managing large groups of immigrants has never been easy in history. Ghettoization has invariably been the result. Whether one thinks of the Jews in Warsaw in WWII, or blacks in slums in the industrial North of America, or the Rohingya in Myanmar, managing large groups of immigrants has been problematic throughout history. America, because of her size and abundance of resources, has been better able to absorb large-scale migration better than most countries. Certainly, Germany's Guest Worker Program remains an example of failed assimilation as noted by Prime Minister Angela Merkel, who said as much publicly in 2012. In the German case, this Program was apparently conceived as a temporary employment of low-skilled "foreign workers." The fact that they were placed in urban enclaves initially did not appear to be an issue. The fact that these Guest Workers stayed, reproduced, and gained German citizenship, but continued to live in ghettoes with low wages, and in general not assimilate, proved to be a problem for both the Turks and the Germans.

There are some three million Turks in Germany today with high birth rates in a country with a very low native birth rate, many now possessing dual passports. Turks learning German and assimilating into German society has not been successful for many, not all, with responsibility on both sides. This might also be said of Spanish-speaking immigrants, documented and undocumented, in America. One difference from the German example is that politically America has become accommodative of the notion that these immigrants not be required to learn English. And it follows that if one does not have to speak English to get a driver's license, work, and vote, with official government documents increasingly being offered in Spanish, the incentive to learn English, however potentially desirable in terms of assimilation and upward mobility, remains weakened. Such policies tend to facilitate the "mixing bowl" paradigm and appeals to many Americans, even though they may, at the same time, tend to inhibit the notion of being Americans first, ancestral and cultural allegiances notwithstanding.

Changing Norms – Spanish as a Second "Official" Language in America

For several hundred years, learning English was expected of non-English-speaking immigrants to America. It sometimes took a couple of generations before English took the place of the ancestral tongue. It was not uncommon for grandchildren of immigrants to understand their grandparents speaking their ethnic language, but not be able to utter more than a few words and phrases in the original mother tongue. It was also a badge of honor to be able to speak English. The need for work and the desire for advancement were all the incentive new comers needed. As noted earlier, this aspiration has been diluted in America in recent decades where Latino culture is predominant. To date, no other ethnic group has been so accommodated.

Many in America find this trend to be divisive of the goal of "union," economically and socially unproductive. Others believe that it is practical, reasonable and may bring with it some political advantage. Because of America's historic geographic insularity, others would argue that Americans would be well-served to learn other languages, Spanish, Chinese, or Arabic for example. Whatever the reasons, many Americans in general, more recent immigrant groups in particular, seem to be content, or prefer, to operate almost exclusively in the context of their racial and ethnic affinity associations than was the case in earlier generations of immigrants. As America continues down the road of multiculturalism and identity politics, preserving the notion, architecture, of the Nation State becomes more and more challenging. Again, there are those that find the Nation State an anachronism. The world is complicated.

Turkish Migration to America

The first Turks may have arrived in the new world as rescues from Spanish Galleons by Sir Francis Drake and settled briefly on Roanoke Island off the coast of North Carolina in 1586. The colony did not survive, but some of these Turks are thought to have eventually repatriated to the Ottoman Empire. Throughout the 1800s, small numbers of Turks, mostly men, came to America for work and would after a number of years return to Turkey. Beginning in the 1960s and 1970s, educated and secular Turks began to emigrate to America, and further trained in their fields, mostly doctors and engineers. They led quiet lives and assimilated into their new country. By the 1980s, Turks of all stripes, skilled and unskilled, secular and pious, began to arrive, including large numbers of students. They began to build Mosques and create organizations, initially to promote Turkish culture, and subsequently, some of them were instituted to give a political voice to Turkish-American interests, a counter weight to the Armenian and Greek lobbies.

Of the good number of famous Turks in America, Ahmet Ertegun, founder of Atlantic Record label, Oz Bengur, a second-generation American who ran for Congress in 2006, Muhtar Kent, Chairman of Coca Cola, Dr. Oz, and Fethullah Gülen come to mind. While Turkish Americans live in all States of the Union, the largest concentration is located in the greater metropolitan area of New York City, with nearby Patterson, New Jersey being known as "little Istanbul." Other concentrations are found in the Washington, D.C. area, Rochester, New York, and Detroit, Michigan. As of this writing, recent estimates of people who claim ethnic Turkish extraction suggest that the Turkish-American population numbers about 500,000. As a rule, the Turks tend to follow earlier patterns of migrant assimilation in learning English – with the large majority already speaking English when they arrived in the past few decades. Since the Ertegün family took up residence in the building before WWII (pictured here), Turkey enjoys one of the most magnificent of all Ambassadorial residences in Washington D.C. The building was completed for Edward H. Everett in 1914, the inventor of the crimped, cork-lined, cola bottle cap. The Residence recently underwent a multi-million-dollar renovation and is one of the more beautiful ambassadorial residences in Washington. Turkish-Americans, while more given to the "melting pot" goal of assimilation, have become more

vocal in politics in support of their ancestral land, especially concerning subjects like the alleged Armenian Genocide, a divided Cyprus, and separatist Kurds, in Turkey and along its southern and eastern borders.

In conclusion, it is interesting to consider the melting pot – mixing bowl metaphors in the context of the late Ottoman Empire and the early Republic of Turkey. Arguably, the Empire was a hybrid, a melting pot for Sunni subjects, half a melting pot for Alevi and Kurdish subjects, and a mixing bowl for the *Millets*, Christians and Jews primarily. In the new Republic, supported by the concepts of Namık Kemal and Ziya Gökalp, and the policies of Atatürk and the Nationalists, Turks were not to be defined by religion or ethnicity, but by common geography, language, shared experience, and custom. In short, the Kemalist policies said, in effect, we are all Turks, we should all learn new Turkish (*Yeni Türkçe*), and religion should become a private matter. All will be in the melting pot and all will be equal before the law. The reality was/ is that ethnic differences and religious preferences, the desire to remain in a Caliphate with an association with the Community of the Muslim Faithful (Ümmet) were suppressed in ways that proved, in the end, to be artificial, contrived, unnatural, and undesirable by significant portions of the citizenry of Turkey. In sum, as is the case in America, the melting pot, for somewhat different reasons, in Turkey is in some ways back to the hybrid mixing bowl of the Ottoman Empire with the secularists being the modern equivalent of the "Westernizers" of the late Ottoman period. Extreme polarization better characterizes the mixing bowl of today in both countries.

Secularism versus the Judeo Christian Institutional Tradition in America

The separation of Church and State enshrined in America's Founding documents had always belied the fact of a natural symbiosis of secular humanism and Judeo-Christian principles and practice. The concept and belief in "Liberty" neither precluded nor excluded religious belief. In the American Experience, the Ten Commandments remained as part and parcel of American political norms and practice. The institutions of the American Government  were imbued with a Judeo-Christian ethos, including its national symbols (note the dollar bill below), from monuments to court houses in ways the French for example, after their Revolution, could find offensive. This aspect of American democracy was patently obvious to Alexis de Tocqueville as he travelled pre-Civil War America. This attribute of American secularism was in evidence in the early 1950s when President Eisenhower, under the perceived threat of Communism, urged the addition of "under God", in the American Pledge of Allegiance to the Flag originally created in 1892 – "...*One Nation, under God, with Liberty and Justice for All.*"

Perhaps, as America has shifted from the melting pot to the mixing bowl in recent decades, armed with the concept of "social and cultural relativity," pure secularists have sought to remove all vestiges of the Judeo-Christian symbols and practices in public institutions – most notably the practice of Christian prayer in school or team prayer in athletics. Multiculturalism places an emphasis on, or celebration of, the racial and ethnic differences of Americans. Such differences easily lend themselves to both commercial and political exploitation. In any case, the meaning, or interpretation of secularism, is changing in the America of the 21st century, perhaps making effective governance of the country evermore complex and challenging.

Secularism versus Islam – A Question of Compatibility in the Business of Governance

If one looks at the concept of secularism in modern Turkey, one also sees a struggle for the soul and direction of the country in the 21st century. For whatever its shortcomings, Kemalist secularism very effectively separated Mosque and State. While it took over half a century to re-enfranchise Islam to where it had a legitimate political voice, the pendulum has swung back to a point where Turkish society, the Turkish polity, finds itself increasingly polarized between the more outwardly pious and the less outwardly pious, or plain secular Turk, Muslim by definition rather than practice. The insertion of overtly Islamic beliefs and practices into the workings of Turkey's secular machinery of governance, together with and a foreign policy which now places a special value on Islamic religious affinity, calls into question the subject of the constitutional separation (1927) of Islam and State.

When Americans have sometimes called taxes on alcohol and cigarettes, a "sin tax," the implications are no longer, as they once were, religious (Blue Laws). It has been traditionally "fair game" to raise revenue for national and state government via substantial taxes on these products. One might ask, has the rationale for increasing taxes on these same products in Turkey been solely for revenue generation, or has the rationale been predicated upon the Koranic moral injunctions against the use of either, or both?

The separation of the Church from the governance of a State was long in coming to the West. It was a history replete with sectarian violent episodes – hundreds of years of bloodshed and wars as we have seen. While the ethics of Western law and systems of governance were originally influenced by Judeo-Christian principles, English and Roman law, the secularization of those contributing principles and rules has removed any direct apparent association with religion. Arguably, the adoption of secular Western laws and systems of governance into a culturally and religiously hostile setting, as was the case in Turkey, made the prospects for a successful transplantation more vulnerable to rejection. The freer the democracy, the more challenging the prospects of maintaining secular forms of government in a Muslim culture, and in a Muslim neighborhood, becomes. Tunisia is also currently struggling to find a secular balance in its Muslim culture, by with a degree of success. The radicalization of religion, often related to a failure to govern effectively, further challenges the pursuit of finding a functional balance in business of governance in Muslim society.

Not Quite Separation of Church and State –
The Establishment of Hanefi-Sunni Islam

Not only is the principle of the separation of Islam and State challenging 21st century Turkey, but within Islam, the Sunni persuasion seems to have been, un-officially, "re-established." Tolerance of Christians and Jews and their places of worship has always been difficult for Muslim countries – some more tolerant, some completely intolerant. Turkey is no exception, arguably becoming more intolerant in recent years.

Reminiscent of the Holy Wars in Christendom, the Reformation and Counter-Reformation between Protestants and Catholics, the Sunni – Shia split has no equal for duration of enmity and killing. Its counterpart in Turkey may be seen in the Sunni – Alevi divide. Incidents of tragic proportion, *Kahramanmaraş* in 1978 and the Madımak Hotel in Sivas, continue to remind one of atrocities that may happen when nationalist Sunni crowds are inflamed by provocateurs. More recently, demonstrations over the building of a *Cemevi* (Alevi House of Worship) alongside an existing Mosque, in a single complex in Ankara, illustrate the currency and volatility of the issue.

It has been reported that for decades, long before the administration of the current Ruling Party, obtaining permissions to build *Cemevi*, and be legally recognized by mainstream Sunni Islam, has been problematic. It has been suggested that the situation of Alevis has become more fractious under the rule of the AK Party whose leaders are from the Sunni majority in Turkey. This bias in the domestic context seems to be mirrored in the foreign policy of the Ruling Policy. There are about 15 million Alevis in Turkey of Turkmen, Kurdish and Arab extraction, including the leader of the CHP opposition party, Kemal Kılıçdaroğlu. They remain concerned about the fate of their people in Turkey and of their Alawite and Shia co-religion cousins. The war in Syria and Iraq has only aggravated the concern. Efforts to address this issue, especially by former President Gül and former Foreign Secretary Davutoğlu, as noted by journalist Semih İdiz in an Al-Monitor "Turkey Pulse" article posted November 9, 2013 saying, *"Davutoğlu's recent and unprecedented visit to the holy cities of Najaf and Karbala, and his high profile meetings with Iraqi Shiite cleric Ali al-Husseini al-Sistani and Shiite cleric and leader Muqtada al-Sadr, were major icebreakers between the Erdoğan government and Iraq's Shiite community."* But he goes on to note that it did not help when in June of 2013, then Prime

Minister Erdoğan, in response to the tragic car bombing in Reyhanlı, referred to the victims as 53 Sunni martyrs, not 53 Turkish citizens or Turkish martyrs.

The explosiveness of the sectarian divide, running through Turkey and into the Middle East, the Gulf States and the Saudi Peninsula is foreshadowed by Washington Post journalist Thomas Rick's article which appeared in *Foreign Policy* magazine in June of 2013 titled, "Is Syrian-related violence the beginning of the Muslim world's 30-Year War?" Identity politics remain at the heart of instability in America and Turkey.

Chapter 19

FREEDOM OF SPEECH

"Democracies ... have ever been found incompatible with personal security or the rights of property; and have in general been as short in their lives as they have been violent in their deaths."

—JAMES MADISON

As a prerequiste to many States ratifying the new United States Constitution, it was deemed mandatory that the Constitution be immediately amended to insure a circumscribing of the limits of the Federal Government over Individual and State's Rights. The Amendments became known as the Bill of Rights which become law in 1790. The First Amendment of the first ten amendments follows:

"Congress shall make no law respecting an establishment of religion, or prohibiting the free exercise thereof; or abridging the freedom of speech, or of the press; or the right of the people peaceably to assemble, and to petition the government for a redress of grievances."

This Amendment was urged by Thomas Jefferson and brought to the Congress by James Madison. Both of these men represented the States' Rights, Anti-Federalist faction position. Both contended with the advocates of a strong Federal government led by Alexander Hamilton, the leader of the Federalist faction. On the subject of Free Speech, General Washington in his Farewell to the troops when he resigned his Commission in 1783 at the end of the Revolution said , *"If freedom of the press is taken away, dumb and silent we may be led, like sheep to the slaughter."* Many States, either before or shortly after the Promulgation of the Bill of Rights, had adopted similar language in their State Constitutions.

It was not long before the Supreme Court, via case decisions, placed some restrictions on this Freedom. Speech that was considered to contravene customs regarding obscenity, speech designed to incite unlawful violence, or words calculated to induce violent acts against individuals or slander, was excepted. Criticism of the Government, or Government Officials, was not precluded. In the course of the 18th century, the practice of free and unfettered speech had grown rather freely in the American Colonies. However, once an independent country, and confronted with challenges that bordered on public safety, or might be perceived as such by the Government, the notion of abridgment of these rights appeared. In the eyes of some, or many, such Federal power could lead to government tyranny.

Free Speech Versus National Security, the
Alien and Sedition Acts in American History

The *Alien and Sedition Acts* were passed by the Federalist-controlled Congress and signed into law by President John Adams. These laws were intended to strengthen the national security of the fledgling United States of America at a time when it felt vulnerable in the midst of a "Quasi War" with Post-Revolutionary France (a country with which America had signed a Perpetual Treaty of Peace after its own revolution). These laws prohibited false and scandalous writings with the intent to defame the President and the Government and bring contempt or disrepute, or incite the People towards disobedience of the laws of the Country, or to lead them toward secession.

These Acts seemed to fly in the face of the First Amendment. These laws were immediately opposed by new immigrants, French sympathizers, and the Democratic-Republicans who argued that the laws were used to suppress Anti-Federalist votes. The Acts played a large role in the defeat of the Federalists in the Election of 1800 which brought Thomas Jefferson to the White House. This controversy brought to light the natural tension between State and Individual Rights and the Federal Government. It has been argued by some, such as Jefferson scholar Peter Onuf of the University of Virginia in a Miller Center Forum on December 2, 2014, that Jefferson's concept of Union was predicated on the equality of rights between the States and the Union. Jefferson, he noted, following on the analogy of a hierarchy of rule within the family, local, and State Government, believed that such order was built upon "consent." And it followed that by implication that coercion at the Federal level is antithetical to the very Union from which it derives its power. The author would argue that while one can have coercion without equality, tyranny if you will, the reverse does not hold. Equality, or democratic equality, without a means of government coercion, can lead to anarchy. Finding a balance would be key to a functioning government. That balance is struck by the vote of an equal People (which at his time excluded blacks, non-substantial land holding whites and white women) based on a majority of the voters. The results of the vote are assumed to contain within them the "consent" of the People, whereby the winners may legally coerce the losers on subjects that were at issue in the election, checked by the power of the Judiciary and the Bill of Rights.

When Jefferson came to power, he released most of those being held at the time under the Sedition laws. However, as observed by eminent historian Ron Chernow in his book, *Alexander Hamilton*, Jefferson used these laws to jail or fine a number of his critics just before and until the Acts expired.

It is also worth noting that during this period, while the Vice President of the United States, Thomas Jefferson, with the help of James Madison, secretly authored the controversial "Virginia and Kentucky Resolutions," which advocated the right ofstates to disagree with and "nullify" Federal Law. In fact, in one of Jefferson's drafts, the right to secede from the Union, if disagreement were serious enough, was justified. Jefferson's famous biographer, Dumas Malone, argued that his Resolutions, written during his Vice Presidency, might have gotten him impeached for treason had it been known that he, Jefferson, was one of the authors. Chernow goes on in this same book to state, *"He [Jefferson] wasn't calling for peaceful protests or civil disobedience: he was calling for outright rebellion, if needed, against the federal government of which he was vice president."* It is not far-fetched to suggest that the Virginia and Kentucky Resolutions' logic contributed to the planting of seeds that led to Secession and the Civil War some sixty years later.

One of the more interesting of those jailed under the Alien and Sedition Laws was James Callender, a Scotsman who had been exiled by the British for his polemical political writings. He came to Philadelphia and later to Northern Virginia where he wrote a book titled, *The Prospect Before Us* (apparently approved by Vice President Jefferson before publication), in which he characterized President Adams' administration as a *"continual tempest of malignant passions"* and the President *"a repulsive pedant, a gross hypocrite and an unprincipled oppressor."* Under the Sedition Act, he was fined and sentenced to nine months in jail.

Again, in time of war and uncertainty, the First Amendment has been set aside for particular reasons as it was in the Espionage Act of 1917 for example. The purpose of the Act was to facilitate military operations, including recruitment, and to prohibit the support of enemies during wartime. In 1919, under challenge, the U.S. Supreme Court unanimously ruled in *Schenck v. United States*, that it did not violate the Freedom of Speech principle for those convicted under its provisions.

Even before the "Red Scare" following the Bolshevik Revolution in the spring of 1917, President Woodrow Wilson, in his December 7, 1915 State of the Union address, asked Congress for legislation to protect the national interests of the country saying:

> *There are citizens of the United States, I blush to admit, born under other flags but welcomed under our generous naturalization laws to the full freedom and opportunity of America, who have poured the poison of disloyalty into the very arteries of our national life; who have sought to bring the authority and good name of our Government into contempt, to destroy our industries wherever they thought it effective for their vindictive purposes to strike at them, and to debase our politics to the uses of foreign intrigue...*
>
> *I urge you to enact such laws at the earliest possible moment and feel that in doing so I am urging you to do nothing less than save the honor and self-respect of the nation. Such creatures of passion, disloyalty, and anarchy must be crushed out. They are not many, but they are infinitely malignant, and the hand of our power should close over them at once. They have formed plots to destroy property, they have entered into conspiracies against the neutrality of the*

Government, they have sought to pry into every confidential transaction of the Government in order to serve interests alien to our own."

Beginning in 1919, with the sentencing of Socialist Congressman Victor Berger, and Joseph Rutherford of the Watch Tower Bible & Tract Society, and communists Julius and Ethel Rosenberg, Pentagon Papers whistleblower Daniel Ellsberg, "Cable Gate" whistleblower Chelsea Manning, and NSA contractor Edward Snowden, America has struggled with the First Amendment. When it has been seen by those governing as being in conflict with National security, the Amendment has been suspended. The debate continues over Free Speech as it relates to contenton the internet deemed to be incite hatred. The internet is a boon to mankind with enormous destructive potential at the same time. Now let us turn to another form of Free Speech, Free Expression, and dress codes.

Head Scarves as Symbols – Turkey and the West (France)

Say to the believing men that they should lower their gaze and guard their modesty: that will make for greater purity for them: And Allah is well acquainted with all that they do. And say that the believing women that they should lower their gaze and guard their modesty that they should not display their beauty and ornaments except what (must ordinarily) appear thereof; that they should draw their veils over their bosoms and not display their beauty except to their husbands,

their fathers, their husband's fathers, their sons, their hus-
bands' sons, their brothers or their brothers' sons, or their
sisters' sons, or their women, or the slaves whom their right
hands possess, or male servants free of physical needs, or
small children who have no sense of the shame of sex; and
that they should not strike their feet in order to draw attention
to their hidden ornaments. And O ye Believers! Turn ye all
together towards Allah, that ye may attain Bliss.—Sura 24
(An-Nur), Ayat 30-31, Koran

Is "modesty" in the eye of the beholder, the beheld or
both? Clearly, covering one's head for reasons of modesty
may be exclusive to Muslim women today, but has not
always been. Head covering for Western women, Christian women, going back in America's case to its Puritan
Founding, was considered the norm. Whether for reasons
of fashion, modesty, status or a combination thereof, head
covering in the West was preferred by men and women
West for centuries. The issue of covering the face, however,
was and remains an Islamic tradition with one notable
exception, Christian women being veiled until the point
at which vows are to be exchanged in a wedding ceremony.
For all its exceptions in practice, the white wedding dress
and veil are intended as symbols of chastity and purity.
The tradition of keeping the groom from seeing the bride
on the day of the wedding until she makes her entrance
into the church is yet another vestige of that same tradition. Conflating the Islamic and Christian traditions here
is only intended to remind one that customs and traditions,

particularly of a religious nature, are symbols which, to one degree or another, tend to survive secular efforts to preempt their practice. Resultingly, in the eyes of the law, in Turkey, Europe, and America, a marriage must be registered with the Civil authorities to be deemed official.

Clearly symbols matter. As discussed earlier, Mustafa Kemal's Hat Law was intended to change the way one perceived one's self and how others perceived you, and by extension, a nation is perceived. He also understood the limits of trying to dictate women's dress. In the case of Turkey, the wearing of the headscarf, and more particularly, the veil, while serving in official State capacity is one issue, veiling while attending a public institution as a student is another. As a matter of Freedom of Expression, in theory, there should be no difference. The 1960s through the early 2000s, with the Turkish Military still very much in the picture and continuing in their perceived role as defenders of the secular Republic, supported by secularists, bans were placed on the wearing of headscarves for students at public universities as well officials of State government.

With the rise of the Justice and Development Party, pressure to relax the rules commenced. The ban, with the exception of military and judicial service, was officially lifted in 2013. Then Prime Minister Erdoğan announced, in a message to Parliament, *"A dark time eventually comes to an end, Headscarf-wearing women are full members of the republic, as well as those who do not wear it."*

The issue of freedom to choose to wear, or not to wear, headscarves and veils again brings the question of who is doing the choosing. Girls as young as ten in Turkey are now permitted to wear headscarves at public schools. Certainly, the French Parliament, under Prime Minister Sarkozy, in dealing with five million Muslims in France, elected in 2013 to ban the wearing of face-covering veils (*naqab, peçe*) and full body burqas as being contrary to France's founding principles of Liberty, Equality, and Fraternity. Additionally, some European governments, in the face of terrorism, have also banned the headscarf and veil in public spaces.

Ayaan Hirsi Ali, Somali-born, former Member of Parliament in the Netherlands and now, in America for reasons of safety, became an outspoken critic of Islam and sees the religion as being incompatible with Western values. At the behest of her own grandmother, while her father was opposed to the practice but was imprisoned at the time by the Said Barre government in Mogadishu, she was a victim of the practice of female genital mutilation. She became a secularist and an advocate of Women's Rights. For her, the Burqa is a symbol of oppression of women and makes the case that such dress contributes to segregation and the maintenance of parallel societies. Her sentiments have been echoed by Prime Ministers Merkel and Cameron in 2014 in admissions of the cultural failure of integration of their respective countries' Muslim immigrant populations.

In response to the French ban, American President Barack Obama stated in a press conference as reported in the Christian Science Monitor, *"Our basic attitude [in America] is that we're not going to* tell *people what to wear."* His statement notwithstanding, the headscarf and veil are a potentially stigmatizing form of dress to many Americans who equate it with a commitment to Islamic practices and the institution of Sharia Law in the public arena which run counter to the secular principles undergirding the Rule of Law.

The debate continues in Turkey and the West. It will continue to have a polarizing effect on the challenge of Muslim integration and assimilation into American culture. Freedom of Expression is a fundamental Civil Right under the U. S. Constitution. Efforts to fundamentally undermine the secular law upon which the Union is based will, in practice, trump the First Amendment as do other beliefs and practices which are perceived as threats to individual and national security. Finding a balance remains one of the greatest challenges to 21st century democratic society.

"Turkishness" as Sacrosanct – Limits on Civil Rights

The Kemalist revolution, supported by the writings of "nationalist" Ziya Gökalp discussed earlier, was faced with a problem at its inception. No longer an Empire, the Kemalist Reformers were tasked with defining the essence of a modern State. They were not faced with the task of making something from nothing. The task was more complicated. They needed to construct something else, something profoundly different from the centuries-old Ottoman model. What they struck upon as a new rationale for governance, the unifying concept *du jour* of Nationalism, popularized since the independence movement in Greece in the 1820s, andwrit large in the Wilsonian principle of "self-determination." But self-determination in the Turkish case was not to be based on racial, ethnic or religious criteria, but rather on a common culture, language and sense of belonging. The geographic boundaries of this entity would provide the borders within which this sense of being "Turkish" were to be nurtured. Achieving that group sense of "Turkishness" (*Türkçülük*) would require the suppression of other forms of identity, religious, ethnic and linguistic. It was thought that the benefits of one might term "national secular homogenization," would redound to the benefit of peoples whose fates had been so ill-served in the latter stages of the Ottoman decline. The process would be painful for some whose religious, linguistic, ethnic, and cultural preferences would be inhibited, constrained or outlawed. The Kemalists believed the results, the advantages to the majority, would become obvious, and self-sustaining in time.

In hindsight, in the context of modern understanding of individual civil rights, one can argue about whether or not the benefits to the modernization of Turkey outweighed/outweigh the costs. While to a lesser extent in recent years, the fact that a public debate can take place in

Turkey on its streets, in its courts, at the ballot box, and in Parliament, without a civil war, is a tribute to Atatürk's longer-term legacy of democratic secularism. More recent developments in Turkey, with the attempted coup of July 15, 2016 and its aftermath, have called into question how resilient that democracy is in the face of more autocratic forces. Protections of Civil Rights and Freedom of Speech/Press are routinely being suspended in the name of security in the post-coup world of Turkey. Only time will tell if the new system of governance established on June 24, 2018 in Turkey will survive beyond President Erdogan's term of office. If a more autocratic style of governance was justified, at least for a time, during Atatürk's One-Party rule as it struggled to replace Islamic governance, its reappearance in the guise of a Republic with functioning checks and balances, after decades of parliamentary rule, albeit fitful, certainly seems to be unacceptable to approximately half the voters in Turkey today (arguably possibly more than half since those elections). The internal and external threats to post Great War modern Turkey's founding were often used to rationalize some of the draconian measures of the Kemalist Reformers. The argument that Turkey has been facing comparable threats, calling for similarly autocratic governance in current Turkey seems exaggerated by comparison. Nonetheless, this argument resonated with the base of AKP and MHP Parties.

Neither the Armenians and Kurds within Turkey and their respective diasporas are content with the status quo.

The Kurdish issue also brings with it international political implications related to EU entrance and Human Rights considerations.

After 35 plus years of violence and more than 40,000 deaths on both the Kurdish and Turkish sides of the dispute, in keeping with the Copenhagen criteria, then Prime Minister Erdoğan announced a "Kurdish Opening." "Buy-In" for this policy had not be sought in advance with the main political opposition parties, the Peoples Party and the Nationalists. The entire Opening backfired after the government had agreed to pardon and welcome home 33 PKK terrorists. The optics of their return proved to be explosive as noted in an article in *Open Democracy* by Selin Bölme and Müjge Küçükkeleş published on April 23, 2013, "Turkey's recent Kurdish opening: opportunities and the challenges ahead."

> *"On 17 August 2012, members of the Kurdistan Worker's Party (PKK), which has been fighting an armed struggle against the Turkish state since 1984, intercepted the delegation of the Peace and Democracy Party (BDP), the main Kurdish representation in the Turkish parliament, at a road junction in the Hakkari province of Turkey and embraced them. The images showing BDP members hugging PKK militants (considered as terrorists by Ankara) drew harsh criticisms from the prime minister, who later called for judiciary action against BDP members, implying that his own Justice and Development Party (AKP) would act to lift their parliamentary immunity."*

The authors went on to refer to the content of a letter from the jailed leader of the Kurdish movement, Abdullah Öcalan, broadcast to the public as follows:

On 21 March 2013, Turkey entered a new period when a letter by Öcalan was read to crowds gathered in Diyarbakır, the largest Kurdish populated city in Southeastern Turkey. In this brief, yet historic letter, Öcalan called for a cease-fire and asked PKK fighters to withdraw from Turkish territory. The letter did not contain the technical details of the withdrawal; nonetheless Öcalan's remarks of "opening the door that leads from armed struggle to a democratic struggle" hinted at the idea of an autonomous Kurdistan being abandoned.

Dealing with minorities, specifically the Kurds, prompted a revision of the 1982 Constitution in 2008 of the definition of a citizen of Turkey that sought to remove the ethnic implication that all Turks are ethnically Turkish. The infamous Penal Code article, 301, by which alleged enemies of the State can be accused of insulting the Republic of Turkey, its government and/or its leaders, was amended to read the "Turkish Nation."

Political will on the part of all Parties will be required to find a peaceful and democratic solution to the recognition of citizens of Kurdish origin, some 20% of the population, and their desire for some degree of autonomy or special rights and privileges regarding their language and culture. The fragile political situation in Iraq notwithstanding, the tacit recognition of a semi-autonomous Northern

Kurdistan within the Iraqi Federation has been accepted. With oil flowing from the Iraqi Kurds into Turkey, the economic incentives to find a solution will continue to argue for some solution to Turkey's burden of resolving this conflict within her borders. However, the continuing war in Syria, as of this writing, suggests that any domestic resolution of the Kurdish issue will be contingent upon Turkey's sense of security along her borders with Kurdish peoples in the relevant neighboring States.

The uncertainties surrounding a domestic resolution to this problem continue to be highlighted as seen in Turkey's National Election of June 7, 2015. Election results brought the first seating the Peoples' Democratic Party (*Halkların Democratik Partisi*, "HDP", a largely Kurdish Party) with over 14% of the vote, which angered the Ruling AKP of Prime Minister Erdoğan whose share declined quite significantly down to 41%. Nationalist Party ("MHP") was also dismayed. Bloody events would soon appear in the *Suruç* attack, officially blaming the Kurdish Separatists, in July of that year, setting off the recommencement of a low level, but deadly, civil war between the Turkish State and the Kurds. The lure of untangling, or severing, this "Gordian knot," and prospect of a Nobel Peace Prize for the one(s) who achieve it, continues to remain as elusive.

Journalists, Hrant Dink, and the *Heybeli Halki* Seminary

Freedom of the Press, a sacrosanct element of democracy in the West, is an aspiration which has always been found to be problematic for those ruling politically unstable countries. If Free Speech was not always upheld by previous Turkish governments with the military looking over their shoulders, a 2013 Freedom House Report suggests that Turkey has been trending the wrong way regarding restrictions on a free press.

> *"The Turkish authorities continued to use the penal code and an antiterrorism law to crack down on journalists and media outlets in 2012, leading Turkey to imprison more journalists than any other country in the world. According to the Committee to Protect Journalists (CPJ), 49 were behind bars as of December.*
>
> *Constitutional guarantees of press freedom and freedom of expression are only partially upheld in practice. They are generally undermined by provisions in the penal code and the criminal procedure code, and by the country's strict, broadly worded antiterrorism law, which effectively makes many types of investigative or critical journalism tantamount to terrorist activity. The restrictive penal code continues to overshadow positive reforms that had been implemented as part of the country's bid for European Union (EU) membership, including a 2004 press law that replaced prison sentences with fines for media violations."*

In an October 22, 2014 article in Al Jazeera-America, the title and byline follows:

> *"ISTANBUL — With 19 journalists jailed, about 150 awaiting trial and 400 forced layoffs and resignations in the last*

year, according to media watchdog Bianet, Turkish journalists say media freedom is at its lowest point in decades."

In a January 23, 2019 article by an Ankara-based reporter, Ayla Jean Yackley, appearing in *The Atlantic*, she reports that the number of journalists now in prison is sixty-eight, claiming that number represents a quarter of all journalists behind bars in the world. She tells the current story of journalist Pelin Ünker, a former *Cumhuriyet* newspaper reporter and now a freelance, who was brought to trial for exposing alleged tax evasion at the highest levels of the Turkish government through offshore investments. She has been tried, convicted and is appealing her sentence saying in a phone interview with Yackley,

"My stories contained no slander, because the claims are not disputed, and not a single word of insult. This sentence isn't just about me. It's punishing the act of journalism to intimidate others who might report this kind of news."

Bringing these concerns to the post-July 15, 2016 coup and beyond, the trends could not be less favorable regarding the protection of democratic notions of free speech. While officially explained as the unfortunate necessity of stabilizing democracy in Turkey under a continuing threat of "Gülenist terrorism," the lockdown on the Freedom of Speech, Freedom of the Press, and the abeyance of the Rule of Law, under a continuing State of Emergency lifted only on July 19, 2018, has even the Ruling Party's staunchest supporters beginning to question the degree and the direction of the crackdown. The lifting of the State of Emergency, if one is following the news, seems to have changed nothing in the autocratic practices of the current government. This subject will be further discussed in the chapter concerning the subject of overweening governance in Turkey and America.

If one combines the treatment of journalists with the treatment of Christian minorities, one is immediately struck by the tragedy of Armenian Journalist Hrant Dink. Dink established a newspaper in 2007, *Agos*. One of the purposes of the paper was to convince Turks that Turkish Armenians were being falsely accused of collaboration with PKK terrorists against the Turkish Government. He also used the paper as a platform to call attention to what he termed the Armenian Genocide of 1915. It has been suggested that the first purpose placed him in the hostile sights of the military. The second purpose placed him in harm's way with the ultra-Nationalists, and the AKP Party and its then Gülenist partners. He was charged twice under Penal Code Article 301 of being guilty of denigrating the "Turkishness" clause – of being a traitor. The first charge was dropped. The second charge held, but was appealed to the European Court of Human Rights where it was dismissed as being groundless. A third charge under Article 301 was being prepared when he was murdered by a young ultra-nationalist in January of 2007. Public outcry followed, not just by the Armenian Turkish community and the Armenian Diaspora, but by Turks themselves and around the world. His assassination was a source of deep national embarrassment for Turkey. It is interesting to note, that the sympathy expressed by hundreds of thousands of mourning and protesting Turks was duly noted, coupled with news reports that the popular reaction and sympathy was greatly appreciated by the Armenian Community worldwide.

Freedom of Religion in Turkey suffered an earlier blow in 1971 when Turkish authorities decided to close the official seminary for the Eastern Orthodox Patriarchate known as the *Halki* Seminary on *Heybeli* Island at the Marmara Sea mouth of the Bosphorus. The closing was, of course, symbolic. It served no demonstrable security purpose. Was, and does it remain a useful bargaining chip to address alleged restrictions on Turkish mosques in Greece, perhaps. Has anything been gained beyond political fodder for some elements of Turkish society? The closing has certainly focused questions on Turkey's commitment to religious tolerance and freedom of expression. In 1998, both Houses of the U.S. Congress voted to encourage Turkey to reopen the Seminary. President Bill Clinton visited the Seminary a year later urging then Turkish President Demirel to re-open it. U. S. President Obama, in a speech to the Turkish Parliament in April of 2009, also urged the Turkish Government to re-open the Seminary saying,

> *"Freedom of religion and expression lead to a strong and vibrant civil society that only strengthens the state, which is why steps like reopening the Halki Seminary will send such an important signal inside Turkey and beyond. An*

enduring commitment to the rule of law is the only way to
achieve the security that comes from justice for all people."

These efforts notwithstanding, it would appear that the Islamists, the Nationalists, and Center Left party, albeit it for somewhat varied reasons, have continued to agree that the Seminary remain closed.

The recent Turkish Law, "Law amending the Law on State Intelligence Services and the National Intelligence Organization," number 6532, enacted in April of 2014, following then President Gül's ratification, was very controversial. As noted in the summer of 2014 "Newsletter on Turkish Law Developments,"

"The new law raises serious concerns about state account-ability. Media freedom and the right to privacy by increasing MIT's data collection powers, granting MIT personnel immunity from prosecution coupled with the absence of effective executive and judicial scrutiny. The new legislation thus brings into question Turkey's compliance with international human rights law."

Turkish government efforts to shut down selected websites and social media during the controversy surrounding alleged government corruption at the highest levels leading up to the 2013 Mayoral Elections, only serves to highlight the undermining of the Rule of Law. Such practices continue and have become increasingly pervasive in recent years.

On matters of government overreach and an unwarranted circumvention of citizen privacy rights in America, the following judicial ruling in December of 2013 by U. S. Judge Richard Leon, illustrates the same Orwellian prospect of unrestrained government powers of surveillance, even if the purposes may be said to differ as between the Turkish and American cases. At the end of the day, both abuses would be, and are still, "justified" on grounds of National Security.

"December 16, 2013: U.S. District Judge Richard Leon rules that the NSA's bulk collection of phone-call metadata violates privacy rights and thus is unconstitutional. The judge's preliminary ruling favors five plaintiffs challenging the practice, but he limits the decision only to their cases, saying:

"I cannot imagine a more 'indiscriminate' and 'arbitrary invasion' than this systematic and high-tech collection and retention of personal data on virtually every citizen for purposes of querying and analyzing it without prior judicial approval. Surely, such a program infringes on 'that degree of privacy' that the Founders enshrined in the Fourth Amendment."

These issues continue to attract public disapproval domestically and internationally. One need only look at the public embarrassment for the U. S. Government over the "illegal" surveillance of the private phone conversations of Prime Minister Merkel of Germany, among other high-level Allied European officials, by American Intelligence Services. The blessings of cyber technology bring with them the seemingly ineluctable temptations to abuse that capability in the name of security, possibly the 21st century's greatest dilemma. Yet, whistle blowers, such as Julian Assange, illustrate that the risks cut both ways. Allegations of Russian cyber malfeasance and interference in the 2016 Election in America abound. Similar "attacks" are said to be coming from China (the Sony case) among other offenders.

In conclusion, it is fair to say that at different times, both the governments of America and Turkey have justified the suppression of Freedoms of Speech and the Press and at times justified the suspension of the Rule of Law. These policies have always been aimed at minorities, racial, ethnic, and religious, or those accused of undermining National Security. Government surveillance of suspected groups continues to threaten the civil rights of citizens in both countries. Although, a case can be made that they differ in degree between the two countries.

Chapter 20

SHIFT AWAY FROM STATISM
IN TURKEY AND THE WESTERN
BUSINESS RESPONSE

America going off the Gold Standard in the early 1970s, together with war and uncertainty in the Middle East and OPEC's dramatically raising of oil prices precipitated two Energy Crises. Economic stagnation followed around the world. Turkey and America were no exceptions to this condition of financial malaise. The West found itself in the grips of stagflation and the rest of the world suffered along with it. Living in Ankara in the late 1970s, the author witnessed the results of economic and political dysfunction, interest rates in the 70% range, power outages, sugar and coffee shortages and unemployment pressing Turkey ever closer to the prospect of civil war. With these conditions only worsening as the 1980s unfolded, the Turkish military again stepped in and declared martial law in 1980. A new Constitution was drafted under military oversight which gave little quarter to individual rights, freedom of speech and any movements that smacked of radicalism, Marxist or Islamist. Suppression of disruptive forces, of any stripe, were harshly dealt with. To their credit, the military and others realized that the sacred Kemalist goal of "Statism" and an insular economy based on "import-substitution" would never allow Turkey to move beyond the roller coaster of rapid growth and unavoidable cycles of rapid decline. Into this crucible stepped a highly respected technocrat, Turgut Özal, whose talents and vision had been identified by military and some civilian leaders.

The Opening of the Turkish Economy under Prime Minister Turgut Özal

Turgut Özal was not the product of any elite. Born in Malatya in Eastern Turkey, he graduated from Istanbul Technical University in 1950 with a degree in Engineering. From there he went on to study in the United States. By 1959, he worked in the Turkish State Planning Organization. Later he worked for the World Bank between 1971 and 1973. He then returned to Turkey and chaired several private sector companies and went to work for Prime Minister Demirel in 1980 as an Undersecretary until the Military Coup of September 1980. During his brief term in that role, he launched substantial economic reforms moving Turkey toward an export-led growth economy.

In 1983, Özal launched the Motherland Party (ANAP) and won election to the position of Prime Minister. During his tenure: he devalued the Turkish Lira; instituted flexible exchange rates; maintained tight monetary control; freed prices for the product of State Economic Enterprises; removed many government subsidies; instituted tax reform; dramatically modernized and expanded the Turkish Stock Market, and encouraged the attraction of Foreign Capital. He introduced the Build Own Transfer (BOT) model for infrastructural development and allowed Turkey's international debt to float in the world market. He instituted a VAT tax, Income Tax Funds and promoted touristic development. He initiated a serious program of Privatization. Being a banker in Istanbul for four years (1988-1992), the author experienced these ground-breaking developments first hand.

In addition to his far-reaching economic liberalization programs, Prime Minister Özal also undertook significant efforts to treat with the Kurdish problem (Kurdish strains in his background) and the Armenian problem. He was a pious man personally and enjoyed consulting with Sufi leaders in the *Nakshibendi* order. While religion informed his decision-making, it never interfered with his engineer's logic in seeking the best, or most practical solution to a problem. Through CNN television coverage during the First Gulf Crisis, Özal became the face of America's NATO ally Turkey. He enjoyed good relations with Presidents Ronald Reagan and George Bush the Elder. His Foreign Policy reflected a world view which is well-summarized in the following excerpt from a USAK Yearbook of International Politics and Law, Vol. 2, 2009.

"Turkism constituted one of the main elements of Özalism. However, his Turkism was neither irredentist, like Enver Pasha's Turkism, nor isolationist, like Kemal's. For Ottoman Turkists, the ultimate aim was a Turkish Empire covering all Turkish tribes who were under Russian, Chinese and Iranian rules. On the other hand, as a reaction to adventurist Turkism, Atatürk developed an isolationist Turkism, viewing the outside a potential danger for the Anatolian Turks. Hence Atatürk's Turkey had no interest in the other Turks outside, and gave no support for Turkish resistance against any power, like the Azerbaijan is against the communist attacks in the 1920s. Conversely, for Özal Turkism was an important element in Turkish citizens' identity and in Turkish foreign policy particularly after the Cold War, when the new world order was based on economic alignment and solidarity among kin states. As a result Özal saw Turkism as one of the cornerstones of Turkish modernisation inside and of the transformation of Turkish foreign policy."

Turgut Özal was above all moderate and practical. He could work with any person or party regardless of their religious or political ideologies. He died in his third year as Turkey's President. His legacy as a leader for positive and constructive change and modernization of Turkey's politics, economics, cultural life, and foreign policy were extraordinary. Certainly, he was the greatest leader Turkey had had since Kemal Atatürk. History will tell us how President Erdoğan will be compared with him.

Supporting Legal Reform – The Laws on Foreign Capital

Various business-oriented reforms, from Land Registration, to laws governing foreign capital, foreign-owned companies, joint ventures, capital markets, capital and dividend repatriation among other laws were the hallmarks of his years in power. These reforms succeeded in attracting foreign capital and international banks flocked in to provide advisory and financial intermediation services.

Turkey's First Investment – Turk Merchant Bank

Prior to the late 1980s, large Western banks confined most of their services to the Turkish Government. As an example, Bankers Trust Company (acquired by Deutche Bank in 1993), had since the 1970s enjoyed a significant position with the Government in leading their International Debt/Bond sales. In the face of energy crises, recession and then inflation, the late 1970s had been a difficult time for Developing Country debt issuance, and debt service performance. Turkey, Brazil and many countries defaulted on their international debt. In turn, major Western banks were preoccupied with writing off Developing Country bad debt, creating special markets for the sale and trading of their discounted debt. Bankers Trust Co. of New York was among those struggling with a sea of bad Developing Country foreign loans. By the mid-1980s, Bankers Trust was then leading 33% of all dollar-denominated Turkish debt, and 25% of the total the Country's total offshore debt issued.

Up until that time, banking to developing country governments was done through Representative ("Rep") Offices in the capitals of these countries or in centrally located city/country for a region. These offices would be supported from banking centers such as London, Tokyo, and Paris which would fly specialized teams in to the developing country capitals, and together with the local "Rep," would offer their services. Working together with large international corporate law firms, a consortium of banks brought debt developing Country debt offerings to the international market. Advisory legal and financial fees for delivering these services from outside the host country were high. Their advisory and success fees were even higher. Whether, for example, it was Bankers Trust, Citi Bank, BNP Paribas, Rothschild Bank, Lazard Frères, or Goldman Sacks, their teams of experts would fly in, conduct research, and advise their findings to the host governments. This was a process involving multiple expensive hotel stays. Similar costs and procedures were part and parcel of large multi-National corporates which also had their Rep offices, when doing deals with the Turkish Government, Turkish Private Sector corporates, or in consortium with one another in the BOT (Build Own Transfer) projects. The time and costs (hard currency being paid out) precipitated the development of similar services supplied by in-country Turkish banks and advisory firms, especially those banks with teams of technical teams that could be flown in when needed. This new niche served to raise the bar of financial sophistication of in-country investment banking services.

With the changes designed and executed by Prime Minister Turgut Özal, liberalizing the economy and beginning to streamline the movement of Foreign Capital and Services, whether it was government privatization or private sector joint ventures or mergers and acquisitions, investment banking opportunities proliferated. In Turkey and other Developing Countries, where Commercial Banks had old and strong underwriting and banking relationships with governments and large Corporates, respectively, it was often Commercial Banks which took the lead in offering investment banking services, Bankers Trust Co. arguably taking the lead at the time.

Bankers Trust (BT) set up a Rep office in Istanbul and began, together with BT London and New York, to look for Joint Venture Partner(s). Having had an old relationship with Turkey's largest Private Sector bank, İş Bank (founded by Atatürk), negotiations with them began. A Joint Venture was agreed with İş and Dış (an İş Bank subsidiary bank engaged in Trade Finance) banks having 40%, Bankers Trust 60% and the management contract. With these partners, Turk Merchant Bank (TMB) was created. Hired away from a very successful Trade Finance bank, Dr. Vural Akışık was brought on board to be the Chairman and CEO.

I received a call, while working in the Wall St. Corporate Finance Division of Bankers Trust three weeks after the 1987 October stock market crash, from people on the International side of the bank. I was advised that a Merchant/Investment bank was being set up in Istanbul to take advantage of the economic liberalization program underway in Turkey. After several interviews, the I accepted the offer. Nine months later, with a young family in tow, we moved to Istanbul in August of 1988 and placed the children in the International Community School. And, not without some anxiety about the future success of both the bank and my own as a manager of a new breed of banking in Turkey, I dug into his new task.

The bank began business in the *Teşvikiye* area of Istanbul. A year later, it moved to a totally renovated nineteenth century villa in *Bebek* overlooking the Bosphorus, including a state-of-the-art trading floor and code-secured entry into the various departments. This is noted because, at that time, TMB was establishing a new look in "sophisticated" banking. Curiosity about how the bank would fare in the financial services sector was high. Turning that curiosity into paying clients, especially in the Corporate Finance piece of the business, would prove both challenging and exciting.

The Bank began operations in 1988. Inflation rates were in the 70% range. Initial business and income came from Treasury Operations and Trade Finance. In time, the new Corporate Finance Department obtained retainers from a number of Turkish Corporates and the Ministry of Privatization. Growing explosively in overhead and personnel, the Bank grew from ten employeesto over forty people within three years. While the bank successfully engaged in traditional Trade Finance and Money-Market operations, the Corporate Finance and Advisory business operated in what felt like a pioneering experience. Until then, such services had been "flown in" from outside. It was exciting work if difficult to generate substantial sustainable profit. But, the Corporate Finance/Investment Banking business certainly added to the aura of the Bank as a new kind of financial services institution in Turkey. Other banks, domestic and foreign, would soon develop similar Advisory businesses to augment their more traditional banking lines.

The Lafarge Coppée Acquisition of Aslan Çimento from İş Bank, 1991

At that time, the Swiss Holcim cement company was the largest in the world followed by Ciments Français and LaFarge Coppée. With foreign investment capital beginning to surge into Turkey in the late 1980s, Ciment Français turned its attention to the potential of the Turkish market. Using CitiBank as its representative, the Turkish Government, through the Privatization Ministry, acquired five cement plants in Turkey. They were purchased serially and not all within a year. That acquisition then represented the largest "block purchase" of Turkish assets by one single foreign buyer.

Bankers Trust in New York had represented the Paris-based Lafarge Coppée cement company in a number of acquisitions of cement companies in Canada and America in the late 1980s and early 1990s. Through Bankers Trust London, TMB received advice that LaFarge Coppée was interested in an acquisition of an Istanbul-based cement company. Lafarge then sent in its chief of acquisitions and TMB was put on Retainer as an Advisor. The bank found a suitable target, Aslan Çimento, an Istanbul cement company. After further due diligence and protracted negotions, a purchase was concluded. With the completion of that transaction, $90,000,000 in 1990 in one payment, that then became the largest "single entity" acquisition on record in the Privatization Program in Turkey at that time. TMB received a handsome Success Fee, not inconsiderable notoriety, and the Corporate Finance team members received a nice year-end bonus that year.

Having the lead on this acquisition, I was both challenged and stimulated by the cross-border, cross-cultural, challenge of translating the "personalities and intentions" of the key French and Turkish players to each other, beyond the matter of mere numbers. Helping to shape the chemistry of the negotiations, if the deal was going to come together, was key. Success in this regard was its own reward, even when I was used as a "bumper" to satisfy the need to attribute misunderstandings, cultural translation errors as it were, to the banker mediator. If the deal was meant to be, keeping one's eye on the prize was the overarching consideration. Some bruised ego along the way was par for the course.

As exciting as the business was, it continued to be hard to repeat that success in the Turkish market at that time. After the first Gulf Crisis in January of 1991, the market in general began to falter. In fact, that Gulf War brought in its wake a challenge the likes of which the author had never experienced. The instability in the region was seized upon as the right time to grab headlines for a Marxist-Leninist terrorist group, *DEV SOL*, with its anti-capitalist, anti-American cause. To that end, they gunned down the British general manager in Istanbul of what they apparently thought it was an American company because of its corporate name being in English. It was actually an English reinsurance company.

Within a couple of days, Turkish detectives found the suspected, but abandoned terrorist house, and a list of fourteen targeted American corporations in Istanbul. The list included Coke Cola, Citibank, and Bankers Trust Co., my parent bank, among others. I remember the General Manager of Coke evacuated his family back to Atlanta within a couple of days. The day after, he hosted a farewell party for his corporate peers wearing a bullet-proof vest, and left the next day. Within two weeks the two Bankers Trust Rep officers had relocated to London. For those of us who remained, our companies, with the help of the Turkish authorities, organized body guard teams, with former army officers leading, two, two-man teams of former soldiers, providing daily coverage. For seven months, before stepping out of my apartment in the morning, a dolly with a mirror on it was run under my corporate car looking for bomb material. The driver would then start the car, and then I would emerge and head off to work. When I/we went out in the day or evening, we were tailed by a guard car. With the bank by then functioning successfully, four years into the assignment, and concerns about the safety of my family, it was agreed that my presence was not worth the continued risk of remaining in harm's way. *

The 1990s, ending with an earthquake in Istanbul, the crash of the Asian Tiger market and the Techno Bubble burst causing the American market to plummet, proved to be calamitous for markets around the world, not least of all, the Turkish market. Nonetheless, Turkey's more economic structure and supporting institutions were poised to provide a modernized platform for an economic "miracle" that would materialize in the early 2000s.

*Having routinely kayaked back and forth across the Bosphorus for years with our children following me with binoculars from the balcony of our apartment, I decided to make the legendary swim across the Bosphorus with its notorious five-knot current running along its edges. One of the body guards insisted that he join my anxious wife and our Irish Setter in a hired 18-foot caique which followed alongside as I swam the mile and a quarter, from East to West. The sight of my panicked wife waving a towel to alert an oncoming cruise ship to my presence in the water, as though the captain could even notice me, or that he could safely alter course in the narrow straits, became an indelible, and amusing, memory. Bless her heart, I thought, and kept swimming. As to the current, while I thought I was swimming directly across, I touched the European side some 500 yards farther south from my starting point.

Chapter 21

TURKEY, THE EU, AND AMERICA

"History is a lie agreed upon."

—NAPOLEON BONAPARTE

In an opinion piece in the *Hürriyet*/Daily News on December 18, 2014, Semih İdiz brought the prospects for positive strides in Turkey's EU Acquis process into sharp focus when he noted,

> It is ironic that it is only at times like this that the EU starts waving the big stick, warning Ankara that if it does not fulfill its obligations in terms of democracy, human rights, and the rule of law it will endanger its membership prospects.
>
> I am convinced, however, that President Recep Tayyip Erdoğan expressed the view of the majority of Turks at that time when he blurted out, in response to the reactions from Europe to the operation against the Gülen movement's media outlets, that "Turkey does not have an EU problem."

Five years later, relations between Turkey and the EU have only further soured. Both sides seemed to be locked into the business of holding each other hostage, Turkey over Europe with the threat of reopening the Syrian refugee floodgates, and Europe over Turkey on the VISA Free travel and restarting the Acquis process. In the interim, President Erdoğan has cast about in search of alternative partners, including Russia, China, Qatar, and some countries in the Horn of Africa. He has continued to bandy about the prospect of a Referendum whereby the people can vote to continue the Acquis process, leave it in abeyance, or abandon the prospect formally. While some might argue this is nothing more than a negotiating tactic with the EU, others might suggest that his purpose is to realign Turkey's alliances, formal and informal, with the Muslim world, as though the Sunni Caliphate could be conjured into a 21st century manifestation.

The economic and political ramifications such a realignment would bring in its path include both economic costs and security concerns. A political realignment calls into question the NATO security pact upon which Turkey as a regional platform for Western economic investment is based. Were such a shift to occasion the prospect of a Turkey without NATO participation, without Article Five (mutual protection) NATO Alliance guarantees, would leave Turkey more, not less, isolated. Neither Erdoğan nor his supporters can actually believe in the wisdom of substituting two Communist powers and a series of essentially unstable Arab allies in place of the EU and NATO. The tight corner Turkey's leadership is placing the country in is, in no small way, the result of some questionable decisions taken, directions embarked on, by the President. Others are and will be blamed, but it is hoped before too many bridges are burned with the West, cooler heads will prevail in Turkey. Until both sides are pushed even further to the precipice and make some profound existential choices, Turkey will find itself in increasingly precarious circumstances. As of this writing, the economic costs of unsound politically-motivated fiscal management of the country are painfully obvious in the 4th Quarter of 2018, with prospects for 2019 according to recent IMF forecasts even more dire.

Customs Union Versus Membership –
The Acquis Process
Through the mechanism of the Customs Union, trade between Turkey and the EU is strong and critically important to both. A significant rupture in trade between the two would be very costly to both, prohibitively so for Turkey. Timely development of functionally offsetting and equally-sized markets would be virtually impossible for Turkey. Accordingly, the advantages to both suggest that the Customs Union will continue without noticeable disruption, but with real prospects of Turkey's membership in the EU being put in cold storage for decades.

Turkey now has a resilient and capable business class which continues to innovate and respond to changing market conditions. Having said this, IMF forecasts of the rate of Turkey's growth in 2019 will likely further shrink dramatically. Recovery will be slow at best. Improving trade balances notwithstanding, Turkey's recovery looks to be protracted and may have some consequences for the political strength of the Ruling Party. The primary drag on the economy will come from its foreign currency debt burden together with difficulty in attracting foreign capital at the levels of the first decade of this century.

Its main trading Partner, the EU, is also dealing with both debt burden problems in the Southern Tier countries, compounded by political instability occasioned by Middle East Refugees absorption challenges. Its current political problems, especially post-BREXIT (if there is a BREXIT), are making the attractiveness of Turkey's belonging to the EU not only more questionable for Turkey but also, other EU member States are showing reservations, as evidenced by the December 2016 Referendum in Italy giving anti-Euro and Nationalist leanings a serious voice, echoing similar patterns in some "old line" European countries.

Looking at the June 24, 2018 elections in Turkey, Islamists and Nationalists have formed a coalition similar in effect to the Nationalist parties in Europe. Given these political developments, a period of lowered expectations for Turkey's joining might be good for Turkey and the EU in the near term. In short, it might be useful for both sides to take a "time out," while re-visioning processes clarify policy directions. If this process is, in the best sense, a cathartic experience, America is now also so engaged. All three entities, without anyone imagining that they can disengage from the world, might be well served to focus on internal healing. Emotions and expectations are presently at dysfunctional levels in the post WWII International Order in general. This may be a needed and useful "correction" that has finally come to pass in the Post-Cold War world – fraught with marvelous, and technologically malevolent, challenges to the International Order.

Currently, proponents "for" and "against" Turkey's joining the EU are presently locked in a "no-win" situation. This checkmate is happily accepted by Nationalists in both the EU and Turkey. Both are motivated by chauvinistic, cultural, and religious reasons. However, Centrist secular parties in both see more advantages than disadvantages.

For years, many in Turkey and Europe believed that the Acquis process, strengthening secularism and a commitment to fundamental Western concepts and practices of the Rule of Law, was desirable, regardless of whether or not Turkey were finally offered membership. Whether or not Turkey would choose to accept, if offered, was less important than the fact of Turkey going through the exercise of the Acquis process. In and of itself, the process alone was thought to be worth the effort, with a by-product of strengthening its orientation to the West. Certainly, EU Membership would draw Turkey more closely into its NATO commitment, but the point now seems moot. By late in 2018, President Erdoğan was proposing/threatening to put EU membership to a referendum. On the EU side, the leading candidate to become the European Commission's next leader, replacing Jean-Claude Juncker, is the head of the European People's Party, the largest group in the European Parliament, is Manfred Weber. According to a *Guardian* news article, dated November 4, 2018, titled "European Commission presidential candidate will end Turkey's EU bid if elected" stated, *"As the European Commission chairman hopeful I would exert efforts to end talks for Turkey's EU membership."* Clearly, there is some brinksmanship at work here. In any case, Turkey's president might prefer to " reject" the EU first, before it can be rejected by the EU if the President determines that there is a chance that a vote against Turkey's membership were seen to be in the offing.

Setting aside the commercial advantages, the political constraints, the surrendering of sovereignty to a supra-national body, is already difficult for many of the Member States of the current Union. For Turkey, for cultural and strategic reasons, many in Turkey would argue that finding commonality with EU supra-national interests would on many fronts be axiomatically problematic. Its geographic location alone would dictate different, if not opposing imperatives. Trying to harmonize Turkey's National interests, with EU interests, which are not on so many foreign policy matters even close to being homogeneous, *vis à vis* Greece, the MENA, Israel, Iran, Russia, and China, is perhaps a bridge too far. In the end, however complicated one wishes to make the analysis of the pros and cons for both sides, the elephants in the room are religious and cultural, compounded by European concerns regarding the prospect of unrestrained labor movement from Turkey. It is a country of 80 million people. These are stumbling blocks which might have a solution in the future. They may not. Either way, NATO-EU security issues remain complicated and potentially dangerous.

What are the risks for Europe, and America by extension, of not continuing a policy of encouragement and incentive for Turkey's joining? What are the risks of Turkey not continuing to seek EU membership in good faith, in spite of anti-Islamic, anti-Turkish sentiment in Europe? The implications of abandonment of the goal of membership are undesirable for both entities. In the vernacular, cooler heads must prevail, no matter how Sisyphean the task. Certainly, for Turkey, increasing reliance on Russian, Arab and Iranian support, is predictable and fraught with instability and intractable conflict.

However constructive the policy of isolation and independence was in the early decades of the Republic, the temptation for Turkey to go it alone has in the long run proven to be unsustainable. Atatürk's "peace at home, and peace abroad," echoing President Washington's admonition to be wary of "entangling alliances," worked for a time. Isolationism *vis à vis* conflicts outside America's borders has always persisted as a piece of the fabric of the American political ethos. One saw it in both World Wars and it continues to have its proponents today. Whatever geographic and resource blessings the United States enjoyed in its infancy, its commitments and opportunities to expand the "economic pie" precluded its remaining insulated while engaging the wider world. Having said that, adventurism has its costs. In any case, one might observe the larger the country, the larger its population, the larger its economy, the less freedom it has to maneuver independently of external considerations, whether one's neighborhood is global or regional. One of those external considerations, for both Turkey and the EU, is the future of a divided Cyprus.

Cyprus, an Achilles Heel

The Turkish military "intervention" on the island of Cyprus in 1974 was justifiable from a Turkish point of view. However, the world will never know nor care about the circumstances giving rise to an action characterized as an "invasion" in the West. The fact that the American CIA was operating in collusion with the Greek military Junta leader George Papadopoulos and his successor, Dimitrios Ioannidis, in supporting a coup to overthrow Archbishop Makarios, President of the State of Cyprus, is only known and remembered by interested International Relations academics and Middle East commentators. When Guarantor Power England failed to act in response to these developments on the island, Prime Minister Bülent Ecevit ordered an intervention to protect the Turkish Cypriot minority (20%) which had been suffering abuse at the hands of Greek Cypriots since 1963 and the outbreak of a civil war (*Kanlı*

Noel, or Bloody Christmas). The leaders of the Coup, as confirmed later, had every intention of returning Cyprus to the control of the mainland of Greece – fulfilling the Junta goal of *"Enosis"* – the reestablishment of greater Greece in conformity with the ambition of *"Megali Idea"* (the irredentist claim to a Greater Greece).

Turkey exercised its right of intervention in accordance with Article IV of the Guarantee Treaty of 1960, (Resolution 573, Standing Committee of the Consultative Assembly of the Council of Europe, 29th July 1974).

Long after the fact, in 1976, the UK House of Commons Select Committee on Cyprus found (HC 331 1975/76 para. 22) that Turkey had proposed joint Anglo-Turkish action under the Treaty of Guarantee. On 14th August 1974 (Daily Telegraph 15th August), Prime Minister Ecevit confirmed that he had indeed traveled to London to urge Anglo-Turkish intervention. However, the British Labor Government led by Harold Wilson refused to take any effective action, in spite of having troops and aircraft available at their Sovereign Bases in Cyprus.

Turkish Cypriots continued to be massacred by the Greek side, especially in the Paphos and Farmagusta areas, as reported by the *Times of London* and the *Guardian*, where upon the Turkish military pushed farther inland, finally  securing about 37% of the island's territory. Efforts to find a diplomatic solution failed during that fall. By February of 1975, the new leader of Northern Cyprus, Rauf Denktaş, declared a Turkish Republic of Cyprus. A Green Line *(Yeşil Hat)*, dividing "no man's land" area to be policed by the U.N., was established.

In response, under pressure from the Greek lobby in America, President Lyndon Johnson, with Congressional support, ordered an arms sale embargo on Turkey, a NATO ally. It was quietly lifted a few years later, but real damage had been done to Turkish perception of America. The days of the Marshall Plan and fighting alongside one another in Korea gave way to an enduring distrust of American commitments to Turkey.

In 1978, the author quietly visited Cyprus for a closer look and was introduced to the English-trained barrister, then President, Rauf Denktaş. After agreeing to some advisory work, arrangements were made for me to have a tour of some of the battleground areas, including the "off limits" abandoned "ghost town" resort city of Varosha, complete with bullet-pocked hotels/casinos. The degree of structural decay in so short a time was disturbing and eerie. Having a graduate school classmate and dear friend living in *Girne* (Kyrenia), I have returned many times over the years.

While prospects seemed bright in 2004 that a solution would be found, unfortunately, negotiations again broke down in November of 2016. The impasse continues. The situation on the island is complicated, not least of all by property claims of displaced people on both sides, Greek Cypriots in particular. The possibility of discovery of offshore gas deposits on the coasts of the island may prove to be a mixed blessing. If substantial resources are found, and can be raised economically (in the $75+ /barrel range), if claim disputes could be resolved between Greek and Turkish Cypriots leavened by oil revenues, such a scenario might serve to thaw an impasse otherwise now "frozen" in time. As reported in the *Guardian* in an article titled "Turkey warns oil companies against drilling in Cyprus" on November 4, 2018, President Erdoğan warned foreign oil companies against energy exploration near Cyprus, describing those who defy his warning as "bandits of the sea." The warning notwithstanding, Exxon is moving a drilling platform onto station off the Cyprus coast. Other major oil companies, including Total and ENI, are committed to drilling near Cyprus. And Turkey itself, has dispatched its new drilling ship to an area North of Cyprus within its own territorial waters off its Mediterranean shore. Tensions in the area are mounting, and include both Egypt and Israel whose territorial waters overlap those of Cyprus.

In the meantime, the Turkish Mainland is subsidizing the Turkish side of the Island, investing in resorts and gambling casinos which has attracted regular travel from the Mainland. There are now daily flights, multiple on the weekends, coming from five cities in Turkey, as far away as Trabzon. When last there, in 2016, the author learned that in response to these investments, Northern Cyprus is now being "colonized" by under-employed Turks from the South coast of Turkey, principally Mersin and Adana. Additionally, with a large Gülenist University with 25,000 students in *Lefkoşa* (North Cyprus capital) as the primary magnet, there are steady revenues coming from a growing student population coming from distressed areas in the Middle East, Syria in particular, and Nigeria in Africa. In August of 2016, an undersea pipeline was completed to the island bringing desperately needed water for agricultural development.

With Mainland Greece under financial distress and Greek Cypriot banks near bankruptcy in recent years, support from Greece has been spotty at best. However, with Greek Cyprus having a much larger population than Northern Cyprus, and being a member of the EU, it is now also enjoying an influx of foreign students. And, unlike Northern Cyprus, Greek Cyprus also receives a substantial boost from European tourism. Additionally, Southern Cyprus continues to host both British and American Naval bases, in close proximity to Russia's naval base in Latakia, Syria, reminding one of the strategic significance of this island.

Greek Cyprus has repeatedly used its veto power over the continuing of the Acquis process for Turkey. It is often supported by France, Holland, and Austria where Turkey is concerned. State pride, the history of death, loss and suffering on both sides, being passed down to subsequent generations, is likely to keep the issue frozen. The solution could be imposed from the outside, but that would require an agreement between Ankara and Athens. It is in this sense a situation like the Armenian Nagorno-Karabakh enclave in Azerbaijan, with both stalemates likely to remain frozen.

Western Perceptions of Muslims Through the Prism of Radical Islam

Earlier we have discussed the subject of Western perception of Islam. It was seen how trade and commerce tended to be supplanted by historic perceptions derived and "handed down" stemming from the Crusades, pitting Christians and Muslims in violent conflict with one another. Arguably, in simple terms, losing Jerusalem and then Constantinople may have left a more indelible scar on Western Christian perceptions and imagination defining who and what Muslims are than the Muslim perceptions of Christians and Westerners in the pre-modern era. Western appreciation for the cultural, philosophical, and scientific debts to high Islamic culture, especially during the height of the Arab-Berber rule of Spain (*Al Andalus*), seemed to have been gradually, and intentionally, expunged from historical memory by the Spanish (Christian) Inquisition. Those inclinations were earlier seen with the French Troubadours triumphally heralding the bravery of Christian Knights over the Moors in the Medieval poetry of "*Les Chansons de Roland*," and later and in the same vein, in Pierre Corneille's classic, *Le Cid*. And still, after this play appeared in the late 1630s, though the Moorish Muslim threat was waning in the Iberian Peninsula, the threat perception of Islam was only increasing in the face of Ottoman incursions in the Balkans and their return to the Gates of Vienna in the 1680s.

As threatening as Protestantism was to the Catholic establishment, and as violent as the Holy Wars of the Reformation and Counter-Reformation were, Western-Christendom, in the form of the Holy League, would coalesce to stanch the threat of Islam from the East, the Ottomans. Commensurate with this threat, images of the barbarism and savagery of the "Terrible Turks" could easily be conjured and readily disseminated amongst the peoples of Europe, Christian, Jew, and others.

With an explosion of European industrial and technological prowess, increasingly evidenced by military superiority, the growing confidence in the West eventually made room for a re-balancing of the more monolithic perceptions of the Islamic world of The Middle Ages and the Renaissance. For example, a certain nobility could be seen in Shakespeare's portrayal of Othello "the Moor."

In time, the purely negative stereotypes were not replaced, but augmented, by both a romanticized version of Arab culture in the 19th and early 20th centuries, but also by a paternalistic and patronizing air of Western cultural and religious superiority. While its origins could be seen in agreements respecting Christian pilgrims made between the victorious Saladin and Richard the Lionhearted in the late 12th century, its modern equivalent began with the notion of protecting Christian minorities in Muslim lands in the first Capitulation agreement between Suleiman the Great and King Francis I of France, discussed earlier. These agreements gave preferential treatment of the King's Catholic co-religionists in the Ottoman Empire. These Capitulations, originally given out of strength and confidence, were later extracted in the 19th century out of weakness. Naturally resented by Turks and seen as an affront to Ottoman sovereignty, these Extra-Territorial privileges for the Christian and Jewish People (*Miletler*) came in the course of the European self-appointed mandate to manage the Eastern Question as she dealt with a crumbling Ottoman Empire.

Together with the belated reforms of the Tanzimat Era, these privileges only gave license to the rise of a new trending political construct, the Nation State and the notion of "self-determination," providing the rationale for nationalist movements. Adding further challenge for the Ottoman Government was the tacit support of European machinations to secure their respective, and sometimes, competing imperialist aspirations and their attendant claims to related "spheres of influence." While pejorative Ottoman/Muslim perceptions of Western ambitions surrounding Ottoman lands is fairly levelled, it would be fair to recognize there have also been positive influences, developments and byproducts of Western cultural and technological influences in the MENA.

In the late 20th and early 21st centuries, Westerners have a decided tendency to see Islam and Muslims through the prism of the adherents, and tacit supporters, of radical and violent Islam. The result is the widespread belief that Islam as a religion, based on many Koranic verses, encourages jihad against "infidels" – nonbelievers, not to mention apostates within their own ranks. With similar attacks in many European cities, the "9/11" attack on the World Trade Towers symbolizes in the West the sense that Islam is in fact, and indeed, at war with the West and Western values – the existence of moderate Muslims notwithstanding. To those who argue that such terrorism is perpetrated by a small percentage of Muslims and unfairly characterizes the whole religion and its believers, there is a sense in the West that if that were true, there would be greater outrage from within Islam, not only condemning such attacks, but drying up their financial resources. In fact, many believe that if the majority of Muslims are peaceful, then they themselves are perhaps cowed by and must live in fear of their own radicals, thereby compelling them to acquiescence in silence. This would not be the first time in the history of the East and West, that populations have been held hostage to a radicalized minority.

Many in the West, as evidenced by BREXIT and the election of Donald Trump in America, see these political outcomes as a manifestation of a reaction to a perceived attack on the traditional Western liberal values of the Nation State and National Sovereignty, in the face of a creeping "politically correct" moral relativism, corporatism, and globalism. Taken together, some see these as threats to the long-term viability of the Nation State. And finally, many Westerners, as well as secular Muslims, believe that fundamentalist Islam and Sharia Law are incompatible with secularism. Further, it is believed that fundamentalist Islam is on the ascendant in many parts of the world. There is a perception many of Islam's leaders, spiritual and political, have enjoined its Faithful to seek to insinuate Islamic values, practices and ultimately Sharia Law in the Western countries to which they have migrated. Many in the host countries resent what they believe is an ongoing attempt to take advantage of Western principles of freedom and tolerance in order to institute Islamic culture and practice, inch by inch, over the very Western culture which has taken them in. Perception, fair or not, comes to be seen as truth. And it works both ways.

In a June 22, 2006 article titled "The Great Divide: How Westerners and Muslims Vie With Each Other" Pew Research revealed the following:

"Overall, the Germans and Spanish express much more negative views of both Muslims and Arabs than do the French, British or Americans. Just 36% in Germany, and 29% in Spain, express favorable opinions of Muslims; comparable numbers in the two countries have positive impressions of Arabs (39% and 33%, respectively). In France, Great Britain and the U.S., solid majorities say they have favorable opinions of Muslims, and about the same numbers have positive views of Arabs.

These differences are reflected as well in opinions about negative traits associated with Muslims. Roughly eight-in-ten Spanish (83%) and Germans (78%) say they associate Muslims with being fanatical. But that view is less prevalent in France (50%), Great Britain (48%) and the U.S. (43%)."

It should be noted that this data is arguably the high point, in the sense of acceptance, in such perceptions, especially as Turkey was riding high at that time on an economic and political wave.

Islamist Perceptions of Secularism, Zionism and Christianity and Western Morality

The same Pew research illustrating Muslim perception noted the following:

"In many ways, the views of Europe's Muslims are distinct from those of both Western publics and Muslims in the Middle East and Asia. Most European Muslims express favorable opinions of Christians, and while their views of Jews are less positive than those of Western publics, they are far more positive than those of Muslim publics. And in France, a large majority of Muslims (71%) say they have favorable opinions of Jews. Moreover, while publics in largely Muslim countries generally view Westerners as violent and immoral, this view is not nearly as prevalent among Muslims in France, Spain and Germany. British Muslims however, are the most critical of the four minority publics studied – and they come closer to views of Muslims around the world in their opinions of Westerners."

Perceptions of how each civilization treats its women are revealing.

"The chasm between Muslims and the West is also seen in judgments about how the other civilization treats women. Western publics, by lopsided margins, do not think of Muslims as "respectful of women." But half or more in four of the five Muslim publics surveyed say the same thing about people in the West."

On the subject of terrorism, the article notes the following:

"The belief that terrorism is justifiable in the defense of Islam, while less extensive than in previous surveys, still has a sizable number of adherents. Among Nigeria's Muslim population, for instance, nearly half (46%) feel that suicide bombings can be justified often or sometimes in the defense of Islam. Even among Europe's Muslim minorities, roughly one-in-seven in France, Spain, and Great Britain feel that suicide bombings against civilian targets can at least sometimes be justified to defend Islam against its enemies."

Underlying all Muslim perceptions of the West is the collective memory of European Colonialism, which in its later stages fostered Zionism and sustains it to this day. Subjugation by Christian countries, or indirect subjugation in the form of Capitulations, remains a scar in the Muslim psyche. The Sykes-Picot Agreement (1917) rings as clearly and loudly in the Muslim world as "9/11" does in the West. Its memory is symbolized and sustained in the ongoing

Arab-Israeli struggle over territorial control and power in Israel-Palestine.

Differences in perception between the West and Muslim East are manifest regarding the issue of the American use of drone warfare. Limited collateral damage by many in the West is accepted as a necessary evil. Muslims point to this as a perfect example of Western hypocrisy when crying foul about the loss of innocent life caused by fanatical suicide bombers and car bombings. The West in turn points to the tactical use of children and Mosques as shields by Hamas and ISIS fighters for sympathetic propaganda purposes regardless of the loss of innocent life in their own communities.

Where these self-serving rationalizations leave the world is an increasingly dangerous place for all. In a world where technology has lowered the cost of lethality, making terrorism available to non-State actors and small radicalized groups has forced State actors, large and small, into a world of "asymmetrical conflict" that knows no borders. Coping with these risks will continue to call for both State-sponsored violence and State-sponsored dialogue. Conflict resolution cries out for dialogue. A recognition that no side is innocent, and that human dignity must be found and nurtured in spite of the hostility "rightfully" felt by all parties to any conflict, is accepted by most observers. As important as dialogue is, can it be a solution? If human rights are universally recognized, though not always similarly defined, how can they be guaranteed, how protected, and through what structures?

Nationalism, Sovereignty and Supra-Nationalism – America and Turkey

We have discussed the progress of the concept of sovereignty from the "Divine Right" of kings to a Social Contract where sovereignty belongs to the people, and its elected representatives. In the West, we have seen how the "sovereignty of God" has over the centuries been replaced in temporal affairs by secular systems of governance. If we call this "modernity," we have also seen its appeal in the Muslim world, and we have also seen its rejection in the Muslim world. If we have seen Western Christendom adapt to secular humanism over a long period of time, we are seeing a continued resistance to it in much of the Islamic world. One thing about modernity, from the point of view of the maintenance of traditional value systems in domains outside the West, it does not seem to lend itself very reliably to "cherry-picking." It is as improbable to be half-modern as it is to be half-pregnant. To a large extent, one has to take "the bad" with "the good." Striking that balance requires compromise and the surrendering of sovereignty to secular authority. History has shown us that, while periods of civil war may occur, the Nation State, institutionally, appears to have been the most effective upperlimit of reach of the surrendering of popular sovereignty. Families, communities, districts and tribal units, in exchange for State maintenance of domestic order, the protection of individual rights and safety from external aggression, have accepted the role and function of the Nation State.

Supra-National entities have also been created, from the European Coal and Steel Community to the European Union, from the United Nations to the World Bank, and from the International Court of The Hague to the World Trade Organization. Arguably, they are more effective in Peace Keeping and economic matters, and less so in political matters. There are many proponents of the necessity or desirability of governance by regional and world bodies to the maintenance of world order. In the main, however, it appears that national governments and the citizens of individual countries find it undesirable and ineffective to surrender much national sovereignty to regional or world organizations. Certainly, such institutions have a role to play, and have certain areas in which they are generally seen to be functional and effective. But those who believe in One World government are in a minority. Surrendering political sovereignty to unknown, and unelected, decision makers to world bodies seems to have reached, and perhaps exceeded, it natural limits.

Turks and Americans have limits beyond which the surrendering of national political sovereignty becomes undesirable. Americans are endowed with a strong sense of individual freedom from government enshrined in the Bill of Rights. And, in turn, individual states enjoy rights not otherwise specified to be in the province of the Federal Government. The idea of surrendering significant sovereignty to a supra-national body, other than for limited and specific purposes, continues to be an idea repugnant to many Americans.

Turkey, for a host of good reasons, looks at membership in the EU as desirable in some ways and not in others. Turkish Nationalists and Islamists, for symbiotic but different reasons, find the prospect of joining the EU, while perhaps economically desirable, politically unattractive. It has been the author's observation that while many believe the Acquis process is useful from the point of modernizing Turkish institutions and laws, they are, at the same time, reluctant to surrender sufficient political independence. And finally, there are those who resent the idea of going through a process which in the end may never result in an offer to join. The author's take on this is that if ever offered, Turks would vote not to join what appears to many, not as just a Western Club, but a Christian Club. It may be more likely that Turks will seek to maximize their advantages in the exiting Customs Union. Meeting the criteria to qualify for VISA-free travel might be the upper limit of a Turkish surrendering of independence/sovereignty. Even those criteria may be politically unacceptable, compelling economic and trade incentives notwithstanding.

EU/US Customs and Trade Unions – Implications for Turkey

The proposed Transatlantic Trade Partnership (TTIP), like its counterpart The Trans-Pacific Partnership, represents an effort to boost trade and jobs globally for the signatories to such agreements. Negotiations are ongoing, but will need to be recast in light of BREXIT and Donald Trump's profession that the terms of trade that might have been acceptable in earlieradministrations, might prove to be less so in the current Republican Administration. Even for those who support these efforts, there are significant impediments to achieving such agreements that would need to be approved by the 28-State members of the EU, on the one hand, and on the other hand, approval in the American case by a majority in the Senate. Detractors in both Europe and America, among other objections, are concerned that such agreements will give too much power to large corporate entities over the participating States. Proponents of the TTIP look to the economic advantages of a free trade market which together, the United States and the EU + UK, would represent some 60% of the world's GDP, 33% of the word's trade in goods and 42% in services. The subject of fair trade from the point of view of the American economy, has not been a focus of proponents of multi-lateral trade groupings. Reexamining the nature and level of existing trade barriers needs to be part of the due diligence in forging and rationalizing trade preference groupings in the 21st century.

Chapter 22

THE ARAB SPRING, TWITTER AND THE IDEATIONAL POROSITY OF SOVEREIGN BORDERS

"For maps are a rebuke to the very notion of the equality and unity of humankind, since they remind us of all the different environments of the earth that make men profoundly unequal and disunited in so many ways, leading to conflict..."
—ROBERT D. KAPLAN, *THE REVENGE OF GEOGRAPHY.*

The Arab Spring, West and East

The Jasmine Revolution and the Arab Spring were convenient constructs of Western media creation which comported with President Obama's and Secretary Clinton's foreign policy message at the time. It remains for many who were actually involved no more than wishful thinking. The author was a skeptic from the beginning and said so publically. Uprisings, strong man regime change/replacement and "Arab winters" might be a more apt description.

For this reason, one might aptly think of those uprisings as events in an Arab Spring Process.

Turkey itself, and its domestic constituent political, ethnic and religious sects, were a part of this process initially. However, in the wake of the attempted coup on July 15, 2015, and even before, developments in Turkey seem to suggest that the Process has not been just stalled, but reversed, since trending away from tolerance, civil rights and the Rule of Law. The Ruling Party, with the support of the Nationalist Party, argue that security considerations and the weeding out of Gulenist "putchists" require a suspension of some civil rights. In this charged atmosphere, it would be two years before a State of Emergency, giving the regime virtual dictatorial powers, until August of 2018. Freedom of the Press is at an all-time low in Turkey. On December 4, 2016, a New York Editorial Board article titled "Crushing Free Speech in Turkey," placed Turkey, according to the Committee to Protect Journalists, at the top of the world's list for the highest number of imprisoned journalists, more than China, for example, which has 18 times the population. The article goes on to state that since 2003, Prime Minister, and now, President Erdoğan, "has launched more than 2,000 prosecutions of people who have offended him – from students playing darts with with his photo to someone behind a social-media post comparing Erdoğan to J. R. R. Tolkien's *small, slimy creature* Gollum." Quoted in the same article, according to Twitter's Transparency Report, "*Turkey is No. 1 when it comes to demands for the removal of "offensive" posts, accounting for 15,000 of the 20,000 accounts fingered this year."* Social media has been shut down by Erdoğan's government. Ironically, Erdoğan used social media to mobilize his supporters, through the network of imams initially (reminiscent of the Ayatolla's tactics in the toppling of the Shah, but without the Internet), to take to the streets and face down the military coup-makers on July 15, 2016.

For the first decade of this century, Turkey was widely recognized in the MENA as the model of the hybrid of democracy in a Muslim country. As one approaches the close of the second decade of the 21st century, Turkey as a model of "enlightened Muslim modernity" has been replaced by Tunisia, which enjoyed a peaceful transition of the Islamist-oriented Ennahda revolutionary government to a more moderate secular-oriented government in 2015. Tunisia's achievment in this regard was highlighted in a *Foreign Policy Journal* article titled "How Tunisia's Islamists Embraced Democracy," dated March 31, 2016.

One reason the Arab Spring failed, with results opposite from its lofty goals, is because it was spontaneous and unorganized. The protestors and reformers who filled Tahrir Square were men and women yearning for freedom from oppression, repression, skyrocketing food prices, and massive youth unemployment. They thought they were fighting against government corruption, tribalism (Libya) and religious zealotry, and for more representative government. Perhaps the most disappointed of all the aspirants for democratic change have been the women protestors and reformers who had dreamt of some degree of emancipation and equal rights. Their voices and energy, so prominent in the uprisings, so sympathetically heard by the Western media in particular, were summarily extinguished by reactionary forces.

The Jasmine Revolution, like Pandora's Box, loosed a popular hue and cry for change in Muslim lands. Unlike the "shots heard 'round the world'" at Lexington and Concord in the American Revolution, the forces loosed in Tunisia, with a poor vendor lighting himself on fire, were far from speaking in one voice. The philosophical and intellectual antecedents of freedom, liberty, and popular sovereignty coming down to the West are seen in a yearning for something similar in many of the peoples of the Middle East. Modern Turkey's founding was based on just such ideas. However, there is another yearning that holds sway over many of these same people. That yearning is to live their lives under the perceived simplicity of a rubric, one with the simplicity of only Five Pillars of obligation, under the authority of a Sublime Ayatollah or Muslim monarch. Such peoples take comfort in the notion of a Caliph being the spiritual ruler of the Muslim Faithful, the *Ümmet*. The subtleties, intricacies, inefficiencies and possibilities of democracy seem remote, too unpredictable, and uncomfortable in many of the world's settings.

Islam, Secularism and the Separation of Church and State, of Mosque and State, has yet to find a stable balance, even a dynamic balance in the Middle East. In making that statement, it should never be forgotten that the commonly shared Western sense of the Rule of Law as it is understood today, and republican forms ofgovernment, were only arrived at after many centuries of cultural, philosophical, and violent upheaval. Somewhere between Luther and Erasmus, Cranmer and the Inquisitions, Western European peoples, after horrific bloodshed, produced from this crucible a Western civilization that never quite extinguishes the human propensity to go to war either within itself, or with the apparent enemies of Western Civilization. But from that crucible, with all its shortcomings, the Western Social Contract has yielded better outcomes for a far larger percentage of its citizens than other systems of governance.

Jus Sanguinis and *Jus Soli* – from the Millet System to a Borderless Cyber World

The old Roman Law concepts of *jus sanguinis* and *jus soli* continue to be important constructs through which to view loyalties, tribal commitments, sectarian and religious commitments. The case was made earlier that geographical and topographical contours, rivers and mountains lent themselves better to Nation State formation in Western Europe than in the Levant. While there have always been disputed areas in Europe, from Alsace to Slovakia, tribal and ethnic differences have been easier to assimilate where geographic, topological and resource protection have served to supersede differences of blood and religion. One might argue that European mountain ranges, gulfs, seas and oceans offer more topographical cohesion for the rationalization and maintenance of Western States than the geography of the Levant does for Arab States.

Without overstating the case, the Romans' experience in governing a large multi- ethnic, multi-racial, multi-lingual, and multi-religious empire led them to develop a distinction between the rules and laws governing the Citizens of Rome, wherever they were geographically located, and those governing non-Roman subjects. The concept of *jus soli*, law of the soil or land, lent itself first and foremost to the European provinces of the Empire beginning with Italy. As geographic, political, religious, and sectarian differences in the Eastern and North African reaches of the Empire made the implementation of the Roman Law impractical, the Romans allowed the "non-citizen"-subjects, as long as they paid their taxes and maintained peace within their groups, the right to observe their own laws and customs. This was the law of the blood, *jus sanguinis.* The same practice was essentially later followed by the Byzantines and the Ottomans. While this proved an elegant solution to balancing central authority with local authority for the purposes of maintaining empires where the vast territory could not be "garrisoned" with soldiers, by the 19th century, administrative institutions equal to the task of governing and policing became increasingly unsustainable. In the breach of efficient rule stepped authoritarian rulers in the MENA who relied on shared religious culture and traditions to provide the framework for governance. If the parliamentary system of Lebanon is an exception in the Arab world, it is so because it serves a complex mosaic of Christian and Muslim constituencies within a small geographical confine.

Without going into the details, the current debacles in Syria, Libya, and Yemen clearly illustrate the difficulties of maintaining order in multi-tribal and multi-sectarian States, where the principle of *jus sanguinis* serves to continue to accommodate division rather than national union. It is precisely this concept which flies in the face of geographic borders. Loyalties other than to and beyond, the State flourish. One of those loyalties is religious commitment. In Islam, the very notion of a Caliphate of the Faithful is one that pre-existed the Seljuk and Ottoman Sultanates. The Community of Believers (*Ümmet*), knew, and knows, no borders. The rise and international appeal of ISIS, as a self-proclaimed caliphate, with transnational support and multi-national Jihadi participation is a good example. However, even where *jus soli* rules, in America today, commitments to one's religion or ethnic group, may not only supersede loyalties to the United States in principle, but in practice as well. Certainly, tribalism is not exclusive to Muslim countries as the Nation State model challenge seeks to come to terms with maintaining its own sense of the meaning of sovereign borders in the face of large-scale movements of political and economic refugees.

The rise of the Taliban and ISIS (IS) as transnational entities, with the aid of the Internet, are perfect examples of the ideational porosity of geographic borders. Like Wahhabism, militant Salafism, and the Muslim Brotherhood, a Caliphate is an idea, more an ideology, with a transnational rationale and appeal. Jihadi supporters, via the Internet, are attracted to the principle of dying for a cause to restore the Community of Believers in the House of Islam (*Daral Islam*) and fulfill the prophecies of the Prophet Muhammad. The demise of ISIS does not remove the animus for a Caliphate for those who think that "Islamic" modernity, albeit medieval in its inspiration of rule under the rubric of Islamic Law, is feasible and desirable.

Early support by the Ruling Party (AKP) of Turkey for ISIS, coming in large measure from a sympathy for the concept of a Sunni Caliphate with its resurrected Baathist (Ottoman) roots, illustrates the quandary Turkey finds herself in adapting to Western modernity. Columnist Pınar Tremblay's article in *Turkey Pulse* (*Türkiye'nin-Nabzıı*) posted by *Al-Monitor* on November 10, 2014, titled "Turks increasingly sympathetic to Islamic State," notes the following:

"A Kurdish Alevi soccer player, Deniz Naki, was brutally beaten on November 2nd in Ankara by supporters of the Islamic State (IS) for standing in solidarity with Kobani. Three days after his ordeal, Naki told Al-Monitor that he left his soccer club in Turkey because he feared for the well-being of friends and teammates."

She went on to quote a bookstore owner in the *Fatih* section of Istanbul who said,

"We are observant Muslims here, and we do not believe what was done in 1924 — abolishing the caliphate by the new Republic of Turkey — was acceptable. I became a fan of IS during the first days of Ramadan when the caliphate was declared — now they represent all Muslims on earth and we are all obliged to support [IS]. I speak to you because I want the world to know the twisted image [portrayed] in the Western media. They always claim that men who are drug addicts seeking money and women join IS. This is wrong. My best friend from childhood, who was a ney flute teacher, joined [IS] six months ago. He had a good life here, teaching rich kids and making good money. He preferred jihad. It is about the honor of the caliphate now."

She then quoted Hüseyin Beheşti, a scholar of religion and philosophy, who told Al-Monitor the following:

"Sunni groups such as the Salafists now are highly active in Turkey. After the Syria problem, because of the sectarian policies of the AKP, the Turkish Islamist community is becoming more radical and fundamentalist. The caliphate ideology is currently being discussed by many Islamist groups that have no record of discussing it previously."

And finally, she notes that Beheşti emphasized that the issue of a caliphate is no longer a marginal issue exclusive to members of Hizb ut-Tahrir and argued that the AKP's pro-Islamist policies helped the formation of a Salafist stronghold in Turkey.

Since ISIS turned on Turkey for allowing the U.S.-led Coalition to use *Incılık* Airbase to strike ISIS targets in 2015, official Turkish Government pronouncements have been an unqualified rejection of the idea of an ISIS-led caliphate. On this subject, since that time, there has been complete "official" agreement in Ankara, Tehran, Riyadh, Amman, and the Gulf Emirates.

As one thinks about the role of the Internet and Twitter in mobilizing support for any cause, good or bad, one can only imagine what a difference social media might have had at the Tiananmen Square protest and riot in China in 1989, prior to the Internet revolution. Clearly, the speed of information flow has served to magnify the role of communication in establishing and maintaining critical solidarity, local and international, for any group or movement, and now a government in the case of the 2016 counter-coup in Turkey. It offers a tool of dissent that can be bridled by "authorities" only at the expense of engendering more popular sympathy for the dissenters. Containing social unrest is no longer a matter of controlling physical space, but now cyberspace which is borderless. In fact, there is no State power which can do anything but interrupt the flow of information – and that only for a limited period of time. In the absence of State power, internet communication advantages are relatively more valuable to politically and economically weaker parties in any contest, whether it be protestors in Tehran, Cairo, Baltimore, or Istanbul as examples. Using a military term, cyber communication is a force multiplier.

The Continuing Importance of the Role of Geography, Borders, and Frontiers

There are borders and there are borders, some harder to cross than others. Internet communication notwithstanding, geography continues to play its role in maintaining state sovereignty. As noted earlier in Kaplan's, *Revenge of Geography*, deserts, major mountain ranges and major rivers can serve to give greater and more defensible rationality to the borders of a country.

Among the more formidable borders are oceans and seas. Governed by International Laws of the Sea, conventions and treaties, the coastal and territorial waters of countries have become more useful, and sometimes more difficult to defend. With the advent of offshore oil and gas technology, no longer is it just fishing rights off the coast of such places as the Grand Newfoundland Banks, for example, whereby the Americans were given shared Rights in the fishing of cod in the Treaty of Paris in 1783. It now applies to the Niger Delta, the North Sea, the Gulf Coast of America, the South China Sea, and now the Island of Cyprus, with her overlapping territorial waters with Egypt and Israel. The Cypriot case is further complicated by competing claims coming from Northern Cyprus and her patron state, Turkey. The now historic dispute between Turkey and Greece over Greek Islands but a stone's throw

to the Turkish mainland, is a constant reminder of adja-
cent territorial water issues and the economic and political
disputes that can and do arise.

Consider the implications of the 2010 Turkey-sponsored
Blue (*Mavi*) Marmara Peace Flotilla and its interdiction by
Israel in defense of its territorial waters and its embargo
on the Gaza strip against Hamas. This incident resulted
in the mutual withdrawal of ambassadors between Turkey
and Israel, only reestablished six years later. The combination of then Prime Minister Erdoğan's pro-Palestinian and
pro-Muslim Brotherhood rhetoric going back to the First
Intifada (2003-2004) added another layer of complication to
the issue of a mutually beneficial shared exploitation of
the Cyprus gas fields – otherwise potentially a win-win
for all parties. Insights at the time on the prospects of
resolution of impediments noted by Middle East analyst
Margaret Williams in her June 20, 2014 article headlined,
"Are Security and Energy Concerns Moving Turkey and
Israel Toward Reconciliation?," which appeared in the *IPI
Global Security* were telling:

> *"Earlier this month, about 3,000 people marched through
> the streets of Istanbul in memory of the eight Turkish cit-
> izens and one Turkish-American killed by Israeli Defense
> Forces when the Mavi Marmara ship, known as the Gaza
> Freedom Flotilla, tried to break through Israel's naval
> blockade of the Gaza Strip in May 2010. The incident
> marked a nadir in Israel's and Turkey's strained relation-
> ship in recent years, and neither country's ambassador*

has since returned to his former post...Four years later, a possible reconciliation agreement between these former allies has fueled speculation of a normalization of relations between the two countries.

This small bit of momentum has prompted analysts to ask what may be driving this rapprochement and what may deter its realization. A multitude of factors play into this equation, but economic and security concerns seem to be at the fore. The discovery of underwater gas fields off the coast of Israel, and collaboration on the construction of a shared pipeline that would bring unprocessed natural gas from the Leviathan gas fields to the shores of Turkey and then on to Europe, are seen as an incentive. If Israel's gas flows into Turkey, "'the Trans-Anatolia Pipeline and Trans-Adriatic pipeline [projects] that take Azeri gas to Europe would provide key infrastructure that would be relatively easy for Israel to tap into,'" said Ross Wilson, former US ambassador to Turkey and now at the Atlantic Council, in a recent interview.

Yet, practical as well as ideological challenges to a shared pipeline are significant. For starters, the underwater pipeline would most likely have to travel through Cypriot waters, due to instability in Syria and Lebanon, thereby requiring some kind of agreement on the Cyprus issue. Add to this, complications arising from Cyprus' recent posturing to Egypt as a possible gas field development partner, and waters become harder to navigate. Furthermore, start-up costs for a shared pipeline would be high, the actual level of gas reserves remains unclear, and, as Dan Arbell, a Senior Fellow with the Saban Center for Middle East Policy at the Brookings Institution, confirmed, Israel may not be interested in any sort of energy collaboration with Turkey until ties have politically normalized, even if a pipeline between the two countries would make the most sense economically. "'If you lay an undersea pipeline to Turkey and from there to Europe, banking on most of your exports going through Turkey, you have to make sure that relations are smoother than they are now.'"

Clearly geography still matters. Cyber communication may serve to distort people's perceptions of geography, but the physics of borders, whether they be porous or substantial, remain. Politicians, and even empires and states, come and go. Mountains, rivers, and oceans remain.

Turkey as a Role Model for other Countries in the MENA

Where does Turkey fit in this mosaic? The Republic of Turkey was established in 1923, the Muslim Brotherhood in 1928 in Egypt. If Turkey is/was a role model for Arab and Muslim countries, why did it take so long for the Turkish model to have notable appeal within Islam? Has its appeal in the East increased as it appears to have moved toward a more Islamist political agenda? European and Middle Eastern perceptions notwithstanding, the Republic of Turkey has had considerable appeal since its inception. Turkey is an amalgam of many faces, political, cultural, and religious. The Turkish model is neither homogenous nor static. Turkey's perceived appeal and perceived short-comings are viewed in both the Muslim world and the West through different and often contradictory prisms. More recent appeal had been fueled by its demonstrably robust economy.

If Turkey is a model, how might it be described? Whether one is looking from the East or the West, the Turkey of the 19th century when it was given the moniker of "The Sick Man of Europe," is anything but in the 21st century, current financial instability notwithstanding. While one might argue over whether it is European or Asian, a hybrid, or neither, at the end of the day, Atatürk's famous definition of who his people resemble, *"Biz bize benzeriz"* ("We resemble ourselves") continues to be an apt description, despite an increasingly politically polarized society. Beginning with the structural and economic reforms of the Özal years, the changes to the country in the past quarter of a century have been "game changing." Istanbul alone boasts a new subway, a "chunnel" under the Bosphorus and a third bridge over it, and a third international airport opened in November 2018. Until the advent of structural economic weaknesses exacerbated by politically-motivated manipulation in recent years, it had become the 16th largest economy in the world. But, rampant infrastructure spending based on foreign direct investment and international credit, current account imbalances, and artificially high interest rates combined in 2018 substantial downward pressure on the currency, resulting in a downgrading of its international debt and rising unemployment. Turkey will need to find the political will and courage to deal with its economic problems in the near term. To break out of its relative position in the world economy, in the longer term, Turkey must successfully address her Achilles heels, namely the Kurdish, Cyprus, and Armenian issues. Making gains in any of these areas will serve to begin to restore its *bona fides* as a stable regional investment platform. This had been Turkey's comparative advantage since the 1980s.

Turkey continues to struggle to evolve into her 21st century skin. While the so-called Arab Spring is about Arabs, and not Turks, they did, and do, share Islam in common. Ottoman Turkey was for centuries the political center of the Muslim World Community. The Turkish Model, in its current manifestation, governed in the context of an Islamist agenda, may now better resonate in the MENA. The crux of her relevance to different segments of Muslim society turns on the issue of secularism and where it fits in the balance of governance. For some countries, Sharia will remain the primary source of law. Where that is the case, the Turkish model, even with its Islamist cast to secular underpinning, will have a qualified appeal. However, clearly, the degree of appeal in the Muslim world will vary with her economic strength.

Turkey's regional economic prowess has contributed to an enhanced view of itself. While Turkey has serious internal contradictions, the popular TV series (now on re-run), *Muhteşem Yüzyil* (The Magnificent Century), the story of

Suleiman the Magnificent, has not only domestic appeal, but strong appeal outside Turkey, especially in the Balkans. This popular appeal reflects a national self-perception of a Turkey on the ascendant, though now tarnished since 2013, to pick a date, by political and social turmoil, the war in Syria and the low-grade civil war against the separatist Kurds. This is a Turkey whose regional and international view of itself, and by its neighbors, is now more Ottoman-esque, more robust and more prideful.

President Recep Tayyip Erdoğan in many ways symbolizes the new Turkey (*Yeni Türkiye*). Much of his support comes from religiously conservative voters and was fueled by the "Anatolian Tigers," Islamist-oriented businessmen, whose base, or original base, is/was in the heartland of the country, including the Eastern and Southeastern parts which border Iran, Iraq, and Syria. These businessmen have cultural, religious, and affinities to the MENA, serving to augment, and counter-balance (not in total value of trade, of course) the historic European trade bias. In 1997, Erdoğan himself was convicted of subversion and briefly jailed by the Kemalist Secularists, backed by the military, for having quoted from a poem at a political rally in Eastern Turkey (Siirt) saying, "*The mosques are our Barracks, the domes our helmets, the minarets are our bayonets, and the faithful are our soldiers.*" Erdoğan has long had ties to the Moslem Brotherhood. So, when he defied Israel, both at Davos over the Gaza Peace Flotilla (*Mavi Marmara*) incident several years ago, and continues to condemn Israel's

Palestinian policies, giving visible support to Hamas, it is no wonder his, and Turkey's, image in the Muslim world has risen.

The author was in Palestine in 2010 and saw posters everywhere with Erdoğan's picture in a Muslim Brotherhood-style "fist pumping" pose. Further to the point, at that same time, the Turkish Economic and Social Studies Foundation undertook a poll in seven Arab countries plus Iran and found that 66% of the respondents believed that Turkey represented a "successful blend of Islam and democracy," with only 15% disputing the assertion.

How difficult is it for Turkey to role model to its neighbors in the MENA? To say that Turkey is between a rock and a hard place is more than cliché. Balancing the demands between and among its "Western," "Northern," and "Eastern" interests, in fact, places Turkey on a fine line in every move it makes. One example is sufficient to paint the picture of complexity. Recognizing that the Iran nuclear threat is more proximate for it than it is for Europe or the United States, giving rise to a reluctant agreement in Madrid with NATO to base a part of the short-range missile defense system in Eastern Turkey, had to be balanced against the fact that 97% of its energy requirement comes from foreign sources, including Iran, sources often opposed to Western European and American policies. The President Obama-led Iran Nuclear Deal shifted the American political center of gravity from Riyadh to Tehran. As many questioned whether or not Iran's nuclear genie was, in any meaningful sense, put back in the bottle in April of 2015, Turkey felt jilted by the apparent shift to a White House Shia bias in the Middle East. In response, Turkey scrambled to find and reprioritize direction. Turkey has since been walking an ever-finer line with its NATO allies, with Russia, with Egypt, and Israel. When AKP came to power in 2003 with a robust policy of *"Zero problems with our neighbors,"* its image enjoyed a ten-year rise in domestic and international appeal. By 2013 and the excessive suppression of the Gezi Park protest, Turkey's foreign policy has spun 180 degrees to be currently defined as, no neighbors without problems.

Contest for Regional Hegemony, Turkey Versus Iran – Sectarian Identity

To the extent that Turkey is competing in the Arab world for regional hegemony with Iran, without the advantage of substantial oil reserves and revenues, or the desire to develop nuclear weapons, places it in a tight spot. In the Islamic Crescent, Turkey's historic and religious sympathies with Sunni Muslims, all the more so under the Islamist predilections of Turkey's President Erdoğan, as opposed to Iranian Shias or their Syrian Alawite cousins in Damascus, Turkey must play a delicate game. Like all the "players," it must be prepared to speak out of both sides of its mouth. It must be able to change course in a hurry as events change on the ground, to wit the recent rapprochement with Russia and Israel. In both cases, whether Turkey is signing the Turkish Stream pipeline project or pitted against Russian policies in Syria, or promoting security business with Israel or railing against their policies towards the Gazans, Turkish policies must be transactional, not country-specific. And, Sunni proclivities notwithstanding, Turkey itself has Shia-Alevis and Shia-Kurds to consider when making foreign policy decisions. One need only remember the international Public Relations nightmare for Turkey, with pictures of its tanks sitting idly on the border, within range of ISIS, and the Alevi blow-back during the ISIS siege of Kobani (*Ayn-al Arab*) in the Rojava Kurdish area of Northern Syria in the fall of 2014. The siege was finally broken by YPG Kurdish and Peshmerga Units, together with U.S. air support, in the spring of 2015.

At least since the 16th century, in the military contest between the Saffavid and Ottoman dynasties, one Turkic-Persian and Shia, the other Turkic and Arab Sunni, the battle for control of the hearts and minds of the peoples of the Middle East has ebbed and flowed. In more modern times, Iran proved to be blessed with an abundance of oil; Turkey not so blessed. One is geographically linked to Southwest Asia, the other to Europe and North Africa, with the Levant being the dividing line, with Syrian and Iraqi the historic and present killing fields in between. What happens in, and to, the States in between them is critical to this contest and drives their respective foreign policies in the Levant, with Sunni-Shia sects and tribes serving as an historic fault line. The roles that NATO, Russia, Saudi Arabia, the Gulf States play, the sides they support, remain critical to the contest. The barbarous Khashoggi assassination in the fall of 2018 is a perfect example of transactional diplomacy. The Turks were able to exploit the world approbation at the expense of their rich Sunni co-religionists, the Saudis, where otherwise they are often allied on various regional issues.

The policies and behaviors of Iran and Turkey have become arguably increasingly opportunistic, confrontational in some areas and accommodative in others. Religious and ideological goals can mutate, making them strange bedfellows when tactical conditions on the ground warrant, to wit mutual opposition to Daesh, or Turkey's eventual temporary alliance with Peshmerga fighters for Kobani in exchange for an uninterrupted flow of Kurdistan oil. Such opportunism is as old as international relations, and survival for that matter. Its current practice has resulted in a weekly-changing political high wire act between Tehran and Ankara, and each other's proxy forces in the region. But these arrangements are temporary in nature, subject to ambiguity, obfuscation, denial, or reversal. These are more pragmatic situational tactical responses. What drives the essence of the contest is more enduring, more strategic, and more ambitious. It is the power and prestige which the two contestants enjoy in the eyes of the Community of the Faithful. With 80% of Muslims being of the Sunni persuasion, this is a competition that Turkey has held the upper hand in for centuries. But, in the battle ground states of the Middle East, the contest is more even, making the role of outside powers all the more significant. Ideas and ideologies are powerful drivers, whether in Turkey's or America's Founding, or today in the Regional and Global contests for hegemony.

Regarding the above noted age-old contest between Turkey and Iran, arguably Turkey would be well served to return, when and where possible, to its earlier foreign policy of "Zero problems with our neighbors." Ataturk's dictum, "Peace at home...Peace abroad" might yet serve the country well. The business-led, business-driven pragmatism of the early years of AK Party Rule was a constructive path. But, first it must move beyond the trauma of the July 15th Coup and Counter-Coup and related Gülenist battles, real or concocted, both at home and abroad.

Chapter 23

ECONOMIC AND POLITICAL DISINFRANCHISEMENT, AND THE LIMITS OF GOVERNANCE

"Let me never fall into the vulgar mistake of dreaming that I am persecuted whenever I am contradicted."

—RALPH WALDO EMERSON, 1838

"You and I, and our Government, must avoid the impulse to live only for today, plundering for our own ease and convenience, the precious resources of tomorrow."

—PRESIDENT DWIGHT EISENHOWER 1961

A Polarized America, Traditional vs. "Progressive" Values and Policies

The November of 2014 off-year Congressional elections in America, while some would argue that the outcome was based on a referendum regarding President Barack Obama's policies, domestic and international, is in any case very revealing about the changing demographic trends in America. The bottom line is that it is as difficult to find a Democrat member of the House of Representatives in the South as it is to find a Republican Representative in Southern California. Pew Research describes this trend by saying, *"Political polarization – the vast and growing gap between liberals and conservatives, Republicans and Democrats – is a defining feature of American politics today, and one the Pew Research Center has documented for many years."*

A look at the Mid-Term 2014 Elections split between Blue State (Democrat) and Red State (Republican) for Upper House elected officials provided a telling indication of an increasing Red State orientation of the country.

In the 2016 Presidential Election key previous Blue States shifted to Red States, notably Florida (29 Delegates), Ohio (18), Pennsylvania (20), Michigan (16) and Wisconsin (10). The Electoral Map shifted dramatically in 2016, with Donald Trump taking Electoral 306 votes to Hillary Clinton's 232.

The 2016 map of Red/Republican to Blue/Democrat, by county, tells another interesting story. There are 3,141 counties in the United states. Trump won 3,084 of them. Clinton won 16.

Recognizing this shift from Blue to Red states, if one just looks at the popular vote, Hillary Clinton should have won. The popular vote favored Democrat Candidate Clinton by some 2,000,000 plus votes. In a pure democracy, Clinton would have won. It is noteworthy that by Clinton winning four of the five boroughs of New York City, she secured more than a two million vote margin. Those five counties encompass 319 square miles. The United States encompasses 3,979,000 miles. It is a story of voting population density. And, it is precisely for this reason that the Founding Fathers established the Electoral College as another layer of safeguard that all America would not be ruled by the voting strength of a few hugely populous areas. It is the reason why the number of seats in the Lower House of Congress is based on a State's population. Whereas the Upper House, the Senate, provides for enormous California and tiny Rhode Island equal representation, exactly two per State. It is worth remembering that one of America's greatest Presidents, Abraham Lincoln, was elected with only 39% of the popular vote, but became President by having more Electors in the Electoral College.

By any measure, Donald Trump's victory, came as a shocking surprise to the professional pollsters and to the political elites and to the establishment in America. Clinton's having won the popular vote has engendered a call on the Democrat left for the abolition of the Electoral College. Yet both sides knew the rules. The Democrats unexpectedly lost the popular vote in just enough populous States to put Donald trump into the White House. If one were to argue that Donald Trump does not have a real mandate, such as the one Republican President Ronald Reagan enjoyed in two popular "landslide" victories in the 1980s, as he did not win the popular vote, it should also be noted that the

Republicans held onto both Houses of Congress that they had secured in the 2014 "off-year" elections.

To Donald Trump's credit, he came with a refreshing message, "Make America Great Again." He was a "political outsider," beholden to no lobbies or interest groups, and he promised to tackle government corruption and "insider business as usual" politics in Washington that had turned Congress into a "dead-locked" hamstrung and ineffective Branch of the Government in the 21st century. His message resonated with much of Middle America, derisively described by Coastal elites, as "Flyover America." That term might account for his turning the corner in Ohio, Michigan, and Wisconsin, flipping them from the Democrat to the Republican column, but does not explain flipping Pennsylvania and Florida. He improved Republican margins from the preceding Republican Presidential hopeful, Mitt Romney back in 2012, by attracting more votes than expected from White women, Seniors, Blacks, Hispanics, and Millennials.

It might be argued that the 2016 Presidential Election was Clinton's to win or lose. She had the money, the ground teams, most of the media and establishment and the prospect of being the first woman to win the White house. She had "issues," "baggage" and failed to connect with many Independents and managed to lose 5% of the Black vote Obama had, dropping from 92% to 87%. The Obama legacy proved to be a little less appealing by the end of his Administration. Economic recovery had been painfully slow, especially for Blue Collar workers.

In the end, it was a pitched and vicious battle in a "house divided." Many in the Country were deathly frightened of trends away from the "traditional values" and "family values" that had made America different from Europe and the rest of the world. Conservatives were keenly aware that appointments to the Supreme Court, with several aging Justices, were at stake. Liberals were equally keen to break the tie in the Court with prospective Clinton appointments. The stakes for the "Contending Parties" could not have been higher.

The aftermath, the trauma on the left, especially among the college youth, was palpable. One would expect the professional political classes and their interest groups to prepare to battle the Republican incumbents in the coming "off year" election in 2018. What was not expected is the sustained rancor by Liberal Youth, especially on college campuses, and measures that might best be described as "coddling" on some campuses.

Certainly, for all its advantages, arguably, social-media is proving to be a mixed blessing in the sense that the heat of battle, once waged, is not allowed to end and dissipate naturally. There are those committed to stoking the fire, even when a peaceful transition of power has been affected, allowing for the population to get back to the business of governance, working and living. America will never be the same. It is not clear that one party going in, or out, of power has ever produced the same degree of what appears to be enduring disillusionment and malaise, except perhaps during Franklin Roosevelt's Presidency in the midst of the Great Depression. Significantly, there was no social media and the people had to get back to work, where possible, in order to survive. America then and now could not be more different. This observer would like to be wrong. The attempt to capture the essence of the 2016 Election here is limited, cursory at best, hopefully shedding some light on an infinitely complex set of facts and varied perceptions.

At the heart of the "Great American Debate" is a controversy about the role of the Federal Government in the governance of the citizenry as a whole. This is a struggle that began in the Constitutional Debates of 1787-1788, between those favoring a strong central government and those wanting power, except in matters of defense and foreign policy, to be in the hands of States and Individuals. After President Washington stepped down, the battle royal commenced in earnest, most notably in the rancorous controversial Election of 1800 that brought Thomas Jefferson to the White House, but only after the Fourth Ballot in a tie-breaking House Vote.

Fast forwarding to the 21st century, when it comes to excessive Federal Government spending, the Republicans think of themselves as holding the moral high ground in this area. In practice, both Parties, when in office, act similarly. Neither side can resist the temptation to raise Government spending by well more than the average annual inflation rate. They differ in the allocation of spending, and there only by degree. Republicans are more reliable spenders on defense and the Democrats on social welfare programs. But even those generalizations vary in some areas of the country, depending on the location of military bases where politicians of both stripes will advocate for military spending within their jurisdictions.

The net result is the same. Too much of the spending, beyond tax income and other revenues, tends to be made up through the printing of more and more money. The result is an artificial increase in the money supply, to service the interest on the ever-mounting Federal deficit and Federal debt, pushing American debt holders (from around the world) ever closer to abandoning the dollar as a reserve currency. Arguably, the only reality keeping this from happening is the dollar, on a relative basis, continues to offer more stability than other major trading currencies.

The burden of such spending policies falls disproportionately on the productive, tax-paying, middleclass workers. While the following is subject to differing interpretations, the 2013 Census in America showed that there were more "means-tested" welfare benefits recipients in America, (109 plus million) than there were full-time workers (106 plus million). Nuancing the interpretation does not essentially change the basic math. This imbalance is fundamentally unsustainable without printing money and growing the deficit. In less robust economies around the world, Borrowing Countries pay a steep price for such imbalances in the form of inflation and higher interest rates.

The growth and the abuse of entitlements is one of those flashpoints around which Democrats and Republicans clash – the latter believing that the resulting liabilities are burdening future generations – weakening America as a country – while satisfying the needs of current generations. Regardless of where one stands in this debate, the imbalances are better met in a growing economy, with more jobs for more of the people. Certainly, failure to meet this demand, increases social unrest, especially in un- and under-employed youth. The cost of this reality is even greater in Developing countries. Persistence of high youth unemployment in inner cities in America is just as worrisome as it is in Developing countries. The success, or lack thereof, of national governments in dealing with this challenge is critically important. If government seems to be intrusive in one's private life and fails to effectively facilitate economic growth and employment, it is a recipe for social malaise and youth violence.

In America, polarization between the two major political Parties, and the society as a whole, also centers on the extent of government intrusion into the province of State's Rights and the rights and privacy of individuals. Government intrusion, at both the Federal and State levels, has been an historic hot-button item since America fought and gained independence from England. The basis of this conflict goes to the Founders and Framers of the Constitution and their intent for the three Branches of government, the Executive, the Legislative, and the Judicial, to serve as a check and balance on each other.

Waging modern war, especially undeclared war, beginning with Vietnam, and dealing with National Security, especially since 9/11, has occasioned the relative power of the American Presidency. Legislative "gridlock" arguably has contributed to the strengthening, by default, of both the Presidency and the Judiciary. Judicial activism and the politicization of courts is one of the by-products of gridlock, as is the resulting tendency for Executive Orders to come out of the White House. The net result is a weakening of the intended balances between, and among, the three Branches of American Government. Both of these tendencies, in the Executive and Judicial Branches, were again at issue in the 2016 elections, Presidential and Congressional.

In conclusion, recent elections in America seem to be turning on an equation of governance which follows two general approaches, one being more "Traditional" republican (with a small "r") values and practices, and the other, which is more "Progressive" – following in the paths of the Roosevelts, first "Teddy" and later Franklin Delano. Both Parties have a "populist" appeal, but aim at different subsets of the populace. Appealing to the Middle Class is common to both, but here, drilling down, one sees differing solicitations to different subsets of the Middle Class. Rather than trying to characterize those differing publics, rich and poor, White-Black-Hispanic-Asian, Upper and

Lower middleclass, legal vs. illegal immigrants, Christian-Jewish-Muslim-Agnostic-Atheist, income tax payers and non-payers, corporates vs. private citizens, "Wall St." vs. "Main Street," urban vs. rural, Blue vs. Red States, suffice it to say that the "sides" are rigidly drawn. The political contests, in large measure, boil down to both Parties seeking to sway the "Independent" vote, to one side or the other over the top.

The American Debate has been aptly described by the relatively new term "Culture War(s)." One example of the complexity of this debate is the subject of government surveillance which gives rise to conflicts over the First and Fourth Amendments of the Bill of Rights, in particular, the Freedom of Speech and protection against "unwarranted or illegal search and seizure" clauses. Of course, most people "want their cake and eat it too." The 9/11 tragedy, the Boston Marathon bombing, and the identification of violent criminals all argue for more surveillance cameras in airports, on street corners, shopping malls and now attached to a policeman's belt. On the one hand, police seizing a suspect's cell phone without a warrant, the National Security Agency tracking all citizens and/or their phone calls and storing the information for years, all in the name of National Security, simply adds to the Orwellian fear of "Big Brother" being privy to private lives, behaviors, and travels. That trend is opposed by "concerned" citizens. On the other hand, if cyber war is a fact of human existence going forward, and an ability to counter or respond to cyber- or physical-attacks requires that the government whose first charge is to protect its people, then citizens are likely to rationalize and accept this invasion of their privacy.

Many, however, are asking if the price of freedom is being purchased at the price of that very freedom. Finding the balance, recognizing that government oversight it is not static but dynamic, varying with apparent threat levels, is tricky. Arguably, if left to its own devices, the Executive Branch will be prone to "Water Gate" its own people in the name of providing safety, or worse, as has been alleged in recent years, for political purposes. Resistance to government policing powers has grown. This is especially true in the apparent selective enforcement of certain laws, such as in the area of illegal immigration and IRS investigations. Both the appearance, the potential threat, and the actual overreach of government power constitute a legitimate concern for the citizens of all countries, especially where some sense of democracy and the rule of law is constitutionally authorized.

Clearly, NSA spying in and outside America is a cause for universal concern – even if some level of it is, and always has been, seen as part of "the intelligence game," but government overreach has its limits.

Polarized Turkey, Secularists vs. Islamists and Nationalists

Extreme polarization began to dominate Turkey's political life in 2013. Based on a thorough reading of the Turkish and Foreign Press in late May and early June of 2013, what started as a simple protest by "Greens" in Taksim Square, Istanbul over the Municipal plan to remove the trees in Gezi Park, and replace them with yet another upscale commercial building, triggered an unanticipated and widespread popular response. What followed might be seen as Turkey's response to the Arab Spring movement – a popular outcry against government overreach into the private lives and lifestyle preferences of many of its people, especially those who had grown accustomed to "freedoms" associated with democratic and secular governance.

Government infringement of Free Speech, Freedom of the Press, and the Rule of Law, however justified or rationalized by the Ruling Party and its Leadership, will continue to generate social unrest in the Country and have undesirable long-term effects for Turkey at home and beyond its borders. Current trends going into 2019 and beyond suggest that the suspension of civil rights and the rule of law, in the name of national security, is taxing the credibility of the notion of an operating democracy in Turkey. To date, however, a majority of the people of the Country find such overreach either tolerable, necessary, or desirable. Such a Social Contract is showing signs of weakening in the face of economic stagnation.

Elections have consequences. The Ruling Party (AKP) has enjoyed more than seventeen years of success at the ballot box (2003-2019). But, a Republic, by its very definition, is bound to protect the rights of its minority parties.

This is the important distinction between a republic and a pure democracy. Its importance was noted by America's Founding Fathers as a system of government which should provide safeguards against what was then termed "mobocracy." The People should elect representatives, and through them seek democratic governance. Opposition Parties in Turkey are currently ineffective.

In conclusion, both America and Turkey need to recognize the need to "curb" the policing powers of their States. It is this very unconstitutionally justified power-grab that animates a significant portion of the American Electorate to continue to lobby to protect the 2nd Amendment Right for the citizenry to bear arms. Police forces in both countries, from a technology and firepower point of view, have become paramilitary organizations. Their appearance, against unarmed protestors, can be a frightening prospect when unleashed against one's own population. Having said that, an angry citizenry acting illegally in either country, and armed with Social Media, stones, clubs, and possibly Molotov cocktails, is surely a threat to orderly society. If unchecked it can lead to anarchy. Failure to find a reasonable balance poses potentially even larger threats. Certainly, one of the antidotes to frustration of the youth in particular lies in channeling their energy into productive jobs, making them "stakeholders" in the search for peaceful and democratic outcomes. This is especially true for those who feel, or are in fact, economically, or otherwise disenfranchised.

Chapter 24

RECENT ELECTIONS IN TURKEY AND AMERICA AND THE JULY 15TH COUP

"The arrogance of officialdom should be tempered and controlled, and assistance to foreign lands should be curtailed, lest Rome fall."

—CICERO, 55BC

In response to a conversation which took place between Richard Falk and Prime Minister Ahmet Davutoğlu on September 28, 2014, Bill Park, Senior Lecturer at Kings College authored the following on December 17, 2014:

"The AKP's success also owes much to the personality cult that has grown up around former prime minister and now president, Recep Tayyip Erdoğan. He is seen by his supporters as a man of the people, blunt spoken, nationalistic, and sharing their prejudices and preferences. They don't mind that he has built himself a Ceausescu-esque palace. He is their Sultan. Whether the AKP could fully survive his political or physical demise has yet to be seen.

Turkey before the rise of the AKP was generally regarded as an 'unconsolidated democracy.' It was characterised by repeated military interventions in the political process, the banning of especially Islamist and Kurdish political parties and media outlets, and a sinister 'deep state' rooted in the judiciary, the bureaucracy, the security apparatus and even the media and academia, that was associated with the unexplained deaths, disappearances, and the intimidation of critics that punctuated Turkish political life. Turkey was ruled less by independent institutions, the rule of law or by elected politicians than by an interlocking network of well-placed Kemalists, presided over and ultimately protected by the General Staff."

The analysis noted above that Turkey, under the Ruling Party and its leaders, operating a more open democratic process of governance, may have been premature, even then. Those observations and opinions are now five years old. Today, one might ask if the Kemalists and Secularists have simply been replaced by a new "deep state" led by a new cadre of Islamist-oriented operatives. Has the Ruling Party become more authoritarian, less democratic, less transparent? According to the Ballot Box, with a slight set-back in the June 2015 National Election, support for the Ruling Party was reaffirmed in the snap Election of November later that same year. While studies show there are definite areas of the country where the AK Party does not enjoy even a plurality of the vote, where opposition to the AK Party is strong, the electoral map of Turkey does show geopraphically widespread support for President Erdoğan's Party. One must never forget that President Erdoğan has been seen as a savior for the pious elements of the population whose beliefs and practices had been shunned by a secular elite for decades. One must also remember that he presided over what appeared to all the world as an economic miracle for a decade. Those successes have been unravelling to some extent in the past few years. Two thousand nineteen is a critical year for the Ruling Party to see if the difficulties can be staunched. In any case, President Erdoğan will have a few years to right the ship before the next Presidential election.

Government Overreach, Tolerance, Transparency and Trust

In the preceding Chapter, we looked at the Turkish Government's response to popular unrest. We saw that protests, together with a sympathetic Media and Social Media, may gain and immediately engage a wide audience, well beyond those directly involved.

Racial unrest in America and Freedom of Speech in Turkey are abiding issues with staying power. Whether or not perceptions of these problems are distorted, fair or not, they are legitimate and will not go away. They may be principally domestic in nature, but they tend to be international in scope and implications. On certain issues, there are times when the governments of both countries can be hardpressed to find friends outside their respective countries.

Perceptions have everything to do with where one sits, politically, socially, ideologically, economically and geographically. It is hard for people living in New York or Boston to have the same perspective on the security and safety of America's borders with Mexico, as those living on and near those borders. Looked at another way, if Canada and Mexico were reversed geographically, arguably, Vermonters and New Yorkers might feel a different sense of urgency and concern on the subject of illegal immigration.

Similarly, it is hard for Americans, so many thousands of miles away, with a large ocean in between, to appreciate the considerations and calculus the Turkish Government is making with respect to its policies toward Kurdish Separatists within its borders, and Separatist sympathies of Kurdish peoples just over their borders in Syria, Iraq, and Iran. Not to overdraw the analogy, but for illustrative purposes, if Mexican Americans were seeking autonomy, or independence, in southern Florida and California, Americans might have a better sense of Turkey's historic preoccupation with the perceived Kurdish threat.

When constituent elements of the population of one's own country are at odds with its government policies, and when sympathetic Social Media and/or the Official Media link those domestic opponents with sympathetic international constituencies, the business of governance becomes impossibly complex, as it has become in the

Internet Era. The temptation to shut down media, social and official, and the internet, in the name of "national security," seems to have been overwhelming in Turkey. The abuse of government power is a charge that can be levelled against the American government as well. One is reminded of Lord Acton's famous observation, *"Power corrupts. Absolute power corrupts absolutely."* Perhaps the following quote of unknown authorship is apropos of the next topic of discussion, *"Corruption is authority plus monopoly minus transparency."*

Constitutional and Legal Reform in Turkey

Those Fundamental American Principles of Liberty and Equality have found their way, in various forms, to so many countries with a written constitution ever since America's Founding. Modern Turkey is one of those countries, a Republic established in 1923. Constitutional and Legal Reform began during Kemal Atatürk's tenure as President and has continued. Its most recent Constitution was crafted and promulgated under Military Rule in the wake of a coup in the early 1980s. It continued the Kemalist secular tradition and favored a strong military involvement in the governance of the people. Prior to that coup, the political system was dysfunctional at best. It may be easy to criticize the 1980 coup in hindsight, but the author's personal experience, living in Turkey at the time, and recollection of the dysfunction and corruption of the government of the late 1970s, and the related political and economic strife, the violence and killings, taken together, surely exposed the Republic to the risk of chaos and civil war in absence of the coup.

With an increasingly widespread belief that Turkey's 1982 military coup-fostered Constitution, written with the Army as an open Guarantor of secularism and stable public discourse, and a general recognition that the military was guilty of excesses in dealing with those it perceived as enemies, the Turkish Parliament agreed in 2007 to undertake the redrafting of a new constitution. More recently, the AKP Ruling Party has, by Presidential Decree, fundamentally changed the laws governing Judicial, Public Prosecutor, and University Rector appointments. These appointments have since become more political. Or, at least the politics of appointment have shifted from Kemalist and secularist to more Islamist for now more than a decade.

The Opposition thought it had dodged a bullet in the June 2015 election, where the AKP, hoping to gain a supra-majority of the 550 seat Parliament, even attempting to bargain with the pre-dominantly Kurdish HDP Party, actually suffered a humiliating loss. Not only was the HDP seated with slightly more than 14% of the vote, but the AKP lost almost nine points, dropping to just over 41%. Under suspicious circumstances, the Government's "cease fire" with the PKK Kurdish Separatists broke down in July following the June election in Suruç in Southeast Turkey. Turkish Government policies in the Syrian war continued to leave the country between a rock and a hard place vis à vis the Kurds, the Iraqis, Israel, the EU, NATO and America as well. President Erdoğan's personal popularity notwithstanding, the cohesion of the Ruling Party was at risk from its, by then, open split with the Gülenists beginning in 2009. He launched a purge of fellow Islamist AKP Party teammates, the Gülenists. As a team, they had together worked so effectively to dismantle and emasculate the Kemalist and secular military officer and judicial ranks, using patently trumped up and falsified charges in operation Ergenekon.

In this politically charged atmosphere of the summer of 2015, President Erdoğan launched a snap Election in November, whereby, with an anxiety-ridden population, with civil and internecine party warfare seemingly out of control, the AKP re-affirmed its majority at the ballot box. Heading into 2016, with Turkey and America at loggerheads over Syrian-ISIS policy priorities, Turkey and the EU at odds over VISA-free travel for Turks in exchange for holding back Syrian Refugees from the Gates of Europe, back door channels with Russia and with Israel were quietly reopened in an effort to diffuse internal and external tension at the margins. Being backed into a corner, in significant measure of its own making, the government of Turkey began revisiting former Prime Minister Davutoğlu's original policy going back to 2002 of "zero problems with its neighbors."

The attempted military coup of July 15, 2016, played nicely into the increasingly authoritarian hand of President

Erdoğan, a "gift" as he is reported to have said. And when it failed, as it surely would post-Ergenekon purges of old-line Atatürkists and Gülenists, he was prepared to act swiftly, under the powers of a State of Emergency. Even in the absence of the coup, he was already planning to purge the military of suspected residual Kemalists and Gulenists in the August Supreme Military Council (Yüksek Askeri Şura) a few weeks later. And the ax came down, perhaps with more force than had been anticipated prior to the coup.

What has now happened, in effect, is a civilian "Counter-Coup," with no need to exit after stabilization as was the military tradition, with "civilian government imposed" consequences in terms of torture, imprisonment, further military, judicial, police, and academic purges with no end in sight. While there was a great deal of political and social unity in Turkey following the early weeks and maybe a month or two following the failed coup, there is some evidence to suggest that there was a significant "buyers' remorse" heading into 2017, as sober reflection began to take stock of the authoritarian practice of the President of Turkey. Further still, these "Presidential prerogatives" were soon to be in process of becoming codified as discussed below. It is no longer unusual to encounter, as happened to the author who was teaching there at the time, to meet people who quietly voiced the opinion that the military coup might have been preferable to the civilian coup. Either way, there is concern, at home and abroad, about the future of secularism, if not in theory, but in practice, in the Republic of Turkey. Late in 2016, the Ruling AK Party, with the help of the Nationalist Party, began to openly move forward the process of Constitutional Reform with proposals to fundamentally enhance the powers of the Presidency, abolish the office of Prime Minister, and diminish the role of Parliament. It was touted by its proponents as being a system based on the American model of an Executive Presidency (Başkanlık Sistemi). Again, in the name of National Security, this concentration of Presidential power, de facto, has been in effect at least since 2015.

On December 10, 2016, twenty-one Constitutional Amendment recommendations were put forward in Parliament with the signatures of all AK Party MPs, with little or no input from Opposition Parties, which were in any case, opposed to the proposed Presidential system. In essence, it was argued that Turkey was not ready for such a system.

Controversy surrounds the concentration of power, and "partisan power" envisioned by proposed Article 104 in particular. By its terms, the President would become both the Head of State, the Head of Government and, the Head of his Party. The position of Prime Minister was to be abolished as were the military courts. The President would have a wide scope of appointments of ministers and senior positions in the bureaucracy. And, ministers would no longer be accountable to Parliament.

The timeline for this process began with the Parliamentary majority approval on December 10, 2016. The stated plan was that, over the course of the first three months of 2017, the General Assembly/Parliament would take up consideration of these proposed 21 Amendments in two General Sessions. In the First Session, consideration would be given the entire set of Amendments as a whole, and then, individually. Amendments to the Amendments were to be entertained. The Second Session, to follow, was intended to determine if any proposed Amendments to the Amendments had the support of a majority, allowing for an appropriate restatement of the original Amendment in question.

With this process complete, a vote on the whole 21 Amendments, with some revisions, was completed by April of 2017. These Amendments (Constitutional reforms) were then scheduled to be voted on in Parliament on a majority basis. The AKP Party then had 316 votes. As the Opposition Parties, the CHP and the HDP opposed the proposed Amendments, the AKP needed the allied vote of the MHP (Nationalists) who controlled 39 votes. In order to enact the law without a Popular Referendum, 367 votes were necessary to achieve a two-thirds Supra Majority. The AKP and MHP combined with a total 356 votes, falling short of the 367 needed. Perhaps to cover for an expected shortcoming in the required majority, both President Erdoğan and the AKP Party officially stated that they wanted a Referendum regardless of the outcome of the Parliamentary Vote.

Failing to line up a majority vote, the Ruling Coalition initially set a date where a Referendum on the Constitutional Reforms would be held in conjunction with local and national elections all to be held on the same day. A majority vote on the Referendum would permit President Erdoğan to run under the new rules, allowing for two consecutive five-year terms if elected in 2019 and re-elected in 2024. The outcome of these new rules could mean that he could serve until 2029 (age 75). The original date was set for the late spring of 2019. History would advance the date of these elections due to growing opposition and economic problems which were gradually coming to the surface, to the attention of the public.

This entire political process took place during a declared State of Emergency which ended in August of 2018, just weeks after the Referendum and National Elections were held on July 24, 2018. The elections were held in an environment where political dissent was/is barely tolerated, a record number of journalists are being held in prison, and grave concerns for basic human rights are being expressed by many in, and outside, Turkey, including by many friends of Turkey in the West.

With each successive political victory of the AK Party since 2007, concern slowly turned to anxiety for many, and the opposition (CHP, HDP). The fear was, and is, an "institutionalization" of AKP rule for the foreseeable future, and the implications that such a development might slowly erode the secular Republic. The question was being asked in some quarters, is Turkey headed toward becoming a, de facto, Islamist Republic, headed by a President with unchecked Executive powers? Will such a proposed governmental restructuring, in the absence of "operative" American-style checks and balances, result in an existential change for the Republic as it was conceived and founded nearly a century ago? What are the risks? What are the rewards? Voters, and not the Army, will decide going forward.

To get a better picture of the political environment leading up to the July 2018 Elections, below are relevant excerpts from two noted journalistic commentators in Turkey.

"The proposals face stiff resistance at this first stage from the two biggest opposition blocs in the 550-member parliament. Secularist and pro-Kurdish lawmakers slammed the ruling Justice and Development Party, or AKP, and nationalists for seeking to impose an autocratic regime in the wake of the failed putsch...Just like we stood against the coup attempt, we will also fight against this arbitrary, authoritarian understanding," said Levent Gök, parliamentary whip of the main-opposition Republican People's Party, after the AKP introduced its proposal.

"This will further polarize Turkey," said Emre Peker, in the *Wall Street Journal*, December 11, 2016.

And, on the subject of the possibility of Turkey becoming an Islamic Republic, consider the following observations of Mustafa Akyol, Al Monitor – *Turkey Pulse*, December 12, 2016.

"Moreover, the presence of the MHP [the Nationalists] in the constitution-making process further guarantees that the principle of secularism will remain in its place. The MHP is a party that appeals to Turkey's conservative Sunni masses, but it has had fewer problems with secularism. In fact, the leader of the party, Devlet Bahçeli, made it a precondition for talks with the AKP that the republic's founding principles enshrined in the first three articles of the constitution, which include secularism and "Mustafa Atatürk's nationalism," would remain untouched. Current reports show this precondition has been observed."

While 2018 Elections took place, the Referendum passed with the slimmest of margins, Erdoğan was elected President, and the Ruling Party, together with its Coalition Partners (MHT Nationalists), barely won. Election irregularities in tightly contested precincts around the country were claimed, and widely accepted. Clearly, on the subject of the future of the Republic of Turkey, the jury is still out.

Constitutional and Legal Reform in America

In an article appearing in The Globalist on October 10, 2013, outspoken critic of a "strict constructionist" interpretation of the American Constitution, author Uwe Bott, in an article titled, "The Need for US Constitutional Reform" notes:

"If anything, the chronic re-occurrence of the U.S. government's failure to approve a budget as well as the repetitive

quarrel over raising the country's debt ceiling demonstrates one thing clearly: Constitutional reform is the priority in the United States. Without it, the U.S. will indeed become a failed state."

The drafting, debating and struggle for ratification of the U. S. Constitution by the original Thirteen States was contentious, protracted and challenging beyond imagination as discussed in earlier chapters. There were only Thirteen States and an elite spanning the geographic, economic, and political interests of a population of fewer people than currently live in the metropolitan area of Washington D.C. The fact that the Constitution has been so seldom amended, since the first ten known as the Bill of Rights, is a testament to the reverential esteem in which the Founders' creation is held, and the durability of the Constitution and its content. Having said this, the debate about whether the Constitution is a "living" document, subject to modernization if you will, or whether it is an almost immutable document, in the absence of super majoritarian approval by the Federal Government and the acceptance of Fifty State Governments, continues.

Various causes and efforts to reform or amend the American Constitution in recent times center on desires to: limit the terms of Supreme Court Justices from the current lifetime appointments to ten-year terms; limit the number of terms that can be served consecutively by Senators and Congressmen, and abolish the Electoral College. Regarding the institution of the Electoral College, it is argued that it is anachronistic, designed to function in an age of horse power for communication. To date, four American presidents have won without a popular majority. Other reform causes include the requirement that the passing of an annual budget be mandatory, with the previous year's budget continuing until a new budget is actually passed. And, in the interest of streamlining the legislative process, all Bills should deal only with the subject matter of the Bill, without Riders by which special interests and their Legislative Representatives tend to compel Legislators to vote special provisions not germane to the Bill in order to get the primary thrust of the Bill itself passed. Finding agreement on any of these issues, at both the State and Federal levels, would seem to require a *"force majeure."*

Like all political outcomes, there are always winners and losers. Stalemate in all democratic systems of government, to the extent that they are democratic, is endemic. Winston Churchill's dictum comes to mind here, *"Democracy is the worst form of government, except for all others that have been tried."* For any shortcomings that might be posited, it is remarkable that the American Constitution, which came into force the year the French Revolution began, 1789, is still operative. Its durability is a function of the genius of its design for the American people, who have also benefitted from their geography and resources, human and otherwise, that have helped to sustain the Great Experiment. Its survival is also due to the fact that there are bodies of law, and laws, which surround the Constitution – Federal, State and Local, Administrative, Legislative and Executive. However inelegant and impractical, the "living law" surrounds the Constitution whose fundamental Principles endure – even where some believe they might be enhanced, or altered, in light of modern experience.

The 2018 Mid-term Election in America

The hype and hysteria surrounding the November 6th Mid-Term election, the amount of money expended into the outcomes, especially in advertising, surpassed all expectations, and all previous American Mid-Term elections. Voter turnout for a Mid-Term election also set a record. Millennials, young people born in years on either side of the turn of this century, also turned out in record numbers (maybe for the first time). The election outcome yielded a reversion to the norm in America, a House divided. The Democrats took back the Lower House of Congress. The Republicans added to their thin margin of control in the Upper House, the Senate. Both sides rightly claimed victory. The popular vote, as determined by the population of a State, gave the Democrats control of the House (from D/195, R/240 to D/235, R/199). 218 Congressman of the same party constitutes a majority. The popular vote as apportioned to all States equally, two per State, resulted in the Republicans gaining a stronger majority (from D/49, R/51 to D/47, R/53).

Whether the outcome, with a Republican President sitting in the White House, will result in classic gridlock, bringing the constructive output of Congress to even lower levels, remains to be seen. The day after the election marked the beginning of the 2020 race for the White House. The Democrats will be in search for the candidate who can mount the most effective challenge to President Donald Trump. Early on, Hillary Clinton appears to be the front runner in a crowded field reminiscent of the one facing Donald Trump leading up to his nomination by the Republican Party in 2016. The pyrotechnics, the vitriol, and the unbridled political warfare is expected to bring little honor to the democratic process, or peace to a deeply divided country.

Recent elections in Turkey have revealed a similar degree of polarization of the people, divided in ideology. But, the kind of political stalemate related to the system of "checks and balances" that characterize the American polity are not in evidence in Turkey. Turkey today, is more similar to modern Turkey at its Founding, ruled essentially by one party led by its charismatic leader, Recep Tayyip Erdoğan.

While unlike Turkey's June 24th election, which was national in scope with the additional issue of profound constitutional reform, America's Mid-Term did not have the Office of the President on the ballot. That fact notwithstanding, the election was in many of the races a referendum on President Trump. The same was true of his predecessor's first Mid-Term in 2010, when Barack Obama was, for all intents and purposes, on the ballot after his 2008 election as President, where the Democrat losses in the House were even greater than the Republican losses in this election.

One of the upshots of this American Mid-Term is that the Urban versus Rural split in America has become even more pronounced. The Republicans lost some of the bridge-land between urban and rural, namely the suburbs, with increases in college-educated women moving away from the Republican Party. Arguably, their move was less from the Republican Party than from the sometimes-boorish style of Donald Trump.

The June election in Turkey evidenced a similar increase in rural support for President Erdoğan and the AKP, albeit for different reasons. Here, some key cities around the country, including Istanbul, swung in favor of the opposition. They did so less in response to competent leadership within the opposition parties than as a rejection of the agenda and authoritarian leadership of the President and the Ruling Party. The cities hold a large amount of Turkey's Middle Class and tend to support secularist policies at odds with the Ruling AKP Party.

Issues capturing the American public shifted in priority in the six months leading up to November. Each Party sought to gage the pulse of the electorate and capitalize on perceived differences in voter concerns. While it is hard to generalize, the adage that 'All politics is local....' and, 'It's the economy stupid....', while in evidence earlier in the year, especially as record economic recovery, lowest unemployment, lowest Black and Latino unemployment in decades statistics were unfolding under the President's business-friendly Executive Orders, shifted in July. The debate and the issues moved away from those 'chestnuts'. Democrat pre-occupation with alleged Russian interference in the 2016 Presidential election, and the claim that between the Russians and the "outdated, outmoded" Electoral College, the Republicans and Donald Trump had stolen the election from front-runner Hillary Clinton, also began to lessen in favor of other issues and tactical election opportunities.

Fraud was claimed in both the 2016 election in the U.S. and in the 2014, '15, and '18 elections in Turkey. In many democrat quarters, Donald Trump's presidency was/is thought to be illegitimate. Unlike the elections in Turkey, where voter fraud is thought to have been widespread, there is no hard evidence to date to support such a claim in Trump's 2016 victory. The fact that there are those who believe and profess that it was rigged will continue to push that contention publicly across all forms of media.

A hallmark of American democracy is the notion that when the bitterness of an election process is over, and the results are in, that the people accept the verdict, get on with life while waiting to have another crack at the winners' column two or four years later. While the aftermath of elections in America continues to have avoided civil war, an acceptance of the ballot box results seems to be no longer uniformly binding. This phenomenon might be said to have begun in Al Gore's loss to George Bush in the 2000 election, which was then the fourth Presidential Election where the winner lost the popular vote, but won in the Electoral College. Donald Trump's 2016 win is now the fifth. In the past, the viability of the implication of an "illegitimate" presidency was kept alive, but ultimately ineffectively, by the losing party's political party machinery. Such messages are now much more effectively sustained by a range of powerful outside forces behind the parties themselves.

Issues driving the debate leading up to the 2018 Mid-Terms might usefully be divided into international and domestic considerations. Interpretations of these issues and events largely came down along party lines, with various publics being mobilized in the contexts of their respective "identity" groups. Depending on the issue or event as noted below, there was some party line cross over.

On the international front, though lower down on the scale to hot button domestic issues, President Trump taking America out of the Paris Climate Accords, out of the Iran Nuclear Deal, out of Transpacific Trade Partnership (TPP) and renegotiating the North American Free Trade Association (NAFTA) all brought cheers in some quarters, trepidation in others. The decision to move the American Embassy to the political capital in Israel, from Tel Aviv to Jerusalem, long promised by previous presidents in their campaigns, was met by horror in some quarters, and praise in others. This decision was an example of a crossover issue where predominantly Jewish support for the Democrat Party was given to President Trump on this matter.

Another issue in the spring and summer 2016 headlines that rattled world stock markets was the hard line taken by the President against the regime of Kim Jong Il of N. Korea – only to yield an historic initial thawing in the U.S. and South Korean relationship with N. Korea. Whether and when that diplomatic approach might begin to bear more permanent fruit remains to be seen.

In the run up to the election, the international issues that seemed to have the most traction with different factions were the American relationship with NATO (weakening versus rebalancing economic burden) and the EU (terms of trade rebalancing), disagreement about how to deal with Putin and Russian territorial designs in Syria and the Middle East, the Crimea and Ukraine, and Eastern Europe and the Baltic States. The other military and strategic hot spot issues centered on China's territorial claims in the South China Sea, the new Belt and Road Initiative ("BRI") through Central Asia, and its strategic resources grabs and infrastructure projects in Africa and Latin America. Also competing for headlines was the Central American "human caravan" reigniting the debate regarding national sovereignty and border protection issue in the context of the immigration controversy. And finally, the Saudi assassination of the Saudi journalist Jamal Khashoggi, exploited to the hilt by President Erdoğan, added, and continues to add, strain to the Saudi-American relationship. This is a relationship, which, under the direction of President Trump, had been resurrected, following the previous administration's reorientation away from Riyadh to Tehran.

While this list of issues is most surely not complete, the one's selected, and President Trump's policies regarding them, their alleged success or failure, seriously added to the continuing polarization of the American public. The polarization is not new, but has intensified. It can be argued that it began to take on a more intractable character beginning with the Speaker of the House Newt Gingrich era Congressional challenge to President Clinton's administration.

On the domestic side, the Republicans were riding strong gains in employment numbers, public confidence in the economy rising, and commensurate gains in the stock market. The Democrats seemed to be focused on allegations of Russian collusion in the unexpected Trump election victory, a pardon, or a pass, for Hillary Clinton's security breaches while Secretary of State, and a general shift in momentum to the left, to the Bernie Sanders and Elizabeth Warren wing of the party.

The Democrat focus then shifted to the Senate hearings regarding inappropriate sexual behavior, and rape charges, directed against President Trump's Supreme Court Nominee, Brett Kavanaugh. The charges against him dated back to high school and college. The television theatrics were riveting. In the process, Judge Kavanaugh appeared to be judged guilty in the court of public opinion. A presumption of innocence until proven guilty in these extrajudicial hearings was not evident. With all due respect to the primary accuser who has suffered from an attempted rape experience while still in high school, discrepancies in her testimony, and an inability to establish any compelling evidence that young Brett Kavanaugh was guilty of said charges, or even present, resulted in a party line vote, for and against, with a thin margin confirming his nomination. He was sworn onto the Supreme Court a day later by the President.

Probably the most compelling vote in favor of his Supreme Court confirmation came at the end of the hearings by the Senator Susan Collins from Maine. She had a history of being a "swing voter" on various issues, sometimes crossing the aisle and voting with the Democrats. In a 45-minute speech, she carefully reviewed all the testimony she had heard, including that of the primary accuser, Mrs. Christine Blasey Ford], and concluded the following: "*I believe that she [Mrs. Ford] is a survivor of a sexual assault and that this trauma has upended her life.... Nevertheless, the four witnesses she named could not corroborate any of the events of that evening gathering where she says the assault occurred.*" She added, "*I do not believe that these charges can fairly prevent Judge Kavanaugh from serving on the Court.*" With her October 5, 2018, "yes" vote, the Democrat Senator from West Virginia, Senator Joe Manchin of West

Virginia, crossed the aisle and also voted "yes". The logjam was broken and Kavanaugh was confirmed.

As this drama played out just a month before the election, many in the country, with all due respect to Mrs. Ford, were appalled by the treatment, the defamation, and character assassination of Judge Kavanaugh, based on unproven allegations going back to his adolescence, in the face of an illustrious career on the bench without a hint of racism or sexism. Many in the country, not just Republicans, were ashamed of the unbridled, merciless, *ad hominem* attacks on his character, his morality, and his suitability for the highest court of the land based on alleged "drunken" behavior as a teenager. He and his family were pitied by many for what they saw as a politically-motivated hatchet job done on him. It resulted in the "Kavanaugh effect," which had the effect of stimulating the Republican base going into the election.

Having lost this battle for yet a second Trump-nominated Justice, the Democrats changed gears and began to focus on Health Care, alleging that the safety net for persons with "pre-existing" health issues, would, under Republican policies, be removed. There is no indication that such an assertion was true, but it was political high season and the media messaging came through loud and clear, perhaps swinging some independent voters into the Democrat column.

Finally, the issue of immigration rose in the context of a caravan of over 7,000 Central American refugees making their way into Mexico and bound for America where they would seek political asylum. Stories of their political oppression and poverty played out on the news, sometimes hourly. Their plight was used by the Democrats to highlight the implied "un-American" Republican position of strong borders, walled borders, and fear of criminal and terrorist aliens being part of the mix of those seeking to cross the Southern border into the U.S. The whole issue of immigration and "sanctuary cities" (cities where local and/or State government determined not to enforce certain immigration laws), and the political divide on how to best protect the security of American citizens, stimulated both the Left and the Right going into the election.

These international and domestic hot-button issues, each with overlapping implications in many cases, served to raise the heat of the debate to fiery levels, including unfortunate and libelous discourse and some violence. Every indication is that this level of political bashing and coarseness continues to simmer, ready to come to a boil with the least provocation, real or professed.

Turkish-American Relations – Governmental versus People to People

Turkish-American relations exist on many levels. The most obvious is the Government-to-Government relationship. Within that stratum of relations, one might further divide political, economic, and military relations. Since the halcyon days of the Marshall Plan and the Korean War, official political relations between the two have ebbed and flowed. The personal relations of the leaders of both countries have similarly had their ups and downs. Through it all, it might be fair to observe that the military relations, while not without some controversy, have over the years been steadier than the political relations. Perhaps this is because the basis tends to be more strictly professional. *Ipso facto*, it goes without saying that the National Interests of any two countries cannot be perfectly parallel. One perfect example is the controversy surrounding the strategy and priorities regarding the war in Syria between NATO Allies Turkey and America. Another reared its ugly head with the Centennial of the Armenian Tragedy in April of 2015, a perennial bugaboo of Congressional deliberation every April.

However, there are so many areas of cooperation and agreement between the two Governments that never reach the headlines. Turkey and America are NATO allies, though presently seriously strained. Both countries have any number of Bi-Lateral Treaties which govern a myriad of commercial and administrative relations designed to enhance cooperation and facilitate business.

Another layer of Turkish-American relations is Business to Business. While not as substantial as Turkey's relationship with the EU, it is nonetheless significant and growing. American business investment in Turkey began in earnest in the 1950s and rose dramatically from the 1980s onward. From that same period of time, Turkish investment in the United States, albeit on a much lower base, began to grow as well. The largest and most successful of the trade associations with other countries based in Washington has for many years been the American-Turkish Council (ATC). Even here, this organization has certainly been affected by the political relations of the two governments, Ankara and Washington. While the ATC members were originally dominated by major Corporates (especially infrastructure sector), Banks, and Defense-oriented companies from both sides, the membership has broadened in the 21st century to include Services, Technology sector and medium-size businesses, especially in the Tech sector. There are also significant Chamber of Commerce relationships between the two countries. And since the 1980s, American-Turkish interest groups, both political and cultural, have grown dramatically.

And finally, individuals making friends while studying, working or traveling in one another's countries add positive, and in some ways more enduring, dimension to the relationship. While anecdotal, this author's observations span over forty years now. It seems that nine out of ten Americans traveling to Turkey come away with great appreciation for the charm of the people, the natural beauty of the myriad landscapes, the plethora of antiquities, the rich history of Asia Minor going back to the bronze and iron ages, the variety and wonders of its extraordinary-multi-ethnic cuisine, or a combination of the above.

The number of Turks studying, working, and in many cases, now living in the States is a testament to America's appeal (though shifting back to Europe, often because it is more affordable, in recent years). It is at this level that one feels confident that American-Turkish relations are flourishing, deepening and broadening, irrespective of the political vicissitudes of "official" relations. Every group of people from wherever they come bring with them pre-conceived notions of what America and Americans are like. Similarly, each group to have come to America's shores arrived with certain stereotypes already in the mind. As an example, the vision of "Terrible Turks" on one hand, and "Yankee Go Home" on the other, are phrases loaded with centuries of "cultural baggage". These are historical artifacts that can be dredged up when tensions run high between any groups, local, national, and international. People to people relationships tend to dispel negative stereotypes, and should be encouraged.

Growing the Middle Class in Turkey and America

Growing the middle class is essential to maintaining order in society. This is where the bulk of "stakeholders" agree, by social contract, to abide by the law, work, pay a reasonable amount of tax for the public good, and raise children who will accept similar terms in due course in their lives. Here labor productivity, tangible evidence of the fruits of one's labors, and a sense of dignity and belonging represent the backbone of a well-functioning society. Turkey's commitment to social and political order is a prerequisite to progress and a predictable modicum of stability. Societies where that is being achievedserve to attract human and financial capital which, in turn, serves to further stimulate the economy and progress.

In an Ernst and Young ("EY") blog titled "Middle Class Growth in Emerging Markets – Hitting the Sweet Spot," the changing prospects for much of the developing world are highlighted.

"Since 1800 the world has seen two great middleclass expansions, and we are living through a third. The nineteenth century industrial revolution created a substantial Western European and American middle class, which grew again after the Second World War – a spurt which this time included Japan. Today this is happening in the emerging markets (EMs). In Asia alone, 525 million people can already count themselves middle class — more than the European Union's total population. Over the next two decades, the middle class is expected to expand by another three billion, coming almost exclusively from the emerging world."

The emergence of a Global Middle Class was highlighted in a report coming out of DAVOS in 2012 written by David Rohde.

"For the first time in history, a truly global middle class is emerging. By 2030, it will more than double in size, from 2 billion today to 4.9 billion. Brookings Institution scholar Homi Kharas estimates that the European and American middle classes will shrink from 50 percent of

the total to just 22 percent. Rapid growth in China, India, Indonesia, Vietnam, Thailand, and Malaysia will cause Asia's share of the new middle to more than double from its current 30%. By 2030, Asia will host 64% of the global middle class and account for over 40% of global middle-class consumption."

In a blog prepared for UHY, a network of accounting and consulting firms, mega-investor George Soros is paraphrased about the prospects even for Africa, describing it as 'one of the few bright spots on the gloomy global economic horizon.' The Report goes on to say,

China's latest GDP forecast? Growth from one of the Asian tiger economies, maybe?

"No. Soros is talking about Africa. It's a continent wracked by poverty, where electricity is intermittent, where corruption soaks up development funding, where political instability and tyrannical governments undermine confidence, and where kidnapping of Westerners is rife. Or, at least that's been the stereotypical image of African countries international investors are waking up to the potential from Africa's imminent boom in consumer spending, which is set to rise from USD 860 billion in 2008 to USD 1.4 trillion in 2020, according to the McKinsey Global Institute till now among Western investors. The Chinese have invested in Africa's natural resource extraction for more than a decade...."

The middle class, in both Turkey and America, is growing. To the extent that the growth of the middle class is not enjoyed equally between the sexes in either country is a concern that was recognized and addressed early on by President Kemal Atatürk at the beginning of the Republic. We have seen that women only had the right to vote in America a decade before the same right was granted in secular Turkey. While it can present some challenges during the child-bearing and child-rearing years for women and for young families, an economy cannot achieve near its full potential if women are not encouraged to, and actually participate in all sectors of the economy. While no earth-shattering revelation, it must be reiterated that education, flexibility, adaptability within a framework of supportive government policies, are a pre-requisite to growing a stable middle class. The current leadership of Turkey is not, in principle, particularly committed to women's contribution in either the public or private sector. Evidence of declining participation of women, from the Parliament to the workplace, is readily apparent. In an *Al-Monitor – Turkey Pulse* article, written by Radia Azimov Akyol, titled, "Why Turkish Women are Opting Out of the Working force," using the results of a Kadir Has University research report released in March of 2016, states,

> *"Public perceptions on gender roles and the status of women in Turkey" study released in March 2016, based on data gathered from 1,200 people in 26 districts show that for 77.8% of respondents, the most important problem women face in Turkey is violence. Among female participants, other burning issues included "inequality" (41.8%),*

"lack of education" (34.8%), "peer pressure" (30.7%) and "family pressure" (26.5%)."

The article goes on to say,

"One thing is clear, according to the Global Gender Gap Report of 2015: Turkey ranks 130th out of 145 countries on this issue. In a written statement on the occasion of International Women's Day, the Turkish Industry and Business Association (TUSIAD) reminded Turkey that 33.6% female labor participation is very low, and that 11.5 million women cannot join the workforce due to obligations at home."

A *Daily News* article dated December 14, 2016, notes that, *"The literacy rate for women is five times lower than it is for men in Turkey, according to data from the Turkish Statistics Institute (TÜİK). Some 9.2 percent of Turkish women could not read or write in 2014, versus just 1.8 percent for men, for a combined average of 5.6 percent, TÜİK said, adding that men were also three times more likely to have a job than women."*

From this perspective, without casting judgment, Turkey's and America's trends in this area are diverging significantly. Without a change in the policies and pronouncements of government leaders in Turkey, traditional "mind sets" on these issues are unlikely to change.

Chapter 25

TURKEY AND AMERICA – WHERE THE TWAIN ARE MEETING

"The Past is not dead, it is not even past."

—WILLIAM FAULKNER

"Oh, East is East and West is West, and never the twain shall meet, Till Earth and Sky stand presently at God's great Judgment Seat; But there is neither East nor West, Border, nor Breed, nor Birth, When two strong men stand face to face, though they come from the ends of the earth!"

—RUDYARD KIPLING, 1889

Differences and similarities in the experiences of both countries have been examined through the prisms of major events, ideologies, movements, technologies, and key leaders. Issues common to both countries, such as geography, religion, sovereignty, nationalism, governance, liberty, the rule of law and human rights have been considered. Fairness would suggest that both countries have struggled with each of these issues over the centuries, and still do. Both countries have memories that bring great pride. What Turk cannot look back with pride at the conquering of Istanbul, the architectural elegance of the *Suleimaniye* Mosque, the rule of a vast empire, the defeat of the Allies at Gallipoli, the defeat of so many enemies in Turkey's War of Independence and the more recent stunning economic growth and development in the 21st century? What American cannot stand a little taller in the memory of the many trials of its first colonists in Jamestown and Plymouth, her War of Independence, America's Founding documents, the Declaration of Independence, the Constitution and the Bill of Rights, her coming to the rescue of Western Europe in two World Wars and putting a man on the moon? Both Republics were built on the shoulders of towering figures in World History, George Washington, and Mustafa Kemal Atatürk.

America and Turkey also have memories of events in their histories, which haunt them – memories that have tarnished the esteem of both countries, both in the eyes of its citizens and in the eyes of others around the world. Both Governments have established and implemented policies that have discriminated against minorities including black slaves, blacks, and Native Americans in America, and Kurds, Armenians, Jews, and Alevis in Turkey. In thinking of these sad events, as noted in an earlier chapter, one is reminded of William Shakespeare, who over 400 years ago, brings to our attention that discrimination is an old affliction in the history of tribes and nations.

"I am a Jew. Hath not a Jew eyes? Hath not a Jew hands, organs, dimensions, senses, affections, passions? fed with the same food, hurt with the same weapons, subject to the same diseases, healed by the same means, warmed and cooled by the same winter and summer, as a Christian is? If you prick us, do we not bleed? if you tickle us, do we not laugh? if you poison us, do we not die? and if you wrong us, shall we not revenge? If we are like you in the rest, we will resemble you in that

—WILLIAM SHAKESPEARE, THE MERCHANT
OF VENICE, ACT I, III – SHYLOCK

Too often there is a "disconnect" between intentions and results, sometimes hostage to the law of unintended consequences. Changing course in an effort to rectify bad policy sometimes requires a catastrophic event like war, a civil war, or a world war. The fact that it is harder to rule effectively than it is to sit in judgment of those in power is patently obvious, and sometimes sophomoric in effect. Actually, ruling is much more complicated and challenging, as incumbents always learn after assuming public office. So, when Rulers get it right, by design or by chance, at least in the eyes of the majority of the ruled, they must be lauded as was aptly noted by Edward Gibbon in, *The Decline and Fall of the Roman Empire,* quoted below.

"The policy of the emperors and the senate, as far as it concerned religion, was happily seconded by the reflections

of the enlightened, and by the habits of the superstitious, part of their subjects. The various modes of worship, which prevailed in the Roman world, were all considered by the people, as equally true; by the philosopher, as equally false; and by the magistrate, as equally useful. And thus toleration produced not only mutual indulgence, but even religious concord."

We have examined the role of geography, where Americans are fortunate in the resources, size and relative isolation and insulation of its development in the process of Nation building. Robert Kaplan makes this point in stark terms in, *The Revenge of Geography.*

"For maps are a rebuke to the very notion of the equality and unity of humankind, since they remind us of all the different environments of the earth that make men profoundly unequal and disunited in so many ways, leading to conflict..."

Turkey's greatest geographic advantage as the East-West crossroads is also its greatest liability. Call itthe challenge of dealing in the world's toughest neighborhood. It is at once, both the beginning and the end of the Silk Road. As the site of the Eurasian land bridge, it has also been a geographic choke point and killing field. Turkey is only the latest country/civilization, to occupy this particular fault line.

While geography has an important role to play, both Turkey and America know the importance of ideas, the men who put them forward, and those who execute the ideology, "revealed by God" or "revealed by man." Here geography and borders might be crossed with ideas, directly into the hearts and minds of people. What is born of an ideology and carried by the "faithful," pious, agnostic, or atheist, may be benign and generous. Or, it may be pernicious and evil. Those ideas and beliefs may produce harmony or produce conflict. Certainly, religion and its geography have always, and may always, be used to generate periods of conflict in a world of social media which knows no borders. When that conflict reaches critical mass, it may result in what Professor Huntington terms a "Clash of Civilizations." This is not a value judgment of the contending ideologies, but an observation that when such ideologies are "highjacked" by fanatical adherents, civilization as a whole tends to be reduced to national and tribal instincts for self-preservation, or perceived self-preservation. The drama and scope of risks are escalated, and further complicated, when clashes occur within civilizations, or within Nations, where common cause against a larger perceived threat becomes a way to vent the internal spleen of domestic strife.

Terrorism, internal and external, imported or home-grown, is something that modern Turkey and America, and the world, have been dealing with for decades. Islamist "Jihadi" terrorism, a particularly virulent form of terrorism in an age of inexpensive but lethal technology, has become a cancer for which both countries, and the world, are seeking cures.

Militant Islam knows no geographic limitations. On what continent has it not struck?Consider the Paris attack in January of 2015 being as one example. It is believed that it was both "home-grown" from the *banlieue* of Paris, but inspired and assisted by Al Qaeda of the Arabian Peninsula. Immediately, these events were described and interpreted through the prisms of culture and experience noted below.

At that time, Cengiz Candar, columnist for *Al-Monitor's* "Turkey Pulse" wrote an article titled, "Post Paris: Perilous Future for Turkey, Muslims," immediately following the tragedy in Paris on January 7, 2015. His observations underscore the challenge of building understanding, cooperation, and trust between East and West, Sharia and Secularism, Christianity and Islam,

Turkey and Western Europe, and Turkey and America. His reaction was telling.

"When the news of the heinous attack Jan. 7 that took the lives of 12 people including the renowned cartoonists and the editor-in-chief of satirical weekly Charlie Hebdo in Paris reached me, instantly mixed and contradicting feelings passed through my mind. Outrage to the cowardly attack was my predominant thought, but feelings of shame, irritation, fear, and uneasiness were equally strong.

The feeling of shame was because I shared the same religion, on whose behalf the perpetrators allegedly committed their crime. I knew, of course, Islam as any other religion, does not and cannot advocate such senseless criminality and shedding the blood of defenseless individuals. However, I was also very aware that the international media would prominently report — as it was already in the process of doing — that the gunmen of the Paris attack shouted "Allahu akbar" ("God is great") while committing their savagery, alleging that they avenged the Prophet Muhammad and that barbarism would spur already existing prejudices against Islam and Muslims all around the non-Muslim world."

Candar concluded by referencing changes in Turkey in recent years and quoting respected Professor Nilufer Göle.

"However, the Turkey of 2015 is strikingly different from the Turkey a decade ago, despite no change in government. The gap in the Western perception on Turkey and its role in international affairs is emphasized also by professor Nilufer Göle of the Ecole des Hautes Etudes en Sciences Sociales in Paris. Göle is an expert on Islam and modernity and a respected Turkish scholar. On the Jan. 7 attack in Paris, she said, "If in Turkey we still had the AKP government of five years ago that was valued and respectedby the West and if that government would have unequivocally denounced this barbarism, perhaps some things could have changed. But that is not likely to happen. That is why we are in awful shape."

At this same time, on an NBC *Meet the Press* interview, Iranian-American University of California professor and commentator on Islam, Reza Aslan, appeared and pointed a finger at Saudi Arabia and Wahhabism as a movement, which, as we have discussed earlier, has long used its oil fortune to export its puritanical interpretation of Islam.

"There's no question that there has been a virus that has spread throughout the Muslim world, a virus of ultra-orthodox puritanism," Aslan replied. "But there's also no question what the source of this virus is — whether we're talking about Boko Haram, or ISIS, or al Qaeda, or the Taliban. All of them have as their source Wahhabism, or the state religion of Saudi Arabia," he said. "And as we all know, Saudi Arabia has spent over $100 billion in the past 20 or 30 years spreading this ideology throughout the world."

In response to interviewer and newsman Chuck Todd that Islam needs to do some house-cleaning of its jihadi extremists, Aslan said the following, *"Anyone who keeps saying that we need to hear the moderatevoice of Islam — why aren't Muslims denouncing these violent attacks doesn't own Google. ...The answer to Islamic violence is Islamic peace. The answer to Islamic bigotry is Islamic pluralism, and so that's why I put the onus on the Muslim community, but I also recognize that that work is being done, that the voice of condemnation is deafening and if you don't hear it you're not listening."*

In response, many have observed that actions speak louder than words. Some would further argue that the vast majority who are peaceful are cowed by threatening extremist forces within their own communities.

The following exchange was reported on January 12, 2015 on *Identities. Mic.* On the evening of January 9, 2015, Media tycoon Rupert Murdoch weighed in, *"Maybe most Moslems* are *peaceful, but until they recognize and destroy their growing jihadist cancer they must be heldresponsible."*

Highlighting the problem of stereotyping all Muslims as being supportive of a religion, which espouses violent jihad against the West and Christians, Harry Potter author, J. K. Rowling, responded to Murdoch's observation with the following, *"I was born Christian. If that makes Rupert Murdoch my responsibility, I'll auto-excommunicate."* She further supported her response by alluding to an absurdity, *"The Spanish Inquisition was my fault, as is all Christian fundamentalist violence...."*

Other opinions, again within hours or a couple of days of the tragedy, included the President of Egypt, Abdel Fattah al-Sisi, who on behalf of the Egyptian people expressed his condolences to the French people and said, *"Terrorism is an internationalphenomenon that should be faced and terminated through joint international efforts."* During an interview on the Jon Daily Show, former President Jimmy Carter, when asked if the tragedy was fueled by anything other than Islamic extremism, said, *"Well, one of the origins for it is the Palestinian problem, and this aggravates people who are affiliated in any way with the Arab people who live in the West Bank and Gaza, what they are doing now — what's being done to them. So I think that's part of it."*

This series of exchanges illustrates the world of perception as truth, and the varying vantage points from which these perspectives are formed and articulated. Senseless acts of violence are not senseless to all. Indiscriminate killing of civilians by suicide-bombers, gunmen, or drones can all too conveniently be psychologically compartmentalized by sanitized terminology like "collateral damage," "work-place violence," and "just revenge." One person's hero or martyr may be another person's murderer.

The tragedy in Paris is also illustrative of the impact of globalization and the revolution in transportation and communication. Immigration, legal and illegal, afford little or no respect to either the notion, or physical fact, of national borders. Dual passports once not too long ago were thought to be a contradiction in terms, thought to beg the question of divided loyalties. Ease of travel, Skype, the Internet and smart phones allow people to maintain and nurture their familial, tribal, and historic homeland sympathies, grievances and hopes, that physical geography and long separation had earlier tended to greatly diminish within a generation or two.

Concomitant with this technological revolution is a heightened stress on the stability of the Nation State. Deference to national authority, in the hearts and minds of newer generations of citizens especially, seems to be diminishing, now tending to migrate "down," to more local groupings, and/or "out", to transnational, foreign State or group associations. The digital, home-grown Jihadis, are one of the more lethal manifestations of this new phenomenon. National "constituent" populations are increasingly associating by race, ethnicity, religion, ideology, age, gender, and sexual orientation. As earlier discussed, this is the tendency for the American Public to splinter, moving away from the ideal of a melting pot, to the reality of a mixing bowl. Primary allegiances would seem to be shifting, aspirations of many notwithstanding, from *EPluribus Unum* to *E Pluribus, Pluribus*. On a macro scale, one observes this in America, while oversimplified in order to make the point, in the politics and preferences of "Red" versus "Blue" States. Those distinctions are even more telling as seen at the county level. The electoral map of Turkey by department and major city shows a similar diversion in allegiances. Both countries are now as politically polarized, as divided by identity politics, as any time in modern history.

In some ways, these sub-State groupings are a by-product of the "global village" concept of Marshall McLuhan, whereby traditional capitals of political power, federal governments, are not trusted or deemed to be sufficient, if even desirable. The net result is a kind of "back to the future" moment reminiscent of Thomas Jefferson, when referring to his "country" in patrilocal and casual speech, even after the Founding of the United States, as Virginia. Further, history would suggest that when he said Virginia, he may well have been thinking more specifically of the Piedmont and Tidewater areas, plantation Virginia of his day. After all, most of his "immediate" world revolved within those geographic limits with notable interruptions in France and Washington DC. Urban rural divides in many states, Virginia, New York, and Pennsylvania are but a few examples of politically polarized, culturally disconnected, populations within a State.

These centrifugal tendencies away from a Nation-State centerwork to the natural advantage of non-State actors, where one thinks of oneself as Latino-, African- or Asian- American for example. Turkish-German, Muslim-French, in Europe, or Sunni versus Alevi or Kurdish or Arab in Turkey. One might argue that such distinctions have always existed. While that may be true, the degree is significantly different, now technologically nurtured to dramatically new levels.

So where do Turkey and America, Europe and the MENA, East and West meet today? Can Judaism, Islam, and Christianity bridge gaps between and among Believers? Is secularism as an ideology, a form and means of government, sufficient to adequately subsume and accommodate religious, ethnic, and other ideologies, including atheism, going forward? How effective as an organization is the Nation State in a borderless cyber world? In the absence of walls, what, using Ibn Khaldun's concept of *"asabiyya"*, can be the animating force to sustain the Nation State, short of a "clear and present" danger either from without or in response to national disaster? Even perceptions of such threats or actual disasters are instantly politicized, making consensus for more than a few days at a time seemingly impossible.

Assuming that any one group, a *Staatsfolk*, or belief-system, including atheism, has, or can have, a corner on the market of truth and justice now fails by definition. Constructive dialogue and interaction must begin with a humbling truth so eloquently stated by Ralph Waldo Emerson, whose own quest into comparative religion during a period of Evangelical Religious Revival in America of the time led him to the following conclusion. *"Let me never fall into the vulgar mistake of dreaming that I am persecuted whenever I am contradicted."* 1838

The task of building and repairing human bridges, like all human constructs, is in continual need of maintenance, and often overhaul. But, like the journey of a thousand steps, it begins with the first step. Sometimes, that step forward is followed by a step or two backward. Nonetheless, it is a worthy and necessary journey. Civilization is at risk to an extent heretofore unimaginable. As much as the East and the West, Turkey and America, appear not to have in common, there is, of course, much more that they do share in common. One has to be willing to look for it, be heartened and guided by the discoveries, and steeled for setbacks in the albeit Sisyphean process.

In the course of this book, we have seen how conflict and cooperation have characterized East and West empires and cultures, Greek and Persian, Roman and Egyptian, Byzantine and Arabo-Persian, all the while being conscious of being Western versus Eastern since the Homeric and Biblical era. We have also seen how Turks and Americans have fought together, in Korea, Bosnia, Iraq and Afghanistan. Turkey and America have worked together as NATO allies, in Business to Business, academic to academic, artist to artist, and, people to people realms. We have learned that great debts of contribution to the West, in the areas of science, medicine, philosophy, mathematics, and culture are owed to Turkish, Islamic, and Persian civilizations. And similarly, Turkish and Islamic culture has benefitted from European and American civilization far more than one would assume for all the residual and current animosities so painfully obvious.

Trust, like one's reputation, can take a lifetime to establish and may be lost, fairly or unfairly, in an instant. It is essential that mutual understanding and respect be based on open and honest consideration and respect for both cultures, both countries, recognizing that we cannot, and will not, agree in many areas at different times. Both must be open to learn from each other, like grapes mirroring each other as they ripen in the sun together (*Üzüm üzüme baka baka kararır* – to use an apt Turkish expression). If such efforts are likely to fail repeatedly, as they so often have, the exercise beats the alternative, never-attended festering wounds. But what is true for man's relationship to man, beginning with the family, and moving outward in society, and between societies, is the sometimes ugly, occasionally sublime, reality of the process of "destructive creationism" when peace fails, as it will.

Turkey and America must, and should, like all States, look first to their National interests, even when they appear to be at cross purposes as they are in the choice of reliable allies in the war in Syria. Turkey and America must simultaneously work to avoid the burning of bridges between them, including their NATO Alliance, as fraught with contending suspicions as they are at this time. In a November 5, 2018 article by Stephen Cook titled "The Case for Reshaping U.S.-Turkey Relations," written under the banner of The Council on Foreign Relations, he observed the following:

"The divergence between these two NATO allies reflects the changes in international politics since the end of the Cold War nearly a generation ago. Absent the common threat posed by the Soviet Union, there is no strategic rationale for the U.S.-Turkey partnership. The sooner American policymakers understand this fact, the greater likelihood that Washington can pursue a more realistic approach to Ankara, which means working together when possible, working around Turkey when necessary, and publicly opposing the Turks where they seek to undermine American policies and interests."

The Turkish-American strategic architecture must be clearly, and frequently, recalibrated, modernized when needed, and respectfully maintained. Both sides must recognize that the National Interests of Turkey and America can overlap, and legitimately differ, without resorting to unbridled condemnation or demonization by one side or the other. As the discussion of the Charlie Hebdo tragedy in Paris in the previous chapter poignantly brings to the fore, that truth is in the eye of the beholder, and the truth, usually lies somewhere in between contending parties. And both, or all, sides must be able to agree to disagree.

In the Post-Cold War era, the luxury of Bloc consensus, is over. Ally impasses will be destabilizing, as they are on so many fronts in the MENA, in Afghanistan and elsewhere. But, they need not be paralyzing. If there is a high moral justification for breaching the sovereignty of a "failed" or a "rogue" State, then the rationale for intervention on humanitarian grounds may arise. But even that justification is dangerous, as there are often underlying, more Machiavellian, motives cloaked in "high ideals."

The caveat noted above notwithstanding, the "International Order," broken as it is, must face the harsh reality of virulent extremism from wherever it comes. At civilization's ultimate peril does one shrink from calling out evil for what it is. It is an unaffordableand temporary luxury to nuance such threats. In so doing they are nurtured to the point where fear, or misguidedsympathy, allows such cancers to metastasize. Militant Islam is a phenomenon without bordersand leaders with economic resources bent on the exploitation of economic, social, and political despair. They offer the romance of martyrdom to disaffected elements anywhere on the globe. Their glory has become the bane of civil society everywhere. Stop and think of the billions of dollars that the people of this earth are reconciled to spend, every year, for 40 years and more, to make international, and inter- and intra-State travel and related commerce, an acceptable safety risk. The amounts spent are ever-increasing, and the threats mounted, ever more nefarious and widespread. These expenditures, and the related inconveniences and intrusions on individual privacy and State sovereignty, are accepted without objection. These precautions and expenditures were once upon a time temporary, regional or local in times of crises or war. It is as though the people of the world, or the elites, have resigned themselves to a Hobbesian state of permanent war and chaos where Leviathan, the International Order, is mandated to police the movement of all its adherents of the 21st century Social Contract.

America, Turkey, Russia, Saudi Arabia, and Iran, all be they strange bedfellows, need to work together to contain militant Jihad. The *Dar al Harb* (the House of War) and the *Dar al Islam (the House of Islam),* are no longer two significantly different places geographically. The Jihad is being brazenly waged in both the Islamic and the non-Islamic world. The reason to work together in earnest, in spite of all other areas of conflict between and among the national interests of the countries mentioned, as well as others, is because time is not on the side of peace, harmony and disengagement. Failure to act decisively and effectively carries with it the larger threat of conflagration, conventional, biologic, and nuclear warfare, for both Eastern and Western civilizations.

If there can be any resolution to these challenges, Thomas Jefferson reminds us that education and mutual understanding can never be forsaken. Whether in America or Turkey, in the West and the East, "meeting" always requires at the very core an observation of this truth.

"If a nation expects to be ignorant and free in a state of civilization, it expects what never was and never will be. If we are to guard against ignorance and remain free, it is the responsibility of every American to be informed."

This book has been written with the intention of telling a story revealed to me over a lifetime of experiences and studies, which have carried me across the ages, civilizations, continents, and oceans. It is hoped that the reader has been challenged and stimulated to continue to search for benevolent understanding that brings more peace and stability to a world at once latent with an abundance of both hate and love. There is truth in both the East and the West. Each must set her/his compass with bearings that seek to accommodate this illusive reality.

IMAGE ATTRIBUTIONS

p.25 Wiki Common

p. 28 https://www.pinterest.com/
pin/409123947370981262/?lp=true

p. 48 https://www.google.com/search?sa=X&rlz=1C1SQJL_
enUS813US813&q=silk+road+map+printable&tbm=isch&-
source=univ&ved=2ahUKEwimi_TUupPhAhXst1kKH-
STQDEYQ7Al6BAgHEBs&biw=1536&bih=722#imgrc=x-
5d1W8VVT6I5OM:

p. 53 Wiki Common

p. 54 Wiki Common https://en.wikipedia.org/wiki/Alham-
bra#/media/File:Dawn_Charles_V_Palace_Alhambra_
Granada_Andalusia_Spain.jpg

p. 54 Wiki Common https://upload.wikimedia.org/
wikipedia/commons/thumb/9/9e/Seville_panorama.
jpg/1400px-Seville_panorama.jpg

p. 61 Wiki Common Topkapi Palace Museum, Istanbul

p. 87 Wiki Common

p. 99 www.thebyzantinelegacy.com/athos

p. 100 Great friend of ours. Picture – her book cover

p. 110 Author's rug

p. 124 Frontis Piece of Thomas Hobbes' book, the Leviathan,
Engraving by Abraham Bosse

p. 132 Wiki Common

p. 145 http://www.cornucopia.net/magazine/articles/the-
crimean-church-in-istanbul/ Cornucopia Magazine, Vol.
25, 2002

p. 165 https://www.landofthebrave.info/13-colonies.htm
Public Domain

p. 174 Wiki Common

p. 179 Wiki Common

p. 193 Painting by William Ranney

p. 194 Monument to General Nathaniel Greene at the Guilford Court House Battlefied, Greensboro, NC.

p. 200 Painting by Antoine Favray at the Pera Museum, Istanbul. Wiki Common

p. 205 Attributed to Titian. Wiki Common

p. 212 Wiki Common

p. 220 Wiki Common

p. 224 Wiki Common

p. 235 Charles Wilson Peale located in Washington-Curtis-Lee Collection, Washington and Lee University

p. 238 Painting by Emanuel Leutz at The Metropolitan Museum of Art, NYC

p. 247 Wiki Common

p. 250 Wiki Common

p. 252 Wiki Common

p. 262 Front Cover of Time Magazine March 23, 1923 as noted in the text

p. 268 Wiki Common Painting by Joseph Siffred Duplessis

p. 270 Public Domain

p. 278 Both pictures are part of the Public Domain

p. 289 Public Domain

p. 294 https://www.whitehousehistory.org/photos/
james-madison

p. 297 Public Domain Statue of Liberty

p. 301 Wiki Common

p. 304 Wiki Common

p. 305 Public Domain

p.315 Wiki Common

p. 344 Wiki Common

p. 278 Wiki Common

p. 397 Fred Prouser, Reuters

p. 410 Wiki Common

p. 411 pc. Picture of Lincoln – Public Domain

p. 411 pc. The Ride for Liberty – The Fugitive Slaves by
Eastman Johnson. The Brooklyn Museum of Art, NYC

p. 412 Public Domain.

p. 415 Public Domain

p. 416 Wiki Common

p. 425 Public Domain

p.436 Remove picture

p. 442 Public Domain

p. 449 Public Domain

p. 451 Public Domain

p. 482 Public Domain

p. 503 Public Domain

p. 592 Public Domain

SELECTED BIBLIOGRAPHY
BY CHAPTER

1. In The Beginning – The Abrahamic Tradition

Abulafia, David. *The Great Sea*, David Lane, U.K., 2011.

Hilali, Asma. *Sanaa Palimsest – The Transmission Of The Qur'an In The First centuries AH*, Oxford University Press in association with The Institute of Ismaili Studies, 2017.

Holland, Tom. *In the Shadow of the Sword – the Birth of Islam and the Rise of the Global Empire*, Anchor Books, 2013.

Horden, Peregrine and Purcell, Nicholas. *The Corrupting Sea – A Study of Mediterranean – History*, Blackwell, New York, 2000.

Koran: Sura 3 (Chapter), Ayah (Verse) 45; 57/27; 37/112; 5/110, Penguin Classics, Middlesex, England, 1977.

Miles, Jack. *God in the Qu'ran*. First Vintage Books Edition, 1996.

New Testament: John 3: Verse 16; Ecclesiastes 3:1-14; Galatians 4:21-31.

Old Testament: Book of Genesis, 12:2 and 16:3, 7-15.

Reynolds, Gabriel Said. *The Quran and the Bible: Text and Commentary*. Yale University Press, 2018.

Robinson, Chase F. *'Abd al-Malik*, Oneworld, Oxford, 2009.

2. Islam, Christianity and the Holy Lands

Atiyah, Edward. *The Arabs*. Penguin, 1958.

Gascoigne, Bamber. "History of the Caliphs". *History World. Net*, 2016.

Mirmobiny, Shadieh. "The Alhambra". Smarthistory, August 8, 2015.

Nasr, Sayyed Hossein. *Islamic Spirituality: Foundations*. Routledge, 1987.

Naylor, Philip C. *North Africa – A History From Antiquity to the Present.* University of Texas Press – Austin, 2009.

3. Competition and Conflict around the Mediterranean Basin

Asbridge, Thomas. *The Crusades: The Authoritative History of the War for the Holy Land.* Ecco, *2010.*

Ehrlich, Michael. "The Battle of ʿAin al-Mallāh, 19 June 1157". The Journal of Military History, Lexington, Virginia, Vol. 83, No.1, January 2019.

Finkel, Caroline. *Osman's Dream.* Perseus Books group, NY, 2010.

Jones, Dan. *The Templars – The Rise and the Spectacular Fall of God's Holy Warriors.* Viking – An Imprint of Penguin Random House LLC, 2017.

Malouf, Amin. *The Crusades Through Arab Eyes.* JC Lattès, France, 1983.

Markham, Paul. *The Battle of Manzikert: Military Disaster or Political Failure?* De Re Militari: The Society for Medieval Military History, Perth, 2005.

4. Commerce, Caravans and Cultural – Scientific Exchange

Averröes. *The Inchoherence of the Incoherence (Tahafut al Tahafut).* trans. By Simon Van den Bergh, https://iqbal.hypotheses.org/3986.

Brownworth, Lars. *Lost to the West: The Forgotten Byzantine Empire that Rescued Western Civilization.* Random House, Three Rivers Press, NY, 2009.

Chejne, Anwar G. *Muslim Spain: Its History and Culture.* University of Minnesota Press, 1974.

Dodds, Jerrilyn D., Maria Rosa Menocal, and Abigail Krasner Balbale. *The Arts of Intimacy: Christians, Jews, and Muslims in the Making of Castilian Culture.* Yale University Press, 2009.

Doudou, Diene. *"The Routes of Al-Andalus Spiritual Convergence and Spiritual Dialogue."* UNESCO, 1997.

Enan, Muhammed Abdullah. *Ibn Khaldun: His Life and Work.* The Other Press, Kuala Lumpur, 2007.

King, Charles. *The Black Sea: A History.* Oxford University Press, 2004.

Rosenthal, Franz, Dawood, N. J., eds. *The Muqaddimah: An Introduction to History.* The Bollingen Series, 1958, Princeton University Press.

Sobel, David. *Longitude – A Lone Genius Who Solved the Greatest Scientific Problem of His Time.* Penguin Books, 1995.

Stone, Caroline. "Ibn Khaldun and the Rise and Fall of Empires." Saudi Aramco World, September/October 2006, vol. 57, no. 5.

Theologou, Kostas and Michaelides, Panayotis G. "The Role of Jews in the late Ottoman and Early Greek Salonika." Journal of Balkan and Near Eastern Studies, Volume 3, September 2010.

5. Religious Controversy and Wars – The Moslem East and the Christian West

Armstrong, Karen. *Fields of Blood – Religion and the History of Violence.* Alfred A. Knopf, 2014.

Coulson, Noel. *Conflicts and Tensions in Islamic Jurisprudence.* University of Chicago Press, Chicago and London, 1969.

Chejne, Anwar. *Muslim Spain: Its History and Culture.* University of Minnesota, 1974.

Hodgson, Marshall G. S. *The Venture of Islam: Conscience and History in a World Civilization*. University of Chicago Press (3 Volume set), 1974.

Holland, Tom. *In the Shadow of the Sword – The Birth of Islam and the Rise of the Global Empire*. Anchor Books, NY, 2013.

Hughes, Bettany. *Istanbul – A Tale of Three Cities*. Da Capo Press, 2017.

MacCulloch, Dairmaid. *The Reformation – Europe's House Divided*. Penguin Books, 2005.

Nasr, Vali. *The Shia Revival – How Conflicts within Islam Will Reshape the Future*. W. W. Norton & Co., NY/London, 2006.

Robinson, Chase. *'Abd al Malik – Makers of the Muslim World*, One World Publications, Oxford, 2009.

Streusand, Douglas E. *Islamic Gunpowder Empires – Ottomans, Safavids, and Mughals*. Westview Press, Perseus Books group, 2011.

6. Mysticism in the East and West

Babayan, Kathryn. "Mystics, Monarchs, and Messiahs: Cultural Landscapes of Early Modern Iran", Harvard Middle

East Monographs 35, ed. Habib Ladjevardi (Cambridge, MA: Harvard University Press), 2002, xvii.

Bilgin, Beyza. "Mevlana ve Dünya Kültürüne Etkisi." Erdem Dergisi, 10/50 (July 2014).

Emerson, Ralph Waldo, "Nature", Essay (1836) and "The American Scholar" a Speech (1837).

King, Richard. *Orientalism and Religion – Postcolonial Theory, India and the Mystic East.* Routledge, London, 1999.

Hawthorne, Nathaniel. *The Scarlet Letter.* Columbia University Press, 1999.

Jenkins, Jr., Everett. *The Muslim Diaspora: A Comprehensive Chronology of the Spread of Islam in Asia, Africa, Europe and the Americas.* Vol. I (570-1500 AD) and Vol. II (1500-1799), McFarland & Co., North Carolina and London, 1999.

Kidd, Thomas S. *The Great Awakening: The Roots of Evangelical Christianity in Colonial America.* Yale University Press, 2007.

Knysh, Alexander. *Sufism: A New History of Islamic Mysticism.* Princeton University Press, 2017.

McGinn, Bernard. *The Foundations of Mysticism: Origins to the Fifth Century.* The Crossroad Publishing Company, NY, 1991.

Şafak, Elif. *The Forty Rules of Love (Aşk).* Penguin Books, 2010.

Thoreau, Henry David. *Walden; or, Life in the Woods,* 1854.

7. Sovereignty, Secularism and the Rule of Law in the West

Armstrong, Karen. *Fields of Blood – Religion and the History of Violence,* Alfred A. Knopf, 2014.

Hale, Brenda. "Magna Carta: Our Shared Heritage." Journal of Supreme Court History, July 4, 2016.

Hazel, Robert and Melton, James eds. *Magna Carta and its Modern Legacy.* Cambridge University Press, 2015.

Howard, A. E. Dick. "The Road from Runnymede: Magna Carta and Constitutionalism in America." The University of Virginia Press, 2015.

Linebaugh, Peter. *The Magna Carta Manifesto: Liberties and Commons for All.* University of California Press, 2009.

Musson, Anthony. *Medieval Law in Context: The Growth of Legal Consciousness from Magna Carta to the Peasant's Revolt.* Manchester University Press, 2001.

Neil MacGregor, Neil. *Shakespeare's Restless World.* Chapter. 13, "From London to Marrakesh", Viking, 2008.

Phillips, Kevin. *The Cousins' War – Religion, Politics, & The Triumph of Anglo-America.* Basic Books, 1999.

Thomas, Robert. *Civil Society and the English Civil War.* Libertarian Alliance, 1992.

8. The Ottoman Response To Western Industrial-Military Growth

Akgun, Secil. "The Emergence of Tanzimat in the Ottoman Empire." Ankara University, 2015.

Aytekin, Atilla. "Agrarian Relations, Property and Law: An Analysis of the Land Code of 1858 in the Ottoman Empire." Journal of Middle Eastern Studies, Vol. 45, issue 6, 2009.

Banetekas, Ilias. "Land Rights in Nineteenth-Century Ottoman State Succession Treaties." European Journal of International Law, Vol. 26, Issue 2, May 2015, pgs. 375-390.

Danforth, Ted. *The Eastern Question – A Geopolitical History.* Anekdota, 2015.

Davison, Roderic H. *Reform in the Ottoman Empire: 1856-1876.* Princeton University Press, 1963.

Figes, Orlando. *The Crimean War – A History.* Metropolitan Books, Henry Holt & Co., NY, 2010.

Hacak, Hasan. "İslam Hukuk Düsüncesinde Özel Mülkiyet Anlayışı." M.Ü. İlahiyat Fakültesi Dergisi, 29 (005/2), 99-120.

Kuran, Tim. *The Long Divergence – How Islamic Law Held Back the Middle East.* Princeton University Press, 2011.

Kuran, Timur. "Why the Middle East is Economically Underdeveloped: Historical Mechanisms of Institutional Stagnation." Journal of Economic Perspectives, Vol. 18, Number 3, Summer 2004, pgs. 71-90.

Mansel, Philip. *Constantinople – City of the World's Desire, 1453-1924.* John Murray, London, 1995.

Palmer, Alan. *The Decline and Fall of the Ottoman Empire.* Fall River Press, NY, 1992.

Plokhy, Serii. *The Gates of Europe – A History of Ukraine.* Basic Books, NY, 2015.

Reynolds, Michael A. *Shattering Empires: The Clash and Collapse of the Ottoman and Russian Empires1908-1919.* Cambridge University Press, 2011.

Rogan, Eugene. *The Fall of the Ottomans – the Great War in the Middle East.* Basic Books, NY, 2015.

Tanör, Bulent. *Osmanlı – Turk Anayasal Gelişmeleri.* Yapı Kredi Yayınlerı, 2016.

9. America's Founding

Aaron, Larry G. *The Race to the Dan – the Retreat that Rescued the American Revolution.* Warwick House Publishers, 2007.

Allen, Thomas B. *Tories Fighting for the King in America's First Civil War.* Harper Collins, 2010.

Berleth, Richard. *Bloody Mohawk – The French and Indian War & American Revolution on the American Frontier.* Black Dome Press Corporation, 2009.

Borneman, Walter R. *American Spring – Lexington, Concord and the Road to Revolution.* Back Bay Books, 2014.

Chavez, Thomas E. *Spain and the Independence of the United States*. University of New Mexico Press, 2002.

Ellis, Joseph J. *His Excellency – George Washington*. Alfred A. Knopf, NY, 2005.

Feldman, Noah. *The Three Lives of James Madison – Genius, Partisan, President*, Random House, NY, 2017.

Fleming, Thomas. *Washington's Secret War – The Hidden History of Valley Forge*. Smithsonian Books, Harper Collins, 2005.

Hannan, Daniel. *Inventing Freedom – How the English-Speaking Peoples Made the Modern World*, Harper Collins, NY, 2013.

Hoock, Holger. *Scars of Independence – America's Violent Birth.* Crown, NY, 2017.

Jefferson, Thomas, "Virginia Statute of Religious Freedom".

Mayor, Holly A. "Bearing Arms, Bearing Burdens: Women Warriors, Camp Followers, and Home-front Heroines of the American Revolution." War Culture and Society, 1750-1850, Chapter 10, 2010.

O'Shaughnessy, Andrew Jackson. *The Men Who Lost America – British Leadership, the American Revolution, and the Fate of the Empire.* Yale University Press, 2014 and, *An Empire Divided – the American Revolution and the British Caribbean.* University of Pennsylvania Press, 2000.

Paine, Thomas, *Common Sense.*

Philbrick, Nathaniel. *Valiant Ambition – George Washington, Benedict Arnold and the Fate of the American Revolution.* Viking, NY, 2016.

Phillips, Kevin. *The Cousins' Wars – Religion, Politics, and the Triumph of Anglo-America.* Basic Books, 1999.

Quarles, Benjamin. *The Negro in the American Revolution.* University of North Carolina Press, 1996.

Spellberg, Denise. *Thomas Jefferson's Koran – Islam and the Founders.* First Vintage Books Edition, July 2014.

Storozynski, Alex. *The Peasant Prince – Thaddeus Kosciusko and the Age of Revolution.* Thomas Dunne Books, NY, 2009.

The Declaration of Independence – The Preamble.

The United States Constitution and the Bill of Rights.

10. Turkey's Founding – From Sultanate to a Secular Republic

Clark, Christopher. *Sleep Walkers: How Europe Went to War in 1914*. Harper Perennial, 2014.

Fawaz, Leila Tarazi. *A Land of Aching Hearts – The Middle East in the Great War*. Harvard University Press, 2014.

Finkel, Caroline. *Osman's Dream: The Story of the Ottoman Empire 1300-1923*. Basic Books. 2005.

Imber, Colin. *The Ottoman Empire, 1300-1650: The Structure of Power*. Second edition. Palgrave, 2009.

Kaplan, Robert. *Balkan Ghosts – A Journey Through History*. Picadore, St. Martin's Press, 2005.

Lewis, Bernard. *What Went Wrong?* Oxford University Press, 2002.

McCarthy, Justin, Arslan, Esat, Taşkiran, Cemalettin, Turan, Ömer. *The Armenian Rebellion at Van*. The University of Utah Press, 2006.

Merriman, Roger Bigelow. *Suleiman the Magnificent, 1520- 1566*. Harvard University Press, 1944.

Reynolds, Michael A. *Shattering Empires – The Clash and Collapse of the Ottoman and Russian Empires 1908-1918*. Cambridge University Press, 2011.

Toynbee, Arnold J. and Kirkwood, Kenneth P. *Turkey*, Greenwood Press, Westport, Ct., 1976.

Walker, Christopher J. *Armenia – the Survival of a Nation*. St. Martin's press, NY, 1980.

11. Leadership Traits – George Washington, Ft. Necessity to American President

Chernow, Ron. *Washington – A Life*. The Penguin Press, NY, 2010.

Ellis, Joseph. *His Excellency – George Washington*. Alfred A. Knopf, NY, 2005.

Ferling, John. *Almost a Miracle – The American Victory in the War of Independence*. Oxford University Press, 2011.

Fleming, Thomas. *The Perils of Peace – America's Struggle for Survival After Yorktown*. Smithsonian Books, Harper Collins, 2007.

Flexner, James Thomas. *Washington – The Indispensable Man.* 1969.

Lengel, Edward G. *General George Washington – A Military Life.* Random House. 2005.

12. Leadership Traits – Mustafa Kemal, Gallipoli to Atatürk

Bay, Austin. *Lessons in Leadership from the Greatest General of the Ottoman Empire.* Palgrave McMillan, 2011.

Gawrych, George. *Ataturk from Young Soldier to Statesman.* I. B. Taurus, 2013.

Hanlıoğlu, Şükrü. *Ataturk – An Intellectual Biography.* Princeton University Press, 2011.

Lord Kinross. *Mustfa Kemal – Father of Modern Turkey.* William Monroe & Co., 1978 and, *The Ottoman Centuries – The Rise and Fall of the Turkish Empire.* Morrow Quill Paperbacks, 1977.

Mango, Andrew. *Ataturk – The Biography of the Founder of Modern Turkey.* The Overlook Press, 2002.

Milton, Giles. *Paradise Lost – Smyrna 1922.* Basic Books, 2008.

Olson, Lynn. *Those Angry Days: Roosevelt, Lindbergh, and America's Fight Over World War II, 1939-1941.* Random House, 2014.

Volkan, Vamik and Itzkowitz, Norman. *Turks and Greeks – Neighbors in Conflict.* The Eothen Press, 1994.

13. Nationalism Expressed in America

Chernow, Ron. *Hamilton.* Penguin Press, 2004.

Hogeland, William. *The Whiskey Rebellion: George Washington, Alexander Hamilton, and the Frontier Rebels Who Challenged America's Newfound Sovereignty.* Simon & Shuster America Collection, 2010.

Jay, John, Hamilton, Alexander, Madison, James. *The Federalist Papers.*

Romano, Renee C. and Potter, Claire Bond. Editors. *Historians on Hamilton: How a Blockbuster Musical is Restaging America's Past. Rutgers University Press, 2018.*

Winchester, Simon. *The Men Who United the States.* Harper Perennial, 2013.

14. Nationalism Expressed in Turkey

Ahmad, Feroz. *The Young Turks and the Ottoman Nationalities: Armenians, Greeks, Albanians, Jews and Arabs.* The Utah Press, 2014.

Baran, Zeyno. *Torn Country – Turkey Between Secularism and Islamism.* Hoover Institution Press, 2010.

Bein, Ahmet. *Ottoman Ulema, Turkish Republic: Agents of Change,* Stanford University Press, 2011.

Erickson, Edward J. *Ottomans and Armenians, A Study in Counter Insurgency, 1878-1915.* Palgrave Macmillan, 2013.

Hovannisian, Richard. "The Armenian Question in the Ottoman Empire.", East European Quarterly, 6,1 (March 1972).

Lewis, Bernard. *What Went Wrong – Western Impact and Middle Eastern Response.* Oxford University Press, 2002.

Lewy, Guenter. *The Armenian Massacres in Ottoman Turkey – A Disputed Genocide.* Utah University Press, 2005.

Marcus, Aliza. *Blood and Belief – The PKK and The Kurdish Fight For Independence.* New York University Press, 2007.

McCarthy, Justin, Arslan E., Taskiran, Cemalletin, Turan, Ömer. *The Armenian Rebellion at Van.* University of Utah Press, 2002.

McCarthy, Justin, Tutan, Ömer, Taşkiran, Cemalletin. *Sasun-:The History of an 1890 Revolt.* The University of Utah Press, 2014.

McCarthy, Justin. *Death and Exile – the Ethnic Cleansing of Ottoman Muslims, 1821-1922.* Darwin Press, 1996.

"New Judicial Era Dawns in Turkey.", New York Times, January 17, 1926, p. 4, archives.

Oder, Bertil Emrah. "Lecture Notes on Theories of Sovereignty", Oder, Koc University, Dpt. of Law.

Orhan, Mehmet. "Kurdish Rebellions and Conflict Groups in Turkey During the 1920s." Journal of Muslim Minority Affairs, Vol. 32, Issue 3, 12 October 2012.

Sieyès, Emmanuel Joseph. "Qu'est-ce que le Tiers ètat?" Éditions du Boucher, 2002.

15. Turkish Governmental Structures – European Models

"A Turkish Renaissance, the story of Turkey's incredible success." Middle East Business, September 30, 2013.

Ansay, Tuğrul, Don Wallace, and Williams, Henry P. III, editors. *Introduction to Turkish Law.* (6th edition), Kluwer Law International, 2011.

Atay, Falih Rıfkı. *Çankaya: Atatürk Devri Hatıraları* (Çankaya: Memoires of the Atatürk Era), Dunya Yayınları, 1961.

Altunışık, Meliha. "The Turkish Model and Democratization in the Middle East." Arab Studies Quarterly, Vol. 27, No.1-2 (Winter/Spring), pgs. 45-63.

Berkil, Gözde. "The 1921 and 1924 Constitutions – A Legal Revolution Based Upon the Ideas of the Enlightenment." 2016. A paper presented at Koç University, Intl. Rel. Dpt.

Bodge, Charles. "Secularism and the American Constitution." July 18, 2005.

Danforth, Nick. "The Ottoman Empire from 1923 to Today: In Search of a Usable Past." Mediterranean Quarterly, Duke University Press, Vol. 27, Number 2, June 2016.

Fındıkoğlu, F. L. "A Turkish Sociologist's View.", International Social Science Bulletin. Vol. IX, No. 1, UNESCO, 1957. Pgs. 13-20.

Friedman, Lawrence. "Legal Culture and Social Development." *Law and Behavioral Sciences*, Vol. 2, No. 3, 1969.

"New judicial era dawns in Turkey." New York Times, Jan. 17, 1926; "New Codes in Turkey." July 5, 1926 N. Y. Times; "New code drafted which sweeps away laws based on the Koran and ends polygamy." N. Y. Times, Sept. 20, 1928.

Mango, Andrew. *Ataturk – The Biography of the Founder of Modern Turkey*. The Overlook Press, 1999.

Mimarouğlu, Sait Kemal. "Quelques considerations sur le droit civil et le droit commercial en Turquie." Revue de Droit International et de Droit Comparé, 1966.

Rustow, Dankwart and Ward, Robert, eds. *Political Modernization in Japan and Turkey*. Legacy Library, 1964.

Stirling, Paul. *Turkish Village 1949-94*. Weidenfeld and Nicolson, 1965.

"The Place of Islamic Law in Turkish Law reform." Annales de la Faculté de Droit d'Istanbul, Fakulte Matbaası, Vol 8, 1959.

Timur, Hifzi. "Civil Marriage in Turkey: Difficulties, Causes, and Remedies." International Social Science Bulletin, Vol. 9, 1957.

Toynbee, Arnold and Kirkwood, K. *Turkey – The Modern World*. Greenwood Press, Ct., 1976.

Velidedeoğlu, Hıfzı Veldet. "The Reception of the Swiss Code in Turkey." Das Problem der Rezeption in der Türkei im Verleich mit Rezeptionen in Europa, Vol. 75, Issue 1, 1958.

Williams, Henry P. III. "Marriage and Divorce in the Legal Culture of the Old, the Ottoman, and the New Turks." Journal of Turkish Studies, Vol V, 1981, Harvard University Printing Office, Library of Congress 75-15418.

Wing, Adrian K. and Varol, Ozan. "Is Secularism Possible in a Majority-Muslim Country?": The Turkish Example." Texas International Law Journal, Vol. 42:1, 2007.

Yalman, Ahmed Emin. *Turkey in My Time*. University of Oklahoma Press, 1956.

16. Perceptions and Experience- How and When Americans Met Turks

Balı, Rıfat N. *The Saga of a Friendship, Asa Kent Jennings and the American Friends of Turkey*. Libra, 2009.

Davis, Robert C. *Christian Slaves, Muslim Masters: White Slavery in the Mediterranean, the Barbary Coast and Italy, 1500-1800*. Palgrave Macmillan, 2003.

Jennings, Robert L. "Waking the Lion." https://www.youtube.com/watch?v=Ow5hHTpIGg0

Hamlin, Cyrus. *Among the Turks*, Turkish Translation – *Robert Koleji Kuran Misiyonerin Anaların Türkler Arasında*, Meydan Yayıncılık, 2011.

McCarthy, Justin. *The Turk in America – Creation of an Enduring Prejudice*. University of Utah Press, 2011.

McNabb, James Brian. *A Military History of the Modern Middle East*, Praeger, Colorado, 2017.

Oren, Michael B. *Power, Faith and Fantasy – America in the Middle East 1776 to the Present*. W. W. Norton & Co., NY, London, 2007.

Pamuk, Orhan. *Snow*. Alfred A. Knopf, NY, 2005.

White, Joshua, M. *Piracy and Law in the Ottoman Mediterranean*. Stanford University Press. November 2017.

Yılmaz, Şuhnaz. *Turkish –American Relations: Between the Stars, Stripes and the Crescent (1800-1952)*. Routledge Taylor and Francis group, 2015.

17. Slavery, Civil Rights and Minorities – Intolerance in Both Countries

Akamatsu, Rhetta. *The Irish Slaves: Slavery, Indenture and Contract Labor Among Irish Immigrants*. Paperback, 2010.

Chernow, Ron. *Grant*. Penguin Press, 2017.

Demos, John. *Heathen School: A Story of Hope and Betrayal in the Early Republic*. Alfred A. Knopf, 2014.

Jordan, Dan and Walsh, Michael. *White Cargo: The Forgotten History of Britain's White Slaves in America*. NYU Press, 2008.

Lee, Harper. *To Kill a Mocking Bird*. J. B. Lippincott & Co., 1960.

Newton, John andWalker, William. The Hymn, "Amazing Grace".

Purdum, Todd S. *An Idea Whose Time Has Come: Two Presidents, Two Parties, and the Battle for the Civil Rights Act of 1964.* Henry Holt & Co., 2014.

"The Gettysburg Address". President Abraham Lincoln. 1863.

18. Immigration and Identity Politics

Lepore, Jill. "A New Americanism – Why a Nation needs a National Story". Foreign Policy, March/April, Volume 98, Number 2.

Millet, Joyce. "Understanding American Culture – From Melting Pot to Mixing Bowl." Cultural Savvy website, 2000.

Spiro, Peter J. *Beyond Citizenship: American Identity After Globalization.* Oxford University Press. February 1, 2008.

19. Freedom of Speech

Baran, Zeyno. *Torn Country – Turkey Between Secularism & Islamism.* Hoover Institution Press, 2010.

Bennoune, Karima. "Secularism and Human Rights: A Contextual Analysis of Headscarves, Religious Expression, and Women's Equality Under International Law." Columbia Journal of Transnational Law, 2007, Vol. 45:https://papers.ssrn.com/sol3/papers.cfm?abstract_id=989066

Bölme, Selin and Küçükkeleş, Müjge. "Turkey's recent Kurdish opening: opportunities and the challenges ahead." Open Democracy, April 23, 2013.

De Tocqueville, Alexis. *Democracy in America*. Sanders and Otley, 1835-1840.

"Effects of the New National Intelligence Organization (MIT) Law on Privacy." Herguner, Bilgen, Özeke Law Partnership. News on Turkish Law Developments, Summer 2014 issue. Summer 2014 issue.

Federalist 43. Madison, James.

"ISTANBUL — With 19 journalists jailed, about 150 awaiting trial and 400 forced layoffs and resignations in the last year, according to media watchdog Bianet, Turkish journalists say media freedom is at its lowest point in decades." Al Jazeera – America, October 22, 2014.

Knott, Stephen F. *Alexander Hamilton & The Persistence of Myth*. The University Press of Kansas, 2002.

Pope, Nicole and Hugh. *Turkey Unveiled – A History of Modern Turkey*. Overlook Press, 1997.

Winchester, Simon. *The Men Who United The State*. Harper Perennial, 2013.

Yavuz, M. Hakan. *Secularism and Muslim Democracy in Turkey*. (Cambridge Middle East Studies), Cambridge University Press, 2009.

20. Shift Away from Statism in Turkey and the Western Business Response

Hale, William. *Turkish Foreign Policy, 1774-2000*. Frank Cass Publishers, 2000.

Pope, Nicole and Hugh. *Turkey Unveiled – A History of Modern Turkey*. The Overlook Press, 2000.

USAK (Uluslararası Stratejik Araştırmalar Kurumu), International Strategic Research Organization).

21. Turkey, the EU and America

Addis, John Lewis. *On Grand Strategy*. Penguin Press, 2018.

Bacevich, Andrew. *America's War for the Greater Middle East – A Military History*. Random House, 2016.

Caǧaptay, Soner. *The New Sultan – Erdogan and the Crisis of Modern Turkey*. I. B. Taurus, 2017.

Copley, Gregory R. *Sovereignty in the 21st Century and the Crisis for Identity, Cultures, NationStates, and Civilizations*. International Strategic Studies Association, 2018.

Kagan, Robert. *The Jungle Grows Back – America and Our Imperiled World*. A Borzoi Book, Alfred A. Knopf, 2018.

Kissinger, Henry. *World Order*, Penguin Books, 2015.

22. The Arab Spring, Twitter and the Ideational Porosity of Sovereign Borders

Caǧaptay, Soner. *The Rise of Turkey, the Twenty-First Century's First Muslim Power*. University of Nebraska Press, 2014.

Fuller, Graham E. *Turkey and the Arab Spring – Leadership in the Middle East*. Bozorg Press, 2014.

Ganji, Akbar. "Why Secularism is Compatible with the Quran and Sunna – And an Islamic State Is Not." January 15, 2015. Huffington Post.

Kaplan, Robert. *The Revenge of History – What the Map Tells Us About Coming Conflicts and the Battle Against Fate*. Random House, 2012.

Lewis, Bernard. "Islam and Liberal Democracy." The Atlantic. February 1993 Issue.

Macris, Jeffry R. *The Politics and Security of the Gulf – Anglo American Hegemony and the Shaping of a Region*. Routledge, 2010.

Naylor, Philip C. *North Africa*. Op cit.

Trager, Eric. *Arab Fall: How the Muslim Brotherhood Won and Lost Egypt in 891 Days*. Georgetown University Press, 2016.

23. Economic and Political Disenfranchisement, and the Limits of Governance

MacDonald, Heyward Hunter. *Lessons Not Learned, Everything Changed: the Vietnam War and American Culture – Becoming Citizens Again*. Create Space, an Amazon Company, Charleston, SC, 2015.

Snyder, Jack. "The Broken Bargain – How Nationalism Came Back". Foreign Policy, March/April, Volume 98, Number 2.

Whitehead, John. *Battlefield America: The War on the American People.* Select Books. 1st Edition, April 2015.

Williams, Margaret. "Youth, Peace, and Security; A New Agenda for The Middle East and North Africa." Journal of International Affairs, Columbia University, June 6, 2016.

Wimmer, Andreas. "Why Nationalism Works – And Why It Isn't Going Away". Foreign Policy. March/April, Volume 98, Number 2.

24. Elections in Turkey (2014,15,18) and America (2018), and the July 15th Coup

Antholis, William. "Can divided government master the "Art of the Deal?" Director of The Miller Center at the University of Virginia, November 28, 2018.

Barkey, Henri J. "The Kurdish Awakening – Unity, Betrayal, and the Future of the Middle East". Foreign Affairs, March/April 2019, Vol. 98, Number 2.

Hazony, Yoram. *The Virtue of Nationalism.* Basic Books, N.Y., 2018.

Varol, Ozan. *The Democratic Coup d'État.* Oxford University Press, 2017.

ABOUT THE AUTHOR

Phil Williams (Dr. Henry P. Williams III) is currently an Adjunct Professor at the Institute of World Politics in Washington. He is also The American Friends of Turkey's (AFOT) longest-serving Board Member, joining in 1993. In 1977, after completing two Masters theses related to Legal Reform in Turkey, Fellowship in hand, he traveled to Ankara for Doctoral research on the legal-cultural challenges of implementing the Swiss Civil Code, adopted by the new Republic of Turkey in 1926, in a Muslim country.

Upon completing his Doctorate, he left academia to become an Investment Banker and was later sent to Istanbul in 1988 on special assignment from the Wall Street Corporate Finance Division of Bankers Trust Company. There he led the Corporate Finance effort at Turkey's first Investment Bank, Turk Merchant Bank, a Joint Venture with İş Bank. The Bank's clients included the Privatization Authority of Turkey, Turkish, European and American corporations. During that four-year stay, he was also active on the Board of the Istanbul International Community School which his young children attended.

A native of Michigan, Phil is noted for his impressive education and intellect. He has received degrees and diplomas from the Universities of Virginia, Edinburgh (Scotland), Florence (Italy), and two Masters and a Doctorate in International Law and Diplomacy from the Fletcher School of Law & Diplomacy, a joint Tufts and Harvard program. He has been featured and interviewed on National Public Radio, has written newspaper articles on Turkey and the Middle East, and is published in scholarly journals on the subjects of Ottoman and Turkish Law. In a variety of capacities, he has worked using four foreign languages during his multi-faceted career.

Phil is a popular lecturer on Turkey and the Middle East, as well as on the American Founding. He continues to take an active role in civil society, serving not only with AFOT, but also as a past State President of the Sons of the American Revolution, a former National Board member and past Chapter President of the English-Speaking Union, and is a Chorister in his church. He remains an avid sportsman.

He and his wife Marilyn have two children. They are both married, and not surprisingly, are, along with their spouses, engaged in international affairs and business.